ROBBER BARONS AND WRETCHED REFUSE

ROBBER BARONS AND WRETCHED REFUSE

ETHNIC AND CLASS DYNAMICS DURING THE ERA OF AMERICAN INDUSTRIALIZATION

ROBERT F. ZEIDEL

NORTHERN ILLINOIS UNIVERSITY PRESS

AN IMPRINT OF CORNELL UNIVERSITY PRESS

Ithaca and London

First published 2020 by Cornell University Press

Library of Congress Cataloging-in-Publication Data
Names: Zeidel, Robert F., author.
Title: Robber barons and wretched refuse : ethnic and class dynamics during the era of American industrialization / Robert F. Zeidel.
Description: Ithaca, New York : Northern Illinois University Press, an imprint of Cornell University Press, 2020. | Includes bibliographical references and index.
Identifiers: LCCN 2019026759 (print) | LCCN 2019026760 (ebook) | ISBN 9781501748318 (hardcover) | ISBN 9781501748325 (epub) | ISBN 9781501748332 (pdf)
Subjects: LCSH: Foreign workers—United States—History. | Industrialization—Social aspects—United States—History. | Working class—United States—History. | Industrial relations—United States—History. | United States—Emigration and immigration—History. | United States—Ethnic relations—History.
Classification: LCC HD8081.A5 Z34 2020 (print) | LCC HD8081.A5 (ebook) | DDC 331.6/20973—dc23
LC record available at https://lccn.loc.gov/2019026759
LC ebook record available at https://lccn.loc.gov/2019026760

In memory of Elizabeth Ann "Betty" Zeidel, sister-in-law and friend

Contents

ACKNOWLEDGMENTS

No project of this magnitude is solely an individual effort. Over the many years during which I researched and wrote this book, numerous individuals and institutions provided invaluable assistance and support. To one and all, with recognition that I will overlook some of those who aided me with this arduous task, I would like to offer my heartfelt appreciation.

Numerous librarians and archivists helped me locate pertinent materials. Staffs at the Hagley Library, Newberry Library, California Historical Society, Huntington Library, Stanford University Library, Chicago Historical Society, and Minnesota Historical Society offered their expertise in identifying relevant collections and cheerfully retrieved multiple boxes. Other depositories assisted with requests for photocopies. The University of Wisconsin Interlibrary Loan program gave access to books and journals not available at my home library.

Scholars too numerous to note read draft chapters, commented on related conference papers, or responded to research questions. Those who provided special assistance include Kevin Kenny, "Skip" Hyser, Chris Arndt, Erika Lee, Kurt Leichtle, and Melvin Dubofsky. Appreciation also goes to the anonymous outside reviewers, for their insightful comments and suggestions for improvements.

The phenomenal staff at Northern Illinois University Press played several key roles in this endeavor. Years ago, when I was completing a previous book on the Dillingham Commission, the then acquisitions editor suggested "Robber Barons and Wretched Refuse" as the title for that work. Not used then, it planted the seed for this book. Current editors Amy Farranto and Nathan Holmes worked with me to polish the work and make it worthy of publication. Of course, I alone bear responsibility for all statements of fact, interpretation, and opinion, and for any errors or other failings.

The University of Wisconsin-Stout, my institutional home, has provided immeasurable support. My colleagues in the social science department, along with philosopher Tim Shiell, Dean Maria Alm, Chancellor Bob Meyer, and the late chancellor emeritus—and fellow historian—Charles "Chuck" Sorensen, encouraged me to pursue my research and envision successful results. It has been my pleasure to work with all of them and with others in the campus community.

Finally, I owe special thanks to my family and friends. Bob and Glenda Niemiec, David and Melva Radtke, Steve and Barb Diederichs, Gary Johnson, and Laurie Pittman, I cannot thank you enough for bringing vitality and alacrity to my often-solitary scholarly life. You never failed to put a smile on my face. My greatest debt is to my family. My brother, Tom Zeidel, is also a dear friend whose support spans several decades. My daughter, Maggie, a K-12 music teacher, brings constant joy to my life. To my wife and best friend, Julie Stenberg Zeidel, I owe not just thanks for reading multiple drafts of each chapter of this book, but for a life well-lived. My late sister-in-law, Betty Zeidel, read sections that I could not seem to get right and offered keen suggestions as to how to get them to say what I wanted. It is to her memory, to that of a scholar and friend, that I dedicate this book.

ROBBER BARONS AND WRETCHED REFUSE

Introduction

Capitalists and Immigrants in Historical Perspective, 1865–1924

Industrialization and the class structure it engendered defined the United States into which millions of late nineteenth- and early twentieth-century immigrants entered. During the sixty years between the end of the Civil War and the mid-1920s, big businesses replaced small, often family-owned concerns as the nation's primary producers of goods and providers of services. The antebellum milieu, with its putative promise of upward social mobility—at least for white males—gave way to one defined by readily visible and largely insurmountable socioeconomic stratification. People at the top, those who owned and operated big businesses, exercised the era's defining power and influence. For the working class, which included most of the era's immigrants, the consolidation of capital and the rise of large corporations effectively decreed a lifetime of wage-earning and determined the nature of labor.[1]

The era's social and economic changes led to considerable contention. Industrialization created incredible wealth, but questions of its distribution and the treatment of those who produced it engendered persistent social turmoil. Labor naturally desired some voice in wages and working conditions. Management and its supporters habitually responded with a strategy of defining the workers' protests as the product of imported radicalism, and identifying immigrants as the purveyors of these dangerous foreign doctrines.[2] Placing blame for the unrest on foreigners proved to be an effective means of social control. Americans—an amorphous group herein defined as those who considered themselves to be the nation's established population— saw their country as land of liberty, a place to which immigrants could come to satisfy their "yearning to breathe free." Yet this freedom did not include the right to embrace ideologies that condemned US capitalism or criticized the polity that supported it, let alone any efforts to overthrow it. "Natives" judged any such radicalism to be inherently un-American, and business leaders exploited assertions of a cause-and-effect relationship between immigrants and subversion. Concerns about immigrant radicalism emerged in the earliest instances of industrial labor unrest, effectively stifled numerous challenges to managerial power, and eventually contributed to the enactment of extreme restrictions during the 1920s. Ironically, the business leaders who habitually linked immigrants and labor unrest saw their pronouncements used to curtail access to the immigrant labor pool on which they relied.

This study explores how the convergence of class and ethnicity influenced the course of American history during the decades of industrialization, showing how it engendered negative perceptions of immigrant workers, ultimately leading to their exclusion. It examines how and why the tumultuous events that fundamentally and dramatically changed the United States led to class conflict, and how and why Americans came to blame the associated unrest on an alien presence manifested in immigrants. In the words of one naturalized citizen (who ironically professed to be in sympathy with labor), workplace troubles started when foreigners "began coming to the Land of Promise in considerable numbers, and thenceforth incidents of labor violence were frequent." Appreciation of this aspect of American labor and ethnic history broadens historical understanding of US immigration, notably how the resident population has responded to the presence of large numbers of foreigners. Emphasis on the ideological reasons for the denigration of aliens expands on and complements the prevalent "nativist" interpretation, which stresses "intense opposition" to foreigners based on "cultural antipathies and ethnocentric judgments. . . ."[3] Comprehension of how allegations of subversion combined with nativism to taint industrial-era immigrants requires appreciation of three intertwined components: the views and actions of the capitalists who controlled the nation's commercial enterprises; the behaviors and beliefs of the working class, including its numerous immigrants; and the nature of the sources that reveal their histories.

A select cadre dominated America's nascent industrial economy and the decades of its emergence. Their preeminence extended far beyond their great wealth. Although only a few tycoons—the likes of Andrew Carnegie, John D. Rockefeller, and Jay Gould—truly qualified as "robber barons," corporate America's collective management did become the nation's "most influential group of economic decision makers." Simply referring to them as feudal lords connotes their prominence and authority, a hegemony that gave them virtually unfettered control of the workplace and the means by which to overwhelm working-class challengers. If their own capacities fell short, they could rely on sympathetic public officials bringing to bear their police powers, in forms ranging from injunctions to military intervention. Judges and other public officials wantonly condemned any agitation that impinged upon the rights of commercial property holders, especially the owners and operators of large businesses. Those who enjoyed this exalted group were the lords of their day.[4]

Antagonists certainly recognized their adversary's might. It was difficult for laborers to win strikes when they were "confronted by capitalists of unlimited wealth and viciousness," counseled Industrial Workers of the World (IWW) representative Giovanni Di Gregorio. Socialist Max Eastman, writing in the *Masses*, similarly spoke of the "entrenchments of custom and capital and privilege" being so strong as to be "impregnable to our attacks. . . ." Even the less militant American Federation of Labor (AFL) compared Carnegie less favorably to brutal barons of medieval lore. "Money gluttons" of his ilk, decried spokesmen for the railway trainmen's union, could "see a dollar at the bottom of a sea of blood. . . ." Such rhetoric sent a clear message: As the United States became an industrial giant, business interests reigned supreme. Reformers succeeded in imposing some commercial regulations, but this oversight reduced only slightly the power of employers. Progress toward the establishment of industrial democracy occurred, but slowly, and with limited results.[5]

Some historians have downplayed the role of individuals, focusing instead on "forces beyond the control" of any particular person, but history inherently is the product of specific actors and the events they precipitated. This certainly held true for industrial-era business leaders and their proponents. Behavior and planning by distinct entrepreneurs determined the course of America's economic growth. Among those who exercised predominant influence, different types engaged in distinct functions. Capitalists provided the funding, entrepreneurs the vision, and various supervisors the day-to-day management. Businesses themselves differed in size, purpose, and location, and each had its own unique features. Yet collectively they shared a distinguishing characteristic: they controlled the means of production and the distribution of its created wealth. Contemporary references to "trusts," technically holding companies, conveyed the idea their monopolistic power. This gave business leaders influence over not just their own companies, but over the whole of the American economy.[6] Their beliefs and actions shaped the national history, notably in terms of labor relations.

Companies operating under the "freedom of contract" doctrine saw it as their prerogative to set work rules and pay scales. Adhering to the precepts of Social Darwinism, capitalists saw the power to control their businesses as a legitimate accompaniment to their commercial success, and a manifestation of the cherished US right to private property. Industrial barons wanted to make money, lots of it, and they equally relished wielding near-absolute power in their proverbial fiefdoms. Time and again, they and their representatives made clear that they would buck any challenge to managerial authority. When asked by a government investigatory committee to define the underlying premise on which American businesses operated, sleeping-car mogul George Pullman did not mince words: "The principle that a man should have the right to manage his own property." Workers either could accept the offered wages and conditions, or quit. National Association of Manufacturers (NAM) president and wagon manufacturer David M. Parry similarly asserted managers' "unhampered" authority to run their businesses. Fellow NAM representative George Pope rued the lack of cordial labor relations, placing blame on reprobate workers who failed to show a proper "willingness to serve one's employer." Operators, including Pullman in his so-called model village, did try to provide incentives for employee cooperation and loyalty, but not at the expense of managerial predominance. Small wonder that he and other industrialists, who considered their managerial prerogatives to be fundamentally American, would seek to taint as foreign the causes of workplace unrest.[7]

Owners and managers saw themselves as speakers for and protectors of the ideological foundation of industrial capitalism. If employers lost that control of their businesses, George Pullman asserted in rejecting arbitration as a solution to labor conflict, they would become hostages to a "dictatorship" of either workers or the government. This, in turn, would compromise "the interests of every law-abiding citizen of the United States." Steel magnate Andrew Carnegie considered industrialization to be the foundation of his "civilized present," as opposed to what he saw as communism's wont to return mankind to its "savage past." America's recent economic growth had allowed nothing less than "democracy" to triumph, while England and Europe, with their more corrupt politics and mores, continued to wallow in decay. Industrialist Marcus Hanna pronounced capitalism's alternatives "repellant to American ideas of integrity and honesty."[8] Radicalism, regardless of its particulars, had no place in the Great Republic.

Characterizing the leftist doctrines as "imported" and un-American, which immigrants both personified and brought to the United States, deflected any consideration of faults or inequities within the US economy. Workers' adherence to pernicious isms, employers made clear, could not be said to have stemmed from exploitative company policies. Instead, labor insurgency and immigration went hand in hand, one emanating from the other. This was not universally true—many immigrants were not radicals and many radicals were native born—but the linkage of foreigners and worker unrest conveyed a message that business leaders could and did exploit. NAM spokesman John Kirby Jr., writing in 1904, referred to the era's large number of southeastern European immigrants as "nothing but seeds of socialism and anarchy with which to thistle our fertile fields." Of an unspecified socialist parade held in Chicago, Andrew Carnegie wrote that there was "probably not an American in the array—a parcel of foreign cranks whose Communistic ideas are the natural growth of the unjust laws of their native land. . . ." Nothing in the United States had induced their unseemly behavior. Identification of the marchers as "cranks" limited Carnegie's indictment to select foreigners. Otherwise, he would have tarred himself—an immigrant from Scotland—and many of his employees, instead of only those with subversive inclinations.[9]

   This distinction allowed employers both to condemn radicalism and continue to hire foreigners. America's rapid commercial expansion had created a pressing demand for labor, especially in large-scale manufacturing, mining, and transportation. Domestic sources filled some of the need, but when these would not suffice, employers turned to the seemingly limitless supply of foreign laborers. "It is scarcely possible to see how we could have accomplished this work without immigration," observed political economist Richmond Mayo-Smith. During the first two decades after the Civil War, employers could seek out potential migrants in their native lands. Even after 1885, when it became illegal to hire workers in foreign countries or otherwise induce their emigration, businesses and their agents could not "resist the temptation," in the words of labor economist John R. Commons, and continued their overseas recruitment. They also used fellow countrymen and family members to make connections with potential immigrants, informing them of job opportunities in the United States. Missives sent from the United States circulated widely in the home countries, inducing others to come to America. Resulting chain migrations ensured a steady stream of new workers. But managers expected foreigners to provide more than mere able bodies.[10]

   By hiring immigrants, business leaders hoped to satiate their twin desires for cheap labor and tractable workers. Trusts, decried a spokesman for the Brotherhood of Locomotive Firemen, "desire to flood the labor market with the cheapest kind of labor." "One grand, effective motive, that of making profit upon immigrants," concurred John R. Commons, had inspired the recruitment of alien workers. An abundance of different ethnic groups allowed managers to identify those willing to work for lower wages, and in the end, "the race with the lowest necessities displaces the others." During strikes or lockouts, managers regularly hired the most recently arrived foreigners as "scabs," or strikebreakers, while trying to avoid groups that had developed reputations for combativeness. "We must be careful," wrote William R. Jones, the superintendent of Carnegie's Braddock Steel Works, in 1875, "of what class of men we collect." Experience had convinced him "that Germans, and Irish, Swedes, and what I denominate 'Buckwheats'— young American boys, judiciously mixed, make the most effective and tractable force you can find." Scots also did well, the Welsh could be tolerated in "limited numbers," while Englishmen comprised "the worst class of men." The target groups might change, but Jones's basic premise, especially his emphasis on "tractable," remained constant.[11]

Employers could choose from among the thousands of immigrants who arrived annually in the United States. The majority, reported the Dillingham Immigration Commission in 1911, were "impelled by a desire for betterment" and came to the United States seeking monetary gain. America's great "prosperity and business enterprise," contended General Nelson A. Miles— who would command troops mobilized to quell the 1892 Pullman Strike— had attracted the millions of foreigners who now called the United States home. John R. Commons and sociologist Henry Pratt Fairchild concurred. Both described the immigration that had taken place between 1840 and the early twentieth century as "an economic phenomenon," with the volume of entry and return migration controlled by commercial conditions. To be sure, persecution did push some migrants to leave their homelands and come to the United States, where they hoped to "breathe free," but in most cases, it was anticipation of material advancement that pulled foreigners to America's shores. The United States, in the words of Chinese immigrants, became "the land of Golden Mountain," where all could find prosperity. Gold, as immigrants quickly learned, did not literally pave American streets. Instead of finding instant riches, most alien arrivals joined the ranks of wage earners, a condition that merged with their foreign origins and cultural differences to determine how America's so-called native population perceived and reacted to them.[12]

Foreigners who came to United States, as Carnegie Steel boss Jones colorfully acknowledged, emigrated from several continents and represented a host of nationalities, ethnic groups, and cultural backgrounds. So-called old immigrants from the British Isles and western Europe predominated until the 1890s, when groups from southern and eastern Europe started to provide the largest numbers of new arrivals. Chinese and later Japanese crossed the Pacific, and Mexicans—today generally called Latinos—either already lived in the United States as a result of earlier territorial acquisitions or entered by crossing its southern border. Cloaked in unique cultural attributes, their admixture added considerably to the heterogeneity of the US population. Contemporaries, it should be noted, frequently referred to the distinct groups using *race,* a clearly outdated term that should be read as *ethnicity.* Distinct characteristics and national origins defined the aliens in the eyes of the native population, but so too did the commonality of their socioeconomic status.[13]

Class, specifically membership in an industrial proletariat, determined the immigrant's place in industrializing America. For this study, laborers are defined as wage earners who had neither control nor ownership of the means of production, and only the slightest chance of joining those who enjoyed such authority and privilege. Contemporaries across the ideological divide recognized the division between the "haves" and "have-nots." Knights of Labor leader Terence Powderly evoked the idea of a distinct and recognizable working class when in 1885 he wrote of an "Army of the Discontented," comprised of skilled and unskilled laboring men and women. Powderly may have been overly sanguine in assuming labor's solidarity, as differences in status and treatment did exist. Yet he correctly identified the existence of a distinct working class. Editors of the *Nation,* whose early interests included trade and finance, pronounced the working class a fixture in American society as early as 1867, deeming its arrival as the coming of "the great curse of the Old World."[14] The fact that such distinctions long had existed, at the very least in the form of antebellum slavery, seems to have been conveniently forgotten, but in terms of their present, the commentators correctly deduced the growing visibility of class. Phrasing it negatively, as a "curse," exemplified the era's tendency to see workplace contention as both foreign and subversive. This focused attention on the millions of industrial-era immigrants.

Managerial dominance of the workplace—over such matters as who got hired or fired, and why—must not obscure the agency or solidarity of this working class. Business leaders never had absolute power, and labor could challenge whatever control managers did wield. Laborers, declared AFL leader Samuel Gompers, intended to use their clout both to get more money and to "determine the conditions under which we are going to work." Gompers hardly qualified as a subversive agitator, but his assertions exemplified the rhetoric that engendered operator's concerns about labor radicalism. Strikes and other violent events attested to workers' willingness to fight—often literally—against specific employers, and more generally to challenge what they saw as the forces of exploitation and oppression. Regardless of their ethnicity, they also demonstrated a sense of class-based unity that was often overlooked. Many, including notable numbers of immigrants, openly called for revolution.[15] While history would show that labor agitation never came close to overthrowing American capitalism, post-facto analysis must recognize the significance of industrial-era worker protest, as did the business interests that they opposed.

Similarly characterizing immigrants as proletarians, or "wretched refuse" in the epic words of Emma Lazarus's poem, "New Colossus," does not demean them. Lazarus penned her sonnet as a tribute to her fellow Jewish immigrants from Russia, whom she saw as destitute and haggard. Not bad people, they owed their impoverished condition to the pogroms from which they were escaping. Contemporaries did use similar verbiage to denigrate recent arrivals, implying their inherent depravity, but Lazarus's phraseology connotes their working-class status. It properly differentiated them from the more well-to-do business operators for whom most would work. Some immigrants did start their own successful businesses, and others climbed the virtual corporate ladder to lofty heights. Ironically, the former included Max Blank and Isaac Harris, who owned the Triangle Shirtwaist Factory, in which 146 workers, most of them immigrants, died in a tragic 1911 fire.[16] Its victims represented the vast majority of America's foreign-born residents, men and women who worked for wages building America's railroads, making its products, or providing its services.

Other groups also belonged to the proletariat and as such influenced worker-management relations. African Americans comprised, at least potentially, another component of the industrial labor pool. The Civil War and Reconstruction had freed them from slavery, but emancipation did not fully integrate former slaves into the American mainstream. Economically, a relative few African Americans did work for large companies, a practice that in some instances had antebellum roots, and managerial correspondence regularly made reference to them as possible employees. Unfortunately, this included their use as strikebreakers, which exacerbated tensions with white workers. Operators, insisted a union spokesman in 1898, "imported colored miners from the South to take the places of miners on strike for living wages." Immigrants especially viewed black workers as competitors, but others saw this as a specious perception. Following the 1863 draft riots, free-black Presbyterian minister James W. C. Pennington declared "ridiculous" the notion "that there is not room enough in this country" for immigrants and black people. Some instances proved this to be true. More commonly, the presence of African Americans in the workforce complicated the industrial era's already complex relationship between ethnicity, or race, and class.[17]

Women occupied an intriguing place in the ethnic and labor dynamics of the time. Many females, including immigrants, worked for wages either in a domestic capacity or outside of the home. Their employment included factory work, notably in the textile trades, but very few labored in the so-called heavy industries—such as railroads, mining, or steel production—which dominated the late nineteenth- and early twentieth-century US economy. But women did have a presence. The Pullman Company, for example, employed about two hundred women to work with fabrics, as did many large textile producers. Female participants appeared in accounts of major strikes and other seminal events. Generally unflattering, if not downright derogatory, descriptions of these women, usually immigrants, conveyed the idea that they did not adhere to proper social decorum. Their aberrant behavior, similar to that attributed to European leftists, added a gender-based component to assertions of immigrant-worker radicalism. The centrality of such females to some strikes, and the leadership of firebrands such as Elizabeth Gurley Flynn, would reinforce these negative perceptions. "Red" Emma Goldman, a Russian immigrant, took the notion of subversive-alien womanhood to the extreme. By combining class-based militancy with rejection of sexual mores, Goldman—more than any other person of either sex—came to represent all that was pernicious about foreign-born malcontents.[18]

Interpreting how and why the involved components came together to shape the history of American industrialization poses several methodological problems. Given the power held by business leaders, sources that reveal their attitudes and behaviors provide unique insight. Research therefore centered on company papers and corporate leaders' public testimony. Due to the concentration of industrial growth in the Northeast and Midwest, businesses and events in those regions received predominate attention.[19] Reactions to other large concentrations of immigrant laborers, notably Asians working in the West, also warranted coverage. No doubt consultation of other collections could have enhanced the narrative and analysis, but those that were used reveal consistent patterns of how business leaders dealt with foreign-born workers.

Numerous industrial-era big businesses left significant archival collections, but their contents often proved to be of minimal use for the study of labor issues. In many cases, corporate leaders apparently preserved records in anticipation of the type of history they wanted to see written, or perhaps that they expected others would want to write. Existing manuscripts tend to tell stories of economic imperialism, of corporate growth through acquisition and merger, and of the increased output and profitability they provided.

The files typically lack documents that reveal how the companies interacted with their employees or responded to labor unrest. This is especially frustrating when dealing with the records of companies that employed large numbers of immigrant workers. Records of the Bethlehem Steel Company at the Hagley Library provide a typical example. A 1913 memorandum calls for the translation of a "General Safety Rule Book" into the various languages used by the company's ethnically diverse workforce. Yet among the extensive collection of corporate papers, that is the single immigrant-employee–related document. Extensive records of this multiethnic workforce could have served as an excellent source of information about industrialists' treatment of and attitudes toward immigrant workers.[20] Unfortunately, the lone reference is all too common.

In cases where collections do have pertinent materials, care must be taken in using the documents, be they corporate memoranda or managers' personal papers. They provide the best sources for determining how American capitalists and company officials thought of and reacted to their workers, including matters related to their ethnicity, but businessmen often wrote with a succinct, practical purpose. They intended their correspondence to conduct business, not convey deep philosophical meaning. This inclination requires the historian to deduce larger ideological significance from frequently terse prose. Conversely, Gilded Age and Progressive Era owners and managers exhibited much more candor than would their more closely scrutinized successors, who would live in the much more publicity-conscious and litigious-minded future. The Robber Baron generation wrote much more openly about ethnic and racial perceptions, albeit using rather pithy language.[21]

Published sources, especially the writings of leading industrialists, hearing transcripts, and periodical literature, supplement manuscripts and archival materials. Andrew Carnegie, for example, commented extensively on the industrial milieu that he was helping to create, and numerous of his peers, especially at times of social stress, used the popular press to promote their views. Frequently more editorial than factual, their pronouncements provide important insights into capitalists' thoughts and feelings about the contentious aspects of labor, class, and the distribution of wealth and power. Finally, the extensive digitalization of historical newspapers makes readily available their accounts of key events. These were not objective reports, as business leaders often controlled key newspapers and used them to disseminate their biased and self-serving perspectives, but they tell the stories and offer the interpretations that would have been read by the larger public. Newspapers also contain information not elsewhere available.[22]

Regardless of the sources consulted, no single chronicling can include all aspects or every instance of immigrant involvement in American industrialization. Complex change over time involved countless events, included innumerable men and women, and spanned more than six decades. Any investigation of their historical interconnections must be selective. Coverage of even the most seminal events cannot be exhaustive, but synopsis can provide a context in which to interpret and analyze the attitudes and behaviors of those involved. Prudent use of salient examples, ranging in time and place, make it possible to write "a coherent collective" study of Americans' efforts to deal with increasing ethnic diversity during a time of dramatic economic change.[23] May this attempt do justice to those involved.

Argument - p. 2 - idea creation of
link b/w immigrants + industrial
workplace radicalism - used to
tamp it down + led to immign. exclusion

paradox - owners wanted immigrants -
pliable workforce that used
foreignness to denigrate workforce -
use of "cranks" p. 5

p. sources - Industrial papers -
not reliable

CHAPTER 1

Harmonic Dissidence

Immigrants and the Onset of Industrial Strife

"Capital and labor have no dividing here. Like the colors on a dove's neck, they join and unite everywhere," wrote former abolitionist and leading social commentator Wendell Phillips of American worker-management relations in 1878. Phillips's commitment to the eradication of the South's peculiar institution had made him a champion of free labor, which he saw as the basis for uniting all Americans and propelling the nation toward unparalleled greatness. He earlier had made clear that the opportunity to share in this bounty extended to immigrants, whether "Chinese or Irishmen." Now, despite the previous year's unprecedented labor unrest, Phillips continued to expound on the seemingly outdated notions of amity that Americans had associated with the pre–Civil War workplace. He specifically rejected the emerging perception of class division between those who owned the means of production and those who did the producing, as well as the perception of the presence of European-style radicalism among American workers, even those of foreign birth. Those who bred communism, a decidedly alien doctrine, were not present in the United States. Using the first-person plural to speak of himself, he asserted: "We have mingled fully with working-men, and never met one who did not believe and proclaim that the interests of capital and labor were one."[1]

Developments during the preceding thirty years, culminating in the Great Railroad Strike of 1877, called such optimism into question and set the stage for future immigrant-related labor strife. During those years, American industrialization began in earnest, engendering a host of socioeconomic changes. Increased large-scale production led to a growing demand for workers, and when the domestic labor force could not meet employers' needs or would not accept their offered wages, business leaders turned to immigrants. The pull of American economic opportunity, coupled with the paucity of that which was available in the Old World, attracted the first waves of industrial-era aliens. In some cases, groups and organizations actively recruited them. Coming from a host of foreign nations, their presence would create an increasingly heterogeneous population. This in and of itself troubled some Americans, but industrialization also spawned the creation of a nascent proletariat, an effectively permanent working class. As tensions rose between it and the agents of capital, culminating with the Great Strike, employers increasingly emphasized a connection between foreigners and worker radicalism. Business leaders recognized immigrants' essential contribution to American commercial growth but also identified the foreigners and their imported ideologies as the reason why the United States appeared to be on the eve of destruction. Associated developments would set the stage for succeeding decades of ethnically influenced and class-based economic tensions.

Immigration increased dramatically after 1840. Over the next thirty years, 7.2 million foreigners entered the United States, and the percentage of foreign-born in the overall population rose from just under 10 percent in 1850 to 14 percent in 1870. With the Civil War acting as a deterrent, the number of arrivals declined during the early 1860s, but then rose again following the Union victory at Appomattox in 1865. Irish and Germans predominated, along with other ethnic groups from the British Isles and western Europe. Northern states, from New York and New England west to the Mississippi Valley, attracted the largest numbers, but after the Civil War, southerners also sought to recruit immigrant labor, mainly as an alternative to the freedmen or recently freed slaves. The era's immigration also included Chinese, the first Asians to come in large numbers to the United States (see chapter 2). Various entities used guidebooks and recruitment agents to induce would-be emigres to come to a certain place or for a specific job, and while these enticements no doubt had their appeal, the great majority of foreigners came to the United States of their own volition, often lured by letters from friends and family members who had emigrated previously. By 1870 foreign-born workers constituted a third of the industrial labor force and were beginning to dominate some types of manufacturing and mining.[2] Not everyone reacted favorably to their growing numbers.

Prior to the Great Strike, concerns about America's increased ethnic diversity centered on sociocultural factors, especially religion. Contemporaries pointed to Catholicism, which predominated among recently arrived Irish and Germans, as justification for immigrant denigration. Religious publisher M. W. Dodd advertised one of his recent works as one that set forth "the dangers of popular liberty from foreign influences, especially Romanism. . . ." and a concurrently published sermon characterized the Catholic Church as "one of the greatest evils and dangers of our times." A story originally from New York's *Evening Mirror* praised a Catholic woman for promptly paying her subscription and then pronounced "the 'Mother Church' as the mother of abomination. . . ." Its orthodoxy and priestly hierarchy allegedly engendered social decay and threatened to corrupt America's republican virtues. Catholics lacked the protestant "work ethic," believed to be a prerequisite for commercial success in America's free labor economy. Critics accused the congregants of participating in a papal plot to take control of the United States and place it under the Vatican's dominion. Writing in the 1850s, future President Rutherford B. Hayes succinctly captured the era's nativist sentiment by noting, "How people do hate Catholics."[3] Immigrants embodied this sectarian menace.

While religion offered a convenient and simplistic target for antebellum xenophobes, partisan politics provided the battleground. Democrats, with their emphasis on individualism and egalitarianism, welcomed immigrants into the fold, sharing with them a dislike of the seemingly puritanical and aristocratic Whigs. The latter, who took their name from the British opposition party, castigated aliens for alleged voter improprieties. When Democrat James K. Polk narrowly won the 1844 presidential election, Whigs claimed that manipulated foreign-born voters had corrupted voting in key states. This, they argued, imperiled the nation's political process and otherwise threatened its values and institutions. Animosity toward immigrants eventually engendered the Know Nothing movement of the mid-1850s. Touting itself as the guardian of America's values and virtues, imperiled by the threat of "rum and Romanism," Know Nothings achieved considerable success in the 1854 elections but thereafter faded amid the growing sectional debate. Some of the initial Republicans similarly foresaw the destitute Irish as a permanent underclass whose presence compromised the party's free-labor presumption of upward social mobility, but others looked upon immigration more favorably. Staunch emancipation advocate William H. Seward of New York contended that the North's continued economic expansion required an uninterrupted influx of immigrants, as did the expansion of free labor into the western territories, where the foreign-born could join northerners in blocking the introduction of slavery. The need to confront the peculiar institution's greater evil eventually would lead most Republicans to reject nativism, or at least mute their criticism of foreigners.[4] Yet as emancipation came closer to reality and the nation ultimately abolished slavery, many of those who had campaigned for its end confronted a world where recent immigrants clashed with African Americans, whom they saw as economic competitors.

Recognition of immigration's importance for economic growth prompted private groups—railroads and other companies—and government agencies to recruit foreigners. During the 1850s, abolitionist editor Zebina Eastman and world-peace advocate Elihu Burritt contemplated a "transportation scheme" to entice English settlers to US homesteads. The Illinois Central (IC) Railroad, finding itself in need of workers and settlers along its route, hired "an American writer" to publicize in Europe the state's economic potential. IC literature, sent to Norway and Sweden, greater Germany, the British Isles, and French-speaking Canada, extolled the benefits of the Illinois prairie. Advertisements offered "permanent employment" at $1.25 per day, along with low fares for those coming from New York City. The Pennsylvania Railroad, in hopes of emulating the success of its competitors, also appointed an immigration agent to promote its services to new arrivals. In 1852 Wisconsin appointed a Commissioner of Emigration. Residing in New York City, his office printed thousands of pamphlets, in several languages, for distribution locally and in Europe. Wisconsin also briefly opened a branch office in Quebec. Recruitment centered on northern and western Europeans, mainly Germans, Scandinavians, and British Islanders. In the first year of operation the Commissioner estimated that some sixteen to eighteen thousand Germans, four to five thousand Irish, three to four thousand Norwegians, and two to three thousand others went to Wisconsin, an overall rise of 15 percent from the previous year. Due to the convergence of pre–Civil War political concerns and a precipitous national decline in immigration, Wisconsin discontinued its recruitment in 1855, but the abandonment proved to be temporary. The program would resume after the Civil War, coinciding with the start of similar endeavors in several neighboring states.[5]

Economist Henry Carey, whose extensive writings critiqued America's emergent industrial capitalism, spoke for those who considered immigrants to be beneficial to the nation's workforce. Committed to the concept of shared owner-worker interests, Carey envisioned the foreigners contributing to expanded US productivity, with "an increase in the return to labor . . . and an increased facility of accumulating capital." Immigrants transformed the value of the nation's machines from potential to actual. In agricultural regions, a larger population brought more land, and that of lesser quality, into productive use. The newcomers also acted as consumers, amplifying demand for "the quantity of food, fuel, cloth, and iron given in exchange for labour." Writing in 1851, at the height of the Know Nothing movement, Carey asserted that the United States had "instantly absorbed" hundreds of thousands of foreigners—notably the often denigrated Irish—with no adverse effects; if the number of annual arrivals were to rise to one million, the effects would be universally positive to both workers and employers. Finally, immigrants demonstrated both America's economic strength and the opportunities that it offered to advance one's fortunes, as foreigners only would come to the US when wages and the employment prospects were high.[6]

When Carey articulated these assertions, the United States remained overwhelming rural and agricultural, but as the Civil War drew to a close he used his influence among Radical Republicans—whose congressional dominance elevated the economist's stature—to extol the virtues of both high tariffs and voluminous immigration. In 1865, as Speaker of the House Schuyler Colfax and other party leaders tried to garner the traditionally Democratic Irish American vote, Carey repeated his earlier conviction that immigrants contributed numerous economic benefits. Acting as both producers and consumers, they made and used American goods, grew and ate American food. The Civil War had been a catalyst for economic growth, accelerating industrial expansion and creating an increasingly proletarian workforce. While some looked askance at these developments, they reaffirmed Carey's belief in immigration's positive effects. The United States, he believed, needed to find ways to encourage more men and women to seek its shores.[7]

Toward that end, Carey supported the American Emigrant Company (AEC). Business leaders, described as "New England men of character, standing, and of wealth," created the AEC in 1863 to procure needed workers—"laborers of every kind"—from Europe. "It is proposed to take orders on this side from employers," explained Henry Ward Beecher—moral reformer, middle-class spokesman, and one of America's most influential clergymen—and then use "agents in Gt. Britain & on the Continent, to bring out laborers skilled in the labor required." Those recruited would sign contracts prior to their departure and then be transported to their place of employment, a process by which the involved workers became known as contract laborers. Immigrants who could not afford passage would receive an advancement on their wages. To promote its work, the company prepared the *American Reporter and Intending Emigrant's Guide*, "a journal designed for the exposition of the resources of this country to the working men of Great Britain." Company recruiters believed that their practices gave "each individual employer the opportunity of supplying himself with the exact number and description of operatives he needs." One would-be English agent offered to find "a very respectable class of workers to fill up the void caused by the drain on the labouring classes in the US to suppress the Rebellion." He pledged that those whom he sent to the United States would be of the same high caliber as the foreign-born soldiers, including his son, who had served in the Union army.[8]

At a time when military enlistments and conscription had depleted the American workforce, the AEC operated in concert with the federal government. The 1864 Act to Encourage Immigration, championed by anti-slavery advocate and now Secretary of State William H. Seward, authorized procedures for overseas labor recruitment. The Act gave legal sanction to contracts signed in the emigrant's home country and provided penalties, including liens on property, for those who failed to repay the costs of their recruitment. It also created the position of Commissioner of Immigration, held briefly by Carey's associate E. Peshine Smith, and established a US Immigrant Office in New York City. The latter shared quarters with the AEC, which saw itself as having "the sympathy and approval of the government of the United States," and also "carrying into practical effect the design of the Government in enacting this Law." Company promotional materials listed Supreme Court justices and US senators among its supporters. For its part, the Immigration Office allowed US diplomats, such as Carey's friend and immigration advocate Thomas H. Dudley, American consul at Liverpool, to cooperate with AEC agents and help with their recruitment of foreign workers.[9]

The Emigration Company intended to solicit clients by providing welcome, free passage, and the promise of a job. "Any person whom you desire to confide to our care," John Williams, the company's general agent, assured Thomas Dudley, "shall be protected and employment found for if you will intimate your wish by a note or card of introduction." Recruiters promised to send only the highest quality men, of the same stripe as those who previously had demonstrated their worth to the United States. Yet financial impediments would hamper the company's plan to get migrants to the United States "without any expense to themselves whatever." In one instance, the AEC prepaid passage for one hundred immigrants from Liverpool, but this proved to be the exception. The Act of 1864 did not appropriate any funds for subsidizing passage to the United States, assuming that employers could deduct the cost of an immigrant's prepaid ticket from future wages. Carey tried to raise more private funding through essays in the trade journal *Iron Age*, but with neither federal appropriations nor adequate support from private firms, the company's recruitment efforts ultimately had minimal success. Further, the practice of hiring "contract laborers" aroused worker animosity, on the grounds that it allowed companies to hire foreigners as strikebreakers, and Congress repealed the law in 1868.[10]

Prussian-born political scientist Francis Lieber advocated a different approach to immigrant enticement. A professor and prolific author, whose works included the first thirteen volumes of *Encyclopedia Americana*, Lieber considered migration to be an inherent right. Shortly after his 1827 arrival, he penned *The Stranger in America*, a testimonial to immigrants' generally harmonious integration. His fellow Germans drew particular praise. After arriving at port cities, they quickly left for rural locales, where they planned to become agrarian landowners. Showing their dislike of slavery, they avoided settling in the South. "Universal testimony," he all but bragged, characterized them as "'sober, industrious, and excellent farmers.'" This made them especially valuable additions. In contrast, Irish immigrants tended to stay in congested urban areas. Their choice of residence, Lieber implied, went hand in hand with other negative characteristics, such as sloth and intemperance, which decreased their desirability as additions to American society.[11] This differentiation eventually would change, as new employment opportunities attracted a growing percentage of all foreign arrivals to cities and other industrial areas. Lieber continued to see immigration as a benefit to the United States, and during the Civil War devoted his attention to attracting nonagricultural wage earners.

In August 1862, Lieber drafted "Proposal of a Constitution for an Association to Promote German Immigration." The Civil War North's need for soldiers, he asserted, had reduced the available labor force, "taking men, in their most productive age, from productive employment. . . ." Work in factories and mills remained undone, because employers could not find enough hands, making immigration, "the influx of labor . . . highly desirable." The proposed association would promote the recruitment of Germans, in cooperation with shipping companies operating out of Hamburg and Bremen, by providing information about employment in the United States. Hopefully, the US government would partner in this endeavor. However, unlike the Immigration Act that Lincoln would sign in 1864, Lieber disavowed any intention to engage in contract labor. Those working on behalf of the association would "do anything expedient and lawful, short of entering into actual engagements for their employment here [in the United States], that can promote increased German immigration into the United States."[12] Lieber did not indicate if similar steps should be taken to solicit people from other places, but if so, his language made clear that they should not involve prearranged contracts.

Lieber also hoped to alleviate immigrants' fears of being drafted into the Union Army, but he did not anticipate future developments. When he organized the German recruitment association in 1862, he tried to assure prospective emigres that they would not be conscripted. No less than President Abraham Lincoln, "the highest authority known in this country," he declared, had "sanctioned" the exemption of foreigners from military service. Shortly thereafter, however, the need for soldiers would alter this blanket immunity. The Conscription Act of 1863, while exempting some resident aliens, did apply to those who had declared their intent to become citizens. While this made many foreigners liable for military service, another provision allowed draftees to hire substitutes, and aliens became prime targets for those wanting to use this loophole. As a result, many immigrants were conscripted, fostering resentment toward the draft and its Republican proponents. Resulting riots—such as the 1863 New York City uprising that included large numbers of foreign-born—tainted ethnic communities. Established workers also resented immigrants who filled job openings created by the absence of men serving in the military, an antagonism also directed at free blacks.[13] National policy creating a non-citizen exemption also had ironic results, in that it deterred young men from pursuing naturalization. In later years, Americans would criticize foreigners, particularly laborers, for any disinclination to become a citizen, and would seek to create inducements for initiating the process. But those developments lay in the future.

War's end, coupled with visions of commercial expansion, engendered renewed interest in attracting immigrants. Even as the number of foreign arrivals grew steadily during the summer of 1865, government and business leaders wanted their numbers to increase. Radical Republicans who led Congress foresaw a "purified" nation, void of slavery, where immigrants could pursue upward social mobility, and Secretary of State Hamilton Fish endeavored to eliminate official barriers to immigration throughout Europe. His success, he believed, would benefit not just the United States by securing more foreign-born residents, but all of humanity. The potential presence of increased numbers of aliens apparently did not conflict with his conviction that the United States needed to take all necessary steps to preserve "conservative stability." An 1870 national convention at Indianapolis, Indiana, emphasized the benefits of attracting foreign workers, whom attendees deemed essential to the "development of the vital industries of life." To ensure their continued arrival in adequate numbers, the US government needed to remove any statutory or procedural impediments to their entrance, encourage their distribution to places that wanted either settlers or workers, and secure the passage of federal laws to protect their interests. Various businesses, including the Pennsylvania Railroad, agreed to support these goals. The Pennsylvania, as well as its competitors, the Erie and New York Central railroads, realized that immigrants equaled revenue; transporting more of the first would grow the second.[14] As with others of the era, railroad leaders gave little hint of future negativity toward aliens.

Previous promoters also renewed their campaigns to draw in foreigners. During the late 1860s, Zebina Eastman and Elihu Burritt returned attention to their colonization schemes, and Wisconsin revived its recruitment program. The state's Board of Immigration—staffed by the governor, secretary of state, and six appointees—collaborated with committees in each county. Legislation passed in 1869 authorized the board to offer public assistance, "with such sums as it may think proper," to immigrants who were planning to settle in Wisconsin, and county administrators drew on local residents to help determine potential recipients. Widely distributed publicity, written in English and a variety of other languages, extolled the state's many benefits. Government officials eventually coordinated their work with that of the Wisconsin Central Railroad, which paid for sending an agent to Europe. Other locales—Minnesota (1867), Iowa (1870), and Dakota Territory (1885)—began similar programs. All wanted to attract more immigrants, viewed as a prerequisite for economic growth.[15]

Following the abolition of slavery, the South also contemplated how best to meet its labor needs. Immigrants offered an alternative to the freedmen. Among those who championed the recruitment of foreigners, some envisioned them as small-scale farmers, whose presence would hasten the end of plantations, while others saw them a new source of agricultural and other labor. In an 1867 editorial, *the Nation* projected that numerical influences of black people "will steadily diminish by reason of the increase of white immigration, hitherto kept out by slavery and its concomitants." Most of the former Confederate states engaged in some form of immigrant recruitment, such as South Carolina's 1866 creation of a Bureau of Immigration, and Louisiana's dissemination of promotional materials printed in several European languages. Virginia's Board of Immigration prepared a twenty-page proclamation, including a laudatory history of the state, designed to lure potential British emigrants. The Virginia Board, like Francis Lieber, stressed the importance of voluntary emigration, but the Richmond *Whig* encouraged the state's large landholders to guarantee either employment or land acquisition. In March 1867, the Society's secretary, who had been recruiting in England, expected "a considerable number of immigrants" soon would arrive in Virginia. Immigration conventions met in 1868 at Jackson, Mississippi, and in 1869 at Louisville, Kentucky. Yet getting migrants to settle in the so-called New South had complications.[16]

Racial considerations, frequently linked with ideological characterizations, influenced the region's pursuit of foreigners. Black slaves theretofore had provided needed labor, and their emancipation added a new—and recurring—ethnic dimension to labor relations. Optimistic pundits expected the freedmen to stay in the region and work in agriculture, with large numbers of black people from the North eventually joining them. But the belief that African Americans would not work without the coercion of bondage motivated more pessimistic southerners to pursue alternatives. "Pro Bono Publico," writing in the *Georgia Weekly Telegram*, proposed offering land at reasonable prices and assistance in obtaining live-stock as a "practical scheme by which the sturdy sons of Europe may be induced to cast their fortunes in our midst." However, this raised questions about the "whiteness" of some groups, such as Italians, whom some considered to be predisposed toward anarchism. Elsewhere, Louisiana sugar planters, looking to attract migrants from a different continent, aggressively recruited Chinese, who previously had done similar work in the Caribbean. Planters viewed the Asians, described by a writer to the New Orleans *Daily Picayune* as "faithful and cheap . . . temperate and docile," as a substitute for the recently freed African Americans. Chinese emigre Tye Kim Orr, speaking that same year to a gathering of southern planters and businessmen, described his countrymen as "docile, patient, and susceptible people."[17]

Orr's words captured a commonality between southern leaders and northern capitalists: a desire for, if not expectation of, compliant behavior by immigrant workers. In the South, ideas about owner-worker relations carried over from slavery. Just as they had controlled the bondsmen, Reconstruction-era Redeemers, who campaigned to restore white hegemony, wanted to dictate employment terms. The Immigration Society of Newberry, South Carolina, advertised its services as a labor broker, offering to provide employers with field hands and mechanics. Society publicity suggested a peonage-like arrangement, whereby immigrants would be expected to report to work in March and stay on the job until December. The Society promised to mediate any labor disagreements and compensate employers whose workers left before satisfying the cost of obtaining them. The Atlanta *Financial Index* went further in defining the expected behavior of foreign-born workers, in the process asserting the essence of what virtually all American capitalists wanted from their immigrant employees. The South, the *Index* opined, needed reliable workers but did not have room for the "anarchistic, law-defying, revolution breeding offscourings of Europe."[18] However, if employers wanted a controllable workforce and saw immigrants as a key component, reports or rumors of exploitation or abuse could deter potential recruits.

Secretary of State Fish sought to allay these concerns. A strong nationalist since his days as an antebellum Whig, Fish now concurred with fellow

Republicans who placed imported foreigner-labor among the components necessary for America's continued economic growth. "I am endeavoring to induce the Governments of Europe whence our Emigrants mostly come to set aside tendencies for their prejudices," he reported in 1869. These "imaginary" beliefs, based on tales of immigrant mistreatment in the United States, had fostered reluctance on the part of some governments to let their subjects leave, with the German states having established impeding regulations. Fish believed that diplomacy could eliminate the official barriers, but he worried about the continuation of European "prejudices" against things American. Seeking to combat their negative effects on emigration, he contemplated Francis Lieber's idea of developing a National Board of Emigration, which would complement the work of various state commissions. Intriguingly, Lieber's proposal reiterated his support for immigration but also included reservations as to the quantity and quality of people who should be allowed to enter the United States.[19] His misgivings exemplified those who, even at a time when immigration generally was viewed favorably, had doubts that every new arrival would be a valuable addition.

"No doubt," Lieber contended, "one of the greatest achievements of civilization is the fact that the stranger is no longer the *hostic* of antiquity." Yet, his thoughts about creating a National Immigration Board made clear his disagreements with those, such as former Secretary of State William Seward, who believed that the national government—and by implication the states—should promote immigration. Its volume, Lieber opined, was "quite large enough,—I think, too much so." Rather, a national board should regulate, "morally and physically," the quality of new arrivals. The United States had a legitimate right to "regulate this most awful influx of Whites and Mongolians, insist on sound sanitary laws, to do as much as possible through our Consuls to prevent the influx of released convicts who have served out their time; and to promote as much as possible sound emigration." He also suggested enacting "a law prohibiting the immigration of any but white people." Radical Republicans, such as his associate Charles Sumner (to whom Lieber also conveyed these sentiments) might find the proposal "distasteful" but once they had secured ratification of the Fifteenth Amendment, propriety dictated turning their attention to the pressing matter of Asian exclusion. "Mongolians" Lieber warned, "with their rat-like procreation," had come close to conquering Europe during the Middle Ages, and "they come now from the West (technically heading east across the Pacific) and invade our country similar to the Norway rat."[20] Elimination of the *hostic* label apparently had its limits.

Secretary of State Fish, by failing to intervene on behalf of other would-be emigrants as he had regarding Germans, also exhibited ethnic bias. In

1869, Jewish American groups urged President Ulysses S. Grant to protest formally the treatment of Russian Jews, particularly their forced relocation. Charges against the Tsarist government included the mistreatment of its former Jewish subjects who had become naturalized American citizens and then visited their homeland. The Russian government (like the Germans) refused to recognize the right of emigration. While President Grant and his advisors, including Fish, showed sympathy toward the plight of both Russian and Romanian Jews, there is no indication that the Secretary of State pressed for the liberalization of either nation's emigration policies. Instead, in sharp contrast to his efforts to lobby the Germans, Fish followed his tendency to avoid "interference in social or political questions." Similarly, in 1872 he proved to be intransigent when a delegation of Japanese officials sought to discuss the US prohibition against the naturalization of their nation's immigrants because they were Asian. The Naturalization Act of 1870 had extended that privilege to Africans, but not other nonwhites who had been barred since the Act of 1790.[21]

Along with ethnicity and national origin, other issues—such as sponsored migration of paupers and former convicts, even when it involved otherwise desirable groups—also created contention. After attending a recruitment meeting in London, US Consular Thomas Dudley reported that its only purpose was to "promote the emigration & transportation of the paupers from London," who now numbered some one hundred and fifty thousand. "No doubt there will be some good men & women among them, but the great majority that will be sent, will be those who are worthless paupers and a burden and nuisance to any country they may be sent to." The head of the Poor Law Board purportedly had agreed to pay the British and Colonial Emigration Fund ten shillings for every indigent sent abroad, up to two thousand. To hide their identities, some would "be shipped on vessels that carry real immigrants." Attempts to dispatch the reprobates from the Port of Liverpool already had been made, and given that future cohorts undoubtedly would be sent to the United States, its authorities needed to be diligent in their efforts to interdict them. That Dudley's concerns involved British immigrants, frequently hailed as being of unparalleled usefulness and industry, underscored the seriousness of his allegations.[22]

Such negatives, while harbingers of the future's more pervasive xenophobia, did not diminish overall optimism about immigration. Even those who disparaged certain groups or types found favor with the idea of welcoming more foreigners to the United States. Francis Lieber, despite his earlier tirade against the admission of Asians and expressed concerns about the United States having too many annual arrivals, nonetheless saw immigration as beneficial to the nation. He advocated a universal right of migration, but without clarifying how this could be compatible with his earlier assertion that the US government could legitimately exclude undesirables. Consular Dudley, even as he warned Fish of the growing problem of sponsored pauper migration, wrote almost gleefully of how England's economic problems were spurring "skilled workers and laborers by hundreds" to depart for the United States, where ample employment opportunities awaited them. It seemed to be a perfect scenario, with emigrants leaving because they needed work and American companies having ample jobs for them to fill.[23] Yet even as Dudley implied that the nation's employers would welcome imported hands, developments called his sanguine presumption into question.

Fracturing of antebellum America's "harmony of interests," would challenge this optimism and eventually cause business leaders to question immigrants' desirability. Harmony, economist Henry Carey had written in 1837, grew out of the pursuit of mutual enhancement. Whatever tended "to facilitate the growth of capital" also would benefit labor, "while every measure that tends to produce the opposite effect is injurious to both." Rejection of competing interests supported the quintessentially American idea of the independent producer, whose status as both owner and worker precluded the possibility of the socioeconomic divide. All honest and industrious toilers could aspire to climb the economic ladder and someday own a means of production. "There is no such thing as a man being bound down in a free country through his life as a laborer. . . ," asserted Abraham Lincoln, offering himself as proof of America's promised upward mobility. "Improvement in condition . . . is the great principle for which this government was really formed." Defining "laborer" as a temporary status reinforced the rejection of class differentiation and denied the propriety of owner-worker antagonism. Everyone benefitted from an expanding economy, which effectively fueled upward mobility, and similarly suffered during strikes or other instances of workplace disruption. Unfortunately, the new industrial reality did not conform to this mythology. Wage earners, Reverend D. O. Kellogg told the Philadelphia Social Science Association in 1879, could "no longer hope to become a capitalist and employer himself. The little shop of his ancestors he could aspire to emulate, but the gigantic factory with its larger resources is beyond his hope."[24]

Developments at Westmoreland Coal Company, which would establish a near monopoly as a supplier of coal for gasification on the East Coast, exemplified the roles that immigrants would play in the changing business milieu. Incorporated by a group of Philadelphia merchants on June 27, 1854, Westmoreland soon owned considerable bituminous coal–bearing lands and operated three mines—Irwin, Larimers, and Spring Hill—in western-Pennsylvania's Irwin Basin. During the 1870s, when average-size American firms employed 20 men, nearly 200 worked at the company's properties. Gasworks prized Westmoreland coal, which when coked produced highly illuminating gas, and by 1861, its mines shipped to 69 companies in cities along the Atlantic seaboard. Customers included the Manhattan Gaslight Company, which in 1869 purchased 25,000 tons for nearly a quarter-million-dollars. Railroads also used Westmoreland bituminous for fuel. Early annual reports indicated growing productivity, and directors anticipated a bright future.[25]

Pursuit of harmony dominated Westmoreland's early labor relations. In 1858 the Board of Directors authorized expenditures of $250 "for the moral improvement of our miners and those dependent on them for support," and a year later the Board endorsed operating the county school ten months per year, instead of the current four and a half. The company pledged to meet any financial deficiencies incurred because of the extended academic year. Believing "that he is best served who helps himself," Westmoreland officials "urged the miners to keep their children in school." Even labor disturbances appeared to be minor and relatively short-lived, as when the company agreed to install scales to meet the miners' demands to be paid based on the weight of the coal they extracted or when management exercised its authority by discharging troublesome employees.[26] It is doubtful that the directors envisioned any of their laborers ever serving on the company board or owning large shares of its stock, but they did try to emphasize shared values and mutually beneficial rewards.

Conditions began to change during the Civil War, which increased both demands for the company's coal and instances of labor unrest. Striking miners closed company mines for ten days in September 1862, won a pay raise from thirty-five to fifty cents per ton in November, and then struck for an increase to seventy-five cents in mid-December. Miners' knowledge of wartime demands, particularly the Pennsylvania Railroad's dependence on Westmoreland coal to fuel its locomotives, had—in the eyes of Westmoreland officials—caused the strikes. Since the US government relied on the railroad to transport Union troops and supplies, the Pennsylvania agreed to pay whatever price was necessary to cover the cost of the raises. Miners ceased work again in May 1863, this time demanding wages of one dollar per ton. After consultation with the railroad, Westmoreland directors rejected the "so-unreasonable" terms. Managers viewed their hard-line position as the only way to counter the workers' excessive demands. When the company refused to relent, the miners returned to work at the old rates. Officials also "dismissed peremptorily" those considered to be agitators, sending them out of the region: "It is believed that we shall have less trouble with them [employees] hereafter, and the hope is entertained that we may, ere long, reduce the wages for miners to sixty cents per ton."[27]

Labor shortages, compounded by wartime conditions, complicated this intent. "An unusual amount of difficulty has occurred in retaining men at work at our mines even at very high wages," the Company reported in January 1863, a situation that left the directors "much embarrassed for want of laborers." Enlistments, especially of single men, had depleted the ranks of those locally available, and Pennsylvania governor Andrew Curtin's 1862 call for 50,000 militiamen, to defend the state's southern border against possible Confederate attack, had exacerbated the situation. As demands for coal increased, Westmoreland wanted to raise its output, but only if adequate numbers of "miners and outside laborers can be had at fair rates." Comments about what was perceived as excessive earning of those with only "average ability" indicated additional concerns about their present employees. Frustrated officials first sought to rectify the situation using traditional paternalism, the construction of new company owned housing that they hoped would appeal to married workers with families.[28] However, when this failed to deliver sufficient results, Westmoreland looked to immigrants as an alternative labor source.

Recruitment of foreigners served two of Westmoreland's needs. It helped the company meet growing labor demands and purge problematic agitators from the payroll. "We have received at our mines, and given employment to, about one hundred miners from the British Provinces," officials reported in January 1864, "thus enabling our Superintendent to dismiss all the refractory miners who have caused the troubles of last year." This use of immigrants to combat worker unrest established a pattern. When miners went on strike a month later, the company refused to meet their demands. Directors instead resolved: "That the sum of one hundred dollars be placed at the disposal of the Executive Committee to be used in the dissemination in Europe of a paper encouraging the emigration to this country of miners." These newcomers would effectively serve as strikebreakers.[29] No legal restrictions yet prohibited the recruitment of overseas workers, or contract laborers, and to officials at Westmoreland, the practice seemed to be the solution to the intertwined desires for both a low cost and more compliant labor force.

Reconstruction brought a partial return of Westmoreland's efforts to engender harmony through community largesse, now coupled with recognition of the company's increasingly diverse workforce. In the spring of 1867, the Directors approved a contribution of $250 toward the construction of a Roman Catholic Church intended to serve the Irish immigrants who comprised "a majority of our miners." As growing numbers of Scandinavians joined them during the early 1870s, Westmoreland also sought to meet their cultural needs. In 1873, directors donated $150 toward the building of a Swedish Lutheran Church, "for the accommodation of our miners of that national religion." The company apparently took other steps to make them feel at home amid their new surroundings. Writing some years later, the local Lutheran pastor praised corporate leaders for having helped to welcome the recently arrived Lutheran congregants to "this great American continent."[30] But while these efforts reveal the company's desire to have harmonious relations with the growing numbers of ethnically varied workers, paternalism did not insure workplace tranquility.

A series of relatively minor labor disturbances concurrently plagued the Westmoreland properties. In November 1865, when the miners went on strike for an increased per-ton rate, the company "reluctantly" agreed to the demand, at the bequest of the Pennsylvania Railroad, but in March 1866, management rescinded the raise, without causing any additional work stoppage. Westmoreland thereafter announced that it would cut wages effective March 1, 1867, and when the miners went on strike, the Superintendent correctly predicted they soon would come back at the offered rates. Striking workers successfully challenged an 1868 effort to reduce their wages, but then lost a similar struggle in 1869. Mule drivers fought for a pay increase in 1871, and after a two-week strike by drivers and miners, Westmoreland found itself "compelled to concede" to the workers' demands. But, as economic conditions deteriorated later in the decade, the company appeared to harden its approach, blaming the strikes on "agitators for the Labor Union" and vowing not to accept terms "dictated by a Union."[31] Negative attention quickly focused on things foreign.

Radical ideologies had joined immigrants among America's so-called alien elements. The International Workingman's Association, or First International, began in London in September 1864, and Karl Marx soon became its dominant spokesman. Arguing that the existing industrial system only widened the quality-of-life disparity between capital and labor, his "Inaugural Address" focused on eliminating the poverty of wage earners. The requisite fight against capitalists, Marx exhorted, had "become the great duty of the working class." To fulfill this charge, labor had to defeat the entrenched "economical monopolies" and conquer the political power bases that supported them. To convince American workers to join the revolution, the Association disseminated Marx's messages, including the republished *Communist Manifesto*. Its distribution animated the American left, whose ranks did include a growing number of European-born socialists. While US labor radicalism dated from the antebellum era, the arrival of Marxist doctrines heightened its recognition of class conflict and sharpened its critique of capitalism. It also convinced proponents of the existing commercial order that the growing rift between employers and workers had alien origins.[32]

The 1871 Paris Commune, Europe's most violent nineteenth-century uprising that left an estimated fifteen thousand dead, heightened American concerns about the presence of foreign radicals. Corporate leaders and managers, along with reformers such as Wendell Phillips, feared that similar outbreaks would occur in the United States. The New York *Herald* offered a scathing, yet sarcastic, assessment of their threat. "Cackling Communists" attending a meeting of the Commune's American branch reportedly allowed anyone who wished to espouse all manner of "vile heresies and doctrines." Many of those who uttered disdain for the American government and economy had come to the United States seeking a better life; now, they chose "to curse the country that warmed and fed them." The *Herald* nonetheless continued to promote the United States as a land of asylum for all who sought liberty. So long as they lived within the rule of law, immigrants from all over Europe, and even China, were "free to do as seems to them best." Not even a New York City riot involving Catholic and protestant Irish dampened this pro-immigrant stance. As for radicals, such as those of Paris, the *Herald* offered a tongue-in-cheek twist to Horace Greeley's advice to go west: "We say to the Communists, 'Come,' with as much heartiness as we have said the same thing to the oppressed and unfortunate of every land." If what had been said about them was true, they should have no trouble fitting into the debating and temperance societies of Bret Harte's West. They should "buy land at once," the paper concluded.[33]

Immediately thereafter, the American economy collapsed amid a frenzy of greed and over-speculation, engendering the industrialized nation's first Great Depression. Problems began with the demise of Jay Cooke's financial empire. Cooke had invested heavily in the Northern Pacific Railroad, then under construction, only to find himself overburdened by debt and unable to sell the railroad's bonds, even at a large discount. His Philadelphia banking house, America's largest, closed its doors on September 18, 1873. Panic spread quickly to Wall Street, where railroad stocks tumbled, and then to the larger economy, where for the next five years, commercial failures and the attendant losses remained high. Major industries, including iron, coal, and textiles, declined precipitously. Adversity did not spare the ranks of labor. High unemployment plagued industrial centers, and those who could find work experienced declining wages, although falling consumer prices did offset the lower incomes. While the exact unemployment rate proved hard to calculate, impassioned calls for relief programs in cities such as New York, Chicago, and Boston, indicated a significant problem.[34] Resulting social unrest among idle workers, including many recent immigrants, intensified fears of a working-class insurgency.

Conditions created a dichotomy. Immigration advocates continued to believe that additional foreign-born workers would benefit the United States, but many of those who witnessed the nation's growing labor unrest blamed foreign-born agitators, identifying them as the purveyors of imported radicalism. In January 1874, as workers struggled to make ends meet, the New York City Committee of Public Safety called for the creation of a municipal works program. Their overtures fell on deaf ears. Critics associated the committee with "European socialists," and the unemployed with immigrant poor. As Police Commissioner Oliver Gardner told Committee representatives with whom he met: "The sooner you gentlemen represent the American citizen the better." Similarly rebuffed by other officials, the committee called for a protest rally at Tompkins Square, located amid the city's immigrant tenements. A crowd of about seven thousand dominated by foreign-born workers gathered on January 13, and when police attempted to clear the area, the attendees—notably the German Americans—resisted. The ensuing riot resulted in 46 arrests, 36 of whom were immigrants of various nationalities. In covering the disturbance, newspapers alluded to the role of foreign agitators, the participation of alien workers, and the pejorative influence of the Paris Commune.[35]

Parody

Immigrants also received blame for the class- and ethnic-based violence that intermittently had plagued eastern Pennsylvania's anthracite coal regions since the 1860s. Attention centered on the Molly Maguires, a loosely organized group of Irish Americans who engaged in "retributive justice." The practice, ironically transplanted from the rural, almost feudal, Irish countryside to the rapidly industrializing United States, directed violence against those in positions of authority who abused the underclasses. Manifestations in the United States included assassinations of mine officials and their suspected collaborators. Attacks peaked in 1874–1875, when the Reading Railroad consolidated its control of the lower anthracite region. Concentrated management then rested in the hands of an economic powerhouse, whose determination to exploit the region's resources and maximize profits threatened traditional work practices. Miners challenged the railroad's authority; some tried unionism, but others turned to violence. The Reading, under the leadership of President Frank B. Gowen, acted with equal resolve. Using testimony by a Pinkerton detective who had worked undercover at the mines, Gowen acted as prosecutor and secured the conviction and execution of twenty alleged Molly Maguires. Ramifications, including an emphasis on the perpetrators' foreign ethnicity, would extend far beyond the anthracite region.[36]

Gowen's pronouncements revealed the realities of the new corporate order, including its ambiguous attitude toward immigrants. Reminiscent of harmony advocates, he embraced the idea that labor and management shared interest in their company's success, yet as a business operator, he also asserted an unfettered authority to coerce compliant behavior, with force if necessary, from his unruly workers. Reforming the delinquent, and punishing the incorrigible, was itself an essential business function. The presence of foreigners and their alien beliefs prompted the need for the latter. Gowen characterized those in the anthracite regions whose maleficent conduct had prompted his draconian but justified actions against the Molly Maguires as aliens, Irishmen "brought here for no other purpose than to create confusion, to undermine confidence, and to stir up dissension between employers and the employed. . . ." At their trials, Gowen used their ethnicity as an effective prosecutorial tool, transferring guilt from the alleged Mollies to any and all obstreperous immigrant workers, wherever their location.[37] Nationwide events during the summer of 1877 would make this clear.

Originating among railroad workers, the Great Strike all but obliterated the remaining vestiges of labor harmony. As a result of the Depression, numerous companies cut wages, but retained dividends to stockholders. To impoverished workers, many of whom used some form of *starve* to describe their plight, the time had come to demand more equitable treatment. Unrest began on the Baltimore and Ohio (B&O) at Martinsburg, West Virginia, on July 16, and quickly spread throughout the country. State and local officials, convinced of the need for greater police power, secured the mobilization of militias and federal troops, but this show of force failed to prevent violent clashes in Baltimore, Pittsburgh, and Chicago; a general strike closed most businesses in St. Louis. At Pittsburgh, enraged workers and their supporters—described by one contemporary as "an immense number of vagrants and tramps, idle miners, and roughs of every character"—destroyed 104 locomotives, 2,152 railcars, and dozens of building. The Pennsylvania Railroad estimated its losses at $2,000,000. The city's official death toll stood at 24, but observers thought that count to be considerably low; similarly, Chicago's 18 reported fatalities likely did not include those whose remains were removed by their comrades.[38] To the larger American public, such death and destruction seemed all but unfathomable; yet it was all too real.

Calls for remedial action came quickly. While extreme in its proffered solution to labor violence, the Gatling Gun Company captured the mood of the times. "The recent riotous disturbances throughout the country," wrote company representative Edgar T. Wells to various railroad leaders, "have shown the necessity of preparations by such corporations as the ones over which you preside to meet violence by superior force and skill." The Gatling Gun, a military weapon designed for the rapid fire of large caliber bullets through six rotating barrels turned by a hand-crank, had been developed during the Civil War. Now, in the hands of a few well-trained employees, this forerunner of the modern machine gun could provide a railroad company with the "perfect means of defense within itself" against domestic unrest. "Four or five men only," Wells declared, "are required to operate the gun— one Gatling, with a full supply of ammunition, can clear a street or track and keep it clear."[39] The solicitation did not elaborate as to who, or what kinds of people, would necessitate such forceful "clearing," but others, assessing the recent turmoil, did not hesitate to define more specifically the presumptive targets.

"The worst elements of the Old World," declared author James D. McCabe, Jr., had perpetrated the sordid events. His contemporary account of the Great Strike (published under the pseudonym Edward Martin) exemplified his xenophobic beliefs in immigration's detrimental effects on the United States. In discussing the onset of the strike in West Virginia, and the violence at Baltimore and Pittsburgh, McCabe did little to substantiate his claim, other than making a few passing references to communists, Molly Maguires, and "representatives from abroad." Elsewhere, however, he made more specific assertions. Chicago's violence stemmed from well-organized communists, who conveyed their subversive message in "every language except Chinese." Among the alleged rioters, Poles and "half-savage Bohemians" received the strongest admonition. French, German, and Bohemians dominated the subversive Workingmen's Party in St. Louis. Finally, New York City's large immigrant workforce, "thoroughly imbued with communistic ideas," stood "ready at any time to make war on the existing state of society." A Tompkins Square rally organized by German-born Justus W. Schwab purportedly demonstrated the need for vigilance. McCabe did explain that the Tomkins Square meeting took place without incident, and that only minimal violence occurred anywhere in the immigrant-rich City, but the xenophobic thrust of his work came across clearly. To ensure that readers came away convinced that immigrants deserved blame for the nationwide violence, McCabe concluded his account of the Great Strike with an otherwise unconnected "History of the Mollie Maguires."[40]

A concurrent account penned by newspaperman J. A. Dacus showed more sympathy for the plight of Depression-ravaged workers and much less antagonism toward immigrants. Yet Dacus did emphasize Old World origins when he placed blame for the strike's excesses on the Workingmen's Party of the United States, which had been created by the Marxist "Internationalists," including those from its "German, French, Bohemian, and Scandinavian" sections. He also indicted the "even worse" refugees from the Paris Commune. Yet, only in coverage of the events in Chicago did immigrants receive special attention: "Its great population is, perhaps, as much of a conglomerated mass, of as many races, kindred and tongues, as the inhabitants in any other city in the world can be." Successive mention of the city's immigrants and its "unusually large" contingent of socialists and anarchists clearly linked foreigners with the radicalism behind the recent unrest. Immigrant leftists had participated in the strike at Chicago and elsewhere, but Dacus's descriptions suggested that their involvement sprang from their ethnicity and ideology, rather than from legitimate reactions to employers' oppressions. He also differentiated between the actions of disreputable "tramps" and those of hardworking, and often exploited, American laborers.[41]

Thomas Scott, president of the ravaged Pennsylvania Railroad, similarly implicated "communist orators" in the tragic process by which "a riot" grew to be "an insurrection." A self-made man who had risen from clerking in a Pennsylvania country store to running one of America's largest corporations, Scott chronicled the strike from an industrialist's perspective, one which effectively absolved those like himself. His public pronouncements reflected the managerial presumption that only a small number of railroad employees had taken part in the violence, and while not specifically mentioning immigrants, he did stress the destructive effects of the "vicious and evil-disposed" reprobates who congregated in America's industrial centers. They, the public needed to understand, bore responsibility for what had occurred. Readers no doubt envisioned the residents of immigrant neighborhoods. After cutting the wages of Pennsylvania employees in part to continue paying dividends to stockholders, Scott disingenuously also blamed outside influences when he asserted that US railroad managers had "always endeavored to treat the interests of employers and employed as identical." If the latter had failed to appreciate the veracity of this presumption, someone or something had led them to a faulty conclusion.[42]

Pennsylvania's *Report of the Committee Appointed to Investigate the Railroad Riots* identified foreigners as the incendiary agents. According to witnesses, Germans and Irish had been the rabble-rousers throughout the state, and along with a few black people, they had been "the burners" at Pittsburgh. Scranton owed its tense conditions to the presence of Molly Maguires who previously had been driven from the Schuylkill Valley. Some of the committee's testimony bordered on the ridiculous, such as the witness who claimed that the rioters could not have been Irish, because some of them threw objects at a bishop who was attempting to pacify the crowd. No "good Catholic" would engage in such behavior, "unless he was an Orangeman." As the latter denoted a Protestant, the notion of a "Catholic Orangeman" defied logic, but the committee's conclusions explicitly condemned immigrants for their purported centrality in the violence. Using the Great Strike to assert the necessity of having the state's National Guard ready to assist with law enforcement, it focused on the pernicious presence of "large numbers of illiterates and unprincipled men concentrated in certain localities, many of whom are foreigners, and imbued with the spirit of foreign communism, which is spreading in this country. . . ." This, not struggling workers reacting to conditions in the US, was the culprit.[43]

Others reached similar conclusions. "It is well known that a large portion, if not a large majority of those engaged in the strikes and riots are immigrants or the children of such," opined one observer, who went on to suggest that labor's condition would improve if the United States curtailed the entrance of foreigners who competed for jobs. Workers then would have no reason "to strike, fight, or destroy property, which only disables the employer from giving living wages." Foreigners, the *Boston Daily Advertiser* proclaimed under the banner "Republicanism in Question," promoted ideas of class division that Americans knew to be misconstrued. Acting on these erroneous presumptions, and showing their lack of familiarity with US political mores, aliens during the strike had comprised "the bulk of those who had brought shame upon the name of working-men. . . ." An editorial reprinted in the Boston *Congregationalist* went further, attributing the "mobs and riots" to "mainly . . . foreign-born Catholics and their children" and asserting "a right to hold any religion responsible for the character of those who have been educated under it." Finally, in seeking to explain how and why American workers had embraced unacceptable "communist ideas," the *National Republican* contended that they had been "introduced into our social system by European laborers."[44]

One of the more intriguing strike commentaries came from John Hay, the future US Secretary of State. Hay had entered public life through his association with Abraham Lincoln and secured entry into the world of commerce and business via his marriage to the daughter of Cleveland, Ohio, industrialist Amasa Stone. Also a laureate, Hay's early writings revealed a temperate reformer, one who both could criticize radicals for their excessive behaviors and appreciate their desire to fix inequitable conditions and exploitative situations. Poems from the early 1870s praised a Paris Commune martyr and accepted violence as a sometimes necessary evil in the pursuit of liberty. This outlook changed dramatically when Hay wrote *The Bread-winners: A Social Study,* a fictionalized account centered around the Great Strike. In defending capitalism and moral order against assault, he rebuked society's malefactors but directed his harshest criticism at rebellious workers and machine politicians. After *The Bread-winners* was published in 1883, he would try to hedge its antiunion message, writing that its true intent was to show how radical agitators with illegitimate aims could highjack acceptable associations and mislead their adherents. But his explanations could not obliterate the book's disdain for laborers, whose faults he wantonly revealed through ethnic references.[45]

Virtually all of the angry workers in *The Bread-winners* had an immigrant connection. Andrew Jackson Offitt, the novel's arch-villain who roused his gullible followers "to make war on capitalism," was identified as the son of an Indiana farmer, but a key component in his nefarious plot involved a story that he claimed to be writing for the "Irish Harp." Agitators as a group drew the appellation "'chinny bummers,'" likely a reference to back-country, uneducated English rubes. According to numerous passages, the best way to pacify a worker mob was to make a positive reference to Ireland, implying that most of the rioters hailed from and retained loyalty to the impoverished island. Irish voters also insured the supremacy of corrupt and ineffective politicians: "There was not an Irish laborer in the city [who] but knew his way to his ward club as well as to mass." The generally unsavory behavior of workers contrasted with the "sober" decorum of proper Americans, most notably the veterans who served as emergency constables during the strike, men who came to the rescue when the political hacks failed to do their civic duties. Such descriptions conformed to Hay's general convictions. While not a vicious xenophobe or racist, his fictional portrayal of the Great Strike stressed his beliefs in Anglo-Saxon superiority and the shallow political thinking of foreign residents.[46] Numerous contemporaries concurred with his assessments.

Allan Pinkerton, whose name and detective agency came to embody America's antiradical bulwark, authored a particularly critical account of those "terrible days," the likes of which had "never been witnessed in America." He intended his admonition "to stand as a warning and preventive of their recurrence." Pinkerton, a Scottish immigrant, considered himself to be a working man and claimed to have empathy for his fellow laborers. Yet he placed inexcusable blame for the upheavals on a combination of foreign influences and evil unions. "Vile elements" from the International and Paris Commune had spread their subversive message among members of the Brotherhood of Locomotive Engineers and the Trainmen's Union. Foreign radicals thus became the models for the domestic subversives who led the various strikes. In Chicago their number included the "young American communist" Albert Parsons, whose "flippant tongue" allowed him to "tingle the blood of that class of characterless rascals that are always standing ready to grasp society by the throat. . . ." Parson's influence, more than any other cause, had aroused the city's working class, yet his "devilish ingenuity" continually enabled him to avoid prosecution (a trend that would end with his execution eight years later; see chapter 3). He and his fellow agitators found an army of willing followers.[47]

Immigrants figured prominently in Pinkerton's identification of those who responded to the subversive messages and fueled the "communistic madness." Poverty in their home countries had pushed thousands to come to the United States, many "without means of subsistence and without any possibility of securing a livelihood." Onset of the riots had allowed these tramps and ne'er-do-wells to vent their frustration. In Pittsburgh, the Molly Maguires—a label quickly becoming the universal appellation for any and all Irish American labor activists—came from the nearby collieries to join the mayhem. "Irish and Americans, negroes [sic] and Jews—all classes and nationalities—commingled," he continued, "and all were equally guilty and equally ferocious." Protesters in Chicago hailed from immigrant slums, notably the Bridgeport neighborhood, an Irish American enclave. An organizing meeting of "self-styled working men" took place at the Vorwaerts Turner Hall. But not all immigrants aligned themselves with the wrong side. The sheriff in Toledo, Ohio, appropriated without resistance a cache of arms amassed by local Fenians—Irish nationalists living in the United States—for use by the local vigilance committee. The alien proprietor for the weapons purportedly recognized the sheriff and his posse as "friends." Still, Pinkerton saw the lawlessness of 1877 as "outcroppings" of "foreign-born elements."[48]

Pinkerton also identified African Americans as participants in various riots but did not recognize in them the proletarian danger that he saw in whites. His description of striking sewer workers in Louisville, Kentucky, trivialized their participation in the city's uprising. Members of a "childish and ignorant race," who had been satisfied with their wages, the "Sambos clambered out of the sewers" and "whooped along the street in the highest good humor of themselves." Black laborers working on a nearby reservoir joined "in the pleasing pastime of promenading the streets." "Intelligent" observers regarded it as an amusing sideshow. Blacks did not pose a threat, until a few joined larger numbers of whites in a later demonstration. To the extent that the events of 1877 solidified the idea of a potentially dangerous American industrial working class and attached to it an ethnic component, it did not fully include African Americans. This was an ironic conclusion, considering that southern whites, including those in Kentucky, feared the agency of recently freed African Americans in their traditional role of agricultural laborers.[49] If and how to include them among the ranks of industrial workers remained—and would continue to remain—indeterminate.

The *Chicago Inter-Ocean* extended strike-related ethnic criticism to immigrant women. "Women's Warfare: Bohemian Amazons Rival The Men in Deeds of Violence" announced its often reprinted story. Drawing comparisons to the Paris Commune, the paper provided most unflattering descriptions of Czech and Irish women. "The swarthy features of the Bohemian women were more horrible to look at in that scene than their men at the Halsted Street riots," the *Inter-Ocean* opined, after one particularly violent confrontation between workers and authorities. Gender conventions confined proper—read American—women to domestic pursuits. By taking to the streets in protest, the club-wielding, rock-throwing, profanity-spouting immigrant women—an "un-sexed mob of female incendiaries"—came across as being both unladylike and un-American. The paper even made vague references to sexual impropriety, calling attention to "open busts" and "large underthings."[50] What could have been more unladylike, more un-American? If immigrant women behaved this badly, what hope could there be of their exerting a positive influence on their men and children?

Actions by the Westmoreland Coal Company demonstrated the ramifications of blaming immigrants for strikes. Company employees, who in the months prior to the Great Strike had been willing to work for reduced wages, walked off the job when the Pennsylvania Railroad workers went on strike. The miners also sent a delegation to Pittsburgh "to aid in the riots," in the words of company officials. This left Westmoreland unable to fulfill its contracts, and to get its men back on the job, management eventually had to increase their wages. Assessing what had precipitated this situation, the annual report for 1877 asserted: "Subsequent discoveries show that the troubles at our own mines for years past have been instigated by a small band of so called 'Molly Maguires' who would not hesitate at arson and murder. Efforts are now being made for their arrest and punishment."[51] Blaming immigrants for labor subversion fits the pattern of post–Great Strike commentaries, but in Westmoreland's case, it raises questions about the origins and veracity of its association of class-based radicalism with immigrant agitators.

Circumstantial evidence may have suggested some sort of Molly Maguire presence at the Westmoreland mines, but accusations about presumed Mollys made by company officials more likely indicate the spread of Frank Gowen's vilification of immigrants as the progenitors of labor radicalism.

After 1870, large numbers of Irish did live in Westmoreland County, and many no doubt worked for the mining company. Some of these bituminous miners may have taken to calling themselves Molly Maguires. However, accounts of the Molly Maguires place their activities almost exclusively within a specific part of Pennsylvania's anthracite region, particularly Schuylkill County, and all of the sensational Molly trials involved events that took place in that area. As the group itself kept no accounts of its activities, it is not possible to prove if there was any connection between the condemned Irish radicals and the Westmoreland employees who worked on the other side of the state. The absence of records does minimize the likelihood of a widespread organization, as it would have necessitated some sort of hierarchy and generated some manner of correspondence. Gowen certainly would have raised the specter of a more widespread conspiracy if he had had any inkling that one existed.[52]

There is no ambiguity, however, in how Westmoreland's managers responded. Concurrent with the efforts to remove the suspected immigrant agitators, the directors approved the creation of a Mine Police Force to work in concert with the County Sheriff. Pennsylvania's 1865 Railroad Police Act allowed for the commissioning of private officers to patrol right-of-ways and arrest suspected criminals, and an 1866 supplement extended these powers to any state company owning or leasing a "colliery, furnace, or rolling mill." Applicants had to apply to the governor and pay a nominal fee, but once commissioned, the officers operated with autonomy, responsible only to their employers. Private officers had first appeared in the state's anthracite region, where their presence had engendered animosity among the miners, who saw the officers as agents of the business owners, not the state. Their more extensive deployment in the 1870s coincided with the increase in ethnic diversity among the region's miners and their involvement in seemingly more frequent and intense labor antagonism, culminating in the Great Strike.[53]

This applied to Westmoreland, which had its security force in place by September 1878. Directors made it clear that the deployment was a direct result of what had happened in Pittsburgh and elsewhere the previous year. The company would continue to hire large numbers of immigrants but solely on its terms. For example, when coal output reached record levels in 1881, workers got a raise, but only because the costs could be passed on to demanding customers. Determined operator hegemony had replaced harmony of interests as the company's guiding principal. Ironically, the Pennsylvania Legislature ended the use of this type of private police in 1885. Lawmakers did this not because the officers "were there protecting the property of railroads (and presumably mines as well), but from the fact that they were there as spies and injuring the laboring people of the community" by charging them with trivial offences. This, however, merely caused operators to switch to the use of Pinkerton and other private security agents to act in the same capacity, as would happen at the Homestead Steel Works in 1892 (see chapter 4).[54]

On a larger scale, Westmoreland's reaction typified employers' contradictory attitudes toward immigrant workers. Growing companies needed labor, and immigrants offered a convenient source. Yet the Paris Commune, the Molly Maguire Trials, and the Great Strike had complicated this apparently simple equation. American business leaders continued to employ large numbers of foreign-born men and women, but increasingly saw them as the cause of the nation's burgeoning class conflict. Events of the coming decades would test operators' efforts to reconcile these conflicting beliefs.

Early Years → Immigr. recruitment of societies
– Positive view of immigrants among owners
– Idea of a laborer - temporary condition
→ Civil War labor shortages
→ Immigrants filling in for soldiers / getting drafted

RR + coal industry

– Marxism & Paris Commune = suspicion of foreigners

– Great RR strike – owners / newspapers blamed foreign agitators

CHAPTER 2

No Danger among Them

Asian Immigrants as Industrial Workers

"We want to get a body of 2500 trained laborers," Central Pacific Railroad solicitor E. B. Crocker proclaimed in 1865, "and keep them steadily at work until the road is built clear across the continent, or until we meet them coming from the other side." To satisfy this need, the railroad builders turned to the West Coast's most notable immigrants. "A large part of our force are Chinese, and they prove nearly equal to white men," Crocker explained, apparently feeling the need to justify their employment, "in the amount of labor they perform, and are far more reliable. No danger of strikes among them. We are training them to do all kinds of labor, blasting, driving horses, handling rock, as well as pick and shovel. . . ." Actual Central Pacific needs would exceed Crocker's estimate by more than 10,000 workers, the vast majority of whom were Asian immigrants. Numerous other companies also sought their services.[1]

Western employers viewed the Chinese in the same ways as their contemporaries in other regions saw European immigrants. Although the Chinese experienced particularly negative reactions, they also encountered employer attitudes and behaviors similar to those directed at their non-Asian peers. All of the qualities to which Crocker alluded—efficiency, availability, and manageability, along with the fact that they would work for lower wages than white workers—made the Chinese an appealing source of labor to railroads and other businesses. Yet they remained desirable only so long as they met expectations of compliance and placidity. Employers would no more accept challenges to authority and prerogative from the Asians than they would from members of any other ethnic group. Although the Chinese escaped association with specific radical ideologies, such as anarchism or socialism, managers did not consider their assertions of agency to be any less subversive. Labor radicalism emanating from any source drew censure for being un-American.

To some critics, Chinese immigrants lacked the wherewithal ever to become proper Americans. Their place of origin, sociocultural characteristics, and physical appearance engendered intense bigotry. Prejudice directed against them had multiple origins. Chinese started coming to the United States several decades prior to the onrush of southern and eastern Europeans, whose presence in the United States would amplify identification of cultural diversity even among so-called whites, making the Asians' differences appear that much more stark. Their neighborhoods came to be seen as downtrodden collections of opium dens, gambling parlors, and other houses of vice and corruption. Racially biased perceptions also came to justify animus on the part of other workers, who saw the Chinese as competitors whose low standards of living, greatly inferior to those of American laborers, enabled them to work for significantly lower wages. Enmity ultimately led to statutory discriminations.[2]

Yet in the eyes of employers, neither their cultural nor "racial" distinctions had much significance, except in semantic references to their ethnicity. All that mattered was that Chinese workers filled a void. Journalist Charles Nordhoff's late nineteenth-century promotional tome, *California for Health, Pleasure, and Residence,* captured "John Chinaman's" bifurcated image. To those seeking his services, he was "'patient, docile, persevering, quick to learn, faithful, no eye-servant, the best cook or waiter you ever saw.'" Critics, conversely, saw him as an opium smoking thief and a "'curse to the community.'" He came from a "'vicious and degraded'" race, who offered no useful presence. Nordhoff, for his part, declined to take a side, presenting evidence to support both positions. The Chinese, for example, were not poor, but they lived in squalor. Yet to Nordoff's mind, it was the host society, in its behavior toward Asian immigrants, that would ultimately determine whether the Chinese "shall be a curse or a blessing to us."[3] One's economic status frequently influenced which characterization to embrace.

California's burgeoning economy attracted the Chinese, along with a host of other migrants. Following the Mexican-American War, the United States officially acquired the region via the 1848 Treaty of Guadalupe Hidalgo, and with the concurrent discovery of gold in the American River near Sacramento, tens of thousands of would-be prospectors, literally from around the world, rushed to find the mythical mother lode. In the process, they commingled with the preexisting Mexican—or *Californios*—and Indian inhabitants, creating a truly polyglot population. Connecticut Yankee Charles T. Blake, who arrived in February 1850, described San Francisco, the region's commercial center and principal entry point, as a city "filled with people from every nation under heaven. Thousands of Chinese, Sandwich Islanders, Peruvians, Chilians [*sic*], French, Spanish, Germans, English & Americans jostled one another in the street, and it would have been hard to tell which were the most numerous." These diverse men and women, notably including the Chinese, comprised the region's nascent proletariat, those who would provide essential labor during the subsequent three decades of commercial and industrial growth.[4]

Several factors influenced the hiring practices of West Coast entrepreneurs. Early mining ventures employed local Indians, but by 1860, disease and violence had dramatically reduced their number. Businesses then looked to immigrants—to those from Europe, but also the Chinese—to meet their needs. They needed large numbers, but they wanted to control the terms of employment. The business-funded California Immigrant Union (CIU) condemned area labor leagues, arguing that their campaigns for higher wages and an eight-hour day were driving up costs, making it so that businesses could afford only to make *"what cannot be imported."* League agitation was "choking off all of those branches of manufacturing whose product comes in competition with that of Eastern or Foreign cheap labor." This created a stalemate that curtailed commercial growth. Because they lacked funds to hire sufficient numbers of workers, businesses could not start or expand, but migrants from the eastern US or Europe would not come to a place where they could not find jobs. California's Chinese, numbering more than 20,000 by the early1850s and purportedly willing to work for low wages, seemed to offer an ideal solution. Observers such as US Commissioner of Mining Statistics Rossiter W. Raymond found them to be reliable and hardworking.[5]

Like the other miners who came to California as part of the original Gold Rush, the Chinese originally worked individual claims, but the life of the self-employed prospector quickly gave way to wage labor in a variety of mine occupations. Large-scale operations hired considerable numbers of Chinese to do both construction and extraction. As the price of "white" labor increased, and areas such as Nevada's Comstock Lode came into competition with the California fields, operators found favor with the Chinese because they would work for lower pay. Investigating in the 1870s, Commissioner Raymond found their pay to be half of that earned by "first-class miners," a designation that conveyed their "whiteness" as much as their ability. Raymond, however, did regard Asians as good workers and anticipated an eventual shrinkage of the pay gap. Chinese also found work in agriculture, doing land reclamation, and on railroads. *Hucthings' Illustrated California Magazine* reported that 150 Chinese were building the San Francisco and Marysville Railroad as early as 1859, and numerous other opportunities subsequently would present themselves.[6] But with employment came bigotry.

Nineteenth-century Americans saw the exotic in all immigrants, but the Chinese appeared to be particularly, and perniciously, foreign. "You have no idea of what a nuisance these Chinamen are becoming in the country," complained Charles Blake, who in 1861 saw their presence as the most pressing problem facing his adopted state. This included the pending schism between North and South. An active Republican, Blake understood the importance of keeping California in the Union. Pro-Southern Democrats had dominated California politics since its US acquisition, and after the attack on Fort Sumter, there was talk of the Bay State leaving the Union and forming some sort of Pacific America. In Blake's mind, it was not the Southern cause that might wrest California from its national moorings: "If anything could drive this state into a separate Republic, it would be an interference with us on the Asiatic question."[7] For Blake and others, resolution of the "question" meant finding a way to keep them out of the state. California did not secede, nor did the Asian "question" abate.

Blake's negativity stemmed largely from social and cultural perceptions, verbalized as unsophisticated bigotry. "They are the most selfish, piggish, depraved animals in the world," he wrote of the Chinese. "They are the most impudent rascals in the world too." To demonstrate their uncouth behavior, he recounted an instance when a group of Chinese unnecessarily had forced him into the mire when he and they had met as they tried to cross a muddy street. They also routinely interfered with the loading of freight onto local stages. By prematurely taking seats and then refusing to move, they blocked access to storage areas. The only way to deal with such behavior, Blake averred, "was to take them by the throat and jerk them out." He and many others soon would conclude that "out" should mean out of the country. California had enacted a series of discriminatory "miners taxes," which applied only to the Chinese, but they faced legal challenge. "These animals," Blake concluded, "have got to be driven out of the State one of these days. If no constitutional way of stopping them from coming here can be found, the miners will take matters into their own hands and drive them out." Blake obviously was one of many who simply did not like the Chinese, but his suggestion that it would be miners who would repel them indicates the importance of class in defining the overall negative reaction to Asian immigrants.

To "white" workers, the Chinese appeared to be unfair competitors. Many believed that they had come to the United States as "contract laborers," who had been recruited in their native land to work for a fixed time at substandard wages. This "coolie" myth had little validity in the case of the California Chinese, the majority of whom came of their own volition, seeking economic opportunity in much the same fashion as their European counterparts. Most either paid for their own transportation or came via "credit tickets," funded by brokers to whom the immigrant repaid the cost of the passage plus interest. This differed from contract labor, whereby American employers paid for the voyage's cost as part of a prearranged recruitment deal. Local whites dismissed this scenario, instead believing that some combination of innate characteristics and willingness to work for prearranged low wages allowed them to live in conditions wholly unsuitable for "Caucasians." Prospectors responded by ostracizing Asians from local camps and effectively forcing them to work poor quality claims. As the mining boom dissipated, the Chinese joined whites in moving into other occupations, again sparking concerns that Asians would accept lower wages. Twenty-five years later, a railroad worker wrote of how he and other white laborers had been "replaced by Chinamen." Chinese in many industries did work for less, but employers also found them to be more disciplined. Woolen manufacturers, for example, wanted cheap workers, but also considered the Chinese to be more reliable than the independent-minded white former miners.[8]

Abolitionist turned labor-advocate Wendell Phillips attributed the resentment of the Chinese to a combination of economic fear and ethnic bigotry, even as he tried to separate the two. Although he described the Chinese as "barbarians," he nonetheless believed that those who immigrated to the United States were capable of advancement, but "such immigration to be safe and helpful must be spontaneous." Chinese, like their European counterparts, had to come of "their own free will and motion." Problems arose when capitalists imported them in mass, as so much "human freight." The Sampson shoe factory, in North Adams, Massachusetts, which in 1870 had imported Chinese workers, provided a salient example. According to Phillips, the owners had retained their services, working through a San Francisco emigrant agency, because they would work for less than half the daily wages demanded by local white workers. Fault in this and other instances lay squarely with capitalists: "Indeed, this random and thoughtless cry for *cheap labor* is one of the great mistakes of heartless and superficial economists." Rising wages equaled social advancement. Immigrants themselves posed no threat, and the United States could continue to "welcome every man of every race," so long as the nation enforced a strict prohibition against the importation of any contracted workers. Unfortunately, Phillips—along with many others—erroneously believed that the majority of the Chinese came in this manner.[9]

California governor Leland Stanford echoed both Blake's populist sentiments and Phillips's more reasoned anti-Chinese contentions, and as one of the region's leading entrepreneurs, he did not hesitate to use them to serve his companies' labor needs. On January 10, 1862, as part of his inaugural address, Stanford declared the state's social and economic growth a matter "of the first importance," but warned that "the character of those who shall become settlers is worthy of scarcely less consideration. To my mind it is clear, that the settlement among us of an inferior race is to be discouraged, by every legitimate means." The present threat came from Asia, which had already sent California the "dregs of her population." Unless the State did something to check the arrival of these "degraded and distinct people," their presence soon would "repel desirable immigration," clearly a reference to white immigrants of European ancestry. The Asians also would have a "deleterious influence" upon those of the "superior race" with whom they commingled. "It will afford me great pleasure," he concluded, "to concur with the Legislature in any constitutional action, having for its object the repression of immigration of the Asiatic races." Ironically, Stanford's next paragraph called attention to the importance of trade between California and Asia, and the importance of having American steamships conduct the commerce, although it would seem that their cargo coming from the East should not be of the human variety.[10]

Stanford returned to the matter of Chinese immigration in his first annual message, delivered in January 1863, but in an interesting twist, he did so by making the Chinese into victims. The Supreme Court had invalidated California's 1862 "'Act to protect the free labor against competition with Chinese coolie labor, and discourage the immigration of the Chinese into the State,'" on the grounds that it intended to prohibit immigration, a power exclusive to the national government. Yet by focusing on the legal status of Chinese immigrants, Stanford articulated a line of argument designed to justify exclusion. Since 1790, the United States had denied naturalization to nonwhites. Many of that generation foresaw the immigrants' value to the Republic, but only those of a certain type. Limiting the privilege to "free white persons" likely intended to keep free blacks—or perhaps even slaves—from securing citizenship, now applied to Asians. Americans could debate the "whiteness" of the Irish (and later that of eastern Europeans), but the "Chinaman's" appearance left little doubt that he could not meet the requisite standards and obtain naturalized citizenship. This condition, conveniently imposed by the federal government, provided what Stanford saw as a valid and even compassionate reason for restricting Chinese immigration.[11]

Since Chinese could not become citizens and thus lacked the accompanying rights and privileges, Stanford contended that it was "not humane . . . not in accordance with the principles of justice and or right" to allow their continued immigration. Their inferior status "induces oppression of which they are the victims; and as they are entirely cut off from the rights of suffrage, they are denied, among us, the benefits of freedom, and are compelled to taste, in part, the bitter fruits of oppression and slavery." This, in Stanford's view, impeded the recruitment of desirable labor. Similar to what had happened when free labor had competed with slavery, "it is undeniable that to nearly the extent to which we admit a class who may be called cheap laborers, we exclude the higher and more enterprising and labor-creating class." This clearly meant whites. To correct the situation, which would require interdicting the veritable "human tide" making its way across the Pacific, California needed to find a means of "discouraging," but not illegally "prohibiting," Chinese immigration.[12] Stanford's failure to call for repeal of the national prohibition of Asian naturalization, a reform that would have alleviated the underlying problem, indicates the political prudence of his remarks.

Analysis of Stanford's overarching beliefs about race indicate that his anti-Asian rhetoric stemmed from a desire to appease California's bigoted electorate and garner its support. In his early years, he had shown racial leanings that would make him a Republican. His parents had sent him to study at the Oneida Institute in Whitesborough, New York, which he described as "a throug [sic] abolitionist school," and while he chose to attend another academy, he wrote favorably of Oneida's interracial student body. As an adult, Stanford consistently opposed slavery, believing it to be inherently contradictory to American notions of natural rights. He accused its "Aristocratic" adherents of wanting "to change the character of our institutions." Yet, as a California Republican, he was careful to temper his remarks. Stanford did not advocate abolition, expressing a willingness to let the peculiar institution remain where it already existed. His opposition to slavery, as he explained during an unsuccessful 1857 gubernatorial campaign, centered on keeping slavery out of the territories. Its exclusion would protect "the white man—the cause of free labor." Similarly, he made clear: "I prefer the white man to the negro as an inhabitant of our country." Stanford no doubt tailored his pronouncements to appeal to his constituents, just as he did when referring to Asian Americans.[13] But, Stanford the business mogul displayed quite contradictory behavior.

Stanford's business dealings showed a willingness to embrace ethnic minorities, particularly the Chinese, as workers. Only when politics intruded did he hesitate to employ them. During the 1870s and 1880s, Asians comprised about a third of workers at his Palo Alto horse farm, and for many years they constituted a majority of the hands at his Vina ranch and vineyard. Stanford initially bucked public opposition to his hiring practices, but in 1886, after having been elected US Senator, he bowed to pressure from a local Citizens Anti-Coolie League and fired the Chinese. Arguing as a business owner, he contended that he had every right to employ Asians, but he also admitted to a "race prejudice" that made him inclined to hire his "own people." Stanford reiterated this position during his 1890 Senate reelection campaign, when he reasserted his gubernatorial era support for Chinese exclusion, on the previously expressed grounds that they could not become citizens. Yet the fact that he only exposed these beliefs under political pressure makes questionable their sincerity. So too did the presence of the Chinese furniture at the family's Nob Hill home. Acquired at the Centennial Exhibit in Philadelphia, Stanford purportedly tried to buy the pieces, only to have Chinese officials give them to him, in appreciation for his treatment of their countrymen who were living in California.[14] The gift suggests Stanford's bifurcated attitudes toward Asian immigrants. While he publicly embraced ethnic bigotry when it served his electoral ambitions, his business needs led him to appreciate the value of Chinese labor. This would be most notable in his railroad endeavors.

In 1861 Stanford—along with Collis Huntington, Mark Hopkins, and Charles Crocker, also known as the Associates or the Big Four—became partners in the Central Pacific, which the Pacific Railroad Act of 1862 designated to build the western leg of the Transcontinental Railroad. Their railroad empire would remain the state's largest employer through the 1880s. Crocker, who headed the Associates-owned construction company, experienced typical West Coast difficulties when he tried to secure needed labor, and many of his early hires soon left for the nearby gold and silver fields. Looking for alternative sources, Crocker turned to immigrants, particularly the Chinese. He later would tell how, early on, he had threatened to hire Asians, ostensibly as strikebreakers, to keep Irish workers in line, but continued labor shortages soon made Chinese employment a necessity. Although some supervisors initially doubted that the Asians could do the work, the Chinese showed otherwise. Their number grew from an initial hiring of 50 in February 1863 to over 12,000 by the time of the Central Pacific's 1869 meeting with the Union Pacific at Promontory Point. Stanford, who consistently emphasized the need for rapid construction, recognized the importance of an adequate workforce: "Have Charlie [Crocker] double his energy and do what is necessary to secure what labor is required to push this road to its utmost." Necessity ultimately meant working through the Sisson, Walker & Company to recruit adequate numbers of Chinese.[15]

Governor Stanford delivered his second annual message in December 1863, at a time when political maneuvering had denied him a second term and his railroad had initiated large-scale Chinese hiring. While his remarks highlighted the "great work" of building the Central Pacific Railroad, he devoted only minimal space to the discussion of "Migration and Emigration," and his only complaint centered on those whose constant search for quick riches prevented them from putting down roots. The railroad's importance to California—in the building of its cities, the development of its resources, and marketing of its productions—conversely received considerable attention. Stanford lectured against the "unspeakable regret that it should be delayed in any particular longer than the physical obstacles to be overcome compel." A lack of public funding, he asserted, was the only impediment to the railroad's timely completion, but the need to secure sufficient labor also clouded its future. The Central Pacific's decision to begin hiring Chinese best explains Stanford's failure to mention the "Chinese problem," which had figured so prominently in the first annual message.[16] No existing sources verify that the governor-turned-railroad-president dropped the anti-Chinese rhetoric because of his company's employment practices, but the coincidence certainly suggests that was the case.

So too does Stanford's description of building the Transcontinental. Commencing in 1861, its construction marked the emergence of an industrially based West Coast economy, but laying tracks to the east highlighted California's worker scarcity. Most of the region's "American or white laborers," Stanford contended, chose other—"more congenial"—types of work, such as mining and agriculture, leaving the railroad to turn to the Chinese: "Without them it would be impossible to complete the western portion of this great national enterprise, within the time required by the acts of congress." In addition to meeting their congressional deadlines, Central Pacific leaders wanted to connect to the Union Pacific as far east as possible, which would maximize their statutory remuneration. The Asians allowed the CP to achieve these goals, and they also offered the benefits of being "quiet, peaceable, patient, industrious and economically ready and apt to learn all the different kinds of work required in railroad building." They did all of this at lower wages than those paid to white laborers who were no more efficient. Their low pay may have angered white workers, but Stanford's praise for the Asians, included in an early history of California, led the authors to conclude that not just the state but the entire nation had accrued "great advantage" from "'Cheap Chinese Labor.'"[17]

As Stanford noted, not just availability and their apparent willingness to work for low wages accounted for the appeal of Chinese immigrants; their placidity also endeared them to the Central Pacific officials. Crocker and other on-site managers viewed them as unlikely to strike or challenge authority. In June 1867, Chinese laborers did strike for higher wages and a shorter work day, arguing that what was good enough for "white men" was similarly good for "Chinamen," but Crocker later would say how he had acted forcefully in getting them back on the job. Another CP official would attest that there had been no "trouble with the [Asian] men that damaged or delayed the work." No employees ever "behaved better" than the Chinese. Stanford credited the company's "just and liberal policy" for their successful recruitment and retention. According to management, the only misunderstanding occurred after completion of the initial line, when many of the Chinese believed they were due free passage back to San Francisco, but the company wanted them to stay on the job. The situation apparently was resolved without lingering animosity. Some Chinese thereafter complained about a couple of "no good boss men" among their supervisors, but senior managers had their doubts about the allegations, as the Chinese who continued to work for the railroad during the 1870s seemed content to work under the same two individuals.[18]

The Chinese presence, those employed not only on the Central Pacific but also at other businesses in San Francisco, repeatedly sparked working-class protest. Leaders of the anti-Chinese movement emotionally alleged that the Asians provided a source of cheap labor that prevented whites from getting good paying jobs, and in February 1867, a mob purportedly composed primarily of Irishmen attacked Chinese who were grading land and working at a rope factory. This prompted a backlash by the pro-business press. "California is destined very soon to become a very large Manufacturing State," wrote the *California Farmer and Journal of Useful Sciences*, "and we want all of the help we can get from every nation." Yet even as the paper seemed to endorse welcoming immigrants from Asia, it also acknowledged the popular perception of "filthy" Chinese living in despicable neighborhoods. The San Francisco *Mercantile Gazette and Prices Current*, in language that could have emanated from any business leader in California (or elsewhere), argued that employers always would prefer the "peaceable, industrious and sober" workers, as the Chinese had proven to be, to those who were "disorderly, idle and intemperate." The *San Francisco Evening Bulletin* pointed to the city's wool production as an industry that had provided employment to both white and Asian workers. Universally, the press emphasized California's need for labor, which some thought would come in abundance once the railroad made its connection with the East.[19]

Completion of the Transcontinental in 1869 did not result in the expected attraction of money and people to the Pacific Coast, leading to the formation of the California Immigrant Union (CIU). Representatives of the Baltimore International Immigrant Society [likely the American Emigrant Company] had visited San Francisco, encouraging business leaders to form a branch of the eastern organization, but the Californians decided to create their own association. The CIU hoped to publicize the need for more immigrants and implement a policy for their recruitment. Mining in the state had declined, but the growth of agriculture and manufacturing had engendered the need for more people. To recruit them, the CIU planned to use literature printed in immigrants' native languages to promote the state's economic opportunities; open offices in eastern cities, such as New York, Baltimore, and Chicago, to help direct immigrants to the West Coast; convince large landholders to allow the CIU to advertise and sell some of their lands to immigrants at low prices; and establish "a temporary stopping place" similar to New York's Castle Garden, at a California port. This last would become a reality in Angel Island, which ironically acted more as a detention center than a portal for those trying to enter the US from Asia, at that point primarily Chinese.[20]

Success would be measured not just in the number of immigrants who came to California, but also the extent to which they belonged to the right "classes of laborers." To attract suitable "agriculturalists, servants and mechanics," the CIU distributed 10,000 German- and English-language copies of "All About California," which extolled the virtues of the Golden State's diversified economy. Because the high wages that had been paid during the mining boom could not be sustained, recruits would have to accept lower pay. They also could not harbor dangerous foreign doctrines; instead, they must be "as well qualified to perpetuate American ideas in their purity as the last or present generation of native born or adopted citizens." This included the expectation that they "naturally become American citizens." Since statute forbade the naturalization of nonwhites (a discrimination that Congress would decline to end in 1870), the CIU's definition of acceptable laborers seemingly excluded Asians, but elsewhere their leaders tacitly affirmed the value of having at least some Chinese workers.[21]

The CIU recognized the "strangely divided" opinions about "Chinese labor on American soil" and tried to formulate a balanced position. On the negative side, the Asians did not come to the US intending to stay, bring their wives or families, consume on the level of whites, learn English, or practice Christianity. They did frequent prostitutes. Most important, and contrary to the Reconstruction Republicans' notions of universal manhood suffrage, Chinese should not have political rights, for which they allegedly lacked the capability to exercise properly. The CIU confirmed the economic gain that a "moderate number" of Chinese, a *serviceable makeshift*, " had provided to railroads and manufacturers, and supported their continued immigration on a limited basis. The Six Companies, Chinese American benevolent associations often involved with immigrant recruitment, could continue to assist the coming of their countrymen at present levels, but without any governmental encouragement. As a means of accommodating the Chinese presence, the Union suggested adopting either the Jim Crow South's idea of a disenfranchised labor force or restrictions on the number of Asians living in any one district. But, since neither of these was likely to occur, the CIU concluded that parties engaged in Chinese recruitment posed a danger to the country's future "equally with those slave traders, who, in Elizabeth's time, transported the first blacks to the shores of Virginia."[22]

CIU President Caspar T. Hopkins, a New England Yankee, forty-niner who came with the Gold Rush, and organizer of the California Insurance Company, reaffirmed the CIU's opposition to Asian immigration and sought to distance the organization from its members who had hired large numbers of trans-Pacific migrants. The CIU, he claimed, had been among the first groups to assert "that the increasing Chinese occupation of the state was an evil to be promptly discountenanced, and there exited this hostility to all of the employers of Chinese cheap labor." This included Leland Stanford and Charles Crocker, both of whose names appeared in the CIU's publications, but Hopkins contended that they "were on the honorary committee" and "took no active part" in the group's operation. Indeed, according to Hopkins, the railroaders' association with the CIU had in some quarters provoked opposition to the group's mission.[23] Given the benefits that Stanford and Crocker had derived from the use of Chinese workers (and harsh criticism that Crocker subsequently would make of those who thought California could rely on only white labor), their connection to the CIU and their willingness to lend their names to its undertaking likely stemmed from a shared concern about the need to attract more labor to California. They would not have joined in the Union's condemnation of the Chinese, but they would have agreed with its disapproval of potentially disruptive workers.

"Our work," Hopkins explained in *Common Sense Applied to the Immigration Question*, "is to try and fill this vast empty territory with the men and women of those liberty-loving races *whose descendants we are ourselves,* and in whose hands, and those of their children, can safely be entrusted the custody of American institutions." He also noted how some of those who opposed the CIU's mission objected to the recruitment of " 'foreign' ideas to California!" The stated and implied notions of aliens who were dangerously *foreign* and *un-American* reeked of anti-Asian bigotry, but they also suggested ideological threats. Hopkins's response to an 1869 strike by the Knights of St. Crispin against San Francisco boot and shoemakers made clear this concern. Writing in the city's *Daily Evening Bulletin,* he described the Knights as primarily wanting "to establish in the mind of the members that the employer is the enemy of the employed." Other editorials similarly accused the workers of trying to subvert workplace harmony. The Knights, in their own articulation of anti-Chinese vitriol, complicated matters by accusing employers of wanting to replace white workers with "Mongolians." Restoring harmony, manufacturers responded, would alleviate any need to dismiss existing workers, effectively eliminating the need to find substitutes.[24] Management may have harbored its own anti-Chinese bigotry, but if the Asians comported themselves appropriately, while whites behaved in confrontational ways, the former were more desirable workers.

An 1876 California State Senate investigation of the social, moral, and political effects wrought by the Chinese joined laborers in castigating employers' behaviors. Not surprising for an inquiry intended to engender working-class support for state Democrats, numerous witnesses testified as to the Asians' generally negative qualities. Lem Schaum, a "Christian Chinaman," whose assimilated status likely added to his credibility, denigrated the San Francisco based Chinese benevolent associations. Those who violated a company's rules, he claimed, became "assassination" targets. Other witnesses, including a number of clergy, told of the wonted "enslavement of Chinese women for prostitution." Although almost certainly exaggerated, if not completely fabricated, such testimony made an impression on the lawmakers. In a report intended to be a petition to the US Congress, the Special Committee tried to make the case for Asian exclusion by asserting that California's Chinese population included a preponderance of "extremely dishonest" laborers and "a large number of professional thieves and fighters." These criminal classes outnumbered the honest men and women "in the proportion of seven to one."[25]

Most serious were the effects of the Chinese on the "industrial classes," dangers "of such huge proportions, and such practical and pressing importance, that we almost dread to enter upon its considerations. . . ." Yet enter they did. At an earlier time in the state's history, "when white labor was not attainable," Chinese had been "of great service, and lent expertise" to railroads, mines, and other businesses. Managers had found them to be readily available, easily managed, and inexpensive; the latter traits, however, had allowed the Asians to "live like vermin." Conversely, because the lifestyles of white workers required higher wages, they could not compete with the so-called Celestials, a satirical term for the Chinese. This led to high unemployment among "our own people," including recent European immigrants. Corroborating testimony came from a Presbyterian minister, a former chief of police, a current police officer, and a "distinguished gentleman" who had traveled in China. Notably scarce were the voices of employers, and the witness list did not include anyone associated with either the Central Pacific or any other railroad.[26] This did not stop the committee from rhetorically asking capitalists to prove that they could not function without Chinese labor.

Two businessmen who did address the committee—lawyer James Galloway, who also owned a mine in Sierra County, and a Mr. Altemeyer, who represented boot and shoe manufacturers Einstein Brothers & Company—spoke disparagingly about the Chinese. Galloway described them as "dirty in their habits, filthy around their camps; generally living on rice but occasionally indulging in fresh pork, or a nice fat dog." Yet he also said that their employment had been profitable for the company and that they soon became good miners, "generally sober, patient, and slow, but constant workers." Altemeyer's company had employed 200 to 350 Asians, hired through a Chinese company for two-year terms. They initially got paid 50 cents per day, but gradually could raise it to a dollar per day, an amount that was still less than what whites could earn. When asked if hiring Chinese was "detrimental to the employment of white labor," Altemeyer replied, "Yes, sir; there is no question but that it keeps white men from coming here, while those who are here cannot get work." However selective and limited, not to mention overtly bigoted, such testimony no doubt resonated with West Coast white workers.[27]

Agitation associated with the Great Strike of 1877 provided them with an opportunity to vent their displeasure. When unrest reached California on June 22, worker resentment centered on the Chinese. In language similar to the testimony before the Special Committee, disgruntled laborers asserted that the Asians' cultural (if not biological, or "racial") characteristics allowed them to live degraded lives, to exist in surroundings wholly unsuitable for whites. Allegedly this allowed the Chinese to accept lesser wages and thereby replace other workers. Resentment abounded, fueled by demagogues such as worker advocate Dennis Kearney, himself an Irish immigrant. After attending a rally of the Workingmen's Party, white laborers vented their anger by ransacking San Francisco's Chinatown and attempting to destroy local businesses such as steamship companies, which they thought were responsible for the Asians' presence. Leland Stanford, believing the threat to his home and that of Mark Hopkins to be credible and serious, asked the chief of police to provide "a proper guard." The riots reinforced the simmering anti-Chinese sentiment among California's working classes, who blamed them for any and all of their misfortune.[28] The workers' calls for remedial action would lead to both state and national anti-Chinese policies, developments that clashed with the wants and needs of employers.

When California adopted a new constitution in 1879, it included several provisions designed to appease disgruntled white laborers. Part of Article I, ironically titled Declaration of Rights, conveyed to foreigners eligible for naturalization the same property rights as native-born citizens, which by implication denied those protections to Asians. Article II forbade any "native of China," along with idiots and criminals, from voting. Under the subheading Chinese, Article XIX empowered the legislature to create guidelines for determining "which persons may reside in the state" and which should be excluded. The constitution rationalized this discrimination by denigrating those not wanted—the Chinese—as likely to become public charges. How this applied to a group that earned its bad reputation for repeatedly taking jobs away from other workers defies logic. The second section targeted employers, by prohibiting any "corporation now existing or hereafter formulated under the laws of this state" from employing "directly or indirectly, in any capacity, any Chinese or Mongolian." The next section specified a similar prohibition against the employment of Chinese on public works projects, and a final provision deemed Chinese "to be dangerous to the state" and allowed for their removal. Federal appeals courts largely invalidated these obnoxious provisions, on the grounds that they violated the immigrants' equal protection, but national lawmakers soon would take similarly draconian steps.[29]

The Exclusion Act of 1882, signed into law on May 5, prohibited "the coming of Chinese laborers to the United States. . . ," on the grounds that their entry "endangers the good order of certain localities within the territories thereof." The law was the product of nationally pervasive racial bigotry, manipulated by politicians seeking to gain labor votes. California laborers had vilified Chinese since the days of the Gold Rush, and tried to make their exclusion a national labor issue, but other than in the West, workers saw contract laborers of any ethnicity (such as those recruited by the American Emigration Company) as being a much greater threat to their economic security. Instead of addressing that issue or taking any substantive action to address labor's growing ire, congressmen seized upon Asian exclusion as a means of placating angry proletarians. Entry restrictions applied to "skilled and unskilled laborers and Chinese employed in mining." Other provisions set forth procedures for the reentry of resident laborers who resided in the US at the time of the law's passage, established fines for those who tried to import Chinese illegally, and reiterated their ineligibility for naturalization.

The restrictions would remain in place for ten years, but could be renewed, as they would be in 1892 and1902, until they were made permanent in 1924.[30] In most of the United States, the new law would have minimal effect, but on the Pacific Coast, where workers no doubt were pleased, the statute would deprive capitalists of an important labor source.

The Exclusion Act's passage came amid the Central Pacific Associates' efforts to expand their railroad empire, another labor-intensive undertaking. Writing in 1875, Stanford had been blunt about the opportunity to enhance their wealth by expanding into Oregon and the Southwest: "We can develop an empire in that extent and control its carrying trade." Since the completion of the Transcontinental, they had built the Western Pacific Railroad from Sacramento to San Jose and added lines to the port cities of Oakland and San Francisco. They also acquired the California and Oregon Railroad (C&O), incorporated in 1866, which would extend their growing system through northern California and provide entry into the Pacific Northwest. It also came with a large land grant, which would be conferred, apportioned per mile, as construction was completed. Finally, the Associates gained control of the Southern Pacific Railroad (SP), incorporated December 2, 1865, to be built from San Francisco to San Diego, and then east to the state line. It would eventually extend through the Southwest and connect with New Orleans. By the 1870s, Stanford saw SP as a particularly valuable property, and wanted to press its construction. "Can't we brase [sic] ourselves up with our old spirit," he urged Huntington, "and be equal to the occasion." Such determination would let them best competitors Jay Gould and Thomas Scott. "Let us believe that we can and determine that we will," he concluded, "and the fight would be ours."[31]

To make that happen, to expand their commercial empire and capture the financial gain, the Associates would need workers. Charles Crocker, who again managed construction, looked to a familiar source, the Chinese. As his nativistic rhetoric made clear, his enthusiasm for their hiring stemmed solely from his want of their labor. After touring a stretch of the Mojave Desert near Needles, California, Crocker described the territory as "the most dreary piece of country that I ever went over, except the worst part of the Colorado desert towards Yuma." Derogatory descriptions of the inhabitants—both two- and four-legged varieties—accentuated his point: "I saw nothing living, except chinamen [sic], four cows, and a little stump-tailed squirrel near the river, for the whole distance of 240 miles." Clearly the reference to Asians was not a testament to their fortitude or resourcefulness, but rather verbal imagery intended to show that the region where he had seen them was inhospitable to all but the lowest forms of life. It was not land that would be suitable for "white" colonization. Crocker also recognized the contempt that other workers had for the Asians, fearing a conflict when "our Chinamen" met the crews building from the east.[32] Yet the Chinese had proven themselves to be good workers who were readily available, and when Crocker sought labor, he aggressively pursued their employment.

By late summer 1881, the Southern Pacific had extended into the Arizona Territory close to Tucson, where bad weather and labor scarcity were hampering productivity. "It is almost impossible to get men," Crocker complained. He anticipated finding more workers once the harvesting and thrashing seasons had ended, but he did not think that even these additions would provide the necessary manpower. He thus intensified his efforts to secure Asian immigrants. "There are three hundred Chinamen on the 'Oceanic', to arrive in a couple of weeks," he informed Huntington in mid-September, "and they will be followed soon by the remainder of the two thousand men whom I ordered." James Strobridge, the foreman who initially had opposed Crocker's plan to hire Chinese to work on the Central Pacific, now believed that their addition would accelerate construction considerably and allow the SP to build quickly toward Texas. Given the challenge presented by Scott and Gould to the Associates' desire to control transportation through the Southwest and into California, Strobridge's belief that his crew could outpace any other involved more than just bragging rights. Hasty completion would block competitors and, as Stanford and his partners well understood, provide considerable profit.[33]

Rough terrain exacerbated the paucity of local workers and complicated the prospect of hiring the Chinese. Crocker had believed "that the 1,000 men I ordered from China would be sufficient," but the Operating Department had appropriated many of these for section work, leaving "only about 400 of them" to do construction. In a testament to their work ethic, he pledged to hire more of the Asian immigrants, but even their recruitment proved to be troublesome. "We are so far away from our base that it is difficult to get Chinamen, or any other men down there to work," an exasperated Crocker explained to Huntington in January 1882. The partners had wanted to complete the SP's western segment by that fall, but prospects for realizing that goal seemed doubtful. Paying higher wages, which did not appeal to Crocker, appeared to be the only practical solution. As he explained to Huntington: "It may be all right & as cheap as [we] can get the work done. . . ."[34] The employment of additional Chinese would have been much more palatable, but the isolated work site was not the only complication. If passed, the Chinese Exclusion Act would limit employment to those already living in the United States.

Trouble
vol Chinese
exclusion
Act

The possibility exasperated Charles Crocker. Not only would its passage personally hurt the Associates in their capacity as "Railroad Builders & Oriental Steamship owners," it would also deleteriously affect "the industrial interests of this coast" and wreak havoc on California's "general prosperity." It would certainly exacerbate the already difficult task of recruiting essential labor that faced regional-employers. This produced something of an alliance, at least in the pursuit of a common goal, between Crocker and the "local Chinese," whose anti-exclusion circulars Crocker forwarded to his partner for use in his lobbying efforts. Working in Washington, Huntington believed that he could scuttle the bill's passage by convincing key legislators to let it "sleep in the hands of the Committee," but by late January 1882, telegraph dispatches from Washington had convinced an angry Crocker that the House of Representatives, by one means or another, would pass the legislation. "Our ships are occupied to their full capacity now by Chinese coming to California," he noted, "for it is feared that they will soon be prevented by law."[35] The immigrants, like the employer, anticipated the worst.

Interestingly, while Crocker fumed about the possibility of Asian exclusion, he seems to have had little concern with the fact that he may have been contributing to a more generalized call for immigration restriction, specifically a prohibition against contract laborers. The practice of hiring abroad had increasingly alienated labor, which found the nationwide practice much more objectionable than the presence of Chinese workers. Accounts differ as to whether the Central Pacific recruited Chinese in their home country, or from the ranks of those already in the United States, but entry figures for the years of its construction suggest the latter. In September 1881 and January 1882, however, Crocker made clear that he had "ordered" men directly from China by the thousand. Need blocked any consideration of the larger ramifications. To Crocker, immigrants—Chinese or otherwise—were a commodity, and he viewed that commodity strictly in the context of a capitalist employer. If companies required labor, and immigrant workers could serve the need, then Crocker wanted policies that would not interfere with their solicitation.[36]

Chinese exclusion also threatened to dash the Associates' intentions of increasing their involvement in transpacific shipping, specifically the hauling of Chinese immigrants. As Congress debated the prohibition, the railroad moguls' existing vessels, filled with immigrants, raced toward California in an effort to beat the impending legislation. Plans called for refitting two ships, so as to provide the Asians with "standee berths and opium smoking rooms." Crocker seemed to have no problem with accommodating the latter vice, likely because only the transportation of Chinese would provide a return on their investment. "If it were not for the imminence of a change in the law, preventing the immigration of Chinese, I would not hesitate for a moment to say that it would be a good thing to do," he said of refitting the ships in January 1882, "but if they pass a law stopping Chinese immigration, this session, our steamers will barely pay expenses." A year later, after the Chinese Exclusion Act became law, the straight-talking construction manager determined that operation of the ships would no longer be possible. The Associates had lost both their source of labor and the profits to be made from transporting the workers to the United States.[37]

Crocker continued his blunt criticism of those opposed to Chinese immigrants as the Associates shifted their attention to construction of the California and Oregon. When track-laying began in early 1882, he had no concerns, in contrast to the work on the SP, about obtaining the necessary labor. "We will have no difficulty in getting all of the men we want to work here in California," he informed Huntington, "as they are willing to work anywhere except in Texas. It is almost impossible to get men to go there." To outpace their competitors, who were building south from Oregon, Crocker anticipated that he would need five to six thousand men, but even with that number, progress would be slow. Eighteen months later, when Huntington pushed for accelerated construction in order to claim the first part of the land grant and issue bonds based on the first miles of completed track, Crocker reversed himself and complained about a labor shortage: "I thought that we would have no trouble in getting all the men we wanted, but I find that now we have got about 3,500 men on the work, it is about all that we can get." An insufficient workforce had become a serious problem.[38]

Multiple considerations made the Chinese the preferred solution. Although the Exclusion Act prohibited the importation of more workers from China, Crocker anticipated "a great influx of chinamen [sic]" would make its way to northern California, once the men had finished their work on the SP, "but unless there is we cannot hope to increase our force much beyond what it now is, except [if] we offer much higher wages." White laborers, by implication, would comprise the ranks of the these more expensive workers, and for Crocker and his partners, their increased cost made them a less desirable option. Workers had to be available, and they had to be cheap. To keep building costs low, Crocker looked to any and every cost-saving measure. He praised one of their engineers who, having taken charge of construction, was "cheapening it very much and building just as good a road." Yet they could not overcome the lack of labor.

When meeting both conditions proved to be difficult, the Associates directed their frustration at those deemed too myopic to realize the value of the Chinese. Personally, they stood to lose valuable land grants, due to a short-age of workers, and on a larger scale, the inability to find enough Chinese could jeopardize completion of tracks that would connect California to the Pacific Northwest. But, in making their case for the benefits brought about by Chinese immigrants, the Associates tried to stress their universal value.

"It is impossible in my opinion," Crocker fumed to Huntington, "to build railroads in this country with white labor entirely." In this case, he directed his criticism toward xenophobic Californians, whose narrow-minded bigotry intended to deprive him of his preferred source of workers. The problem was the same as that which had vexed area entrepreneurs since the Gold Rush days: "The fact is that labor is scarce in California, and the action of our New Constitution makers has prevented many from coming." The offending document was the 1879 Constitution, with its restrictions on both Chinese and the companies that would hire them. Although the courts had begun to strike down many of the discriminatory provisions, on the grounds that they infringed on powers delegated to the national government and violated the Asians' federally guaranteed right of equal protection, it did not assuage Crocker's frustration. Any interference with immigration, particularly that of the Chinese, retarded growth and prosperity, by depriving businesses of an essential commodity.

Yet Crocker's embrace of the Chinese depended on laborers comporting themselves in a manner acceptable to employers. When those on the California and Oregon challenged the operators' authority, Crocker's response to the obstreperous immigrant workers resembled that of Frank Gowen and other hard-line corporate leaders. In July 1883 the eagerly awaited completion of the first 20 miles of C&O track hit a snag. The "chinamen" had gone on strike. Nothing had been done for two weeks, as the recalcitrant laborers sought a 25 percent pay raise, a 10 percent reduction of the standard workday, and what Crocker described as "many other privileges which we would not grant." "In fact," he continued in his report to Huntington, "we will not grant anything, as you well know that if we should grant them 10%, it would be an incentive for another strike at some future time." Moreover, Crocker believed that obdurate tactics would soon yield the desired results, as the Chinese were "pretty well starved out" and would be back to work "within a few days," under the old terms.[39] As with European immigrants in the East, availability and low cost were only some of the attributes that made the Asians desirable workers; compliance with management authority over wages and working conditions were others.

These narrowly defined expectations made it more difficult for California employers to find suitable workers. Passage of the Chinese Exclusion Act may have provided emotional satisfaction to xenophobes, but it eliminated any growth of one theretofore tapped resource. In 1883, the year after the Act's passage, the California Immigration Commission of the Central Pacific Railroad mounted an aggressive recruitment campaign "to settle up the vacant lands of California & there by add to the prosperity of the state. . . ." Wealthy businessmen supported the efforts to attract needed labor. Advertisements in the United States and abroad promoted the Golden State to would-be migrants as a place "of wonderful resources & industries," where "pecuniary success is more certain and life more enjoyable" than in other parts of the West. Railroad officials anticipated attracting large number of foreigners, not explicitly stated but understood to be replacements for the Chinese, but residents would have to do their part, by welcoming the immigrants and selling them land at reasonable prices. Various schemes had denied this last opportunity to Asians. Proponents may have been optimistic, but at least one long-time employer saw less than satisfactory results. Five years later during congressional testimony, Collis Huntington would decry California manufacturers' lack of labor, an insufficiency due largely to the barriers to more Chinese immigration.[40]

Even Denis Kearney, a leader of the movement to exclude Chinese laborers, would acknowledge the void created by their proscription. Following the death of Leland Stanford, Jr., Kearney offered to supply domestic help during the family's time of bereavement. The former labor leader, who now ran an employment and general business agency, did not stop with this overture, and offered commentary on prevailing economic conditions. "Our state is entering a degree of prosperity this year never before known in her history. . ." he opined, but more needed to be done. "The gap made by the departing Chinese will have to be filled." The law did not in fact expel the Asians (although some who felt unwanted may have left), but prohibiting the entrance of any new laborers would effectively reduce the number of those available to employers. Kearney claimed to be doing his part to fix the problem, by publishing editorials in US and English newspapers extolling the opportunities that awaited laborers on the Pacific Coast. One can only wonder if his efforts to recruit more workers led him to reconsider at least some of his antagonism toward the Chinese, as clearly they neither had taken every jobs away from whites nor prevented them from demanding higher wages for much needed service.

One can only speculate on how Leland Stanford, Sr., may have reacted to Kearney's words. Certainly as a businessman Stanford would have shared the employment broker's exuberant promotion of California's economic prosperity. Yet when it came to finding the necessary workers, the railroad magnate would have recognized the extent to which the now excluded Chinese had been responsible for building its major transportation arteries. These thoughts may have evoked bitterness toward Kearney and his ilk for contributing to their restriction. Stanford also may have wondered how the former sandlot xenophobe hoped to find adequate numbers of workers, as employers had struggled to solve this dilemma since the Gold Rush days. California habitually had needed labor, and previous schemes to attract more laborers had failed to alleviate the problem. Even if adequate numbers of workers could be obtained, they had to be available at affordable costs. The Chinese had filled this bill, as Stanford and his associates repeatedly had demonstrated.[41]

Although, as Kearney himself had demonstrated, laborers also had to be of the right temperament. In 1877, when the Great Strike and its attendant violence had reached San Francisco, Stanford had specifically mentioned "Kearney and his friends" as comprising the "mob" that had threatened his and Hopkins's property. The Irishman had been the very type of unruly immigrant on whom industrialists such as Stanford placed blame for any and all labor disturbance. These foreign-born malcontents, wherever they might be found, comprised an element much more dangerous, at least in the eyes of business leaders, than any ethnic group. Succinctly put, a good worker would neither strike nor sow disharmony.

These expectations applied to all workers. Anti-Asian bigotry plagued Chinese laborers and led to their restriction decades before Congress passed similar measures targeting other ethnic groups. The Chinese also encountered experiences in America similar to those of their peers, immigrants who had crossed another ocean or traveled from contiguous territory. They most importantly shared the status of wage earners. As such, the Chinese typified what it meant to be a foreign-born laborer. They served managers who expected them to work long hours, for relatively low pay, under conditions unilaterally set by their employers. Events to the east that involved their non-Asian contemporaries would confirm this universality.

CHAPTER 3

Alien Anarchism

Immigrants and Industrial Unrest in the 1880s

"Dynamite Explosion," Chicago businessman Charles A. Heath wrote in his diary on May 4, 1886, enlarging the letters and highlighting the black script in blue. Heath, a pious family man who managed a seed company, devoted most of his daily entries to routine family matters such as church meetings or walks with his wife. Today was different: "A bomb thrown by unknown parties into a company of Police men sent to disperse a crowd of Socialists in the old Hay-Market. 40 Policemen wounded. 1 killed."[1]

Repercussions would reverberate across the nation. Called by one commentator "the most significant event that has occurred in this country since Sumter was fired on,"[2] what happened during and after the Haymarket Square rally would solidify the presumed connection between aliens and undesirable worker radicalism. Reaction to the Molly Maguires and the Great Strike had established the practice of blaming immigrants and associated foreign ideologies for the industrial era's loss of workplace harmony, but the stigma did not prevent employers from fulfilling their growing labor needs by hiring large numbers of alien workers. Those recruited regularly included strikebreakers whose presence angered established workers. Through the early 1880s, laborers—not capitalists—tended to harbor animosity toward recent arrivals. When the Haymarket affair renewed and intensified fears of working-class violence, employers resorted to the pattern of implicating the immigrants who labored at their mills, mines, and factories, even as they continued to employ them.

During the years between the Great Strike and the reappearance of economic depression in 1883, the pace of American industrialization accelerated significantly, as did the consolidation of capital and the creation of ever larger firms. The factory system, declared Massachusetts labor economist and US Census supervisor Carroll D. Wright in February 1882, had "found its most rapid extension in the United States," enabling the nation's manufacturers "to become successful rivals in the mechanic arts of any country that desires to compete with them." Wright did pose the question of whether America's industrial success was "a power for good or evil," to which he provided his own answer by deeming factory production as the "most potent element in promoting civilization." He concurrently dismissed "the schemes of socialists or the insane panaceas of quack economists," neither of which offered anything capable of improving American commerce. Other writers offered more critical assessments of corporate greed, but joined Wright in marveling at the array of goods and services increasingly available to American consumers.[3]

Statistics offered empirical evidence of the country's burgeoning economy. Between 1877 and 1883, the value of cotton textiles—the nation's oldest factory-produced commodity—rose by 26.5 percent, from $10.2 to $12.9 million. Tonnage of steel railroad bars rose 238 percent, from 385 thousand to 1.3 million long tons (each of which equaled 2240 pounds), and the volume of refined petroleum products jumped from 10.8 to 26.6 million barrels, a 146 percent gain. The increased steel production served the needs of a still-growing railroad system, one that by 1886 had created a unified network with a standard track gauge and established time zones. Shippers of raw materials and manufactured products could now send them virtually anywhere in the United States; at its ports, a fleet of modern vessels stood ready to transport the various articles of commerce to world markets. Concurrent expansion of another popular commodity perhaps indicated the wants of the growing working class: during the six years after the Great Strike, the volume of intoxicating beverages—beer, wine, and liquor—grew by 250 million gallons. Other major industries also showed impressive gains.[4]

More production meant more jobs, which drew foreigners to America's shores. Construction and manufacturing, asserted famed Civil War–era journalist Charles Carleton Coffin, "called for such a vast number of laborers that we could not supply the demand and we summoned them from other lands." Come they did. In 1877, the year of the Great Strike, approximately 142,000 foreigners entered the United States, but that number more than quadrupled, to over 602,000, in 1883. At Castle Garden in New York City between 1878 and 1879, the number of immigrants doubled. Most of the immigrants continued to hail from places that traditionally had sent the largest numbers, with England and Germany predominating. Sweden sent the third-most immigrants, but Italians, part of what would come to be called the new immigration from southern and eastern Europe, trailed by only a few thousand. As expected, most of the immigrants settled in industrialized regions in New England, such as Massachusetts, Rhode Island, and Connecticut. Alien residents in Massachusetts, with its large textile mills, rose by almost 100,000 between 1870 and 1880, when they comprised about a third of the population. To the west, Chicago also attracted large numbers of immigrants as it built itself into a major industrial center in the middle of the continent.[5]

A few commentators continued to portray immigrants as hearty pioneers coming to the United States with the traditional intent of homesteading western lands, but more insightful observers recognized that most foreigners now came to the United States intending to work for wages, usually in industrial centers. Pro-capitalist spokesmen emphasized the immigrants' commercial contributions. "In the long run," editorialized the conservative magazine, *The American*, "to which all wise economy looks, all classes benefit by the influx of new labor and would-be citizens from Europe." Available alien workers had allowed companies to expand their economies of scale, their rate and efficiency of production, and immigrants also had increased the nation's consumer base, which generated even more commercial activity. Some commentators had doubts about the Chinese, but others saw even them as having economic benefit. Writer Albion Tourgée, a consistent champion of justice and equality for African Americans, made no distinction among ethnic groups when he characterized 1880s immigrants as "among the most enterprising, far-reaching, and determined of their respective classes." In direct rebuke of those who would condemn immigrants as a threat to the nation's mythical Anglo-Saxon roots, he compared contemporary arrivals favorably with the foreigners who had been coming to North America since the colonial era. Interestingly, Tourgée did not raise the issue of immigrants possibly taking jobs away from African Americans.[6]

Tourgée lived in North Carolina during Reconstruction and later depicted his experiences in the fictionalized *A Fool's Errand*. The book chronicled his diligent yet frequently fruitless efforts to create a progressive, interracial New South. Combining tenets of pre-war Jacksonian democracy and abolitionism, Tourgée wanted to unite the freedmen's interests with those of working-class whites. This seemingly should have led him to encourage employers to hire African Americans and to see them as a readily available labor force, ready to meet the needs of growing businesses. Seeing and using them in this way would have alleviated at least some of the need for foreign-born workers, a point that Tourgée could have made in his commentary on immigration. But he also believed that the former slaves would need time to adjust to freedom, both politically and socially. Given this qualifier, it was hardly surprising that "the Fool" wanted immigrants to come to the South, to labor in its newly established manufacturing plants. How their presence might impede the freedmen's economic advancement does not appear to have crossed his mind.[7]

As to the potential for employment competition between immigrants and native whites, Lucy Larcom, a nationally esteemed poet and partici-pant observer of the factory system's early days, summarily dismissed that threat. Larcom, one of the "Lowell Girls" who had worked in the city's tex-tile mills during the 1840s, contended that the Yankees of her generation had not intended to toil permanently at their looms and shuttles. They also had higher expectations for their daughters, such as school teaching or com-munity service. In their absence, businesses would have to seek labor from other sources, specifically the "underdeveloped population of Europe" that supplied "the factory workers of the Old World who now fill our mills." Rather than vying for jobs with the upwardly mobile Americans, the aliens filled jobs that natives willingly vacated. Larcom foresaw only one serious problem: the immigrants' potential failure to assimilate higher US standards of living. To prevent the foreign-born from becoming lower- class objects of contempt, and encourage them to strive for high levels of manhood and womanhood, Americans had an obligation to provide immigrants with edu-cational opportunities. Thus Larcom did not see immigrants so much as a threat, but rather as an issue in need of attention.[8]

Corporate practices, however, did create tensions between immigrants and established workers, who in response developed some of the earliest concerns about the influx of alien workers. An 1882 strike by freight han-dlers against greater New York City railroads exemplified this trend. Work-ers struck for higher wages, and even in the face of criticism, the involved companies refused to accede to their demands. "There is no doubt," claimed the *St. Louis Globe-Democrat,* commenting on the strike's detrimental effects on national commerce, "that the delay of freight is due to the refusal of the roads to pay sufficient wages to get the job done." Local workers similarly sympathized with their striking comrades, making it difficult for the railways to find replacement laborers. "Their only resource," reported *Frank Leslie's Illustrated Newspaper,* "was to seek recruits from the throng of immigrants who are passing into the city, and among these the Italians and Russian Jews were the only class which furnished hands." Thousands of these able-bodied laborers passed daily through the Castle Garden immigration station. While one report ridiculed the immigrants' almost buffoonish lack of proper training, resulting in "Jew, truck and boxes going to pieces in one grand catastrophe," managers did hire these "scabs" in large numbers."[9]

Animosity developed quickly between the strikers and the alien replacements, with the voices of capital and labor offering varied interpretations. *Leslie's Illustrated Newspaper* depicted an Italian immigrant defending himself against a mob of strikers, described as "hoodlum assailants." Accompanying prose explained how the threat of violence compounded the already difficult situation for men who could not speak English: "Moreover, most of them were nervous and timid, and they soon became so fearful that they would be killed by the strikers that a large proportion deserted after the day's work was done." Labor spokesmen saw things differently: "The raw immigrants from European cities are brought here by padrones, and others, and these poor creatures, unacquainted with our language or customs, are taken off the ship and put at work without being allowed to converse with anyone who would be likely to explain the real situation of affairs," decried representatives of the Freight Handlers Central Union. Those who the strikers did manage to inform frequently left the job site, and in some cases, they joined the strikers.[10]

Concerns about the use of aliens as strikebreakers led to condemnation of recruitment in their home countries. Companies "summoned" immigrants by offering them contracts, presumably at less than prevailing American wages, prior to their departure. Beginning in the 1860s, labor leaders saw this practice as management's most effective weapon for exploiting workers, as it allowed employers easily to replace workers who struck or otherwise challenged supervisory authority. Adding insult to injury, businesses that benefitted from tariff restrictions on foreign goods could freely import cheap labor. William Sylvis, head of the National Labor Union, initiated the campaign to restrict their entry, but he carefully differentiated between the employers, whose greed he condemned, and the unknowing immigrants upon whom they preyed. Congress in 1882 sought to appease labor by barring most Chinese, but American workers demanded a more broad prohibition. To them, it mattered not from where the foreigners came, but under what circumstances. At its 1881 convention, the Federation of Organized Trades and Labor Unions (precursor to the AFL) called for the "prevention of the importation of contract labor."[11] The issue intensified with the onset of another depression during the early 1880s.

Between 1882 and 1886, American business activity declined precipitously. Commerce contracted, production of durable goods fell, and nearly ten thousand companies failed in both 1884 and 1885. Economist Carroll D. Wright, who only a few years earlier had praised US industrial growth, now announced the onset of the nation's first industrial depression. Conditions created what Wright called an "apprehensiveness on the part of all classes," but it especially affected working men and women, who needed to earn money in order to subsist. Numerous surveys, including one done by Wright in Massachusetts, found double-digit unemployment. Almost 30 percent of the Bay State's labor force had been out of work for at least four months, and those who remained on the job experienced significant wage reductions. New York State experienced a similar rise of "men walking the streets looking for something to do." The resultant "army of unemployed," in the words of Knights of Labor leader Terence Powderly, developed a "deep rooted feeling of discontent." Business owners and managers drew much of their ire, but many of the voices that decried the dire state of America's working class directed their frustration at the presence of foreigners. Powderly himself, in his subsequent career as a US Bureau of Immigration official, pursued restriction as a means of protecting US labor from cheap foreign competition.[12]

Other critics of immigrant workers included spinners at the fifty-two textile mills in Fall River, Massachusetts. In 1880 their collective output comprised more than 60 percent of the nation's print cloth, and the city had the highest percentage of foreign-born residents in the nation. Employment prospects had attracted the aliens, but in mid-December 1883, on the eve of an unsuccessful strike, the *Raleigh News and Observer* reported on the Fall River Spinners' Union plan to settle excess foreign workers in the South. English textile mills had expanded considerably in recent years, but many of the country's spinners still could not find consistent work. Fall River seemed to offer an alternative, but with the onset of the depression, Union leaders worried that the unemployed Brits were "coming in direct competition with labor here, crowding our factories and in no small measure to increase the burdens on our operatives." The Spinners' plan called for the establishment of a cooperative in the US South, "colonized by the unemployed operatives from this city, whom we could send there from time to time when the conditions of the labor market warranted such action." Many of the colonists so envisioned would be recently arrived foreigners, whose presence in Fall River would make it more difficult for the unionized employees to exert pressure on management.[13]

Results of an 1884 strike demonstrated the importance of worker solidarity. The spinners walked off the job in February 1884, but by mid-May management had broken the strike. A glut of cotton cloth in a saturated market hurt the workers' cause, as did the fact that the spinners comprised less than five percent of the area's mill workers. They tried to organize a union of the more numerous weavers, but this "army" of less skilled laborers apparently did not support the spinners' cause, at least to the extent that they were willing to join the walkout. Rumors circulated of a pending general strike involving all mill workers, but it never materialized. No reports specifically mentioned any attempt by operators to recruit immigrants as replacement workers, but any perception of immigrants impeding workers' advancement could not help but intensify anti-alien sentiments. Mill managers' ability to keep their plants running showed the value of having ready access to a surplus labor pool.[14]

Importation of immigrant workers did figure prominently in the 1884 Hocking Valley Coal Strike, where miners lost a bitter struggle to protect their wages. Over 100 regional mines, employing 4,500 workers, annually extracted 2.5 million tons of bituminous coal. Simmering tensions erupted when the owners' syndicate attempted to lower per-ton compensation, claiming that the reductions would make their coal competitive with that from other regions. The ensuing conflict, called by one contemporary "the bitterest strike in the entire mining industry of America," prompted the operators to recruit Italians—and by some accounts also Hungarians and Poles—who would accept the lower pay. Workers initially warned "that no foreigners will be allowed in the mines." However, immigrant scabs—characterized by union leader John McBride as having been deceived by the owners—did start to arrive by mid-July, and the *Milwaukee Sentinel* reported on the operators' plans to have "3,000 more foreigners to go into the mines in a few days." The concurrent appearance of Pinkerton detectives intensified the standoff, and in early September when the situation turned violent, Ohio governor George Hoadly mobilized the state militia. Calm did return, but for workers, it came with the loss of the previously higher pay.[15]

Immigrant recruitment to the embattled Hocking Valley mines stemmed from management's deliberate attempt to find compliant—and lower-cost—workers, but reports indicate that the foreigners may not have provided the desired panacea. "The Italians who had been brought in to work the mines," reported the *Michigan Farmer*, "quit in body after four days work, and marched to the depot to take trains for Columbus and Chicago." Other papers reported similar scenarios. Accounts did not say if those who left comprised all or just some of the strikebreakers, and if they left from more than one mine, but their departure appeared to vindicate labor advocates, who saw their exodus as the result of having learned the truth. For example, reports by future Haymarket principal August Spies, of "hundreds of lives in the process of slow destruction" as a consequence of the strike, appeared in foreign-language newspapers and purportedly contributed to the formation of a local German-speaking chapter of the International Working People's Association.[16]

Two strikes at the Cleveland Rolling Mill Company showed similarly conflicting immigrant behaviors, as those involved in the work stoppages both supplied the cheap labor that the employer wanted and acted as the alien radicals that they dreaded. The company, incorporated in 1863 and operated by the Chisholm family, made rails and other steel products. During the 1880s, new technologies and methodologies allowed Rolling Mill to replace its skilled workers, largely earlier immigrants from Great Britain who belonged to the Amalgamated Association of Iron and Steel Workers (AAISW), with newer arrivals from eastern Europe. An 1882 AAISW strike accelerated the substitution process. New immigrants, those both already in Cleveland and recruited from other locations, acted as strikebreakers. The company reportedly hired some of the latter at Castle Garden, literally as they got off of the ships that had brought them to the United States. Wherever they might have been approached, their availability, coupled with the AAISW's failure to organize unskilled workers, allowed the company to break the strike and establish a nonunion shop. In an interesting twist, native speakers perpetrated most of the attendant violence when they sought to dissuade the newer immigrants from "scabbing."[17]

The situation changed dramatically three years later. This time, in reaction to a series of wage cuts, Poles and Bohemians—the new immigrants—led the strike. Marching through the plant, angry workers closed not only Rolling Mill but also other companies operated by the Chisholm family. At one of the rallies, which were held in the immigrant neighborhoods, Chicago anarchist William J. Gorsuch—who shortly would be connected to the Haymarket affair—urged the Cleveland workers to rain death on the likes of "the Vanderbilts, the Goulds, and the Chisholms." Shortly thereafter an angry mob again succeeded in closing the reopened Rolling Mill, and Cleveland's mayor, fearing an escalation of violence, convinced the company to settle with its disgruntled workers. The very immigrants whom the company had recruited to crush a previous strike now had mounted a successful challenge to managerial authority. While this no doubt hinted of immigrant radicalism, aliens observed at the various protest rallies generally carried the American flag, instead of the red one signifying socialism. Unfortunately, one son of Polish immigrants would not find contentment in his parents' newfound home. Seven years later, Cleveland Rolling Mill would blacklist Leon Czolgosz for taking part in yet another strike. His lingering resentment might well explain how and why he became an agent of death, targeting not a capitalist but the American president whom he thought acted in their stead.[18]

Others, native-born and immigrant alike, shared Czolgosz's resentment of worker exploitation, if not his ultimate choice of reaction. The rise of the Knights of Labor, coupled with the electoral success of candidates representing various labor parties and the emergence of worker councils in several cities during the early 1880s, indicated the level of discontent. Led by Terence Powderly, the Knights' membership reached 750,000 by the spring of 1885, making the union a force with which to be reckoned. Labor candidates appeared on ballots across the nation, including New York City, where reformer Henry George received about a third of the 1886 mayoral votes. Even theretofore conservative Tammany Hall Democrat "Honest" John Kelly swung to the left, condemning monopolies and supporting labor causes. Some worker advocates denigrated recently arrived foreigners—especially the Chinese and eastern Europeans—as unwanted competition and the docile pawns of management, but others enthusiastically embraced the foreigners who joined labor's ranks and occasionally led what the press called immigrant strikes. Encouraged by the widespread ferment, proletarians envisioned successful campaigns for shorter hours, higher pay, and better working conditions. The Wheeling, West Virginia, *Sunday Register* described the labor question as a "mighty commotion" marking the land.[19]

Contention centered on demands for a shorter workday. Post–Civil War laborers typically worked ten- to fourteen-hour shifts, at an employer-set pace. Resisters, led by Boston machinist Ira Steward, secured the 1886 enactment of an eight-hour standard shift for federal employees, but unfortunately, future presidents and agency administrators seldom enforced the statute. Advocates nonetheless hoped to expand its application to private industry. In 1886 the Federation of Organized Trades and Labor Unions (FOTLU, precursor to the AFL) sought to make eight hours the standard for all American workers, and called for its implementation to begin on May 1. In Chicago, August Spies and others associated with the immigrant-friendly International Working Peoples' Association—who previously had dismissed agitation for a shorter workday as a distractive compromise with capitalist enemies—joined the campaign. Michigan labor spokesman Joseph Labadie viewed the movement as nothing less than a "revolution." Editors of *Science* added their endorsement, but they concluded that the desire to work for one-third of the clock day was a legitimate request, not a "radical" demand.[20] Whether an extreme or moderate reform, by the mid-1880s, labor activists had made "eight hours" their rallying cry.

As the workday protests intensified, labor strife rocked southwestern railway lines controlled by financier Jay Gould, whose reputation as an unprincipled speculator made him the quintessential robber baron. Railroads and telegraph companies comprised his major holdings. Starting early in his career, Gould exploited ethnicity to control labor. He responded to an 1871 miners' strike at Wyoming properties operated by the Union Pacific Railroad by hiring Scandinavian immigrants as substitute workers. When they struck in 1874, Gould vowed that he "would not make any concessions" and requested deployment of troops to deter potential violence. He also approved replacement of the strikers with lower-cost Chinese. Ethnicity became a wedge by which to divide labor, pitting "whites" against Asians and preventing worker solidarity. Ethnic manipulation would allow management to "keep master of the situation" on a "permanent" basis. Resulting lower wages would bolster corporate profits and provide an edge when competing with rival firms. While Gould did confer with Terence Powderly during the subsequent southwestern strikes, he did not waver in his resolve to preserve management's mastery.[21]

Depression-driven wage reductions prompted a series of strikes. Shopmen, who maintained the rolling stock, struck Gould's southwestern railroads in 1885. Their efforts resulted in a victory for the workers, many of whom belonged to Knights of Labor. The next year, dubious disagreements between the Knights' District Assembly 101 and the Texas and Pacific Railroad spread to other Gould lines, including the Missouri Pacific and St. Louis Bridge Company, prompting a determined but ultimately unsuccessful strike by shop mechanics and yardmen. In addition to increased wages, strikers demanded recognition of the Knights as the employees' bargaining agent, creation of an apprentice system, and implementation of a formal discharge procedure for union members. A published list of concerns, called a manifesto by one commentator, conveyed the level of antagonism between capital and labor. It read in part: "in order to meet and defeat these contemptible and blood-sucking corporations and their government allies, and in order to secure redress for grievances and the following demands, we have inaugurated this strike." This radical posturing, coupled with violence at East Saint Louis, Illinois, and Fort Worth, Texas, helped to doom the workers' cause. While laborers had broad public support in 1884 and 1885, local citizens and public officials turned against the strikers in 1886. Bloodshed eroded support even among the ranks of workers.[22]

Placement of blame for the associated violence produced some interesting results. The strike, succinctly postulated Harvard economist Frank W. Taussig—not once, but twice—"was a struggle for power." The "inevitable" confrontation emanated from a test of wills regarding who would exercise what power in management of the Gould lines. Conversely, pursuit of redress for the actual wrongs that had been done to employees played no significant part in the walkout. Others heaped blame on strike leader Martin Irons, characterizing him as a recalcitrant rabble-rouser intent on pursuing his own radical agenda. Interestingly, commentators made no reference to his having been an immigrant, albeit one from Scotland who had arrived forty years earlier at the age of fourteen. His long residence in the United States may account for the omission of his origins from public castigation, as might Americans' generally favorable views of Scottish immigrants at a time when the "new" arrivals began to attract more negative attention. A lack of readily apparent ethnic identity among the strikers also may have muted allegations of alien-induced radicalism. Taussig, for example, makes no reference to the presence of foreigners among the railroad workers. Critics did identify striking African Americans as a particularly disruptive element, making them, not ethnic whites, the target of suspicion.[23]

Strikers themselves used ethnicity to identify a foil. Both blacks and whites vilified Chinese, whom they equated with convict or unfree laborers. Specious accusations charged the Missouri Pacific and Texas & Pacific, two of the Gould lines, with employing large numbers of Asians, to the detriment of hardworking "free" men. A March 1886 Knights of Labor petition called upon fellow employees to drive the interlopers from the railways. Attention centered on Texas, to which Chinese had first come in the late 1860s, when local employers saw them as an alternative to the freedmen. Several hundred initially worked on state railroads, and approximately twenty-six hundred came east during the building of the Southern Pacific in the early 1880s (see chapter 2). Yet the number who remained in the state stayed small; the 316 living in Texas in 1880 comprised only 0.01 percent of the state's population, and while the number rose to 710 in 1890, they amounted to only 0.03 percent. "Only about one hundred Chinese," confirmed a post-strike investigation, worked on the accused railroads, and "they at a remote point."[24] Neither their small number nor their isolation likely mattered to the angry railroaders, as they emulated a typical management tactic by blaming "others" for the fate that befell them.

The strike against the Gould lines influenced labor unrest on other railroads, including the Vanderbilt-owned Lake Shore & Michigan Southern Railway, which terminated in Chicago. On April 17 Lake Shore switchmen struck. Their demands included the removal of eight nonunion employees whose presence angered unionized workers on other railroads with which the Lake Shore exchanged cars. The walkout precipitated six days of minor violence, leading to the intervention of sheriff's deputies and Pinkertons. After reviewing the situation, Governor Richard J. Oglesby (who shortly thereafter would figure prominently in determining the fate of those charged with the

Haymarket bombing), contemplated calling out the state militia, and reports circulated of offers by Jay Gould and Cornelius Vanderbilt II to fund the mobilization. Oglesby ultimately determined not to use the troops, and the strike ended inconclusively, with both sides claiming victory. Regardless of which side had won or lost, business and civic leaders viewed the growing militancy among area workers as matter of serious concern. Diarist Charles Heath, for example, noted the disturbances on the Lake Shore and other lines, commenting on their adverse effects on commerce and trade. Negative attention soon would focus on the city's numerous immigrant laborers.[25]

Labor strife quickly shifted to the city's McCormick Reaper works. One of the city's largest employers and a driving force in the continuing settlement of the vast region to its west, the company steadfastly opposed reduction of its ten-hour workday. Cyrus McCormick, Jr., who had assumed control of the company in 1880, had a history of conflict with the workers. "We have, together, done what we could to uphold the liberality and fairness in our dealings with the laboring classes, so far as our men are concerned," he explained in 1886, "and where the issue was one of principle, we have been unwilling to surrender, whatever might be the cost." Principle here meant the authority to determine conditions of employment, and in this instance, maintaining it would come at a high cost. In February 1886 the company replaced its union workforce, and then hired the seemingly omnipresent Pinkerton agents to protect the "scabs." On May 3, workers who had been attending an eight-hour rally rushed to the nearby McCormick compound. Violence ensued, and Chicago police officers, who had been sent to disperse the demonstrators, fired into the crowd, killing and wounding an undetermined number of protesters.[26]

Those sympathetic to the company quickly placed blame. The unacceptable "outrages" had "originated with the foreign-born." The perpetrators had been "a mob of aliens." "The barbarian attack on the McCormick reaper factory Monday afternoon and the assault upon its workmen were instigated and led by foreign Communists," reported the *Chicago Tribune*, even though the May 3 events had been more spontaneous than orchestrated. Agitators claimed to be protecting American liberties, the *Tribune* continued, but not one of them was "a true American citizen" or had anything in common with those who deserved that appellation. Other accounts similarly identified the leaders as immigrants and noted the prevalent use of foreign languages in incendiary publications. Ironically, a generation earlier, when faced with a similar situation, Leander McCormick had suggested to his brother and CEO Cyrus, Sr., that the company might benefit from finding an agent who could recruit immigrants willing to accept the company's wages and work conditions.[27] Now it would increasingly be foreign-born workers who found themselves the targets of employer distrust.

The next evening a protest rally took place on Desplaines Street, adjacent to Haymarket Square. The gathering proceeded peacefully, with no reports of unruly behavior, but as it neared its conclusion, police arrived intending to disperse those still assembled. As the constables approached the wagon that served as a rostrum, someone threw a bomb into their midst, killing one officer. The ensuing melee wrought more death and injuries, for which eight anarchists were tried, convicted, and punished. On November 11, 1887, four of the alleged conspirators—in the words of Heath—"were hanged at noon in the Cook County Jail." Another—Louis Lingg—had committed suicide the previous day by "exploding a dynamite cap in his mouth," and the remainder were incarcerated at the Joliet penitentiary. "The four men who met death were nothing in themselves," opined the *Boston Daily Advertiser,* "only examples of the most depraved and reckless of the swarm from the slums of Europe which is finding its way to this country."[28] As the editor noted, the anarchists' fates were not a simple matter of innocence or guilt, but also how one more broadly defined the latter.

To Heath and those who held similar opinions, the men clearly deserved their punishments. Their guilt derived not from direct participation in the attack on the police. Instead, what they had done to rile whomever had perpetrated the dastardly deed sealed their doom. Much of the anarchists' rhetoric had called for armed rebellion against the forces that exploited or used violence against workers, such as the managers of the McCormick plant and the constabulary who had acted in their interest. Appeals to revolution permeated their writings. The condemned also had comported themselves as martyrs to the cause of overthrowing American polity and corporate capitalism. Yet their case revolved around the perplexing distinction between advocacy and action. Illinois statute extended guilt to anyone who advised or encouraged criminal actions, so to hold the anarchists culpable authorities needed only to make a connection between their fiery pronouncements, their otherwise legal possession of arms and explosives, and the bomb thrown at the police. Both the prosecution and the public would emphasize the defendants' ethnicity in making the needed link and justifying their convictions.[29]

Seven of the eight alleged offenders were immigrants. Samuel Fielden had come to the United States from Britain, generally thought to be a place that supplied "desirable" immigrants. Oscar Nebee had been born to German parents in New York City, but he thereafter lived in Europe and then returned to the United States as a teenager in 1864. August Spies, Michael Schwab, Adolph Fisher, and George Engel had immigrated from Germany, but all of them had lived in the United States for about a decade prior to the bombing. Hence, even though many of them had brought radical inclinations from Europe, they also had been affected significantly by their American environment. Fielden, for example, had been appalled by the treatment of freedmen during Reconstruction, and Neebe's voracious reading had included works by Thomas Jefferson and Thomas Paine. Finally, ancestors of Albert Parsons, who was considered the anarchist ringleader, had come to colonial America in 1632, and several of his forebears had served with distinction in the Revolutionary War. But these US influences mattered little.[30]

Louis Lingg, the most radical of the defendants, had also emigrated from Germany, coming to the United States less than a year before Haymarket. In many ways—particularly his recent arrival and unabashed endorsement of violent confrontation—he among the defendants most manifested public perceptions of alien subversives. Bomb-making materials had been found when police searched his home. Those frightened by the threat of radical violence saw dynamite as the ultimate menace, because it placed disproportionately destructive power in the hands of a single man, and Lingg made clear his willingness to use it. "I repeat that I am the enemy of the 'order' of today, and I repeat that, with all my powers, so long as breath remains in me, I shall combat it. I declare again, frankly and openly, that I am in favor of using force," he stated in response to his conviction and death sentence, to which he added an earlier declaration: " 'If they use cannons against us, we shall use dynamite against them.' " Although he acknowledged that execution would end his part in making good on the threat, he averred that thousands of others who had heard his message would follow in his footsteps. In a final act of defiance, he committed suicide rather than succumb to the executioner's noose.[31]

Two broadsides connected to the defendants, written in both German and English, reinforced perceptions that the "outrages" had un-American origins. August Spies wrote the so-called Revenge Circular after witnessing the killing of workers at the McCormick plant. A typesetter added the infamous "revenge" across the broadside's top, but even without it, incendiary prose permeated Spies's missive. Both the English and German versions called workers to take up arms against employers and the police who served them. The German prose conveyed especially strong sentiments: "Annihilate the beasts in human form who call themselves rulers!" Initial composition of a second circular, this one announcing the Haymarket rally, also included an incendiary call: "Workingmen Arm Yourselves and Appear in Full Force." In this case, Spies did secure its removal, but some with the original wording still circulated.[32] Close examination of the documents—at least from a historical perspective—makes clear that Spies and his associates were angry at exploitative practices directed against laborers. To challenge the abusive institutions and oppressive authorities was hardly incompatible with US ideals, yet to contemporary observers in the wake of the bombing, their pronouncements equated to criminal conduct. Their message also came across as decidedly un-American, an impression amplified by the inclusion of the German text.

Prosecutors led the charge to connect the defendants' ethnicity with their presumed guilt. Using language reminiscent of Frank Gowen's indictment of the Molly Maguires, lead prosecutor Julius Grinnell referred to the accused as "godless foreigners" and "loathsome murderers," making clear that the two characterizations were inexorably intertwined. Americans had "every right to criticize their nationality. . . ," because they had come to the United States only to sow the seeds of communism and anarchism. No one should consider them to be "part nor parcel of this country." Assistant prosecutor Francis Walker extended ethnic condemnation to defense witnesses, contending that they too were aliens and anarchists who deserved to be indicted along with those who were on trial. Not one of them, he incorrectly proclaimed, was "an American citizen or a naturalized citizen, none of them in this country but two or three years." Even trial judge Joseph Gary, writing seven years later to reinforce the verdict, characterized anarchists as "mostly foreigners to whom the English language was a strange tongue. . . ."[33] Anarchism was on trial in Chicago, and it inherently and unequivocally was foreign to all things American.

Little wonder, then, that Haymarket commentary in the press emphasized the involvement of immigrants and Chicago's large alien population. "The foreign anarchists in America," editorialized the Spectator, "have gradually become more and more fanatic, until they have at last thrown prudence to the winds and prematurely revealed themselves to Americans as they are." In the case of those involved in the rally, not only were they seen as agents of death and destruction, they were primarily Slavs and South Germans. Others identified them as Bohemians. The Troy Weekly Times warned its readers that the bombing should make clear to authorities the danger posed by "organized associations of foreign anarchists and communists." They reported that newspapers written in their native languages spread their diabolical propaganda, and ethnic neighborhoods provided breeding grounds for subversion, especially among those who could not read and write English. Offices of the Arbeiter Zeitung, the German-language newspaper where Spies had served as editor, became a den of iniquities, from whence the nefarious plot had been hatched. Even the Cherokee Advocate, which spoke for its own ethnically-marginalized constituents, identified the rioters as being foreigners.[34]

The murderous acts, asserted *Frank Leslie's Illustrated Newspaper*, emanated from "a social philosophy that is as foreign to the conditions of this free land as cowardly assassination is foreign to the habits of our daily intercourse." Symbolized by the red flag, the associated radicalism had migrated in steerage from the far corners of Europe. True Americans need have no sympathy for the conveyors' "imported ethics." But while "speedy strangulation with good American-grown hemp" would eliminate the immediate threat, its long-term amelioration would require more extensive steps. Modification of the prevailing ideas of free speech would help to silence future troublemakers, but most importantly, elimination of the subversive menace would have to include implementation of immigration restrictions sufficient to impede the "steadily inflowing population of law haters" pouring through America's ports. "Have we reached the point," the conservative weekly posited, "when we can no longer undertake to assimilate to an unlimited extent the foreign element—foreign not in respect to nationality alone, but in ideas, purposes and methods."[35]

Political economist Henry C. Adams, an advocate of state action to promote socioeconomic harmony and cofounder of the American Economic Association, likewise pronounced anarchism, and any behavior that it might engender, as wholly alien to the United States. Those who embraced it, in his estimation, did not comprehend American ideals of freedom, specifically the differentiation between speech and calls to abominable actions. The United States had long operated under the premise that it could absorb all would-be immigrants, but "of late certain Poles, Bohemians, and Hungarians (many of whom, it must be said, were imported by labor-contractors) as well as some Germans who left their own country for their country's good, have proven to be a hard meal to digest." They congregated in ethnic enclaves, failed to learn English, and too often fell prey to agitators. The United States needed to be more selective in whom it admitted, taking specific care to interdict those who would "use infamous weapons to strike terror into the minds of a peaceful community."[36] Yet Adams erred—in both fact and interpretation—in making his explicit connection to Haymarket: "It is a significant fact that of the anarchists now lying under arrest not one is a native American." Albert Parsons may have slipped his mind, or been conveniently ignored, but fully absent from Adams's thinking was any notion that the events may have had an American cause.

Philosopher William Mackintire Salter, who resided in Chicago, lectured for the Ethical Cultural Society, and participated in efforts to secure amnesty for the Haymarket defendants, nonetheless joined those who associated anarchist violence with immigrants. "Many come over here with but the faintest idea of what our government is, the main notion being that they are free to do about as they please," he stated in his lecture, "The Cure for Anarchy." Salter focused his political philosophy on the melding of religion, science, and democracy to create a system of beliefs intended to fit the realities of the modern world. He rejected the dogmatic adherence of most Americans to narrowly defined traditions and instead embraced a plural- ist respect for all human beings. Yet when it came to aliens who had come to the United States, he made clear his belief in the need for assimilation. "They should be taught, they can be," he said in regard to American mores and principles, "and I hold that it would be perfect equality if they were not allowed political function till they were taught, or had taught themselves, and were ready to pledge loyalty to the fundamental methods of our law." He also condemned Spies's "Revenge Circular"—and by extent the immi- grant press—for urging the men who went to the Haymarket rally to come armed and ready for violence.[37]

The condemned anarchists themselves acknowledged the considerable extent to which their ethnicity influenced their destiny. Perceptions of their un-American essence, coupled with the ideology that they preached, became the central issue at their trial. It, rather than any credible evidence, ultimately formed the basis of their guilt. "Grinnell's main argument against the defen- dants was 'they were foreigners. They are not citizens,'" rebutted August Spies. "I cannot speak for the others. I will only speak for myself. I have been a resident of this State fully as long as Grinnell, and probably have been as good a citizen—at least, I should not wish to be compared with him." Michael Schwab attempted to refute claims that the presence of anarchism and other radical beliefs could be linked to immigrants: "The outcry that Socialism, Communism and Anarchism are the creed of foreigners, is a big mistake. There are more Socialists of American birth in this country than foreigners, and that is much, if we consider that nearly half of all industrial workingmen are not native Americans. There are Socialistic papers in a great many States edited by Americans for Americans." George Engel opened his remarks with a reference to his immigration from Germany, and of the fail- ure of the United States to make good on its promise to foreigners like him who now called it home.[38] Few so-called natives wanted to consider that side of the nation's emerging ethnic history.

Concurrent with the Haymarket events, labor violence in Milwaukee, Wisconsin, fostered similar reactions. As part of the movement for the eight-hour day, the city's Central Labor Union and the local Knights of Labor called for a general strike to commence on May 1. Momentum grew slowly, but by May 3, most businesses had closed. Demonstrations at the

North Chicago Rolling Mill, located just south of Milwaukee in the industrial suburb of Bay View, convinced Governor Jeremiah Rusk to mobilize the Wisconsin National Guard, including Milwaukee's predominantly Polish American Kosciusko Guards. On both May 4 and 5, in a strange twist of fate, Kosciusko members guarding the Mill fired into the boisterous crowds, comprised mainly of immigrants. The first day's discharges resulted in no casualties, but the next day, a volley of rifle fire killed five people, one of whom was an innocent bystander in his backyard. The presence of the Guards and other constabulary ultimately broke the strike, and authorities arrested several of its leaders, notably German-born socialists Paul Grottkau and Frank Hirth.[39]

Both men claimed to be of a different stripe than those blamed for the Haymarket bombing. While editor of *Arbeiter Zeitung*, Grottkau had hired August Spies, but when Spies became too incendiary in his anarchist editorials, Grottkau severed his ties with the paper. After the protests for the eight-hour day, he characterized Spies and his associates as a depraved lot, adding that there were no anarchists—except a few cranks who thought that the designation made them sound sophisticated—residing in Milwaukee. Hirth described anarchists as criminals with designs on "murder and robbery." "The great difference of belief between the anarchist and the socialist," he opined "is that the latter think that after a general communistic system is established that a government and code of laws should be maintained, while the anarchist holds that in such a condition of society both government and statute of law will have no meaning."[40] No doubt most of his readers cringed at even the thought of creating a "communistic system," and gave thanks for the Kosciusko Guard and other militia units. This did not stop Hirth from trying to make a case for the compatibility of his political philosophy with American ideals. He hoped to convince them that his beliefs were not manifestations of some subversive foreign ideology.

Critics of the mayhem in both Chicago and Milwaukee did attribute it to an alien presence. Condemnation of those involved by the *Dunn County News*, published in the heart of western Wisconsin's lumber region, resorted to racial slurs: "The expenses to the state for calling out the militia to quell the riotous Polacks [*sic*] in Milwaukee was about 1,800 a day. The whole expenses to the state will be about $12,000." The "foolish strikes" that the foreign malcontents had caused, opined leading local businessman J. Downing, who lived in a hamlet bearing his name, retarded the country's development and hurt laboring men. A *News* reprint from the *Philadelphia Press* made clear that the local editors blamed foreigners for the recent unrest. The time had come, the editorial contended, to "spurn and repel the agitators, thugs, anarchists, and outlaws who have no thought of being settled and law-abiding American citizens and who come here only to discourage honest labor, to flaunt the red flag and wage war on social order and public peace. Shut them up or send them back." Of course, not all aliens were bad. Radical reprobates stood in sharp contrast to the "honest and patriotic" men and women "who seek our soil in good faith to enter into the spirit and body of American citizenship."[41] This, however, posed the problem of how to differentiate between the two types of immigrants.

What *the Nation* called "the horror caused by the Anarchist crimes in Chicago" spurred debate regarding the need for more extensive immigration restriction. Labor issues joined increased concerns about "mongrelism"— the feared result of growing numbers of southern and eastern Europeans coming to the United States—in fueling the discussion. Terence Powderly led those who stressed the familiar working-class argument of the need to protect US workers from low-cost foreign labor, "semi barbarous" men and women who debased the American standard of living. Others emphasized the pro-business assertion that the continued influx of immigrants—with the exception of criminals, the diseased, the vicious and ignorant, and loafers— ultimately would benefit all Americans, by increasing the nation's productivity. Rabbi Solomon Schindler, himself an immigrant from Germany who captured national attention by trying to Americanize his temple, contended that even immigrants who "scabbed" posed no serious threat. Nonetheless, virtually the entire mainstream press agreed on the propriety of barring the "ranting apostles of disorder," who abused their welcome by "cursing our institutions and inciting their dupes to pillage or assassination." The *Nation* advocated close policing of suspected immigrant radicals and deportation of those who acted on their beliefs. Even those who praised immigrants' contributions to the United States expressed distaste for those who belonged to "communistic societies."[42] Opinions about what to do varied considerably.

Writing for the *Harvard Monthly*, future president Theodore Roosevelt gave cursory mention to the importance of excluding "the communists and anarchists . . . the dynamiter in all of his varieties," but employers, more than subversive aliens, attracted Roosevelt's ire. The days when a recent arrival could go west and claim vacant land would soon come to an end, and most immigrants would become wage workers. Given this reality, the United States needed to focus its attention on protecting American workers, both native- and foreign-born, by preventing the entrance of "the cheapest and least desirable foreign laborers." Businesses that imported workers (by that time technically illegal) engendered anger on the part of those already employed, creating a climate where anarchism could flourish. "The capitalist who aids in the importation of cheap labor," TR declared, "with a view to

increasing the 'competition in the labor market,' is, in fact, almost as dangerous an enemy to society as is the scoundrel like Most or O'Donovan Rossa."
These were damning accusations, in that anarchist Johann Most's fiery *Science of Revolutionary Warfare* provided a manual for violent revolution that
had been used to help convict the Haymarket defendants, and Irish nationalist and US resident Jeremiah O'Donovan Rossa advocated the use of dynamite against the British. But Roosevelt minced no words. Instead of having
to deal with the consequences of an ever-growing labor pool—even if this
was what employers wanted—the United Statets needed to secure a gradual
reduction of immigration and insure the proper assimilation of those admitted.[43] Others voiced similar concerns.

Norwegian American writer and college professor Hjalmar Boyesen concurred with those who were concerned about the saturated labor market,
which he saw as a leading contributor to the greater evil of alien radicalism.
His literary works frequently showed disdain for working-class immigrants,
a theme on which he expounded in laying blame for social upheaval. Foreigners had caused "the alarming spread of socialistic doctrines among the
laborers in the great industrial centers." Radical tenets had permeated even
the Knights of Labor, generally considered to be a conservative union. Thirty
percent of the German immigrants, Boyesen alleged, belonged to or had
sympathies for a socialist organization, and each ship brought more potential recruits. To eliminate the problems caused by radical aliens, the United
States had to do more than simply bar those who openly exposed the dangerous ideologies. It had to limit the overall number of immigrants seeking
entrance on an annual basis.[44]

John P. Altgeld, a German immigrant who would eventually become the
governor of Illinois and pardon the imprisoned Haymarket anarchists three
years later, showed much greater sympathy to his fellow foreign-born, and
identified a different source of social unrest. Foreign-born residents and
naturalized citizens had demonstrated their loyalty since the 1860s. They
had secured Abraham Lincoln's presidential election by giving him enough
votes to defeat Stephen Douglas in key northern states, and thereafter they
had fought in the Civil War and produced the materials necessary to wage
it. Voluntary immigration neither rendered a danger to American labor
nor threatened the national tranquility. Riots involving foreigners had been
"nothing but impotent protests, by ignorant but honest people, against
the rapacious greed which took the bread they toiled for away from their
children's mouths. . . ." In addition, close examination would show that at
times of conflict, the number of American-born protesters equaled that of
foreign-born. "Nationality," Altgeld concluded, or what might better have

been called ethnicity, had not been the catalyst for the labor disturbance; rather, the confrontations grew "out of industrial and political excitement." Economic reform, not immigrant exclusion, held the key to preventing future disturbances.[45]

Analysis of what had happened at Haymarket influenced University of Chicago political economist Edward W. Bemis to reach a different conclusion. "In immigration there is much good," he contended, "but in another larger portion there is equally great evil." The presence of the latter led him to believe that the time had come for the United States to reduce immigration significantly. Foreigners contributed a disproportionate percentage of America's insane, indigent, and diseased, and the sheer number of annual arrivals taxed the county's ability to assimilate them. Having a lower standard of living, immigrants depressed American wages; their willingness to accept lesser pay reduced compensation and ultimately undermined the socioeconomic status of all workers. This characterization particularly applied to the newly prevalent ethnic groups, which in Bemis's opinion tended to be impoverished and illiterate. These last were the target of his suggested remedy: "Admit no single person over sixteen and no man over that age who cannot read and write his own language." Over the next twenty years, restrictionists—those who sought the enactment of more restrictive laws—would make this so-call literacy test their preferred method of exclusion. Practicality made it appealing, but the Haymarket events provided the impetus for its inception.[46]

"Everyone knows that it is our foreign born," Bemis asserted, "who indulge in most of the mob violence in times of strikes and industrial depression." Anarchist activity in Chicago, implied to have been wholly the work of foreigners, had led some Americans to call for their exclusion. This raised the question of how to identify such individuals and how to test their opinions and ideology. Even if a method could be found, some of the targeted would avoid detection. A law merely barring anarchists would leave unaffected those who came to be under their sway. "Parsons, Schwab, and Fielden would not have been dangerous," Bemis concluded, "if we had kept out from this country their ignorant and degraded followers by a test which should have excluded them, not as anarchists, but as ignorant and degraded, and had done our duty by the people that already were here." Only by excluding illiterate immigrants could the United States prevent events like the one that had taken place in Haymarket Square and thus eliminate the threat posed by dynamite in the hands of a malcontent.[47] Anarchists might have been the immediate cause of what had happened in Chicago, but the larger danger lay in the masses of uneducated foreigners. They, Bemis believed, the US government needed to winnow.

Lawmakers did take limited steps to stop the influx of presumably dangerous elements, but their actions primarily sought to placate angry workers rather than cater to employers. In addition to the 1882 Chinese Exclusion Act, which prohibited the entry of laborers from that nation (see chapter 2), lawmakers in 1885 passed the Foran Act, barring "the importation and migration of foreigners and aliens under contract or agreement to perform labor in the United States." Principal supporters, notably the Knights of Labor, saw the measure as a bulwark against the perpetuation of "wage slavery." Related legislation enacted in 1887 established an inspector service to query incoming immigrants about their employment status. The subsequent Immigration Act of 1891 simplified enforcement of the entry requirements, by giving the national government sole control, and required steamship companies to transport home any of their passengers who entered the United States illegally or who became "a public charge within one year of arrival." It also excluded polygamists and those suffering from contagious diseases. None of these, however, addressed the growing apprehension of alien radicalism, leading many Americans to concur with Bemis's call for the interdiction of those immigrants who were most likely to embrace the seditious doctrines.[48]

Events in the next decade would reinforce this belief. Class violence would reappear, amplifying notions of immigrant subversives agitating American workers and threatening domestic tranquility. In sensational instances, the turmoil would get personal.

- Growth of Knights of Labor - indicator of Worker discontent

- Haymarket riots 7/8 of those arrested were foreign born - accused of riling up workers - framed as dangerous foreign ideas

CHAPTER 4

Confronting the Barons
Immigrant Workers and Individual Moguls

"The quick importation of 'Pinkertons' aroused every lawless instinct in the men," declared the *Chicago Inter-Ocean*, "for the very name 'Pinkerton' will put a Hungarian or Pole on the warpath." The ethnic labels referred to the violent labor confrontation at the Carnegie Steel Works in Homestead, Pennsylvania, on July 6, 1892. Similarly stressing the rioters' foreign origins, the Worcester, Massachusetts, *Daily Spy* characterized the recently arrived Slavic, Russian, and Polish immigrants as threats to America's well-being. "These men who are coming in such large numbers to this country to collect about our great manufacturing centres," the *Spy* editorialized, "are many of them persons who not only have no respect for authority but hate law on general principles." The aliens were not the sole target of the *Spy*. Given their proclivities, the *Spy* questioned whether the corporate leaders who had attracted them to the United States should share culpability "when such lawless murderous, infamous scenes are enacted" at places such as Homestead."[1] Participants and places changed, but the fundamental question of whether business interests bore responsibility for attracting pernicious foreigners dominated the 1890s.

Personal connections, such as the one between Andrew Carnegie and his steel empire, characterized the decade's labor disputes. Commercial growth and the trend toward consolidation had created large conglomerates, which seemed to signify the nation's coming of age. Edifices such as the Carnegie

Steel Works in Homestead and George Pullman's model community in south Chicago paid tribute to America's rise to greatness, validating the propriety of both its polity and economy. Even so, recurring class violence affected some of the nation's largest and most prominent businesses and cast a pall upon this glittery milieu. Here was the essence of the Gilded Age, incredible opulence coupled with unsightly social unrest. Against this backdrop, Americans of the 1890s struggled to understand why such incidents seemed to occur with increasing frequency. In the minds of angry workers, fault lay with the economic barons, but those barons and their supporters saw things differently, placing responsibility on the very immigrant employees upon whom their companies relied to meet their labor needs. Employers' only transgression seemed to be their unfortunate hiring of alien subversives.

Commercial consolidation dominated the 1890s. The 1889 New Jersey General Incorporation Act allowed industrial empire builders to combine their interstate holdings into a single, legally-incorporated entity. While absolute monopolies—100 percent control of a particular industry—rarely if ever existed, large unified companies now could dominate particular commercial fields. Vertical integration and horizontal combination allowed companies to grow to unprecedented size. Congress attempted to limit monopolization of interstate commerce by passing the Sherman Antitrust Act in 1890, but initially the law would have minimal effect. Center firms—companies large and powerful enough to control a particular industry nationwide—became a prominent feature of the American economy. Men who commanded these commercial fiefdoms—"like the barons," noted one commentator, "which in many aspects they are"—became the personification of big business's power and wealth and hence the focus of public attention and scrutiny.[2] Their names also became synonymous with the labor conflicts that gripped their businesses.

Baronial ranks included "Americanized" Andrew Carnegie, whose expansive iron and steel holdings included the Carnegie Steel Works in Homestead and numerous other mills in and around Pittsburgh. Carnegie epitomized the Horatio Alger rags-to-riches mythology of appropriate and expected immigrant behavior. Born in Dunfermline, Scotland, to struggling artisan parents who had to borrow money to travel to the United States, thirteen-year-old Andrew arrived with his family at Castle Garden in July 1848. Classic push-pull factors had influenced their decision to emigrate. In Scotland, new technologies had effectively displaced Andrew's handweaver father, so the family came to the United States seeking a new start, lured by the promise of economic opportunity. Needing to help support his family, Andrew found employment as a bobbin boy in a Pittsburgh, Pennsylvania, textile factory. There he began his climb up the socioeconomic ladder, finding subsequent employment at the O'Reilly Telegraph Company and the Pennsylvania Railroad. At the latter, Tom Scott introduced Carnegie to investing—the capitalist world of stocks, bonds, and unearned income—that would make him rich. Early holdings included the Keystone Bridge Company and the Union Iron Mills, initial forays into the industry over which Carnegie Steel Company eventually would wield a commanding influence.[3] His life told the story of the good immigrant, one who had worked hard, avoided vice and other temptation, and stayed on the proper path. By availing himself of all that America had to offer, he had received his just reward, and he would come to expect others who came to the United States to follow a similar course.

An ardent defender of the American capitalist economy that had made him rich, Carnegie often used *harmony* to delineate his thoughts on proper industrial-era labor relations. His meaning, however, conflated labor harmony and management's desire for material gain. Given the reality of consolidated wealth, no longer could a worker at a big businesses realistically aspire to own his own plant, and even Carnegie, a supporter of corporate profit-sharing, in the form of employee stock options, understood that only an infinitesimal number of his workers—if any at all—would duplicate his level of fame and fortune. This did not preclude restoration of "a reign of harmony" between those who controlled capital and those who labored under its control. Prudent administration of wealth provided the key to achieving this lofty goal. Those with monetary largesse would act as trustees, expending their fortunes in the interest of the masses and for the common good. Stewardship would create a sense of shared community, one in which both owners and toilers could find common value. Defined by Carnegie as the "Gospel of Wealth," these practices would insure "that the ties of brotherhood may still bind together the rich and poor in harmonious relationship."[4] But as Americans prepared to conclude a century during which their nation had grown from a small, fledgling republic to a global economic leader, this was not to be the case.

Frequent disharmony pushed the industrial leaders and their advocates to explain why class conflict threatened to tear asunder America's social fabric. Writing just before Haymarket, Carnegie optimistically had opined that a combination of grievance arbitration, "beneficial" trade unions, and a sliding wage scale—which rose and fell based on the going price of the employer's products—could eliminate the nation's labor problems and thereby repair the strained relations between workers and owners. Combining these elements under effective management would theoretically offer the best possible benefits to both groups, but Carnegie's abstract visions did not conform to the era's unfolding history. When the ensuing violence in Chicago and

Milwaukee challenged his framework for establishing a new industrial harmony, he penned an addendum, which offered a familiar explanation for the strife: "the mad works of a handful of foreign anarchists . . . who thought they saw in the excitement a fitting opportunity to execute their revolutionary plans."[5] Carnegie had chosen his words carefully. His remarks both placed responsibility for the social unrest on an "un-American" source and guarded against a universal taint of all immigrants, which would have included himself and many of his needed employees.

Speaking in November 1891 to the St. Andrew's Society, Carnegie waxed eloquently about his fellow foreign-born, making the case for what they had contributed to the United States. "The American is great," he asserted, "chiefly because he is a conglomerate of all the races of Europe." Their amalgamation had engendered ethnic improvement, creating a sum that was superior to its parts. Tongue-in-cheek, he referred to the Scottish American— understood to be manifested in himself and his audience—as "perfection at last attained." More seriously, their record of national service dated from the American Revolution. Alexander Hamilton, for example, had "substantially" written the Constitution. Carnegie's praise for his fellow Scot may have overlooked the contributions of James Madison and other convention delegates, but the testimonial did reveal the steel baron's conceptualization of immigrants. Those who had proven themselves to be positive additions had come from Europe, as indicated by both Carnegie's statement to the affirmative and his failure to acknowledge Hamilton's Caribbean heritage. In fact, he had been born on Nevis to a woman to whom his Scottish father was not married and who may have been of Creole descent. Carnegie's immigrants also had added solely to America's order and stability. In Hamilton's case, the contribution came through his connection to the writing and ratification of the Constitution, not his duel with Aaron Burr.[6]

Carnegie also could join his partner Henry Clay Frick in abandoning any and all sentimentality toward foreigners when it came to those who labored at their businesses. Since the 1870s, their labor needs had pushed them to hire, in Frick's words, "a larger percentage of foreigners of necessity." Growing numbers worked at the partners' iron and steel mills and the coke-processing plants that supplied the requisite fuels. Their aggregate included British, Irish, and other western Europeans, often called "old immigrants," as well as members of the "new" groups from Eastern Europe, to whom the press referred generically as Hungarians, or "Huns." Of these, Slovaks and Poles— designations which themselves could refer to men and women of multiple ethnic backgrounds—comprised the largest contingent. Management relied on their labor, and also expected them to behave. Describing an instance of worker unrest at the Edgar Thomson steel mill, Frick referred to the troubles as a "drunken Hungarian spree," which managerial fortitude easily would rectify. Carnegie, despite his public praise for foreigners who had sought America's shores, conveyed similar sentiments, agreeing with Frick that immigrants needed to "learn they can't quit work and riot in this free country." This mentality guided the steel barons' responses to labor conflicts.[7]

In 1886 and 1887, strikes in the Connellsville, Pennsylvania, coke-processing region—home to the H. C. Frick Company, in which both Carnegie and Frick had a financial interest—would test the owners' expectations of obsequious immigrant workers. Keeping iron and steel plants productive and profitable required substantial amounts of coke, which was made by cooking bituminous coal in large beehive-shaped ovens. Mining and processing were centered in and around Connellsville, where the Frick Company controlled over a thousand coke ovens manned by 7,000 laborers. Strikes centering on wages and working conditions began in January 1886 and continued intermittently until June 1887. Because Carnegie wanted his steel mills to have sufficient fuel to stay operational, he pushed Frick to break with other coke operators and settle with the workers, an estimated 20 percent of whom were foreign-born. Carnegie's action reportedly had the immigrant laborers—specifically the ubiquitous Hungarians—dancing "with glee."[8] Perhaps they did indeed kick up their heels, as they had figured prominently in the strikes' progression.

"A howling mob of Hungarians," announced the *St. Louis Globe-Democrat* at the strike's beginning in January 1886, "have congregated in the vicinity of the mines and will allow no one to left [*sic*] a tool." Described elsewhere as a "turbulent set," the Hungarian workers purportedly lacked any sense of "decency or humanity." The "American element" of the labor force similarly attributed the unrest solely to their immigrant compatriots, who were creating a "reign of terror." Initial reports, later repudiated, claimed that the foreigners had looted dynamite from company storehouses and attacked company guards who ventured too close to workers' quarters. The Hungarian Consul at Pittsburgh, Max Schamberg, even as he contended that coke managers had wronged immigrant workers and now threatened to evict them from company housing, tacitly identified his countrymen as troublemakers: "These men are very different from American workmen, because they do not understand American law and cannot speak the language of the country." Schamberg also relayed Frick's suggestion to his transplanted countrymen. Dissatisfied Hungarians should look elsewhere for work. The operator would not, however, pay travel fares for those wishing to leave the coke region.[9]

As the coke strike progressed, the *Globe-Democrat* offered an intriguing assertion. A June 1886 editorial claimed that there were as many anarchists in Connellsville as there were in Chicago: "The composition of the proletariat, as they like to be called, is exclusively foreign—Hungarians, Poles and a few Englishmen. The Americans, as a general thing, keep aloof." Foreign-language publications circulated widely among area workers, and leaders of the various ethnic groups had been the principal agitators during the spring strike. Eerily premonitory of what would happen in the aftermath of the Homestead battle, leading agitators reportedly circulated a picture of Henry Frick, so that "the foreigners" could recognize and then target him for injury or death. Since the settlement of the spring strike, the subversive elements had returned to their jobs, "digging coal in the mines and making converts outside to the doctrine of destruction." The article also alleged that Haymarket anarchist Albert Parsons and his firebrand compatriot William Gorsuch had visited the region in an effort to incite area workers.[10] Such accusations, regardless of their veracity, implied that the coke region easily could experience foreigner-perpetrated violence far exceeding that which had gripped Chicago.

Similar to those engaged in other heavy industries, immigrant workers in the coke region were male, but descriptions of "their women" figured prominently in efforts to portray the strikers as wild-eyed radicals. Hungarians were generally regarded as "hard to handle," and when it came to the perpetration of mayhem, the females were "worse than the men." One Hungarian woman, upon seeing authorities arrest her husband, grasped his body and refused to release her grip. When authorities could not separate the two, "she accompanied his high lord to jail." Another lady, quoted in several papers, declared that her compatriots had "plenty knife, plenty pistol," which they were good and ready to use. Numerous females were said to have joined the men in battling authorities. Even in their purely domestic activities, the immigrants failed to adhere to proper standards of decorum. Their "marriage ties are elastic," reported one paper, insinuating sexual promiscuity on the part of at least some spouses and, unable to stem their lust, they "multiply like rabbits."[11] If the strike made immigrant men appear to be undesirable subversives, their women came across as that much worse.

Accounts of the Connellsville strikes emphasized the Hungarians' radicalism, but a few stories regarding their involvement, and that of other ethnic groups, suggested that they served as strikebreakers. Conflicting scenarios appeared in the press. In January 1886, as some establishments tried to stay operational, management purportedly told "native workers" to return to work or risk losing their jobs to "imported Hungarians." Newspapers reported on owners' plans to recruit Slavic scabs in New York City.

Conflicting stories told of schemes to hire workers from different ethnic groups to replace the malicious Huns. One version had the coke producers procuring the services of Italian immigrants. Conversely, the Philadelphia *North American* quoted unnamed sources as saying that the companies would employ more "negroes." African Americans already working in the region were said to be satisfied with their wages and to have avoided involvement in the strike. Thousands more waited in Lynchburg, Virginia, ready to go to the coke region: "The intention is not to bring in large numbers at one time, but as fast as a family leaves the region a colored family will take its place, and the change will not be noticed until it is made."[12] There is no indication that any of the replacement plans went beyond the hypothetical, but immigrants or other ethnic groups figured prominently in all of the discussions.

Labor disputes concurrently occurred at the Carnegie-owned Edgar Thomson steel mill in Braddock, Pennsylvania, and at the Homestead works. Although immigrants and their children comprised a significant part of the labor force at both plants, their involvement during the late-1880s disturbances received scant press coverage. Then, not even the presence of Pinkerton detectives appears to have prompted the workers, be they aliens or natives, to engage in violence. Rather than having reputations as unruly agitators, the immigrants tended to be seen, at least by their peers, as low-cost competitors recruited by management to take jobs from existing workers. The only press-reported violence involved the beating of three "Germans" suspected of being scabs.[13] But in the summer of 1892, as national attention focused on the conflict unfolding at the business bearing the name of the country's most famous immigrant, foreigners figured prominently.

Carnegie had acquired the Homestead properties in 1883 and thereafter weathered strikes through which the Amalgamated Association of Iron and Steel Workers (AAISW) won concessions from management, including union recognition. Conditions changed dramatically in the early 1890s, when industry-wide overproduction prompted steelmakers, including Carnegie and Frick, to cut wages. They also intended to break the AAISW and the other unions at their plant. When the workers—not unexpectedly—resisted, the operators initiated a lockout, prepared to hire replacement workers, and again procured the services of Pinkerton detectives. Frick had charge while Carnegie was in Scotland, and the latter displayed no compassion toward their laborers. "Am with you to the end whether works run this year, or next or never," he telegraphed Frick. "No longer question of wages or dollars." Showing equal resolve, armed workers confronted the barges that had transported the detectives up the Monongahela River, determined to prevent their deployment at the mill. The ensuing battle claimed the lives of three detectives and seven workers and prompted activation of the state militia.[14] Once again, violence dominated American labor relations.

Associated events featured premeditated violence perpetrated by a bona fide alien radical. On July 23, Russian-born anarchist Alexander Berkman attempted to assassinate Henry Frick. The would-be assassin acted independently, with no connection to striking workers save sympathy for their cause, but he did embrace the anarchist creed of "propaganda by the deed," the use of violent actions, or *attentats*, to promote the causes of the oppressed. Having arrived in Chicago shortly after the execution of the Haymarket anarchists, he later would say that their treatment had destroyed his faith in American liberty. Following the events at Homestead, Berkman posed as an employment agent in order to gain access to Frick's office, where he both shot and stabbed the industrialist. Berkman's efforts failed, as they neither killed his prey nor changed the course of events at Homestead. After helping to subdue his assailant, the wounded Frick made clear the latter. The attempt on his life would not change anything connected to the strike and the company would "pursue the same policy and it will win."[15]

Coverage of Berkman's actions stressed the link between his ethnicity and ideology, a connection that seemed to confirm the general association between immigrants and radicalism. "Desperate Crime of a Russian Anarchist," proclaimed the *New York Times*, even before police were aware of his true identity. He and his ilk were "pestilent creatures," and American workingmen has no worse enemy "than these same ignorant and reckless Socialists and Anarchists of foreign origin, who make so much noise about the rights and wrongs of society of which they have no intelligent comprehension." "Cowardly Attempt at Assassination by a Russian Anarchist," echoed the Portland *Oregonian*, while other papers emphasized that he was a Jew who had immigrated to the United States within the past five years. His actions would give a name and face to immigrant radicalism, and he and his foreign-born lover, "Red" Emma Goldman, would personalize fears of alien subversion for the next three decades.[16]

Virtually all reporting on Homestead similarly focused on the participation of foreigners, variously connecting them to some form of negativity. Initial descriptions of the July 1 lockout portrayed immigrants more as management stooges than strike protagonists. Frick, the *New York Herald* editorialized, had intended to incite violence, leading to mobilization of the National Guard and imposition of martial law. This would allow him to recruit replacement workers without interference. But, because of their non-foreign ethnicity, the locked-out workers would not be duped easily: "There are no excitable Huns whom he has to deal with now, but the very *corps d'Elite* of the army of organized labor." American Federation of Labor leader Samuel Gompers similarly contended that the aborted arrival of Pinkerton detectives would have been "but the advanced guard of a large army of Hungarians and Poles, who were to fill the places of the strikers." They, in contrast, flew the Stars and Stripes above their meeting places. Finally, one of the Pinkerton agents who surrendered to the strikers purportedly remarked: "I was told I was to meet and deal with foreigners. I had no idea I that I was going to fight American citizens."[17] But once gun-fire erupted, the portrayal of foreigners, specifically their role in the conflict, predictably changed.

Arthur G. Burgoyne's *The Homestead Strike of 1892* and Myron Stowell's *"Fort Frick,"* both written immediately after the battle, presented the shifting perception of immigrants, particularly eastern Europeans, as the events unfolded. Discussing the confrontation's first days, Burgoyne alluded to initial fears among Homestead labor leaders that Hungarian workers might break ranks with their compatriots and accept a company offer to return to work. Stowell, conversely, wrote of how the same leaders worried about the foreigners rushing imprudently to violence. But when their narratives reached the point when the violence ensued, the authors portrayed the immigrants, as opposed to virtuous Homestead men—read native-born—as being the source of the most radical behavior. When, at the battle's end, the captured Pinkertons were forced to walk a gauntlet of angry workers, Stowell told how "some Slavs" wanted "to take the scared Pinkertons and shoot them down as they stood." Burgoyne described the perpetrators of vicious and gratuitous violence as "a crowd of Hungarians," who were determined to avenge the death of one of their countrymen. In an interesting admixture of ethnicity and gender, he noted the exploits of a "strongly built" immigrant woman who joined the melee by attacking an agent with a club. Her behavior, and that of other alien women, neither feminine nor civil, contrasted with the conduct of the "honest men fighting for bread for themselves and their wives and children."[18] One can infer that those "American" ladies had done the proper thing and stayed at home.

Economist Edward W. Bemis, whose reaction to Haymarket affair had led him to propose a literacy test for immigrants, reached similar conclusions about the events at Homestead. Frick, due to his unwillingness to negotiate with the workers, bore primary responsibility for the carnage. But, the workers had erred in using force against the Pinkerton agents, who properly had been hired by the company and had a legal right of access to the mill. In making this case, however, Bemis implied that fault lay with the immigrants. Foreigners dominated the ranks of unskilled workers, and they had shown a much greater propensity for violence than had their more skilled native-born colleagues. Aliens thus bore responsibility for instigating the attack on the barges that carried the Pinkertons, and anarchist Alexander Berkman's attempt to assassinate Frick had shattered any hope of a negotiated settlement. Frick's behavior up to that point made any kind of amiable solution highly improbable, but this did not stop Bemis from concluding that the attempt on the chairman's life had significantly poisoned the situation. Labor's connection with "anything savoring of anarchism" set back its cause. Yet Bemis refrained from identifying Berkman as an immigrant or attributing his actions to ethnic causes.[19]

Bemis also returned his attention to restriction, tying its need to deteriorating labor relations. The rising numbers of foreigners from eastern and southern Europe reduced the living conditions of all workers by their willingness to work for low wages. Low-paid immigrants did little more than increase the wealth of "church supporting millionaires." In the end such gains were transitory. "It may be for the temporary advantage of single employers to secure the cheap help," Bemis asserted, "but in the end it reacts on the employing class, since the consequent lower standard of life calls for fewer purchases of goods." On the job, immigrants lacked disciplined work habits, and they did not form beneficial, "wisely managed labor organizations." They instead fell under the sway of diabolical, but hard to exclude, alien radicals. Restriction could, however, keep out the masses of their followers. If only native-born Americans comprised the labor pool, any shortage of workers would accelerate the invention and installation of laborsaving devices, without decreasing wages. Employer and employee both would reap fiduciary benefit.[20] Although Bemis did not use the word harmony, he clearly believed that proper restriction of immigration would return that quality to the American workplace.

To the Reverend W. F. Crofts, a conservative reformer best known for preaching proper reverence for the Sabbath, Homestead became a symbol of national lawlessness. The minister had contempt for big business's practice of operating seven days a week, rather than closing the plants on Sundays, but he directed most of his post-battle vitriol toward immigrant workers. Their presence had occasioned the unrest: "One-third of the men in the town are not only foreign but unnaturalized, and probably a majority of the others are not of American birth." Suggesting that the United States was essentially a Protestant nation, Crofts believed that the unruly Homestead immigrants lacked a properly evangelical religious orientation. Most of them did have at least a nominal church affiliation, but if it were Roman Catholic or Eastern Rite, they still lacked Crofts's sense of suitability. In any case, they failed to respect Sunday as a time of worship and exhibited wanton intemperance.

If the United States wished to eliminate disturbances such as the one that had flared in Homestead, all of its people had to show proper reverence for the Sabbath, prohibit or otherwise curb the use of intoxicants, and restrict immigration. The last, in Crofts's mind, would help considerably to advance the other two causes.[21]

Homestead itself epitomized the nation's industrial centers, or in the words of essayist Hamlin Garland were "American only in the sense in which they represent the American idea of business." Men of the "discouraged and sullen type" comprised the resident "gangs of foreign laborers." To some, Garland's characterization may have stigmatized the immigrant laborers, by implying that only they would work and live in such terrible surroundings. But his overall message of exploitation conveyed the opposite; these were immigrants who struggled against the ravages of an inhospitable workplace in hopes of making a better life for themselves and their families. To the question of whether nature or nurture had produced the man, one Homestead worker, identified only as "L. W.," answered, "A strange character surely; a creature who seems to be made by the work, and not for it."[22] Following this logic, the immigrants who figured prominently in the confrontation with Carnegie Steel management did not act on account of any foreign attribute. They instead responded to the environment in which they worked and lived. Others clearly saw their unruly behavior as inherently alien.

Government scrutiny allowed several Homestead participants to offer their assessment of the recent violence. The battle hardly had ended before various congressmen called for an investigation of its causes. When US House and Senate committees subsequently held hearings, their attention focused on the use of Pinkerton agents, at Homestead and in general, and on the effects of the steel tariff, but immigration and the behavior of foreign-born workers attracted frequent interest. The Senate Select Committee to investigate the use of private detectives made clear that it was not charged specifically to examine immigration, but nonetheless asked several witnesses about related matters. It even recalled one of the labor leaders to ask specifically what he thought the nation should do in regard to immigration restriction. House Judiciary Committee Chair William C. Oates at one point said that he had "been requested" (by some unidentified source) to ascertain the ethnic composition of the AAISW membership. The role of immigrants at Homestead was not, he explained, "so very important," but he also saw "no harm" in querying witnesses about aliens' involvement in the troubles. Regardless of why he posed particular questions, the negative answers no doubt influenced his committee's report. For example, House investigators concluded that the "indecent and brutal" injuries sustained by the captured detectives had been inflicted "principally by women and boys. We are loath to believe that any of the women were native Americans."[23]

The questioning of strike leader Hugh O'Donnell denoted the inquisitors' disposition. Chairman Oates asked him about the "Slavs and some others who were firing" on the barges that were attempting to ferry the Pinkertons to Homestead: "Do you know what proportion of the populations down there are alien or native born?" When O'Donnell estimated that about forty percent had been natives, Oates queried him about the nationalities of those comprising the other sixty percent. "I should say Slavs and Hungarians," O'Donnell replied, "not many Hungarians, a great many Slavs, Irish, English, Welsh and Germans." Slavs and Hungarians, along with others, also had fired pistols to warn of the barges' impending arrival. O'Donnell did not indicate the ethnicity of those involved in the infamous gauntlet, saying only that they had been "irresponsible people," not union men. Surprisingly, given the questions about other participants, no one asked him if they were foreigners. Chairman Oates did get O'Donnell to make one more significant revelation: few immigrants worked in the departments directly affected by the company's new wage scale, which implied that they had no legitimate reason to wreak violence on their employer.[24] The presumed gratuity of their actions added to their culpability.

Henry Frick espoused much the same thinking. When Senate committeemen asked him when his companies first experienced labor trouble and whether it emanated from "native or the foreign labor," he minced few words. After indicating that the need for workers had led his various businesses to employ more foreigners, Frick said that he and other managers preferred to hire natives. However, in times of scarcity managers of necessity turned to aliens, some of whom were secured through recruitment agencies. Their presence had led to problems. In the 1880s, Frick contended, unrest among coke workers began when the companies refused to allow the wives of foreign workers to help in the yards. Pennsylvania law prohibited women from engaging in this labor, but many of the immigrant women wanted to help their husbands. Since the men were paid by the amount of coal they processed, having the extra hands would increase their remuneration. Did this mean, the committee pressed as it sought a broader indictment, that labor troubles generally originated with foreigners? "Largely," Frick replied, returning to the problems at Homestead, "although a certain percentage of American born were troublesome people." He did not elaborate on the number or role of the natives, but "largely" spoke volumes regarding the ethnic identity of the recalcitrant.[25]

AAISW president William Weihe also criticized immigrants, but he blamed their undesirable presence on the machinations of greedy businessmen.

There were some "restless, mischief-making men," at Homestead and else-where, who agitated their colleagues and urged them to commit violent acts, Weihe testified, but they were a small minority. Among them, certain groups—he designated Hungarians, Poles, and Slavs—included individuals who "feel like doing in this country things that are not peculiarly American." Foreigners who did not know English and lacked familiarity with US laws and customs tended to make the most trouble, and they also showed less willingness to mediate their differences with management, even though the latter's actions had created this situation. When asked if the United States needed more immigration restriction, Weihe said that additional exclusions were necessary to protect labor's interests. Large corporations used steam-ship companies and other immigrant recruiters to secure low-cost foreign workers, especially during strikes. Solicitation of foreign workers violated contract labor laws, Weihe acknowledged, but that did not deter employers. Once hired, the immigrants became little more than paupers, "at the mercy of unprincipled capital or unscrupulous corporations." This provoked other workers, who had little choice but to accept similarly exploitative condi-tions. For the sake of all workers, Weihe concluded, the practice needed to be stopped.[26]

Representatives of various detective agencies used immigration, in a countervailing manner, to boost their reputations. As the title of the Sen-ate committee indicates, investigators from both chambers had serious con-cerns about bodies of armed men being transported across the nation with virtually no oversight. One commentator compared them to Middle Ages "freebooters," who sold their martial services to the highest bidder. These characterizations placed the detectives in the position of having to defend their practices, but—ironically—questions about whether they hired aliens gave agency officials a chance to emphasize their patriotism and prudence. "About what proportion of your men which you have employed are citizens of the United States," Representative Case Broderick asked William Pinker-ton, regarding the company that bore his family name and had sent the men to Homestead. All of them, replied the detective, to which his brother Rob-ert Pinkerton added: "They have got to be citizens as far as we know." Matt W. Pinkerton (no relation), head of the United States Detective Agency, simi-larly said that his company determined citizenship prior to offering employ-ment. Finally, when asked if the Pinkerton Detective Agency would hire women, if they "possessed the necessary qualifications," Robert Pinkerton said no, because females "are sort of unreliable and you cannot depend on them, you cannot bet on them."[27] Agents who had experienced the wrath of the Homestead women may have offered a different assessment.

While engrossing, these anti-immigrant perceptions of what had happened at Homestead did not necessarily agree with reality. Worker solidarity, not ethnic division, characterized the labor force. At the time of the lockout, the community's approximately 1,000 eastern Europeans shared with their British, Irish, and native-born colleagues a desire to earn a living-wage and provide for their families. Various nationalities attended the same churches and drank at the same bars. During the 1882 strike, which predated Carnegie's purchase, the initial Slovaks and other "new" immigrants had coordinated with other laborers under the auspices of the Irish National Land League. Ten years later, the most recent arrivals held unskilled positions, but as the conflict unfolded, their status did not divide them from their more highly trained compatriots. All felt threatened by Frick's actions. If eastern Europeans did indeed initiate the conflict and then dominate the various violent incidents (the gunfight and the gauntlet), they used incredible stealth. Of the more than one hundred indictments of workers on charges of murder, treason, and conspiracy or riot, none were eastern Europeans, who would have been the most "foreign" of the immigrant workforce.[28]

Xenophobic rhetoric provided various commentators with convenient explanations for why the Homestead violence had occurred. It allowed them to avoid making any systemic indictment of Carnegie, Frick, and their fellow industrial employers. Accounts of immigrant maleficence dominated press accounts, and the Pinkerton hearings indicated governmental interest in assessing the connection between the immigrant working class and the recent labor turmoil. Yet instead of considering possible new restrictions, Congress had more inclination to continue addressing workers' concerns about the importation of contract laborers. The Immigration Act of 1891 had banned advertising for US jobs in foreign nations and prohibited transportation companies from soliciting passengers through promises of American employment. New legislation, under consideration during the Homestead strike and passed in 1893, dealt mainly with bureaucratic matters. Some lawmakers, such as Henry Cabot Lodge, wanted to include new restrictions, but those in opposition included Representative Oates and Senator William Peffer, each of whom had served on their respective chamber's Pinkerton committee and frequently posed questions about immigrants. The answers did not cause them to join with their restrictionist colleagues. Writing for the *North American Review,* Oates leveled criticism at Frick for failing to negotiate with his employees and importing the detectives, and at the laborers for impeding the entry of replacement workers, but he said nothing about immigration.[29] Not even Berkman's attack on Frick pushed Congress to include a prohibition against the entry of alien anarchists; lawmakers would take that step only after another anarchist assassin—with a foreign-sounding name—killed President William McKinley in 1901.

Corporate leaders also considered what to do regarding immigrant labor, including possible alternatives. In 1893 Illinois Central Railroad managers, whose predecessors had pioneered the recruitment of immigrant workers and settlers in the 1850s and 1860s, contemplated recruiting immigrants to work on its lines running through the Mississippi Delta. Advocates emphasized the region's need for "industrious, frugal, white people." Germans and Italians attracted particular interest, and at least one labor broker offered to provide the needed numbers of "good hard working" foreigners. But IC managers in the Delta also acknowledged the potentially "great evil" of flooding "our country with worthless, undisciplined tramps from the north." Illinois Central president Stuyvesant Fish generally supported immigrant importation, but he also worried about how the arrival of Europeans would redound on the freedmen. "Are they to remain in enforced idleness roaming about the country," he mused about the latter, "or like the Indians be settled on reservations[?]" Their employment by the railroad could provide an alternative to either of these depressing scenarios.[30]

As business and governmental officials condemned worker unrest as "blood-thirsty lawlessness" perpetrated by "hoodlums and anarchists," with the last characterization connoting immigrants, Fish pondered the proposition of using African Americans as industrial workers. Southern railroads since the antebellum era had relied on blacks for construction and maintenance work, and to a more limited extent as firemen. Still, Fish followed his predecessor and former slaveholder James C. Clark in seeing in them at least the potential to do more. "The experience of every Railroad manager with whom I have come in contact confirms my own that for the wages paid him the negro [sic] is as good a hand as we can get," Fish responded to a query about plans for immigrant importation into the Delta. "Surely wish that we could employ more." Unfortunately, among the freedmen, "few of them have risen above ignorance of all laws of health, thrift, and self-reliance in which emancipation found them." Fish qualified his impressions, acknowledging his limited personal interaction with black workers, but nonetheless pressed subordinates in the Delta "to encourage the black labor which you have, to habits of frugality and thrift, and to protect them from the 'sharks' of one kind or another who prey upon their simplicity and childlike appetites for sweets and gewgaws." This, in theory, would make more of them suitable for railroad employment.[31]

Fish's mulling preceded by two years Booker T. Washington's call for "a new era of industrial progress" in the South. Speaking at the 1895 Atlanta

Cotton States Exposition, Washington emphasized the idea of blacks forgoing political participation and social equality in order to pursue economic gain. He urged white employers to look beyond "the incoming of those of foreign birth and strange tongue and habits" when filling their labor needs and instead hire the region's readily available African Americans. To a much greater extent than recent immigrants, blacks had proven their loyalty. In the "Standard Version" of his remarks (which appeared in his *Autobiography*) Washington added a statement regarding how blacks had contributed to the South's economic success "without strikes and labor wars." Promises of accommodation and compliance might not appeal to all African Americans, but Washington had a clear purpose. Like Fish, he wanted to promote their economic success. Yet both men's relatively benign sense of racial propriety paled in comparison to that of most southern whites. Those living in the Mississippi Delta, during and after Reconstruction, had made clear their antipathy to sharing either political or economic opportunities with the freedmen. "The determination of the whites of the south," perceptively observed former abolitionist Frederick Douglas, "is to keep the black man down."[32]

This mentality, which extended beyond the South, should have increased the desirability of immigrant laborers, but the 1893 onset of yet another depression intensified negative reactions to their presence. Business failures and currency problems had engendered general economic decline. "Industry has been practically stopped," noted Ohio governor William McKinley. "Labor has found little employment and when it has been employed it has been at greatly reduced wages." Pundits disagreed as to the severity, but virtually all commentaries acknowledged the centrality of unemployment and growing worker discontent. Both businesses and labor organizations came to fear that immigrants were swelling the ranks of the jobless. Their rhetoric followed familiarly divergent patterns. When labor advocates promoted the need to limit the influx of foreigners, they based their advocacy on the supposition that capitalists used the present labor surplus—to which immigrants who had been recruited by employers allegedly contributed significantly—to drive down wages. Offering an alternative argument, a spokesman for the AAISW asserted that thousands of immigrants had "come not to work for a living but to stir up strife and to commit crime." Commission of their subversion had exacerbated—if not caused—the depressed conditions. Everyone, it seemed, could find reason to blame immigrants.[33]

Reactions to the 1894 march of Coxey's Army demonstrated the continuing designation of labor unrest as foreign. As the depression persisted, relatively wealthy Ohio businessman Jacob S. Coxey led a march from Massillon, Ohio, to Washington, DC, to call attention to the plight of those looking for work and to prompt the federal government to appropriate $500,000 for road improvements. Other groups, mainly from the West, attempted to join this commonweal, or "crusade of the unemployed." Some of the associated "armies" commandeered trains and a couple of them attempted to build boats and float down the Missouri and Platt Rivers. Although there were confrontations, such as the arrest of Coxey—essentially for walking on the grass—as he attempted to speak from the Capitol steps, the marchers tried to show the utmost decorum and thereby distinguish themselves from any and all revolutionary types. When the march started, Coxey stressed its "peaceful purpose," saying, "No criminals or anarchists will be allowed to mingle with us." His purpose, he stressed, was not revolution but the "salvation of the republic."[34]

Contrarily, critics saw the marchers and their message as the antithesis of and a threat to "true Americanism," despite contradictory evidence. *Engineering Magazine* described the participants as the "American representation" of European socialists. If so, they also were mostly homegrown Americans. Few surviving records give detailed information about the marchers, but a survey of the participants conducted by Drake University president B. O. Aylesworth does indicate nationality. Students questioned 763 men, of whom 549 identified themselves as native-born American; of the immigrants, most were British or German. Other observers noted a significant African American presence. Most importantly, the marchers' grievances emanated from American economic conditions and frustrations with US public policy. And yet this did not prevent social critic Thorstein Veblen from offering his own florid assessment of the un-American essence of the Coxey movement. The marchers embodied a "cis-atlantic line of socialism of the chair," which he equated with various European forms of despotic government. The economic depression may have triggered the protest, but a reading of the various critiques gives the impression that its ideological roots originated in foreign lands.[35]

Depressed conditions also influenced the nation's next major labor confrontation. The 1894 Pullman Strike, similar to Homestead in its connection to a specific industrialist, centered on George Pullman's Palace Car Company. The quintessential entrepreneur, Pullman had perfected the primary sleeping car used on American railroads. Success propelled him into the ranks of America's leading capitalists, with all of the attendant trappings. "Among your other good qualities I have always thought you were a well dressed man," commented former President Benjamin Harrison, indicating Pullman's pursuit of highbrow bearing proper for one of his economic standing. "You told me that you had a New York tailor who was responsible for your good appearance and I wish that you would give me his address, as I may want to have some clothes made in New York." At the time of the strike, Pullman Palace Car had a capitalization of $36 million, with an additional $16 million in accrued profits. As the depression worsened, Pullman acknowledged that "business is not in a very satisfactory condition," but one would not know it by the amount paid in corporate dividends, which increased, even as workers' wages declined. Deteriorating commerce also did not keep Pullman and his wife from planning a grand European excursion. When the strike began, he reassured her that the troubles would not interfere with their travel plans.[36] The sleeping-car baron and his baroness clearly lived in a world far removed from the one inhabited by those who labored at his company.

By 1894, Pullman Palace Car employed 5,500 workers, women and men, most of them skilled or semiskilled, who labored in shifts of 10 hours and 45 minutes. Management exerted total control, not just over the workplace but also the namesake town, where many of the workers lived. The company owned all of the housing, which employees rented, and also the bank, commercial property, and even the church building. The so-called public library charged an annual fee for adults and children. During abortive strikes in 1880s, Pullman made clear that he never would allow laborers to encroach upon his dominance. He also used a local detective agency to monitor his employees. Visiting the town in 1885, labor economist Richard T. Ely noted Pullman's attempt to furnish his employees with "the best homes under the most healthful conditions," but Ely also concluded that the company's unmasked power made "unavoidable that the idea of Pullman is un-American." In May 1894, facing wage reductions and diminished hours, but no decrease in rents, exasperated Pullman workers decided to confront their hegemonic employer. When they chose to strike, it would be the workers and their supporters who found themselves stained with Ely's pejorative designation.[37]

Immigrants comprised 72 percent of the town's residents. Scandinavians, the largest component, were said by various clergymen to be "industrious, good mechanics, and sober in their habits." They harbored only a few minor grievances prior to the depression-induced wage cuts. When critics took issue with the strikers' white ribbons, saying that the insignias were un-American, William H. Carwardine, pastor at the Methodist Episcopal Church in Pullman, forcefully disagreed. The strikers, who had been ground "unmercifully" by George Pullman's Palace Car Company, exemplified US patriotism. Certainly no one should call them anarchists, with its alien and seditious connotation. This was especially true in regard to the company's Scandinavian,

British, Irish, and German employees. According to Carwardine, some foremen preferred the immigrants to native-born workers because the latter were "too d—d independent." The bosses could more easily coerce the foreigners, if not outright abuse them. "Some of the foremen use the vilest epithets toward them, and even attempt to kick them," Carwardine asserted, implying that their native-born compatriots would not tolerate such behavior. But sometimes the immigrants' own habits, including good ones, contributed to their exploitation. They saved more than "American mechanics," and as a result lived in conditions that the Americans would not accept. The immigrants' low standards of living, Carwardine illogically concluded, indicated a lack of aspiration and a willingness to accept lower pay. Yet, this did not make them subversives.[38]

Activities in Pullman seemed to prove this, as the strike remained peaceful in the town, but the dispute had ramifications far beyond the factory site. Because the Pullman Company operated a few miles of track, it qualified as a railroad in the eyes of the American Railway Union (ARU) led by Eugene Debs. In 1894, the ARU organized the company's employees into affiliated locals. When the Pullman workers struck, protesting pay reductions with no corresponding drop in rents, the ARU supported their efforts, calling on its members to refuse to operate any train that included a Pullman sleeper. Union involvement transformed what would have been a significant local strike against one of America's leading corporations into a nationwide conflict. Violence erupted at several locations, which the Reverend Carwardine attributed to "mob elements, the rabble, and cheap foreign labor" imported by greedy businesses. Regardless of its origins, at least 12 participants had died and 515 had been arrested by the strike's end. The ARU's action, opined the *New York Times*, did more than demonstrate sympathy toward the Pullman workers; it created "a struggle between the greatest and most powerful railroad labor organization and the entire railroad capital," which would determine the future strength of those on both sides.[39] The paper would have been no less accurate if it had redacted much of the verbiage and simply called the Pullman Strike a defining struggle between capital and labor.

The ARU's sympathy strike, beginning on June 26, quickly spread across the central and western US. It primarily pitted the union against the Chicago General Managers' Association, representing 24 different rail lines with terminals in that city. Organized during the unrest of 1886, the Association devoted much of its attention to defeating union initiatives, and as the Pullman strike commenced, it gained considerable support from the federal government, most notably President Grover Cleveland and Attorney General Richard Olney. Illinois Central's railroad leaders, for example, showed no sympathy for its striking workers, anticipated that the government would act decisively to support the businesses, and worried only about the size of the available military force. Would it be large enough, they wondered, to quell the disturbance? Railroad officials worked in concert with Olney to secure injunctions, based on violations of the Sherman Antitrust Act, for purportedly obstructing interstate commerce and interfering with the transport of the US mail. In response to what he would call "acute and determined defiance of law and order," President Cleveland, over the objections of Illinois governor John Altgeld, approved the mobilization of US troops. The courts ultimately jailed Debs for contempt due to his defiance of an injunction that ordered him to stop inciting interference with rail travel. The strike, contended Olney, had brought the country "to the ragged edge of anarchy," engendering the need for strong action.[40]

For many, this meant reducing immigration and Americanizing those already in the United States. General Nelson A. Miles, who commanded the US Army forces, characterized the strike as a "reign of terror" and joined others in blaming misguided immigrants. When necessary, America had to use force to protect law and order but only as a last resort. Other means could eliminate the need. Had not the time come, Miles asked, as it had previously in regards to the Chinese, to end "the importation of the vast hordes of cheap and degraded labor unloaded on our Atlantic shore?" The nation should accept no more foreigners than it could readily assimilate. US Commissioner of Railroads Wade Hampton believed that the country had become a "dumping ground" for Europe's communists and anarchists, who had caused most of the recent violence: "It was announced that in some instances the mob of rioters who committed gross outrages was composed entirely of foreigners, none of whom could speak our language." In contrast, Miles and Hampton, along with AFL leader Samuel Gompers and *Railway Age* editor Harry Robinson, took care to differentiate between these undesirable aliens and honest American workers.[41]

George Pullman made clear his conviction that business interests bore little responsibility for the recent turmoil. All of the company's efforts to resolve the differences with its workers had been "fruitless," he complained, even though he steadfastly had refused any and all overtures to submit the dispute to arbitration. Instead he exhibited unfailing determination to exert his unfettered will. "Of course, there is nothing to do but fight it out," he ruminated, even as the ARU's strike crumbled, "and I will probably feel better after the fits commences than I have during these days of great suspense." Garbled prose did not obscure the sleeper-car baron's position. He did not care if angry workers threw "fits" and fully intended to assert his hegemony as he deemed appropriate. Palace Car Company shops had by then reopened with a reduced workforce made up partially of replacement workers, but many old hands continued their struggle. If Pullman did feel better, he did so as the striking workers starved and many left his model community in search of more fair and equitable treatment. They received no sympathy from their former employer. If the employees had stayed on the job, he contended, they would have had money to buy food. Pullman unfortunately did not indicate who, beyond labor in general, bore responsibility for the sorry state of affairs, but those with whom he corresponded left little doubt as to the culprits' identity.[42]

"The world seems to have gone wrong since you and I were young," surmised Southern Pacific Railroad superintendent A. N. Towne, as he joined others in attributing the attendant social decay to the work of subversive agents. In his view, these individuals had undermined beneficial managerial authority. In the past, business operators like Towne and Pullman had imposed discipline on the "great armies" of labor, and the harmonious results had advanced "the good of society." Workers had appreciated the owners and bosses who provided employment. "All this feeling of cooperation and unity of interest seems to have been lost," Towne lamented, and workers now sought to define their terms of service "in defiance of all reasonable governing conditions. . . ." This had happened because laborers had allowed themselves to fall under the control of "traveling agitators," who advocated the use of "brute force." Rockford, Illinois, farm-implements manufacturer William A. Talcott reached similar conclusions, castigating Eugene Debs for having misled "the whole community into this anarchistic state." Another writer blamed Governor John Altgeld's coddling of labor leaders and anarchists.[43]

The ensuing chaos left Pullman with but one appropriate response. "The men have been misled by the professional agitator and now must suffer the consequences," wrote Chicago railroad supplies manufacturer J. McGregor Adams, as the strike commenced at the Palace Car factory. It and other labor conflicts were battles between American values and those of "cranks," the nineteenth-century term for a variety of malcontents. Given the consequences, Adams and several others made clear, Pullman could not waver in his refusal to negotiate with the ARU or any other union. Henry Villard, long-time railroad promoter and director of the Northern Pacific, praised the sleeping-car baron for his resistance to the "brutal attempt to substitute tyranny and terrorism [for law and order] in the United States." An Ohio farmer, claiming that he and his fellow agriculturalists composed "the majority of working men of America," penned support for Pullman's "struggle for right against anarchism, nihilism, and such that seem to be in rebellion against our government." "Every loyal citizen, including every honest and patriotic workman," contended another writer, "will yet thank you for the great and everlasting service you have thus rendered to the stability of free institutions." Finally, a concerned lady drew a connection to Haymarket with her worries about the influences "of such criminals as Herr Most," the fiery German-born anarchist known for his advocacy of "the absolute destruction of all existing instruments of 'order.'" The writer urged Pullman to guard himself against assassination.[44]

Others, both business leaders and their middling supporters, more clearly attributed the unrest to alien sources. The Pullman Strike, hotel developer Frank B. Abbott contended, was part of a larger, "inevitable struggle between the foreign-born element that demands a living without any compensation and the industrious American who desires to be protected in his constitutional right to work without interference of any workingman's union. . . ." "Americanism" faced a moment of truth. The effort to stay the ravages of a "reign of anarchy," advanced by foreign-born radicals and their immigrant followers, could not be delayed or avoided. Procrastination would only result in "protracted misery." A former newspaper editor (who now wanted a job at the Pullman Company) saw a link between the current unrest and the immigrant-connected Molly Maguires and Homestead workers, and an "Old Rebel" from Arkansas pledged his support and that of his fellow southerners should there be a need to rid the United States of its "foreign element." They were the ones, he asserted, who were "kicking up all the fuss." Fear that "blood must flow and flow freely before this issue is settled," led an Illinois railroad official to blame the obstruction of commerce and destruction of property on inadequate immigration laws, a widely shared conclusion.[45]

Investigators and commentators fueled anti-immigrant concerns. The US Strike Commission, chaired by national labor administrator Carroll D. Wright, delineated "hoodlums, women, a lower class of foreigners, and recruits from the criminal classes," along with a small percentage of ARU strikers, as the perpetrators of lawless acts. The hooligans' behavior contrasted with that of the Pullman employees, who comported themselves in a "dignified, manly, and conservative" manner. If one can assume that this also applied to the company's 125 women workers who belonged to the ARU, they contrasted sharply to one group of protesting females, "largely of the foreign type" whose vile language had been "very abusive of the troops." These strong ladies, reportedly by themselves, had overturned two freight cars. One account took care to explain that "Polak" was the common name for Poles and then used the epitaph to identify a striker shot by militiamen as they attempted to protect railroad property. Foreigners, according to another witness, perpetrated the violence at Chicago's Blue Island railroad yards, where one of the city's worst riots took place on July 1 and 2, and those involved were not railroad men. Given the frequent testimony regarding the rioters' knowledge of railway procedures, such as switching and coupling of cars, it is likely that significant numbers of white, native-born railroaders did participate in the diverse violence, but the reporters' accounts revealed the propensity to blame such actions on "others." In addition to targeting immigrants, one newspaperman claimed to have seen a large number of "negroes" among the rioters.[46]

Among the witnesses before the Strike Commission, only labor leader Eugene Debs used the opportunity to call for more stringent controls of foreigners entering the United States. He saw them as corporate tools. "I am not opposed to immigration; on the contrary I think that under proper restrictions there is room for millions of people to come to this country to be good citizens," he told the investigators. But America had become the dumping ground for undesirable foreigners, brought to United States "at the bequest of corporations." In Pennsylvania, for instance, mining companies had imported "the most vicious element of European countries," who had displaced the existing well-paid workers. Aliens elsewhere contributed to high unemployment and gave rise to Coxey's Army. The foreigners' presence, in Debs's opinion, created destructive competition, which inevitably would "degenerate into perfect slavery, if it does not already exist." Debs made clear, as he had in the past, that he supported restrictions only to eliminate this pernicious element. More general calls for exclusion served only to undermine labor solidarity. Yet while Debs may not have been anti-immigrant, he did use his testimony in the Pullman hearings to make a subtle distinction between that which was foreign and that which was American. He was an "American citizen" and not a socialist, as if the two were mutually exclusive.[47]

Despite assertions that there was a nefarious foreign source behind the Pullman strike, it had limited effect on the calls for more extensive immigration restriction. The US Strike Commission did not include any such proposals in its recommendations. It merely acknowledged that the barring of pauper labor had been suggested as a way to address labor unrest. Rather than focusing on punitive actions, investigators instead stressed positive ways to eliminate future conflicts. They favored the creation of a permanent strike commission and state boards of conciliation, greater protections for labor— except when engaged in violence—and recognition of unions. So, too, did

Edward Bemis, who emphasized the need for binding arbitration in disputes involving "public" corporations such as railroads. Unlike his reaction to the Homestead violence, his assessment of the Pullman Strike made no mention of immigration. Perhaps the paucity of foreign-born railway employees, except among track- and shopmen, directed his focus away from the workers' ethnicity. Others, however, perceived a need for more immigration restriction and so looked to his previously proposed literacy test as the most promising method.[48]

In December 1895, Representative Samuel McCall and Senator Henry Cabot Lodge, both from Massachusetts, introduced bills drafted by the Immigration Restriction League that were designed to exclude anyone over sixteen years of age who could not read and write either English or some other language. Lodge believed that the test would exclude the maximum number of unwanted foreigners. Along with other benefits, it would address the concerns of those who feared the presence of alien radicalism and those concerned about the importation of cheap labor, by excluding "a great many persons who are undesirable from both the point of view of citizenship and from the effect of their competition on American wages." Its simple and definitive method would do more to protect the United States from pernicious foreign influences than provisions more narrowly aimed at anarchists or seasonal workers. For the next 18 months, Congress debated the literacy test's merits and refined its particulars, such as who would be exempted and how it would be administered. Some representatives, for example, unsuccessfully argued for excusing women, due a lack of "white" domestic servants. Both chambers passed the bill in February 1897, and it then went to President Grover Cleveland.[49]

Cleveland had acted forcefully during the Pullman Strike, authorizing the use of federal troops and supporting the Justice Department's use of injunctions against the strikers, but his veto of the literacy test bill showed the limits of his concern about immigrant involvement in labor unrest. Voicing several criticisms of the literacy test, he specifically addressed issues pertinent to labor and radicalism. The failure of the nation's economy to provide employment for all who wished to work presented an unfortunate state of affairs, but American workers should not blame immigrants for the overcrowded labor market. A phenomenal business depression had stagnated all types of production. Prudent fiscal policies, coupled with a resurgence of commerce, ultimately would remedy the misfortunes of unemployed workers, and while the depression continued, it would check the influx of foreign laborers. As to the matter of alien subversives, Cleveland believed that it would be much safer to admit one hundred thousand illiterates than one unruly agitator who, though able to read and write, delighted in arousing those peacefully inclined to discontent and tumult. Violence and disorder did not originate among illiterate, working-class immigrants. Instead, they fell victim to the educated rabble-rouser, but this potential for calamity did not justify excluding the unwary.[50]

Andrew Carnegie reached a similar conclusion. Instead of placing blame for Homestead and similar events on elements—immigrant or otherwise—within labor's ranks, the steel magnate offered his much more altruistic "Gospel of Wealth." Speaking in 1894 at the dedication of a public library in Pittsburgh for which he had paid, he articulated a path to the renewal of labor-management harmony. Prudent dispersal of one's "surplus wealth," via the funding of projects that would provide lasting and universal "public good," held the key to up-lifting society. Showing his managerial paternalism, he argued that "adding petty sums to the earnings of the masses" would lead only to most of the recipients frittering away their meager bounty. They would waste it on transient pleasures. Distribution to individuals would lead to "pandemonium," as workers would develop a sense of entitlement and constantly ask for more. Injudicious concession to worker demands also would adversely affect productivity. Operators had to exert firm control over their business endeavors, or the companies would fail, to the detriment of all. To insure universally beneficial results, those of economic means must take steps to bring lasting enlightenment, "the joys of the mind" and "the things of the spirit," to the lives of the toiling masses.[51]

Unfortunately, Carnegie's envisioned enlightenment did not come to dominate the next two decades. Americans instead continued to witness intense and frequently violent class struggles, and as the new century opened, immigrants remained at the forefront of discussions as to how best to alleviate social unrest. During the Homestead strike, the United Brewers Association had voiced its support for the steelworkers in their "resistance to capitalists, some of whom are aliens, who try to contemptuously ignore the constitution [sic] of the United States."[52] The alien reference likely referred to Carnegie, but it would be working-class immigrants whom most Americans would continue to see as acting in a contemptuous manner.

- Homestead Strike / Coxey's Army / Pullman Strike linked to imm. or foreign ideas.
- B.T. Washington's ideas - IL Central in MS
- Still little pressure for Imm Restriction

CHAPTER 5

Into the New Century

Economic Expansion and Continued Discord

On September 6, 1901, at the Pan American Exposition's Temple of Music, Leon Czolgosz fired shots that would kill President William McKinley. The assassin, a self-proclaimed anarchist who had been born in America but bore the foreign-sounding surname of his immigrant parents, provided a simple explanation for his actions. "I only done my duty," he initially told investigators, to which at the time of his execution he added a somewhat more extensive declaration: "I shot the President because I thought it would help the working people, and for the sake of the common people." In his mind, be it addled or calculating, the president both embodied and represented America's monied elite, making his murder—however horrific and misguided—a crime of class-based passion. The killer's name added a misconstrued ethnic dimension to the offence. As America entered a new century, with its promise of material largesse and growing global influence, Czolgosz's words and actions sent a chilling message about ethnicity and working-class radicalism, one that transcended his singular act of violence.[1]

McKinley's assassination reinforced the presumed connection between immigrants and class-based radicalism that had been building for the previous thirty-five years. Concurrent developments, above and beyond the president's murder, would insure continuation of the linkage. With the end of the 1890s depression, the new century's first decade saw the arrival of record numbers of immigrants, increasingly coming from southern and eastern Europe. Return of commercial prosperity cemented employers' need of their labor, but the continued reliance on foreign-born workers by business came amid intensified concerns about the foreigners' problematic behaviors. Over the next ten years, against a backdrop of economic growth coupled with virtually continuous labor conflict, these presumptions would bring heightened calls for immigration restriction, and would push business interests to intensify their efforts to control labor, notably in industries with predominately alien workforces.

Newspapers quickly and incorrectly connected Czolgosz's ideology with foreign ethnicity. Some accounts at least suggested his American birth and rearing, describing him as being of "Polish-German extraction." Reminiscent of the erroneous identification of Haymarket defendant Albert Parsons as an immigrant, other commentaries mistakenly identified Czolgosz as foreign-born. Instead, prior to his birth, his parents had come to the United States to escape the persecution of Catholic Poles in Prussia. Apparently, his last name and beliefs were enough to convince excited scribes, and presumably their readers, that he was an alien. "The Assailant Is A Polish Anarchist Named Czolgosz" proclaimed the *Charlotte Daily Observer*. So, too, the press exaggerated the connection between Czolgosz and Emma Goldman, characterizing the former as her "ardent disciple." Using an alias, he had attended one of her lectures and engaged in a brief conversation with her at a train station in Chicago. The would-be assassin thereafter spent more time with Goldman's fellow anarchist Abe Isaak, who initially thought that Czolgosz might be a police informant. Quite the opposite, the man whose name few could pronounce had murdered the president, and for many Americans, this was enough to link him to an established chain of immigrant-conducted subversion. The connection would have broad implications.[2]

The strange case of Ethelbert Stone revealed the nation's xenophobia. Stone, a native-born ship builder from Camden, New Jersey, had portended McKinley's assassination in a heated conversation with coworkers. The president, he had wagered $5, would be dead before 8:00 PM on the day when Czolgosz shot him. Upon learning of his remarks, the district attorney had him arrested. Police eventually determined that he simply had made "a silly, thoughtless remark," purely coincidental to the assassination, and released him from custody. Yet in initial reporting, the *Philadelphia Inquirer*, after noting that Stone previously had shown no "anarchistic tendencies," explained he had worked at a New York City shipyard with "a gang of Italians and Hungarians."[3] This association with immigrants somehow offered a plausible explanation of how and why someone with an American-sounding name and no history of radical adherence or behavior could have been part of a plot that extended to Emma Goldman, Jonathan Most, and other pro-labor radicals.

Conversely, the Kansas *Emporia Gazette's* epitaph-laced editorial provided an analysis of the assassination's connection to immigration that echoed labor's long-standing concerns. As Americans vented their indignation at the horrific crime and tried to separate it from "legitimate" labor protest, the editors suggested that "it might be well to pause and see if some little blame does not lie somewhere in the system and order of this republic. For half a century the greed of the great captains of industry has been almost untrammeled." Their avarice had resulted in the importation of "millions of Pollaks [*sic*] and Huns and Italians, the very scum of European civilization." Upon arrival, they had displaced "honest, well-paid, intelligent, conscientious, American labor." The induced migrants, a collection of "human vermin," to whom liberty meant license, lacked any and all capability to appreciate US institutions or laws. "The Pollak [*sic*]who shot McKinley is as incapable of understanding American liberty as a tiger is of understanding the beatitudes," the editors contended. However, the capitalists who imported immigrant workers were "in some measure to blame" for the putative alien's crime.[4]

The *Gazette's* indictment bucked the prevailing sentiment. The editors accepted the erroneous assumption of Czolgosz's foreign birth, but they also postulated a domestic cause of his deplorable crime. This was a surprising fact, given that most Americans saw no native circumstances that might explain Czolgosz's actions or mitigate his guilt. For the new President Theodore Roosevelt, nothing in the United States, except a foreign presence, could explain what had happened to his predecessor. Writing shortly after the shooting but before McKinley had died, TR took care to separate the fallen chief executive from capitalist elites and any criticism that they might deserve, even though he very much represented their interests. Roosevelt directed his vitriol solely against the assassin and his creed. Czolgosz was an "infamous scoundrel" and "so crazy a fool." TR lamented only that if, as expected, the president lived, Czolgosz could be sentenced to merely seven years in prison.[5] McKinley's death soon made this a moot point.

Beyond the particulars of Czolgosz's mental state and appropriate punishment, the president's assassination raised broader questions of whether the United States needed new laws dealing with immigrants. The issue had quieted since President Cleveland's 1897 veto of the literacy test bill, but McKinley's assassination renewed discussion. According to various critics, the new immigrants flooded labor markets, engendered unemployment and low wages, and otherwise caused havoc. "These creatures compose the murderous mobs in the mining districts of Pennsylvania, Ohio, and Illinois," editorialized the Portland *Morning Oregonian* in condemning southern and eastern Europeans. More dangerous even than the Asians with whom westerners were more familiar, they cheapened wages, degraded labor, and soon would "defile the ballot box." They needed to be restricted, their critics asserted, but not everyone agreed. The Superintendent of Schools in Cleveland, Ohio, assessing attendance at night classes, characterized recent immigration as "100 per cent better than only a few years ago." Addressing the issue of imported radicalism, a *St. Louis Globe-Democrat* reporter highlighted better enforcement of the contract labor laws as having secured a better class of immigrant workers, who had the "promise to make good citizens." Their quality exceeded that of earlier arrivals, many of whom had made good workers but also had harbored "ultra socialistic and anarchistic tendencies."[6] Both sides of the debate could not be right, and as large numbers of immigrants continued to pour into the United States, policy makers pondered the best course of action.

Presumption of a connection between McKinley's assassination and imported radicalism convinced President Roosevelt of the need to act and reinforced the long-standing restrictionist beliefs of his confidant and United States Senator, Henry Cabot Lodge. Anarchists, a provoked TR averred, comprised a wholly un-American lot, against whom the nation needed to do nothing less than make war. Their plague had to be driven from the land. Replying to his friend's assertion, Lodge moved the focus from un-American to anti-immigrant. Those like Czolgosz were "the enemies of the government, society and patriotism." To neutralize their threat, the United States needed to pass "stringent legislation against them and for the restriction of immigration." Lodge had championed the latter for the past decade, but not even concerns raised by the Pullman strike had been enough to secure the enactment of new exclusions. But now, following McKinley's murder, "there was more reason than ever" for the nation to address its inadequate immigration statutes. TR would concur, at least when it came to excluding anarchists, using his first Annual Message to urge Congress to bar such women and men from entering the United States, allow for the deportation of those who had entered the country, and punish any who stayed. Presumably the latter referred to aliens who promoted anarchist ideas after living for a time in the United States.[7]

Congress would pass a new immigration law but would limit its new prohibitions to anarchists. Four years earlier, in his 1897 Inaugural Address, President McKinley had endorsed the exclusion of any immigrant who came to the United States with the intent of making war upon the national social order, which to most Americans meant anarchists, but Congress had shown little interest in passing this or any other new legislation. Reluctance stemmed in part from the nation's focus on a different foreign concern, the incursion into and occupation of Cuba and the Philippines during and after the Spanish American War. It also reflected employers' continued reliance on immigrant workers. The pro-restriction *Outlook* magazine cynically identified businesses that wanted cheap labor and brewers who wanted patrons as the principal and successful supporters of unimpeded immigration. But in reaction to McKinley's murder, the Immigration Act of 1903 excluded "anarchists or persons who believe in or advocate the overthrow by force or violence of the government of the United States, or of all governments or of all forms of law, or the assassination of public officials." It also allowed for their deportation within three years of entry and precluded their naturalization. Because Czolgosz had been born in the United States, the new law would not have affected him, and Congress declined to pursue legislation aimed at native-born anarchists. Yet the prohibition of immigrant anarchists demonstrated the extent to which notions of "foreign" and "radicalism" had become intertwined.[8]

Other than barring anarchists, the new law did little stem the overall tide of immigrants coming to the United States. Industrialists, including those who concurred with the need to interdict alien radicals, comprised a powerful opposition to the literacy test, or any of the other means of more stringent general exclusion, on the grounds that such measures would limit the availability of needed workers. The Illinois Central Railroad's General Counsel made this clear to Mississippi Senator Anselm McLaurin: "The demand for labor is very large for working people all over the country, North and South" and the literacy test would exacerbate the situation. Education might be beneficial for citizenship, IC President Stuyvesant Fish postulated, but it was not "a desirable requirement for merely coming to the country." The rudiments of education did little or nothing to improve the quality of one's labor, an immigrant's primary attribute, and requiring it for entry into the United States would deter the migration of many aliens. "Such a curtailment of the supply of labor," Fish complained, would be "very detrimental to the interests of the Illinois Central R.R. Co. and other railroads." Boston and Maine Railway leaders agreed. The railroad joined other New England companies in pressuring the region's congressmen to oppose the test, even though Massachusetts' Senator Lodge was its champion, due to fears of its adverse commercial effects.[9]

By focusing its concerns on how restriction would adversely affect the South, the Illinois Central demonstrated the national nature of managerial concerns. Recent high demand for labor in the North had spurred a large

African American exodus from the South. Their absence left the IC with the problem of finding enough "competent hands" (inferring that it had followed through to at least some extent on President Fish's 1893 proposal to use black laborers), and agriculturalists were having an equally difficult time getting enough men to pick cotton. Adequate access to cheap foreign labor held the key to eliminating this predicament. At present, few immigrants went to the South, an unfortunate pattern that Fish attributed to the nation's "idiotic alien labor laws," which prevented companies from recruiting them. New exclusions would exacerbate the situation. "If there is a serious restriction on the importation of labor into the Northern States," an IC official warned, "there will be an increasing demand upon the South for its labor, and as the prices paid are larger, our industries will suffer consequences." Southern business leaders, like their northern counterparts, saw provision of needed workers as immigration's "utmost importance." But as the Montgomery, Alabama, Industrial Association said of its support for immigration recruitment, any who came to the state must contribute to "a patriotic and loyal citizenship."[10] To the north, renewed unrest in the steel industry showed the universality of this expectation.

Harkening back to Homestead fifteen years earlier, a largely immigrant workforce represented by the Amalgamated Association of Iron, Steel, and Tin Workers (AAISW) struck the newly formed United States Steel Corporation in 1901. The conglomerate, which included the former Carnegie properties, epitomized consolidated capital at the turn of the twentieth century. Although organized by banker J. Pierpont Morgan—whom the US press elevated from baron to "Little King" and for whom the British media suggested coronation—US Steel symbolized the movement away from businesses controlled by or associated with singular leaders, such as Carnegie and Frick. Less personal corporations—with myriad stockholders, greater separation of ownership and management, and powerful yet distant boards of directors—increasingly dominated the country's leading industries. Organizers believed that the new business model would increase profitability by promoting efficiency and limiting competition. Beneficiaries generally did not include workers, nor did the changing corporate culture lessen labor tensions.[11] At US Steel, management's response to the 1901 strike followed the pattern established by Frick and Carnegie.

The 1901 strike centered on the AAISW's demand for the extension of union recognition to all of the company's plants, and unlike the Association's past organizing efforts, unionization would extend to unskilled workers, many of whom were recent immigrants. "Several thousand Poles and Hungarians employed as laborers in the tube [steel] works are anxious to strike and will be formed into an organization of their own or admitted to the Federation of Labor," read one account, under the headline "Immense Revolt of Organized Labor." Some immigrants did strike, but others continued to work, amid reports of the company's efforts to recruit Hungarian "scabs." As to the foreigners who protested, sometimes violently, a Pittsburgh magistrate wanted them to know that "any one who is arrested in connection with strike disorder will be made to feel the utmost penalty of the law." While Morgan publicly expressed his faith in an "easily reached" solution, privately he supported the company's determination to avoid any extension of collective bargaining. In this he succeeded, as labor could not even preserve the status quo. Following the strike, US Steel president Charles Schwab rejected Morgan's idea of retaining preexisting collective bargaining agreements and refused to sign union contracts at mills that previously had them.[12]

The Morgan-financed consortium that dominated Pennsylvania's anthracite coal region followed a similar pattern. Since the time of the Molly Maguires, area operators had struggled to secure mutually beneficial cooperation, and between 1898 and 1901, Morgan successfully orchestrated the creation of an association involving eight regional railroads. Organizers used an array of holding companies, binding contracts, and less formal agreements to dominate effectively the production and transportation of anthracite coal. Several railroad presidents, for example, served on the Temple Iron Company board of directors, which provided a forum for discussing any and all matters related to the anthracite trade. It also allowed participants to perpetuate an "understanding," by which each railroad hauled an agreed-upon proportion of anthracite traffic. Not surprisingly, the frequency of board meetings increased during strikes. The consolidation paid handsome dividends, as the price of the coal delivered to New York Harbor increased steadily after 1901 and remained high for the next decade.[13] But the railroad leaders and investors were not the only ones who wanted higher remuneration from the trade in hard coal.

A 1902 strike pitted the anthracite region's multiethnic, 140,000-man labor force—represented by the John Mitchell–led United Mine Workers of America (UMWA)—against a powerful anthracite combination, headed by Reading Railway CEO George Baer. Contention centered on wages, work practices, and union recognition. Emotions ran high, and not just among workers. An absence of coal also threatened to deprive ordinary Americans who lived along the populated East Coast of what they saw "as a necessity of life." The troubling thought of an "empty coal bin" caused considerable public angst. While some observers called for the imposition of new policies to insure that the miners received "reasonable prices" for their labor, Baer adamantly rejected what he considered to be meddling in *"our affair."* Morgan, who publicly declined to get involved and urged those who called for some sort of arbitrated-solution to do the same, reportedly said that there would be no concessions until the miners went back to work. Ultimately, however, he did cooperate with President Roosevelt to orchestrate a mediated settlement, a scenario at odds with the usual practice of government authority and power solely supporting capitalists. The strike also provided an opportunity for a wide-ranging discussion of immigrant workers.[14]

Between 1880 and 1900, central and eastern Europeans had flocked to the anthracite region where, by the turn of the century, they comprised 46 percent of the population. The newcomers encountered numerous discriminations as they supplemented the Irish and English migrants who had dominated the coal fields during the Molly Maguire era. An 1889 state statute required *miners*—a specifically defined occupation as opposed to a general term for those who worked at the mines—to obtain certification by passing a test in English. Although advocated as a safety measure, one that would keep "incompetent persons" out of the mines, the act effectively limited those who were not conversant in English to less ruminative and more physically demanding jobs. It passed the legislature, suggested one supporter, to prevent "the importation of pauper immigrants into the anthracite coal regions. . . ." An even more discriminatory act, enacted in 1897 but soon voided by the courts, taxed businesses that hired immigrants, and companies recouped the assessment by charging the alien employees, further reducing their already low pay. Newer immigrants who could secure status as miners often failed to get assigned to an underground chamber, as these were limited in number and tended to go to "Anglo Saxons," men from the British Isles or of American ancestry. This left the "Sclavs," as one writer identified them in the *Yale Review,* to work as laborers who spent longer hours than miners in the shafts but earned only one-third of the latter's pay.[15]

Evidence of this ethnic hierarchy was widespread. Visitors during the 1902 strike found glaring differences between the communities inhabited by natives and older immigrants, and those that were home to more recent arrivals. The former, asserted social critic Frank Norris, lived in clean neighborhoods with "charming" houses; those of southern and eastern Europeans stood in sharp contrast. "The Polanders of Melonsville," he wrote, using language that suggested ethnic bigotry, "live a great deal worse than any street cur would elect to live if he had his way and say in the matter." Others also noted variations in living standards, but described them with less negative phraseology. Mine work, these writers attested, attracted the less fortunate of all ethnic groups. Their abodes often did not adhere to "conventional standards of living," as judged by most Americans, but this resulted more from lack of adequate wages than ethnic predisposition. According to one writer who had dwelt among the miners for more than twenty-five years, those who lived in impoverished surroundings, including the new immigrants, were sober and law-abiding people: strong, honest, and hardworking women and men.[16]

Observations by John Mitchell, who both represented immigrant workers and took a dim view of those who recently had arrived, addressed the question of who bore blame for mine families living in squalor. Changing conditions, he believed, offered the best answer. During the early- to mid-1800s, the daunting and strenuous transatlantic journey had created a "natural selection" process, insuring that only the Old World's most hearty inhabitants survived the trip. This recently had changed. Faster steamships now allowed those with lower standards of living—but not necessarily moral depravity or mental failings—to cross the Atlantic easily. Willing on arrival to take the first available job, many of the recent immigrants fell prey to "the sweaters and the exploiters." This was especially true of illiterates. In the mining industry, the immigrants acted as a "club," hanging above the heads of existing workers. Threats to hire more foreigners coerced experienced miners into accepting reduced wages, effectively lowering pay for the entire industry. Restriction could act as a preventative, but Mitchell realized that not everyone agreed with its propriety. One group of opponents drew special scorn. "From the point of view of the great employers of labor," he lamented, "there is an apparent advantage in having the doors wide open." It guaranteed a ready supply of cheap labor.[17]

Mitchell and the muckraking *McClure's Magazine* generally agreed about how businesses used immigrant workers, but Mitchell elsewhere offered a contradictory assessment of their behavior. Companies had a right, *McClure's Magazine* editors stated in response to the labor leader's commentary, to hire whomever they pleased. Both Mitchell and *McClure's* stressed immigrants' presumptive role as corporate stooges, cheap workers whose pliability allowed employers to impose their will. Foreigners not only did what management decreed, their presence divided workers along ethnic lines and effectively prevented the creation of labor solidarity. If native workers did try to assert their prerogatives, a virtually inexhaustible pool of aliens stood ready to replace them. This scenario stressed management's exploitation of immigrants, but the conservative Mitchell also viewed them as a subversive presence. While he publicly praised immigrants and their children for being "on average, as patriotic, as loyal, and as valuable citizens as those of native ancestry," he privately made a different case, characterizing foreign workers as akin to "a drove of cattle, ready to stampede" at an agitator's urging. This latter frequently came closer to describing their actual behavior, although the immigrants acted with greater purpose than that for which Mitchell gave them credit.[18]

Immigrants' actions during the 1902 strike contradicted contentions of interethnic strife and showed their propensity to support the UMWA, albeit in a strident manner. Previous strikes, most notably those of 1897 and 1900, had engendered worker solidarity that crossed ethnic lines. "The Sclavs," concluded the *Yale Review* writer, "make the best Union men in the anthracite coal fields." University of Chicago professor John Cummings joined Mitchell in stressing immigrants' tendency to get agitated but viewed their militancy as a contribution to the workers' cause. Alien miners tended to be "lawless and violent," an "immense, isolated group of foreigners, who do not speak our language, and who know nothing of our institutions." Yet Cummings also acknowledged their union memberships and encouraged management to bargain collectively with them: "To bring these men into the country, to build and rent them their houses, to employ them in the mines, is to deal with them." He did not condemn employers for "bringing" foreigners to the United States, nor did he call for more immigration restriction. In contrast to Mitchell's concerns about the immigrants' adverse effects on unionization, Cummings recommended recognition of and negotiation with the UMWA, to which many of the immigrants belonged, as the best way to deal with the foreigners.

Managerial perspectives on the steel and coal strikes reflected the changing nature of corporate hierarchy. Financier J. P. Morgan, a quintessential robber baron who played a leading role in the creation of both US Steel and the anthracite association, dominated American capitalism in the early twentieth century, but unlike Carnegie or Pullman during the previous decade, his involvement in the industrial process was indirect and fiscal. Morgan provided the money, while others ran the businesses. This limited his contact with and commentary regarding foreign-born workers. Although he lived in polyglot New York City, he associated almost exclusively with the men and women of its upper social echelons. Among these, Morgan's frequent references to Jews in anti-Semitic terms hinted at nativism, but his carefully selected business associates included Italian American Egisto P. Fabbri. His charitable giving acknowledged the city's working-class immigrants, but he lived in a different world. Observing his congressional testimony in 1912, a newspaper from immigrant-rich northern Minnesota opined as to how Morgan "talked of millions and billions as if he were a kid on the street counting marbles. The ordinary individual thinks in cabbage, onions and the price of steak for breakfast."[19]

Circumstantial evidence did suggest that Morgan viewed immigrants primarily as laborers who served the needs of America's growing industries. During the 1860s, J. P.'s father Junius had lent his name to the American Emigrant Company's recruitment of foreign workers, but J. P devoted most of his attention to the importation of European capital. His admiration for M. M. Holland Thomas's 1888 novel *Fraternity, a Romance of Inspiration* (republished in 1910), indicated how he likely felt about the working-class *others* who did journey to the United States. The novel's antisocialist plot extolled the virtues of accepting poverty, rejecting conflict with property holders, and embracing an inequitable human fraternity. Endorsement of this message appears to be as close as Morgan came to commentary on contemporary class conflict or its ethnic participants. He did support social reformers who worked with immigrants, hiring and subsidizing the salary of the Reverend William S. Rainsford, an avowed social activist, as rector of St. George's Episcopal Church, which Morgan attended and supported. He also funded Dr. James W. Markoe's efforts to bring obstetric and gynecological care to immigrant women at New York's Lying-in Hospital.[20] These connections showed the financier's awareness of foreign-born Americans but leave vague the level of his interest in their working-class lives.

Ships that hauled immigrants did attract Morgan's attention. Coincidentally, he first addressed the unrest at US Steel after having returned from Europe aboard a liner owned by Hamburg-Amerika, one of the steamship lines that had brought tens of thousands of immigrants to American shores. As he disembarked, reporters asked about the financier's rumored plans to purchase his own transatlantic steamers. Morgan declined comment, but he would in fact organize the International Mercantile Marine (IMM), or what the press came to call "the steamship trust." Because some foreign lines retained their independence, the trust never had the integration or consolidation of US Steel, nor did it become one of Morgan's more profitable ventures. (A 1903 cartoon showed Morgan standing in front of a ruptured ship, as its cargo of coins spilled into the drink.) Unfortunately, coverage of the Mercantile's creation, operation, and ultimate demise dwelt primarily on its management and profitability, with almost no mention of the trust's actual or potential capacity for hauling passengers. Morgan and the other organizers apparently focused their attention on freight. This may have been a costly oversight, as the combine's vessels frequently sailed empty when returning from Europe.[21]

US Senator Marcus A. "Mark" Hanna, a leading industrialist and frequently lampooned representation of ostentatious wealth, did use the anthracite strike to draw attention to the efforts of the Industrial Department of the National

Civic Federation, a consortium of business and conservative labor leaders of which he was president. Its Immigration Department, headed by Chicago banker Franklin MacVeagh, conducted a 1905 conference to explore the nature of American immigration and address its related maladies. Although MacVeagh belonged to the Immigration Restriction League, and Conference Secretary Franklin J. Warne later would write of an "immigrant invasion," numerous attendees spoke of the nation's need for foreign-born workers. Representatives from across the country emphasized demands "for common brute labor, labor of the hand." One called for an end to contract labor laws, which inhibited the recruitment of workers to needy places, and another urged the elimination of prejudice based on an immigrant's nationality.[22]

Linking immigration and labor unrest and reflecting the new century's cooperative approach to commercial enterprise, Senator Hanna emphasized voluntary conciliation as the solution to the conjoined problems. Constructive dialogue, he believed, was the key both to ending labor's resort to strikes and addressing the challenges posed by immigrant workers. The arrival of "all classes and all kinds of people from the four quarters of the globe" was creating a "cosmopolitan" America, which in turn produced unique and volatile labor relations. "It is not an easy manner," Hanna declared, "to assimilate such large numbers of foreign immigrants; they do not understand our language, they are not abreast with the education of a self-governing people; they do not understand our institutions."[23] Something needed to be done to eliminate the associated dangers, and Hanna looked to businesses to provide a remedy.

Employer-directed Americanization held the key to immigrants' repudiation of radical ideologies. Any effort to promote harmony "must necessarily be a work of education," a cause that all business interests would be well-served to embrace. "Everything that is American is primarily opposed to socialism," Hanna proclaimed. Extremists who taught its precepts posed a danger to the country, and they tended to target the "semi-ignorant classes," an apt characterization of Hanna's new immigrants. These vulnerable people, he believed, must be shown that socialism was "un-American and unnatural to us as a people." Learning this and other key lessons would bring immigrants into the fold, allowing them to contribute to the conciliation between capital and labor. But if Hanna had his way, however enlightened, immigrant workers still would be at the mercy of employers, upon whom rested "the responsibility for seeing that the men receive their fair share of its [capitalism's] benefits."[24] Although willing to explore positive means of defusing contentious labor relations, Hanna perpetuated perceptions of radicalism as inherently foreign, and not the product of employers' exploitative practices.

Events involving US Steel and the anthracite railroads took place at venues with established histories of combined immigrant hiring and labor conflict, but the start of the 1900s saw parallel confluences at less familiar locations, notably in the West. The previous decades had seen the region change from being the home primarily to Native Americans to an extension of the nation's industrial economy, particularly in mining. Individual prospectors, searching with pick and shovel for the mythical mother lode, had given way to big businesses with the fiscal resources necessary for large-scale extraction. These companies needed labor, and like their competitors in the East, they sought to recruit immigrants. The pull of economic opportunity attracted significant numbers from both old and new sources. Reporting in 1903, the *Colorado Springs Gazette* praised efforts to "move the enormous Italian contingent now coming to this country" to vacant lands in the West, rather than having them settle "in the already over-populated cities." So-called Mexicans also contributed to the western labor force, and even though many came from families who had been living in the United States since the annexation of Texas and acquisition of other lands through the Treaty of Guadalupe Hidalgo in the 1840s, "Anglo-Americans" nonetheless saw them as belonging to a distinctly foreign and "outside" group.[25] By the turn of the century, the array of foreign-born miners had clashed with management at Coeur d'Alene, Idaho, in 1892; Cripple Creek, Colorado, in 1894; and Leadville, Colorado, in 1896; as well as at other mines or smelters throughout the region.

"Whether in Chicago or in Clinton, in New York or Morenci, it is the first duty of the authorities to maintain law and order," editorialized the Tucson *Citizen* in 1903, talking about a strike by Arizona copper miners in the territory's east-central mountain region. Developments during the previous decades had created labor dynamics akin to those in the East. As the New York City *Worker* explained to its readers in March 1903, with the Morenci-Clinton mine workers on the verge of striking, the men who controlled Standard Oil, US Steel, and National City Bank (a Rockefeller-associated institution) had extended their reach into Arizona's remote copper country. Industrial giant Phelps Dodge effectively controlled the industry. Commercial extraction and smelting had begun in 1873, creating a need for labor. Local Indians long had prospected individually, but rather than becoming part of the industrial workforce, they frequently attacked the growing settlements throughout the 1870s and 1880s. Owners instead turned to Mexicans and Chinese. Construction of the Southern Pacific Railroad had brought the Asians to the area, and for a brief time they also labored in the mines, until the operators abruptly discharged them in 1883. During the next two decades, the advent of new techniques and the arrival of better transportation increased mine productivity, attracting more workers from a variety of ethnic groups.[26]

Implementation of a would-be reform (manipulated by the mine operators) precipitated the 1903 strike. Territorial statute had reduced the miners' workday from 10 to 8 hours, but management offered only 9 hours of pay. As this was effectively a 10 percent pay cut, the miners struck. Coverage of the unfolding events centered on the participants' ethnicity. "The strikers are all armed and very demonstrative," declared the Tucson *Citizen*. "They are mostly Italians and Mexicans, with Italians in the lead and the most aggressive." Stereotypical characterizations abounded: "There is also a rumor in circulation that several of the alleged members of the Mafia society who were driven out of Morenci several years ago have returned with the avowed intention of getting revenge." Acting Territorial Governor Isaac T. Stoddard's telegram to President Theodore Roosevelt, asking for federal forces to help restore order, referred to "three thousand men, mostly foreigners," "armed and in the hands of professional agitators," who were menacing the local communities.[27]

The strike followed a familiar course. Stoddard mobilized the state militia and local authorities, who established martial law, and TR sent federal troops from Colorado. The president's actions, instead of continuing the enlightened behavior that he had shown during the anthracite conflict, repeated on a smaller scale Grover Cleveland's use of the military to defend capital during the Pullman Strike. Labor leader William D. "Big Bill" Haywood declared that Roosevelt had committed "treason to the principles of organized labor." Following the military's arrival and arrest of several strike leaders, the "quiet but sullen" miners soon accepted the operators' terms. But as work resumed, the radicals—identified as such on the basis of their ethnicity—had been purged from the miners' ranks. "The Italians only," reported the press, "are not included in the settlement." Authorities also prosecuted the arrested leaders, all of whom were Mexicans and Italians. In trials that centered as much on the defendants' ideology and ethnicity as on their actions, ten were convicted of inciting a riot and sent to the Territorial prison.[28]

Similar conflict gripped the Colorado coalfields. When commercial mining started there during the 1870s, lead developer William Palmer had envisioned a work environment where "there never would be any strikes or hard feelings among the labourers towards the capitalist," but from the beginning, a series of disputes proved him wrong. Now, in the fall of 1903, the aggrieved colliers demanded better underground safeguards and ventilation, improved compensation, and an eight-hour day. They also called for an end to payment in company scrip. Initiating the walkout, UMWA President John Mitchell defined the strike as an "effort to secure reasonable wages and fair conditions of employment. . . ." The situation, especially at some of the larger companies, had become "intolerable," necessitating the work stoppage. Across the state, an estimated 10,000 workers joined the strike. To the north, operators capitulated to all of the miners' stipulations, except the shorter workday. They even agreed to implement the settlement on a temporary basis, with permanence contingent on its approval by employers in the southern fields, where immigrant labor predominated. Seeing this offer to some as a means of dividing the workers along ethnic lines, firebrand union organizer and worker advocate Mother Jones urged unity between "Americans" and foreigners. Northern miners initially rejected management overtures, out of concerns that a settlement would undermine their brethren to the south, but Mitchell, in a quest for conciliation, called for a second, ultimately successful vote.[29] His efforts may have brought labor peace to the state's northern mines, but not to those in the south.

There, Colorado Fuel and Iron (CFI), a Rockefeller concern that also owned a large steel mill in nearby Pueblo, and Victor-American controlled about 90 percent of the coal output. Blatantly exploiting their largely immigrant workforce, the companies based wages on a heavier "long-ton" instead of the more common 2,000-pound ton, and failed to have a worker "check weigh-man" verify each miner's output. They also paid in company scrip instead of cash and then gouged the workers at company stores. Seeking to help these angry workers and also strengthen its national prowess, UMWA organizers aggressively recruited the westerners. By 1903, the union represented two thousand Colorado and Utah miners, or 25 percent of the regional workforce. The strike started in November, when CFI and Victor-American refused to negotiate grievances, recognize the UMWA, or even to attend a conciliation meeting called by the state's commissioner of labor. In a matter of days, 6,400 of an estimated 6,800 union and nonunion workers came together to shut down the mines. The presence of the more radical Western Federation of Miners (WFM) also pushed the UMWA to act aggressively, so as to retain its members' loyalty.[30]

Immigrants of thirteen nationalities comprised the vast majority of the miners. Among these, about 40 percent were Italian and 20 percent Austro-Hungarian. The UMWA selected immigrants to lead its organizing efforts, chose members from each camp's dominant ethnic group to take charge of local recruitment, and acquired the Italian language newspaper, *Il Lavoratore italiano* (*ILI*) to serve as its official publicity organ. Using a transnational approach, the paper linked the miners' new American home to their country of origin. References to the American Revolution commingled with those pertaining to Italian heroes and their Old World fights for justice. Linkage stressed that immigrants could be loyal to both the United States and their European heritage. To make the case, *ILI* editors tried to combine Old World condonation of radical creeds, such as anarchism, with portrayals of immigrant workers as law-abiding men and women. Recruitment efforts challenged popular notions of the Italians' predisposition to scabbing, and praise for their peaceful disposition dispelled reputations for unruly behavior.[31]

For foreign-born workers who were both incensed by their employers' practices and generally suspected of being subversive, adhering to the positive characterizations was not easy. Addressing the striking workers on December 13, 1903, Mother Jones exemplified their dilemma. Her remarks included calls for nonviolence and respect for law. But she also declared: "Before the warfare will come to an end labor must be given all, capitalism itself must be destroyed and Socialism must take its place." To the tired, hungry, and angry strikers, Jones's words offered hope for a better tomorrow, and they responded with sustained applause at the end of her two-hour speech. Even labor leaders who preached avoidance of unnecessary provocation could not doubt the appeal of her message, even as they grimaced at the likelihood that her words would condemn the alien miners in the court of public opinion. State officials, who called in the National Guard and otherwise contributed to crushing the strike, clearly showed the workers no sympathy. By Spring 1904 the strike ended with the miners' defeat.[32]

Press coverage, with its consistently negative and often misleading references to the immigrant workers, validated the fears of those concerned about the effects of inflammatory rhetoric. Virtually all accounts of violence included an immigrant reference. One headline read: "Six Italians At Starkville, Colo., Assault Coal Company Guards." The perpetrators were not angry workers or frustrated strikers, they were "Italians." Similarly, when wives of striking miners attacked a marshal, "nearly severing one of his ears," the paper took care to note that the mutilation took place in the town's "Italian quarter." According to the *Colorado Springs Gazette*, Italians had instigated the strike, walking out while Mexicans, Austrians, and Japanese wanted to continue working. In another instance, the paper reported African Americans being imported as strikebreakers. In reality, the walkout had broad-based ethnic support, and the leaders convinced some black workers to join their efforts. Mine operators may have planted the more derogatory accounts, seeking to undermine the workers' unity. To counter the negative press, UWMA spokesmen described its members as "law abiding American citizens," but to no avail.[33] The Colorado coalfields may have been thousands of miles from better-known immigrant communities, but the portrayal of striking foreign-born laborers as radical militants was all too typical.

contribution

Disparaging depictions of obstreperous immigrants could differ to the point of contradiction, as shown by those of Italians in southern Colorado and the Pennsylvania coalfields, but they conveyed similarly negative messages. One commentator attributed the scant presence of Italian workers in the anthracite region to the men's lack of "nerve or endurance" in comparison with other foreigners, from both old and new sources. But in the Colorado mines, where they were the largest ethnic contingent, they exuded the western miner's sense of masculine bravado. *ILI* editor Carlo Demolli, whose publication of bawdy letters got him arrested on obscenity charges during the strike, typified the image of "tough guy" courted by western males. Demolli not only wrote for the newspaper, he also boxed. He and other Italians certainly did not avoid the anthracite region due to cowardice or weakness, as demonstrated by their willingness to work in Colorado's dangerous and physically taxing mines. During the strike, they hardly shied away from conflict or otherwise displayed a lack of nerve. Indeed, once the strike began, those earlier described in the press as "clannish but industrious and peaceful" showed a willingness to resort to violence.[34]

Yet another Colorado strike played out in Cripple Creek. There, the Western Federation of Miners (WFM) struck the Standard and Colorado Company reduction mills, demanding an eight-hour day, higher wages, and union recognition. Length of the workday dominated the dispute. Voters supported amending the state constitution to allow laws establishing standard workdays, but the Mine Owners' Association stymied the process. Seeing no alternative, the WFM called for a strike, first against the refining plants and then at any mine that shipped them ore. Contention soon rendered conditions at the camps "little short of hells on earth. . . ." Allegedly to preserve law and order, Governor James H. Peabody sent National Guard troops, and when the Association agreed to fund their deployment, they became the business leaders' private army. Martial law and suspension of *habeas corpus*, coupled with Citizens Protective League vigilantism, led to incarceration and deportation of strikers and their supporters. But radicalism was apparently in the eyes of the beholder. Company G of the Colorado National Guard commandeered the armory at Pueblo when they did not get paid—by either the Owners' Association or the state—after returning from service at Cripple Creek, but they were "obviously" not provocateurs bent on fomenting revolution.[35]

Voices across the ideological divide offered differing opinions of the unfolding events, with one consistently notable omission. The Social Labor Party's *Daily People* described the situation at Cripple Creek as the "mailed hand of the brigand class of capitalism . . . exhibiting itself at its worst."

Disagreeing, Colorado's US Senator Thomas M. Patterson characterized the strike as an unprovoked effort by "Socialists" who were trying to divide the nation. An editorialist, who identified himself only as a miner, referred to the Western Federation as a criminal organization, allegedly responsible for the assassination of 19 nonunion men and the maiming of numerous others. Its intimidating presence kept those like the writer, who wanted to work, away from the mines. Another participant observer, long-time private detective and company guard Stephen Massey, emphasized the role of agitators. "What I have noticed most in these strikes [of hard-rock miners]," he told the press, "is that many of the same men are connected with different classes of strikes wherever they are."[36] Interestingly, neither Massey nor any of the other castigators evoked the presence of immigrant radicals in making their charge.

Likely because most of the hard-rock miners who then belonged to the WFM were either native-born or immigrants of long residence, ethnicity played little role in the Cripple Creek strike, but its saga would have unexpected consequences involving immigrant workers. The complicity of authorities in crushing the walkout convinced many of the miners and union leaders of the futility of trying to reform the existing system. Something of a more revolutionary nature was needed to defeat the perceived combination of government and capital. The Western Federation always had been more radical than the AFL, particularly in its aim of creating an industrial rather than craft-based union and its willingness to engage in strikes or otherwise confront management, and now the WFM would take the lead in creating the socialist-leaning Industrial Workers of the World (IWW) nicknamed the Wobblies. Organized in June 1905, the IWW quickly evolved into a revolutionary group dedicated to the destruction of capitalism. WFM and IWW spokeswomen and men—notably Vincent St. John and Elizabeth Gurley Flynn—would mount a nationwide effort to bring their radical message to the American working class, including miners on Minnesota's Mesabi Range.[37]

There an overwhelmingly foreign-born workforce extracted over 50 percent of the nation's iron ore. Locals initiated commercial mining on the Mesabi in 1890 and controlled the properties during their first years of operation. Soon, however, capital demands—not just to open and run the mines but also to build the railroads and docks on Lake Superior needed to transport the ore—led to investments by John D. Rockefeller, Andrew Carnegie, James J. Hill, and other leading industrialists. Their involvement brought consolidation, and after the creation of US Steel in 1901, its Oliver Iron Mining Company dominated the region. In 1902, Oliver mines produced 60 percent of the Mesabi's ore, and other similarly large corporations, such as Republic Iron and Steel Company, accounted for most of the remainder. While the Mesabi may have been a collection of small towns—like the mining regions of the intermountain West retaining something of a frontier appearance and ambiance—but in terms of the business conducted there, they were very much a part of industrial America. The big businesses that ran the mines followed well-established patterns of rebuking any challenge by their workers.[38]

The Mesabi's foreign-born labor force went "hand in hand with the region's industrial development." "Without immigrants," concluded government investigators, "the mining companies operating on the Minnesota iron ranges would never have been able to open the mines, or if successful in opening them to continue operations." The region lacked sufficient native labor, particularly for the "low class of work demanded in the open-pit mines of the Mesabi range," but southern and eastern Europeans appeared willing and able to fill the void. Finns and Slovenians, for example, purportedly possessed the needed physical stamina. "Most of the men were raw material, new importations from Europe," wrote Minnesota newsman Charles Cheney. "They had been 'induced' in various ways to come, and herded like sheep in the Mesaba district, to furnish a cheap and adequate labor." Cheney exaggerated the extent to which the miners had come to the Range in the traditional manner of contract laborers. Companies did use employment agencies to attract needed workers, but the immigrants came of their own volition or at the urging of family and friends. They knew that they could find jobs. Since area mining companies paid relatively high wages, Cheney also overstated cost as a reason for their recruitment. But he did correctly stress their presence. By 1907, when the mines experienced their first strike, immigrants representing at least 32 ethnic groups made up the workforce, and the Mesabi had become synonymous with its foreign-born population.[39]

Managers may have tried to use ethnic diversity to impede workers' activism, but if so, their efforts failed. Immigrants figured prominently in the Range's growing worker militancy. Starting in 1905, the WFM tried to organize the Mesabi miners, in part to keep them from being brought further west to act as strikebreakers. Federation spokesmen initially had little success, until local Italian American and socialist Teofilo Petriella tailored his recruitment strategy to appeal to immigrants. His messages then found a receptive audience, especially among the Finns and Italians, who had reputations for leftist leanings. "Their leaders were Socialist agitators," wrote Cheney of the striking aliens, "and their 'red flag,' which figured prominently in all dispatches, seemed a warning of bloodshed to native Americans in the terrorized towns." Petriella tried to lessen this subversive imagery, by differentiating the militant miners from anarchists, and local Finn John Maki tried to use an ethnically based explanation to alleviate fears of the red flag's prevalence. It represented all workers: "They cannot take a white flag because not all of the men are white. So they take red, because red is the color that runs in the body of every man." Ironically, arguments based on so-called whiteness unwittingly may have done more harm than good. Critics used a presumed hierarchy of races, based on some combination of culture and heredity, to denigrate certain immigrants as not fully white and call for their exclusion.[40]

Workers struck Oliver Mining Company in July 1907. Dockworkers' strikes in Duluth, Minnesota, and Superior, Wisconsin—ports from which the ore left on freighters headed to Lake Erie ports and eastern steel mills—had curtailed extraction at Mesabi pits, but when the company confined layoffs at its Mountain Iron properties to union men, it precipitated a walkout. The combined strike and lockout, which spread to independent mines, eventually affected almost 15,000 miners. They demanded recognition of the union and reformed work rules. Miners labored six ten-hour days, got paid in gold or silver—not company scrip, and received medical care and accident insurance through payroll deductions. But the workers had no union representation, and some complained about fraudulent employment practices, such as having to give kickbacks to foremen. The main disagreement centered on the contract system, whereby miners got paid for how much they produced, not a per-day salary. Some observers wondered if the miners had been duped by agitators, not understanding that they frequently made more than they would if paid on the salary basis. This interpretation, however, failed to appreciate the importance of reliably constant pay and union recognition.[41]

Clashes occurred between strikers and scabs, but violence was limited. Finns, joined by lesser numbers of Slovenians, Italians, and Croatians, showed a determination to battle the capitalists. When sheriff's deputies disrupted the strikers' peaceful meetings, Petriella exhorted the men, some of whom were armed, to resist any interference with their gatherings. Press reports described how predominantly immigrant strikers at the town of Hibbing "assembled in the streets and after forming marched over the town shouting maledictions at and stoning all who opposed them." US Steel officials feared that there would be more extensive violence and sought to curtail large marches or parades. On the other side, union officials complained about companies using an out-of-state agency to recruit private detectives from Milwaukee and Chicago. Companies hired several hundred guards, deputized as sheriffs, but investigators reported no evidence of their importation from out of state, which would have violated Minnesota law. Despite the tense conditions, managers did not perceive an immediate need for troops, but they wanted assurances from state officials that they would do what was necessary to keep the mines in operation.[42]

Minnesota governor John A. Johnson, a progressive Democrat, hoped to mediate the situation. The Governor enjoyed a good reputation on the Mesabi, where the school at Hibbing had been named in his honor. Now, hoping to change the workers' perceptions of law enforcement as being nothing more than a capitalist tool, he visited the Range. Acting on his observations and advice from the State Labor, Industry and Commerce Department investigators, Johnson promised not to use force against the miners, so long as they remained peaceful. He affirmed the right to work, which meant that strikers could not try to stop anyone who wished to enter the mines. The Oliver Company had made replacement hires, including 1,300 Montenegrin immigrants, who reputedly were stronger and more reliable than Finns and Italians. "They are not pretty to look at, being dark, shagged, stoop shouldered and forbidding," said the Duluth News-Tribune of the recently arrived Slavs, but apparently they were compliant. If you gave one a shovel and told him where to dig, he would "make the dirt fly." The availability of these and other scabs allowed mines to ship their usual amounts of ore. Coupled with Johnson's prohibition on parades and other public demonstrations, the replacements effectively doomed the strike. It ended in August, with a "complete victory won by the operators."[43]

Accounts did not hesitate to stress the strikers' foreign identities and alleged leftist leanings, calling special attention to the "radical tendencies of the Finns." Coverage by the Duluth News-Tribune, the closest large-circulation newspaper, condemned red-flag–waving foreigners for marching through area towns, and criticized local police for failing to interdict the perpetrators of this "outrage of common decency and defiance of American ideals and customs." Reports circulated of a "Finlander" who threatened to blow up one of the independent mines if its workers did not join the strike. According to other accounts, agitation conducted in "blind pigs," the name given to illicit drinking establishments, incited presumably intoxicated Finns and Italians to engage in violent behavior. Austrian Catholics publicly blamed vandalism of their church on marauding Finnish miners, who they said had flung rocks at the building's stained-glass windows. Virtually every reference to Teofilo Petriella mentioned that he was both Italian and subversive, implying a link between his ethnicity and ideology. Even accounts that offered more probing analyses of the reason for the strike seemed compelled to mention some sort of subversive-alien factor.[44]

Other evidence indicated the presence of conservative communities steeped in American values, and numerous indicators showed high levels of assimilation. According to one survey, more than 80 percent of the miners had been naturalized or started the formal process, and in sheer numbers, the allegedly radical Finns bested miners from all other groups in becoming citizens. Many of the mine families owned their own homes. Few children held wage-earning jobs and "members of all races will be found in the class rooms of the public schools." None of the miners' wives worked outside of the home (perhaps due to an absence of opportunity) but many did take in boarders and lodgers. In the days preceding the strike, press coverage of upcoming Fourth of July celebrations lauded the residents' patriotism. Predictions that "flags would wave," while "the eagle will scream," certainly did not refer to all red ones. Business leaders planned to give a prize to the best represented local organization, virtually all of which had some sort of ethnic connection, and a $5 prize for the most handsome baby. Rather than radical agitators, the expected speakers included a minister and a local lass reciting the Declaration of Independence. These prestrike positive characterizations of the miners and their communities contrasted markedly with the descriptions of alien subversives that appeared during the work stoppage, posing the question of how much of the latter rhetoric was hyperbole with its own ideological intent.[45]

In the strike's aftermath, mine operators both praised the immigrant miners' provision of valuable labor and criticized their faults. The latter highlighted distinctions among the different ethnic groups regarding their propensity for causing trouble. With few exceptions, reported an Oliver Mine Company superintendent, "all of the races we have are good workmen." The exceptions were "Black Italians" and Montenegrins, who were "fit only for the most menial work." "Black races," the common parlance for southern and eastern Europeans, generally could not do as much work as a "white man." The official attributed this to the fact that in the underperforming cultures men did little more than gamble and fight; other less productive workers, he believed, simply did not eat enough. A manager at another mine characterized the same groups as "fit for but the lowest grades of work in the open-pit mine." The company tried to hire as few as possible. These criticisms were telling, given that Oliver and other firms had recruited hundreds of Montenegrins when they needed strikebreakers. Reports then, at the managers' moment of need, had lauded their physical prowess and strong work ethic.[46]

Reputations of other ethnic groups also depended on their comportment. The Mesabi Range Finns found themselves praised when they behaved and criticized when they protested. According to one operator, they came to the United States with the intention of becoming citizens and surpassed their colleagues in tolerating "hard physical labor." This alone would have made them preferred workers, but they also were "a surly, troublesome lot, and among the younger men are many who are anarchists." The Oliver superintendent described them as "good workers when they want to work" but generally undependable. Another official concurred with the age differentiation. "Old Finns" were good workers, while the younger ones, "especially those who have received a little education, are troublesome and agitators of the worst type." Scandinavians, called "the most desirable men we employ" by the Oliver manager, received employers' highest praise. They, along with workers from the British Isles, who had come to the United States earlier, dominated the skilled or managerial occupations.[47] These assessments, as the gender-specific language indicated, pertained exclusively to men, but in other industries, immigrant women faced similar scrutiny.

Experiences of female garment-makers exemplified the convergence of ethnicity and gender. From the start of commercial clothing production during the mid-nineteenth century, women constituted a significant portion of the industry's workforce, and beginning in the 1880s, large numbers of these were immigrant Jews from eastern Europe. Influenced by developments in their native lands, many of them harbored leftist leanings and demonstrated a willingness to defy authority. Different organizations, such as those representing cloak or dress makers, struck periodically during the 1880s and 1890s but with minimal success. Discord and ideological differences diminished the workers' effectiveness in challenging owners and operators. All the while, the industry grew, with the number of workers and establishments more than doubling during the century's last decade. In 1900, workers from several related trades organized the International Ladies' Garment Workers' Union (ILGWU or International), which would exert notable force in securing rights for the industry's laborers. Although men led the International, growing numbers of women comprised the rank and file in the dress and shirtwaist trades. In 1909–1910, they would dominate one of two ILGWU-led strikes.[48]

Between November 1909 and February 1910, an estimated fifteen to twenty thousand New York City shirtwaist workers, 75 percent of whom were women ages 16 to 25, waged a successful strike. Most of the participants were immigrants, predominantly eastern European Jews and Italians. Fifty-six hours constituted the standard workweek, and while wages varied depending on one's skill level and place of employment, "regular" laborers earned a reasonable weekly remuneration of between $7 and $12. But, workers also endured seasonal fluctuations, excessive charges for supplies such as needles and thread, and unreasonable fines for spoilage. The ticket system, wherein a worker received a bundle of cloth and a ticket and then got paid for the finished garments only if she returned the frequently lost ticket, also invited exploitation. Managers, opined one source, simply failed to "recognize the girls as human beings." Companies against which the workers struck included the Triangle Waist Company (later made famous for the horrific fire that claimed the lives of 146 workers in March 1911), which helped to start the walkout by discharging union members. The strikers demanded uniform wages, an end to the ticket system, no in-shop subcontracting, and union recognition. Their efforts brought success. With women playing a "preponderant part" in organizing and picketing, the International persuaded the Associated Waist and Dress Makers (which represented the leading employers) to give the workers most of what they wanted, with the exception of the closed shop.[49]

During the strike, employers tried but ultimately failed to exploit ethnic divisions and the immigrants' limited knowledge of American conditions. Manufacturers initially "made clever use of race and religious antagonism to keep the girls from uniting," and the predominantly Jewish workers did fear that Italians would scab. But ethnic solidarity soon prevailed. The shirtwaist local union created an Italian headquarters and recruited over three thousand workers. While some recent arrivals did cross picket lines, they tended to be ignorant of the situation. The women—described by socialist writer William Mailly as "high-strung, intelligent, and courageous girls"—maintained their composure and made their case peacefully, even while being assaulted, injured, and arrested. Reporter Constance Leupp also praised the "Jewish, Italian and American girls from the East Side," highlighting their "generalship, obedience and good conduct under circumstances which would break a less determined and courageous heart. . . ." Their unity and determination could serve as a model to "trades"—read "men"—who purportedly had more knowledge and experience when it came to labor disputes. "The Triangle Waist Company girls have been entirely orderly," agreed the *Survey*, "but police interference has made them appear otherwise." Because many of the strikers were immigrants, employers and their allies attempted to denounce the women's efforts as "'Un-American' and 'un-democratic,'" but to New York City physician and writer Woods Hutchinson, such denigrations were outdated in the multiethnic twentieth-century United States.[50]

The second garment-industry strike pitted 50,000 New York City cloak, skirt, and suit makers against the Manufacturers' Association, representing the trade's largest and most influential shops. Similar to the women shirtwaist makers, Jewish and Italian immigrants filled the ranks of the mostly male cloak-makers. Manufacturers, contended one labor leader, habitually took advantage of poor immigrants who were willing to accept lower wages. Some of those who eventually united in protest had socialist leanings they had acquired in Europe, but their anger toward employers, like that of their more conservative colleagues, grew out of the conditions they encountered in the United States. Grievances, which had been festering for at least a decade, centered on unsanitary shop conditions, nuisance costs, stagnant wages, and the use of subcontractors. To try to negotiate a settlement, Attorney Louis D. Brandeis chaired a conference between representatives of the General Strike Committee and the Association, and German Jewish leaders, such as banker Jacob H. Schiff and retailer A. Lincoln Filene, worked to bring the two sides together. This eventually led to "The Protocol for Peace," which abolished in-shop subcontracting, eliminated many of the petty charges such as that for electricity, established paid holidays, and gave the workers better pay. Most importantly, remembered Russian-Jewish immigrant and International president Abraham Rosenberg, it created a preferential shop, wherein employers had to choose union men when hiring. Shops also stated "their belief in the union and that all who desire its benefits should share it burdens." In the words of the group's official historian, the settlement was "a great step forward in industrial relations in the industry."[51] Immigrants, as both workers and leaders, had made it happen.

The garment workers' strikes succeeded in part because producers needed the foreign-born laborers, a universality that countered the era's growing calls for immigration restriction. The Dillingham Immigration Commission emphasized this in its seminal *Reports*. Congress created the officially designated US Immigration Commission (which from its start went by the name of its Chairman, Senator William P. Dillingham of Vermont) in 1907 and charged it with conducting a thorough "inquiry, examination, and investigation" of American immigration. The inquiry also served as an alternative to immediate imposition of new exclusions, which many in the United States enthusiastically endorsed. Consisting of nine members—three each US Representatives, Senators, and private sector experts—the Commission's inquiry would span the next three years. Resultant recommendations, which eventually contributed to the enactment of the literacy test and quota restrictions, would give the Commission notoriety, but the most extensive part of its inquiry focused on "Immigrants in Industry." Findings, prepared under the direction of political economist W. Jett Lauck, documented the centrality of foreign-born labor to American mining and manufacturing, where immigrant workers and their children predominated.[52]

More than half of the *Reports of the Immigration Commission*, 22 of its 41 volumes, made clear what business leaders long had realized: American industry relied on immigrant laborers. Hundreds of tables analyzed data on numerous employment characteristics, separated by industry, and figures for sixteen major industries, "extensively and intensively studied," made clear the predominance of immigrant workers (see table 5.1). In some occupations, such as Iron and Steel laborer and Bituminous Coal miner, aliens comprised 61 percent of the workforce. Foreign-born women and men were less numerous in Silk, Shoes and Boots, and Shirt and Collar production, but in these occupations, their children figured prominently. If the number of native-born with a foreign-born father are added to those born outside of the United States, more than 50 percent of the industries' workers had ties to immigration. In Sugar Refining, the combination of immigrants and their children accounted for more than 90 percent of the labor force. Commissioners let these numbers convey the immigrants' positive contributions to the US economy but offered more disdainful assessments of occupations with a less permanent, or floating, work force.[53]

"The temporary labor supply," the Commission concluded, ". . . is largely recruited from members of races of recent immigration originating in Southern and Eastern Europe." They built and maintained railroads, dug canals, constructed city water systems, lumbered, and harvested ice. Others did seasonal work on farms or in canneries. Seasonal terms of employment did not indicate a lack of demand for the immigrant laborers, and many so

Table 5.1   Immigrant workers in leading industries, ca. 1910

INDUSTRY	FOREIGN-BORN	FOREIGN FATHER
Iron and steel	57.7%	13.4%
Meat packing	60.7%	14.5%
Bituminous coal	61.9%	9.5%
Glass	39.3%	18.4%
Woolens	61.9%	24.4%
Silk	34.3%	44.9%
Cotton	68.7%	21.8%
Clothing	72.2%	22.4%
Shoes and boots	27.3%	25.6%
Furniture	59.1%	19.6%
Shirts and collars	13.4%	36.5%
Leather	67.0%	15.7%
Gloves	33.5%	15.7%
Oil refining	66.7%	21.5%
Sugar	85.3%	8.4%
Tobacco	32.6%	15.5%

hired effectively had full-time work. The trend held true for all parts of the nation: "Even the South, which in former years depended almost entirely on the negro [sic] for this class of work, owing to its extensive development during the past decade, has found it necessary to employ immigrant labor." While the "negro [sic] is much preferred by Southern contractors," who found black workers to be more productive and compliant than immigrants but also prone to gambling and drinking, particularly right after payday. These latter allegations increased the desirability of aliens. "Any but Italians," declared one southern contractor, describing his hiring preferences, but the number of Italians doing construction work in the South exceeded that of any other foreign group. In Dixie as elsewhere, employment often became a simple matter of supply and demand, and industry demanded immigrants.[54]

While most of the Commission's findings came from original field research, it did invite statements and recommendations. No industrial or trade association submitted a brief, and only the AFL represented organized labor. Many of the respondents did address the subject of immigrant workers, usually ignoring their labor value and highlighting their problematic presence. Junior Order United American Mechanics spokesmen connected foreigners with contradictory evils. Lax laws allowed business to recruit immigrants and then use them to displace higher-paid natives, and "the menace to the peace and good order of our country in times of strikes or labor up-risings" originated among the same aliens. The latter, it claimed, had been the case in Pittsburgh in 1877 and at Homestead in 1892. Logic suggested that employers could alleviate both maladies by paying existing workers higher wages. The Order apparently did not foresee this happening and instead demanded action intended to force businesses to change their evil practice of importing immigrants. Immigration Restriction League leaders, generally the scions of old-stock New England families, similarly explained how big business had championed immigration "to force wages down regardless of the effect upon the community." AFL leaders asserted the benefits of passing a literacy test. Because virtually unlimited numbers of immigrants lowered the standard of living for all laborers, its enactment was essential "for the self-preservation of the American working class."[55]

Other respondents accepted the foreigners' presence but emphasized, in the words of the Sons of the American Revolution, the necessity of "some action toward aiding the assimilation of this vast and motley horde." To some, this meant better distribution. It reflected poorly on the United States, averred YMCA officials, "to have a thousand men idle in Pittsburg [sic] and a crying need for labor in Minnesota." American Jewish Committee representatives called upon government to work with private agencies to ensure

that immigrants got to places where they could get jobs "at prevailing rates."
They then would become "intelligent, industrious, and moral" additions to
their new nation, increasing its "productiveness and general prosperity." The
Council of Jewish Women similarly saw the immigrant girls with whom
it worked in terms that would have resonated with the likes of J. P. Morgan. The young ladies brought "energy, intelligence, high ideals—a capital
which can but redound to the good of the country. . . ." Reaping its benefits
required safeguarding the women, who frequently had fanciful dreams of
what they would find in the United States. Guidance and education would
ensure proper adjustment to life in their new surroundings and accrue benefits to the host society. The YMCA said the same about alien men. Teaching
them English and nurturing their "stature of manhood" would serve the
needs of employers.[56]

Competing calls for restriction and assimilation revealed the Americans'
conflicted beliefs about immigration. Although no business representative
had responded to the Dillingham Commission, employers most certainly
would have joined those extolling immigrants' contributions, or at least their
potential benefits, to the United States. Yet as the most strident critics of
alien-originating radicalism, they also would have agreed with the pressing
need for better "Americanization." To protect their access to an unrestricted
immigrant labor pool, employers would join the campaign to make every
foreign worker who arrived in the United States a true, patriotic, "100%
American." In this they both joined and conflicted with "progressives."

CHAPTER 6

Turmoil Amid Reform

Immigrant Worker Protest and Progressivism

"Some people have expressed fear that there is too much immigration," presidential candidate Woodrow Wilson told the Friendly Sons of St. Patrick in March 1912. "I have the least uneasiness of the new arrivals being gripped as we have been gripped." Those who had come in recent years, Wilson continued, bore witness to foreign-born residents' contributions to American industry and society. A decade earlier, Wilson had been far less sanguine, disparaging recently arrived aliens as "the lowest class from the south of Italy and men out of the ranks where there was neither skill nor any initiative to quick intelligence." But now, as he campaigned among immigrant voters, he tried to clarify his earlier writings by offering explanations that would find welcome among the working class. The people about whom he had written, Wilson explained, largely had been of an "artificial kind," imported by employers, "to displace laborers on this side of the water, and lower the scale of wages." This condemnation did not apply to the working-class women and men currently coming to America's shores. They immigrated under proper circumstances and after arriving behaved in appropriate manners.[1] Unfortunately, several developments would challenge Wilson's positive presumptions.

Wilson's candidacy, along with that of Theodore Roosevelt and Eugene Debs, signaled the height of the Progressive Era, a time beginning in the early 1900s when Americans believed that sufficient application of proper ways and means could alleviate virtually any social or economic malady. Reforms intended to ameliorate blight frequently focused on the presence of large numbers of foreigners and their native-born children. Progressives held contrasting ideas about how best to address immigrant-related issues, especially the extent to which their continued influx would exacerbate a host of problems. Some, like Wilson, saw immigrants as valuable additions to the United States, and emphasized the need to assimilate them properly so that they would come to embody "American" values and practices. Others believed that immigrants contributed disproportionately to social ills, a propensity that justified their exclusion. To these restrictionists, the imposition of more effective ways to reduce the number of immigrants and improve the quality of those allowed in would contribute to national rectification. Businesses in need of immigrant laborers sought ways to allay the restrictionists' fears, but new labor conflicts involving foreign-born women and men complicated their efforts. Two years after the 1912 election, the outbreak of war in Europe exacerbated domestic concerns about the loyalty of foreign-born residents, further complicating America's "immigration problem."

Progressivism's emphasis on reform put businesses on the defensive. Nineteenth-century capitalists had expected government to support their interests, as President Cleveland had done forcefully during the Pullman Strike and other officials had done more subtly in other instances, but the certainty of this favoritism had become less definite during the presidential administrations of Theodore Roosevelt and even that of the conservative William Howard Taft. The trend continued under Wilson. As various constituencies united in their calls to fix the maladies that plagued the nation's industrial order, negative attention increasingly centered on commerce. National Association of Manufacturers president George Pope accused the prevailing national mentality of producing "constant attacks of newspapers and individuals upon the integrity of the great employing interests and especially the manufacturers." Consolidation, or the so-called trust problem, took center stage, but reformers also focused on railroad rates, the tariff, banking, currency, and labor relations. To this list, immigration's critics frequently added working-class poverty and labor radicalism, for which they blamed foreigners.[2] Combined, these factors complicated the already strained relationship between industrial employers and immigrant laborers.

Recommendations by the Dillingham Commission intensified calls for restriction. After finishing their work in 1910, all of the members recommended reducing the immigration of unskilled laborers and all but one endorsed the literacy test as "the most feasible means" of excluding undesirable elements. This engendered a concerted effort by supporters of the test to secure its passage. During the summer of 1912, when Woodrow Wilson faced questions about his views of immigration, advocates barraged President William Howard Taft and his advisors with testaments to the anticipated benefits of the test, including those to labor. The new restriction, argued the Immigration Restriction League, would safeguard American standards of living and citizenship. Detractors mounted an equally intense counteroffensive. Secretary of Commerce and Labor Charles Nagel—a former corporate counsel with generally pro-business inclinations—synthesized opponents' fears, telling the president that the test would exclude too many worthy immigrants who were presumably desirable due to their capacity for labor. In the end, Congress passed a bill requiring most adult immigrants to be able to read, but Taft vetoed it, indicating that he could not endorse a measure that in his mind would not improve the quality of arriving immigrants.[3] Some celebrated his actions, while others grumbled.

As reactions to near-record immigration during 1912 and 1913 made clear, Taft's veto had not resolved the question of whether large numbers of immigrant laborers were beneficial or detrimental to the United States. Sociologist Henry Pratt Fairchild, a leading restrictionist, offered a stinging rebuke to the argument that commercial prosperity required the continued influx of foreign workers. Following recovery from the economic panic of 1907, employers had looked to Europe's "inexhaustible reservoir" to meet their labor demands. Foreigners had filled this need, Fairchild explained, but their availability had stifled any significant rise in workers' wages. Aliens, who continued to arrive in large numbers, were "ready to take any wage that will be offered, just so it is a little higher than the pittance to which they are accustomed at home." This relegated the immigrants to lives of poverty. Conversely, the hiring of native-born workers would result in greater remuneration for all workers, accommodating more saving and consumption. Greater working-class affluence would lead to permanent business success. Unfortunately, the lack of adequate restriction was taking the country down a different path: "Thus wages are kept from rising, and immigration becomes a powerful factor, tending to intensify and augment the unhealthy, oscillatory character of our industrial life." Ethnic factors, specifically the presence of southern and eastern Europeans, contributed to the dreary scenario. Yet while these "undesirables" drew much of Fairchild's scorn, the employers who hired—or rather, recruited—them in large numbers shared the blame for their pernicious effects.[4]

Reaching contradictory conclusions, statistician and social researcher Isaac A. Hourwich, a Jewish immigrant who had fled persecution in Russia, dismissed the purported claims of restriction's economic benefits. Immigrants instead contributed to American prosperity. New arrivals expanded the economy, allowing native-born whites and earlier-arriving Europeans "to rise on the scale of occupations." "There is absolutely no statistical proof of an oversupply of unskilled labor resulting in the displacement of natives by immigrant workers," Hourwich emphatically asserted. The same held true for remuneration: "As a general rule, the employment of large numbers of recent immigrants has gone together with substantial advances in wages." Pay, in fact, increased as the size of the workforce grew, primarily through the addition of immigrants. New arrivals also contributed to labor's betterment by joining unions, an assertion that held true in many but not all industries. Whatever might be the inequities of industrial capitalism, fault lay not with alien laborers.[5]

Hourwich, like his ideological opposite Fairchild, found fault with large-scale employers. Corporate consolidation put wage earners at a disadvantage when it came to bargaining for wages and benefits. Large companies could treat workers as little more than a commodity, easily replaceable should they attempt to assert themselves. This made it difficult for employees to wring concessions. Even when pay went up, Hourwich contended, companies could raise prices at a faster rate, and this effectively took away the increased buying power that might have come with higher wages. Worker exploitation destroyed any sense of harmony. This, not the presence of immigrants, caused labor disputes. Coupled with the lack of any evidence showing immigration's negative economic effects, these truths invalidated the calls for more stringent exclusion. Restrictionists who claimed otherwise, Hourwich concluded, made either invalid or unsubstantiated assertions.[6]

Other immigration proponent focused their arguments on the importance of attracting the right kind of people and insuring their proper assimilation. The 1913 National Conference of Charities and Corrections called upon regional leaders to formulate "safe and practical" schemes for dealing with growing numbers of new arrivals. Those who came to any particular place had to meet its needs. Reactions to the Mississippi Valley Immigration Society's 1913 efforts to bring foreigners to the labor-scarce South fit this pattern. Newspapers in and out of the region commented on the importance of avoiding "the new problems" that recently had plagued the Northeast. There, stated the *New York Sun,* "unassimilable [*sic*] groups of foreign-born laborers" had acted to satisfy their own selfish advantage, "wholly without any conception of the duties of citizens to the State which affords them such opportunity." The Chattanooga *Times of* Tennessee pondered the consequences of mixing immigrants and African Americans. Perhaps, the editors postulated, better treatment of blacks, equal to that given to immigrants, would improve the former's work performance and thereby render a "wonderful service to the South." Speakers at the 1912 Immigration Convention of the Pacific Northwest stressed the importance of directing aliens to the most productive endeavors. Washington and Oregon did not have a lot of factories where they could work, but it did need farmers to develop the cutover lands. Local programs also needed to teach English and citizenship. Pursuing these more positive initiatives, supporters maintained, would produce better results than the more negative restrictionist approach.[7]

Businessmen's responses to the calls for new exclusions varied greatly. Without question, companies continued to want immigrant workers, but employers could not ignore growing public concern about a pernicious alien presence. Some representatives of the business community expressed disappointment with President Taft's veto of the literacy test. Franklin MacVeagh, Secretary of the Treasury and long-time Chicago banker who also had been associated with the Immigration Restriction League, generally favored the proposed literacy requirement. Spokesmen for the Cunard Steamship Line, whose income depended on transporting large numbers of immigrants, also gave the measure tacit support. Although they found some of the bill's administrative features to be awkward, they believed that ticket agents could easily insure passengers' compliance. In opposition, the Italian-American Businessmen's Association of Buffalo, New York, which combined ethnic identity with commercial pursuits, asked Senator Elihu Root, formerly an attorney for several wealthy capitalists, to work against the test's passage. Root initially promised only to give the bill careful considerations. Whether or not this had always been his intent, he eventually supported it, while seeking to add a strange amendment allowing for the deportation of aliens who had conspired to promote revolution in their home countries. To others, a resurgence of domestic violence would validate the reality of the immigrant danger.[8]

On October 1, 1910, an explosion ripped through the *Los Angeles Times* building, killing twenty people and exacerbating the city's already tense labor relations. Harrison Gray Otis, the newspaper's ardently antiunion publisher, attributed the bombing to union saboteurs and hired detective William J. Burns to find the culprits. Burns focused his attention on the International Association of Bridge and Structural Iron Workers (BSIW), which during the last few years had engaged in a bitter struggle against US Steel. Suspecting the BSIW of having perpetrated other dynamite attacks that targeted nonunion employers across the country, Burns eventually linked Association secretary John J. McNamara and his brother James B. McNamara to the *Times* bombing. The brothers, having retained the services of attorney Clarence Darrow, initially asserted their innocence. Hoping to spare the brothers the death penalty, Darrow advised them to plead guilty, a decision he later came to regret. While their incarceration may have been unjust, the sensationalism surrounding their trial did prove to be a catalyst for those hoping to find better ways to deal with the prevailing antagonism between capital and labor.[9]

"The most critical issues pending in modern states," wrote John B. Clark of the Carnegie Endowment for World Peace (an ironic forum for such assessment given events at the benefactor's steel mill twenty years earlier) in July 1912, "are those between employers and employed, and in our own country they are coming to have overshadowing importance." In the aftermath of the McNamara trial, progressives especially longed for ways to alleviate the associated violence. Recognizing the extent to which previous governmental intervention had given at least the appearance—often substantively true—of being pro-business, reformers realized how and why workers had come to distrust laws and their enforcement. Seeking a new approach to dealing with socioeconomic grievances, educators, social workers, and worker advocates petitioned President William Taft to create an industrial commission. Employers added their support. Taft's reply acknowledged the seriousness of the so-called labor question—an issue equal in importance to that of the "trust problem"—and endorsed the idea of a thorough and authoritative investigation, the findings of which would "furnish the basis for intelligent action." Congress in August 1912 approved creation of the Commission on Industrial Relations, with a provision that its inquiry include possible evasions of the Asian exclusion laws. This opened the door to consideration of other immigration issues. Disagreements on staffing delayed commencement of the Commission's work until the start of President Wilson's administration, and before issuance of its final report in 1915, several high-profile events would highlight immigrant involvement in contemporary labor unrest.[10]

During the first weeks of 1912, textile workers in Lawrence, Massachusetts, went on strike. The city's twelve woolen mills employed up to 32,000 workers, mostly southern and eastern European immigrants. They typically earned low pay, experienced wretched working conditions, and lived in squalor. Effective January 1, the state reduced the prescribed-maximum weekly hours for women and children under eighteen from 56 to 54 hours per week. Seeking uniformity, mill managers first applied the standard to all workers and then proportionally cut wages. Lower remuneration triggered a boisterous strike. Troubles started on January 12, at the American Woolen Company's Washington mill at Lawrence, and quickly spread to other establishments. In response, police and the state militia mobilized to preserve order and protect the plants. Prior to the strike, less than 10 percent of the laborers belonged to unions, including a small contingent in the IWW.

The AFL, which represented a few of the highly skilled laborers, saw little value in trying to organize a workforce "so varied in its racial composition," but Wobbly leaders Joseph J. Ettor and Arturo Giovannitti, later joined by Bill Haywood and others, did successfully engender worker solidarity. Supported by a Central Strike Committee representing the workforce's fourteen largest immigrant groups, the IWW led a successful effort to secure benefits including higher wages and overtime pay based on the 54-hour week. Other New England mills then adopted the provisions.[11]

As the events unfolded, virtually every account and commentary emphasized a combined presence of large-scale capitalism, immigrant laborers, and outside agitators. Critics portrayed the mill owners as "feudal barons, living under feudalism and fighting to save it." As their businesses had grown substantially, those in control had failed to embrace "industrial democracy," whereby labor shared in the determination of shop policies and the division of profits. Demand for more labor had attracted foreigners, and the conditions that they encountered had pushed them to the brink of "extreme violence and disorder." Improper coupling of reduced wages with the mandated lowering of hours had then induced the strike. The *Survey's* reform-oriented editors added mainstream labor organizations (most notably the AFL) to the list of culprits, for not helping the workers improve their sordid conditions. The Wobblies had seized upon this failure in order to spread their revolutionary creed. Progressive journalist Walter E. Weyl, while showing little sympathy for the IWW's "supremely dangerous" type of European syndicalism, offered a similar explication of how and why the Wobbly message could appeal to Lawrence's largely immigrant workforce. They were "no more bloodthirsty" than everyday Americans, but they earned "indecently low wages," lived in poverty, and simply wanted to enjoy "decent living conditions." Managers, conversely, engaged in "ruthless, immoral" behavior. "We may not allow men, whatever their intention, to throw matches into explosives," he said in reference to the IWW, but he did not end there. "*Neither may we allow men, however wealthy or respectable, to scatter explosives on the ground.*"[12]

Immigrants, who were "unaccustomed to the English tongue or to American institutions" and who came to see themselves as fighters against "a selfish and heartless capitalist system," comprised a key part of the explosive conditions. According to political economist W. Jett Lauck, who had served as a lead investigator on the Dillingham Commission, comprehension of their involvement was essential for understanding the roots of the unrest. The city's population had become increasingly more foreign during the previous sixty years. In the 1860s, two-thirds of the residents had been "American," but by the time of the strike, those who were native-born of native parents constituted only one-eighth of the total, with immigrants and their children comprising the remainder. They spoke an estimated fifty-five different languages, more than one could hear in any city of comparable size. "There are almost as many nationalities here in Lawrence," reported Weyl, "as in your Babel of New York." Southern and eastern Europeans, said to be more numerous than in any other New England mill town, predominated among the strikers. Italians, for instance, reportedly initiated the walkout at the Washington mill, and speeches by "Italian" Joseph Ettor, a "militant leader," thereafter "hastened the rioting." A January 18 protest march featured: "Strange songs and strange shouts from strange un-at-home-looking men and women, 10,000 of them." At the end, "many tongued cheers" signaled that the two sides had reached an agreement.[13]

Beyond providing a means of identifying the strikers, ethnicity offered one explanation for how IWW leaders—revolutionaries with "no faith in the justice of our country"—had been able to win the workers' support. Foreigners' failure to appreciate American institutions and traditions allegedly made them easy targets for agitators. According to Lauck, less than a third of those eligible for citizenship had pursued it, and the southern and eastern Europeans, in particular, had "very little political or civic interest." Additionally, fewer than half of all non-native English speakers had learned that language. "If the alien influx is permitted to continue," Lauck believed, "it will mean a further degradation of the industrial worker and the intensifying of the conditions of unrest and dissatisfaction which offer such fruitful ground to the Socialists and other revolutionary and radical propagandists." Weyl, too, highlighted how immigrants resided in communities "very remote from an environment conducive to the best American citizenship." This made them easy targets of inflammatory speeches (presumably delivered in the workers' native languages) that, editorialized *the Survey,* "certainly hastened the rioting." IWW leaders themselves, who sought the "final overthrow of the present capitalist system," embodied the worst of European syndicalism.[14]

Others simply viewed immigrant workers as inherently radical. Lorin Deland, the scion of an "old" Boston family, believed that many of foreigners had arrived "saturated with ideas of revolutionary socialism and class hatred." Congregation in ethnic enclaves, where the aliens—on account of their "race and custom"—chose to live as "hoboes and tramps," made their assimilation all but impossible. Surrounding communities suffered as a result. An absence of organizational efforts by more conservative unions did not help. While "Ettor did it!"—that is, organized the Lawrence workers— non-radicals could have done the same and thereby ensured better results. The alien laborers, Deland acknowledged, were not paid enough to have a standard of living appropriate for US residents, and efforts to improve their compensation could change their disposition. "But, who knows," he equivocated, "whether they care for American civilization anyway, or would live to American ideals if they had more pay." An unidentified correspondent to *the Outlook* agreed, not only identifying the strikers as foreign-born but also describing them as being imbued with un-American attitudes and behaviors, which they had learned in their homelands. Now, the writer asserted, they were "training their children to be seditious."[15]

Involvement of these children led to one of the strike's most sensational components. Following a tactic used by European workers, parents sent their children to live away from the commotion. Both the practice and the reaction to it drew sharp criticism. Striking parents and their advocates initially placed 119 youth with similarly ethnic families in New York City. Exodus organizer Margaret Sanger (later known for her promotion of birth control) described them as "pale, emancipated, dejected children," suggesting that the strike had been particularly hard on the affected juveniles. But on February 22 and 24, police arrested additional parents and their children as the latter tried to board trains. Allegations of the children being placed in unsafe and abusive situations circulated in the press. Inappropriate parental behaviors purportedly included placing them with radicals who would inculcate subversive doctrines, part of supposedly seditious training that would make them "veritable breeders of anarchy." Others saw the situation quite differently. Interference with the exodus, averred the strikers' supporters, denied parents their protected American rights. A telegram sent to Socialist Congressman Victor Berger condemned the arrest of the women—some pregnant—and children as a "hideous brutality." Illinois workers accused the authorities, not the foreign-born strikers, of engaging in conduct reminiscent of the worst abuses to be found in Europe, such as those practiced in Tsarist Russia. In response, Berger promised a thorough congressional investigation of the situation in Lawrence.[16]

Reminiscent of the Haymarket bombing, officials arrested two of the IWW leaders, Joseph Ettor and Arturo Giovannitti, for a murder to which their only connection was that of worker advocacy. Annie LoPezzo, an Italian immigrant, had been shot and killed, some said by a police officer, when authorities tried to stop a striker protest. Neither Ettor nor Giovannitti had been present, but the state charged them with having caused the murder by spreading subversive doctrines, which had ignited the riots leading to LoPezzo's death. Although ultimately found innocent, in contrast to the Haymarket anarchists three decades earlier, their incarceration and trial brought stinging criticism. Writers for both the *Outlook* and the *Survey* wondered if charges for indirect responsibility also should be made against the mill own-ers, who maintained the conditions that led to the strike.[17]

Prosecution of the anarchists led some to ask if the American legal system could "discriminate between charges against men as murderers and opposi-tion to men as agitators of an undesirable propaganda." The *Survey's* James P. Heaton—along with the editors of the more conservative *Outlook*—referred to the proceedings as the "Salem Trial," both a reference to the site of the tribunal and a reminiscence of the city's 1692 witch hunt. For immigrant workers, Heaton asserted, the treatment of Ettor and Giovannitti punctu-ated perceptions of an abusive "government of the native-born," which the foreigners also had seen in the form of "the swinging clubs of the police and the prodding bayonets of the militia." Failure to file charges in the death of a striker, reportedly killed by a soldier, lent credence to this perception. Any indication of biased judgment, suggested one commentator, would only reinforce the strikers' belief that they were being oppressed. Still, in the end, when the jury acquitted the defendants, the foreigners also could see how "American justice can weather times of industrial stress."[18]

The centrality of foreign-born workers in the Lawrence strike contrib-uted to the already contentious discussion of America's immigration laws. In the minds of the textile industry's critics, employers used misleading public-ity, which promised ideal working and living conditions, to attract southern and eastern Europeans. Upon arrival, they quickly encountered a far less alluring reality. Angry, they quite naturally turned to the IWW to help them right perceived wrongs, seeing themselves as joining the fight against a "self-ish . . . capitalist system." Flawed policy, the *Survey* editors opined, allowed employers to recruit "an exploitable body of laborers to a mill destination and then leaves [*sic*] them without adequate protection." The editors neither elaborated on specific problems with the current laws nor made specific rec-ommendations as to how they could be fixed, but their overall comments implied the need for new restrictions that would stem the tide of new arrivals and force employers to give their workers better pay and benefits.[19]

More overt restrictionists predicated their advocacy on negative beliefs about the foreigners themselves. Lauck tied the importation of alien labor to tariff protection. The textile industry benefitted from high import duties on foreign cloth, partly put in place to protect American workers' high stan-dards of living, but then hired "pauper" alien labor, effectively pushing out native workers and lowering wages. Recent disturbances at Lawrence, he continued, "are distinctly at variance with the claim that unrestricted immi-gration is an advantage and a protective tariff a necessity to the American wage-earner." Both, in fact, served primarily the manufacturers' interests, to the detriment of their workers. To improve the lot of the working class, the United States needed to check further immigration until those already employed achieved "proper wages and working conditions." "If the alien influx is permitted to continue," Lauck contended, "it will mean a further degradation of the industrial worker and the intensifying of the conditions of unrest and dissatisfaction which offer such fruitful ground to the Socialists and other revolutionary and radical propagandists." Lorin Deland concurred. The continued influx of immigrants was "preparing a very dark problem for the future," and the time had come to address it: "Finally, the presence in this nation of congested masses of vaguely-understood foreigners who absolutely refuse American standards of living should turn us to a careful consideration of our immigrant laws."[20]

Radicalism among the alien workers, especially the most recently arrived, amplified Lauck's concerns. Regarding the events at Lawrence: "The southern and eastern European is normally of a simple mind and of a peaceable disposition. He is usually tractable almost to the point of subserviency. When aroused, however, he will dumbly follow a leader to any length, often to the point of extreme violence and disorder." Immigrants who associated with the IWW demonstrated the veracity of such assertions. In addition to providing evidence of the need for new restrictions, their subversive actions also made clear the importance of addressing the dangers posed by those already in the United States. "Every possible agency," Lauck wrote, "must be brought to bear upon the effort to Americanize the alien." Aggressive assimilation could not wait, and in pursuing it, the United States could not afford to fail. If it did, destructive violence would continue to plague its industrial centers.[21]

Espousing different reasons, business-friendly voices also used the strike to find fault with existing immigration policies. An unidentified Lawrence "manufacturer" pointed to restrictions on contract labor as the law's most salient deficiency. "Except for it," he argued, "skilled operatives could have been hired to come over with their families, but now one must rely on the chance immigrant—ignorant, unskilled, of many undesirable nationalities, ready, for the sake of saving money, to live in very undesirable conditions." As a result, argued Boston social worker Robert A. Woods, they adhered to "the lowest scale of European and even Asian living. . . ." A "mill overseer" agreed, emphasizing similar racially pejorative presumptions. In contrast to "Anglo Saxons," who could and would live well on prevailing wages, southern and eastern Europeans hoarded money in anticipation of returning home. These funds theoretically could have been used to improve their US standards of living.[22] Immigrants did save for return migration and also sent funds to friends and relatives in Europe, but this was not the cause of their

American poverty. It resulted from low pay, and as the overseer's analysis failed to appreciate, increasing the wages of newer arrivals could have remedied their impoverished conditions and mooted their impetus to strike. Also, it had been skilled native-born workers who had pushed for the contract labor law, to protect their interests, and in absence of the prohibition, there would be nothing to prevent employers from hiring more unskilled workers in Europe at even lower wages.

Those speaking on behalf of the mill operators also stressed the need to uphold law and order, especially in immigrant communities and situations involving the IWW. Their combination, declared the usually worker-sympathetic *Survey,* inevitably resulted in a frightening "class struggle" seeking the "final overthrow of the present capitalist system." In response to Weyl's warning to business interests regarding the scattering of "explosives," former Speaker of the Massachusetts House of Representatives John N. Cole found fault solely with the IWW agitators. All "loyal Americans," including manufacturers, wanted to improve immigrants' standards of living, but of necessity it would take time, ending only with passing of the immigrant generation. For now, the real problem in Lawrence, Cole declared, was the establishment "of an anarchistic, Socialistic movement that shall hereafter control the textile business in the State, and ultimately reach out and control other business in the State, and in other States." Only the militia's presence, a frequent visitor to strike-torn Lawrence told readers of the *Survey,* had preserved the peace in the face of an angry mob. Judge Wilbur E. Rowell, who presided at some of the strike trials, dismissed as erroneous any criticism of employers and instead implicated outside agitators. The immigrant workers frequently engaged in litigation, which in Rowell's mind showed "evidence of their prosperity." Apparently only those of relative means, resulting from adequately high pay, would have the wherewithal to avail themselves of the courts. "Decidedly prosperous, happy, though not quite contented," they would not have behaved as they did except for the negative influence of rabble-rousers.[23]

The IWW's successful organizing received special attention, both for its accomplishments and its purported dangers. Other unions had problems recruiting Lawrence's immigrants, especially the recent arrivals, but according to the *Survey,* the Wobblies had attracted many of the aliens by making "common appeal to the polyglot races of the town." Some ethnic groups, such as the Germans and Franco-Belgians, had a history of socialistic or cooperative efforts, and IWW organizers had convinced others, primarily the Italians and Sicilians (designated as distinct groups), to overcome their individualistic tendencies. Unification of these immigrants may well have been hailed as a step toward Americanization, except when it came to the Wobblies. Calling for reform, as opposed to revolution, *the Survey* condemned the IWW's radical orientation, a censure that extended to all with whom it had even a passing association. Most immigrants, fretted one of the journal's reporters, lived "an almost wholly foreign life," and this made it easy for the IWW to lure them with calls for "direct action." He feared this revolutionary approach to labor relations would spread to other regional industries, with serious consequences.[24]

Others disagreed, finding at least some favor with the IWW's recruitment of the foreign-born. Labor organizer Mary K. O'Sullivan condemned the AFL for its strict trade-union orientation. Too often, the practice only resulted in immigrants working as scabs. Lawrence had been different. "This is the first time in the history of our labor struggles that the foreigners have stood to the man to better their conditions as underpaid workers," she asserted, with some degree of hyperbole. Strike supporter and Wellesley College Professor Vida D. Scudder found favor with at least the Wobblies' creation of fraternity among the diverse ethnic groups. It augured "a future when, in America, those differing races shall, indeed, be of one heart, one mind, one soul," united in their quest for a "fair reward for labor and fraternal peace." Subsequent labor unrest would perpetuate the question of whether this would be good or bad. In Scudder's case, public disapproval would lead to calls for the Wellesley trustees to dismiss her.[25]

Events in Paterson, New Jersey, the center of the American silk industry, featured the familiar mix of a primarily foreign-born labor force and an IWW-led work stoppage. Paterson's mills and shops employed approximately 25,000 mostly immigrant laborers as broad-silk weavers, ribbon weavers, and dyers. Aliens, frequently characterized as "non-English speaking," comprised about 85 percent of the workers. In recent years, long hours at abysmal work sites for inadequate pay had engendered multiple disputes and several largely ineffective strikes. Various organizations had tried to organize the workers, with limited results. Starting in 1911, some of the larger employers added to the exploitative conditions by introducing a system of one weaver operating four instead of the customary two looms. This intensified the overall dissatisfaction of laborers. Tensions simmered until February 1913, when disgruntled workers called for a general strike, soon directed by the IWW. "We are going to fight this strike in Paterson until hell freezes over," declared IWW leader Bill Haywood, "and then we will fight on the ice." Protest efforts included pickets, rallies, and parades, all of which resulted in the arrest of several Wobbly leaders. A children's exodus copied that which had been used in Lawrence, but without the draconian reaction on the part of authorities.

Journalist John Reed—an emerging voice of the American left—directed a theatrical pageant based on the strike at New York's Madison Square Garden, drawing critical acclaim but resulting in financial disaster. Ultimately, due to the multiplicity of employers and continued silk production at plants in other areas, the strikers' efforts came to naught. Most had returned to work by late July, with few having secured even minimal new benefits.[26]

Attention paid to the events at Paterson focused on the IWW. The union's success at Lawrence, followed by similar results in textile mills at Little Falls, New York, convinced many observers that at least the East, if not the nation, stood at the brink of the Wobblies' promised revolution. Paterson became Armageddon. There, wrote commentator Gregory Mason for the generally conservative *Outlook,* an "industrial war" had engendered "bitterness and obstinacy" on the part of both labor and capital, the likes of which had rarely been surpassed in the annals of American commerce. Blame rested solely on the IWW, an allegation based on the commonly held presumption of its wanton willingness to use violence and *"sabotage"* to achieve its ends. Social researcher John A Fitch, a student of labor expert John Commons and a sympathizer of working-class causes, disparaged the Wobblies as an "outlaw organization." Unpatriotic, its leaders were "preachers of violence, lawlessness, and anarchy." Defense of rights and privileges did not apply to such individuals, and the arrest of IWW officials and speakers did not constitute abuse of power or deprivation of their civil liberties. To many, convictions of the Wobblies and their supporters, on charges of "hostility to government," properly punished dangerous agitators, whose deserved penalties in no way violated their constitutional rights.

Yet if the IWW posed a grave danger, specifically in Paterson and potentially elsewhere, it stemmed in large part from the ability of agitators to garner support from immigrant workers. The IWW appealed only "to the more ignorant foreign element," the *Philadelphia Inquirer* asserted, and not at all to intelligent American laborers. *Outlook's* Mason thought the same: "The unskilled laborers, and practically all of the foreign-speaking element, the latter constituting about forty per cent of the mill population, have cast their lot with the revolutionary organization." The Madison Square Garden Pageant, where Italians, Germans, and other immigrant workers performed together on stage, demonstrated the dangerous extent to which the Wobbly organizers had been able to meld divergent groups and create ethnic solidarity. To forge their own connection to immigrant workers, employers organized Flag Day, hoping that appeals to patriotism would lead workers to disassociate themselves from the IWW's "'foreign' and 'anarchistic' methods." Immigrants then hopefully would unite under the Stars and Stripes, rather than the red banner of socialism, and return to their jobs. Strikers responded in kind: "We wove the flag; we dyed the flag; we live under the flag; but we won't scab under the flag."[27] The final pronouncement conveyed a militancy that many Americans found disconcerting, but numerous observers did appreciate the seriousness of the underlying issue.

Gregory Mason succinctly summarized the underlying issue: "That something is wrong in the existing industrial order as illustrated at Paterson no man can doubt." He as easily could have substituted Lawrence, or McKees Rocks, Pennsylvania, or Little Falls, New York, or a host of other locations. At McKees Rocks, a combination of native-born and immigrant workers—the latter largely eastern Europeans—struck at the Pressed Steel Car Company (a maker of railroad cars), eventually leading to IWW involvement and violence. It ended with public resentment of the aliens and the Wobblies, and praise for more moderate native-born workers, whose leaders had negotiated a pro-employer settlement. A textile strike in Little Falls, New York, brought attention to the poor treatment of that city's foreign laborers. Sanitary conditions in their homes, according to investigative journalist John Fitch, were "bad in the extreme." So, too, at the time of the strike, had been their wages. When the state government reduced the maximum weekly hours, management punished the workers: "The proprietor of the mills could not take summary vengeance on the law-makers who had passed the law, but he cut wages 10 per cent." Thousands of miles away, the *Idaho Daily Statesman* made a salient observation: "Because these people are foreigners is no reason why they should be underpaid."[28] It was not a question of whether something needed to be done, but rather what it should be.

Private sector philanthropy offered one answer. Concern for the fate of America's foreign-born and their children influenced the behavior of business elites beyond their strictly commercial realm, and during the 1910s, several leading capitalists institutionalized their giving and oriented their contributions toward alleviating major social ills. Others engaged in personal charity. To be sure, some industrialists gave to others in order to placate critics of their wealth—some would say their greed—and project a self-serving image of social concern. But many, even if they had virtually no personal contact with the working-class recipients of their largesse, did have a genuine interest in human betterment. One could see this in Andrew Carnegie's provision of public libraries beginning in the 1890s. (His workers, however, would have preferred better wages and working conditions, along with the right to unionize.) The 1910s saw the maturation of capitalist-funded philanthropy, exemplified by the case of Standard Oil mogul John D. Rockefeller and his son, John D., Jr.—often called Junior.[29]

Significant Rockefeller philanthropy, after 1907 institutionalized through various family foundations, centered on helping immigrants. Successful applicants who intended to work with foreigners or their children ranged from those who wished to address socioeconomic problems by ameliorating the difficulties faced by new arrivals to those who wished to pursue aggressive Americanization programs. Until the end of World War I, the Rockefellers showed a liberal or progressive bent, indicating respect, even admiration, for diverse cultures. They tended to fund requests through which the recipients would work within ethnic communities, intending to improve the lives of their members rather than change their culture. One of the earliest recipients was Hebrew Technical School for Girls in New York City. The school received $15,000 to support its mission of combining "a general and up-lifting education" with training in skills that could be used to support the students and their families. Rockefeller advisor Starr J. Murphy lauded often-maligned Jews as having "a splendid strength of character, a toughness of moral fiber, and a relentless determination to take advantage of every opportunity for uplift which is available." Junior suggested an even larger donation.[30]

In 1909, the Society for Italian Immigrants, which furnished "temporary lodging and emergency advice" to indigent new arrivals, requested $10,000 in Rockefeller philanthropy. Funded services would benefit some of the "new immigrants" whom many wanted to exclude. The Society operated a school for compatriots who were working on the upstate Ashokan Dam, part of a project to bring fresh water to New York City. They also ran the Casa boardinghouse at South and Broad Streets in lower Manhattan. Society leaders most valued "the moral benefit derived by the multitude of Italians that pass directly or indirectly under the influence of our institution where they are honestly treated and thoughtfully advised." Testaments to the good results came from such notables as *Outlook* editor Lawrence F. Abbott. Initially the Italian government had pledged to support the group's work, but domestic problems in that nation had delayed payment, forcing the Society to take out a loan and seek other funding.[31]

Although the Rockefellers would dismiss any responsibility for the Society's indebtedness and give considerably less than requested, they "happily" began a series of annual contributions with a $1,000 donation. Foundation leaders deemed "the work of the Society . . . to be of value" in helping the needy, and its various endeavors, especially among "sick and destitute laborers," "looks to be worthy and on general principles ought to be commended." The Society used Rockefeller donations to provide help to Italians who wanted to return to Europe, clothing to those detained or deported, general assistance to those struggling with banking and other financial matters, and aid to those under quarantine. The Casa boarding house eventually opened its doors to all nationalities and furnished some impoverished Italians with free lodging. Rockefeller support continued for several years, until World War I reduced the number of Italian immigrants. Declining need for the Society's services led the Foundation in 1918 to discontinue its support, "dropped in view of dwindling usefulness." This did not, however, signal an end to the Rockefeller contributions to immigrant-related philanthropy.[32]

Social reformer Frances A. Kellor also secured Rockefellor support for immigrant assistance. Kellor saw immigrants as the victims, as opposed to the cause, of America's urban-industrial turmoil. Rather than being manipulated by agitators, as critics averred, the alien worker had become a "pawn in the industrial game." Numerous bad experiences had corrupted their views of the United States. Poor conditions abounded at the camps that housed construction crews on railroad, highway, and public works projects. Employers frequently relied on the padrone system, whereby an immigrant would subcontract to provide workers from among his countrymen. Those recruited typically received despicable food and lodging and endured threats or lies to prevent their desertion, all with the blessing of the employers. Exploitation did not stop at economic abuses. Isolated and interactive solely with other foreigners, the immigrant workers also had little opportunity to Americanize. "Now, is not this system poor economy and bad Americanism of the kind which breeds anarchy?" Kellor rhetorically asked a frustrated public.[33]

Elimination of the padrone system, establishment of municipal and state agencies to assist alien job seekers, and creation of a distribution bureau to direct arriving immigrants to regions needing workers would rectify the situation. Better employer treatment of foreign-born laborers would result in more productive workers and go a long way toward preventing what had happened at Paterson and Lawrence. "Shall we leave the fixing of living standards to the Industrial Workers of the World to be worked out in terms of war," Kellor wondered, "or shall we Americans work it out in terms of peace, utilizing to the full for American progress the splendid vitality, courage, loyalty, and intelligence which these men and women from abroad came here prepared to give to America?"[34] Her appeal to the Rockefellers offered a plan for fulfilling the latter scenario.

Headed by Kellor, the New York Committee of the North American Civic League for Immigrants, which eventually became the Committee for Immigrants in America, sought to pursue the twin goals of eliminating exploitation of immigrants and securing the expected benefits of effective Americanization. Efficiency, research, and planning, Kellor believed, would ensure the realization of both pursuits. In November 1910, after having studied the frauds perpetrated upon recent arrivals "by those taking advantage of their ignorance of the language and the laws and customs of the country," she and the New York Committee wanted to establish a guaranteed $30,000-per-annum immigrant assistance fund. Primary expenses would go toward investigating problems, such as how to get foreign-born and first-generation American-born children into schools, and aiding immigrants as they passed through Ellis Island. Plans called for coordination with the New York State Bureau of Industries and Immigrants, other government agencies, businesses, and philanthropic institutions.[35]

Kellor's revelations of extensive immigrant exploitation garnered support from the Rockefellers. "Although this is a new work," foundation advisor Starr Murphy said of the New York Committee's plans, "it is so promising and occupies a field where something of the kind is so greatly needed that I think we should take a share in it." He suggested up to $10,000. The Rockefellers, taking into account the belief that a donation equal to one-third of the group's planned expenditures was too much for any one patron, and expressing concerns about the lack of a clear plan for spending the intended $30,000 budget, pledged annually to match one-fifth of the other contributions, not to exceed $5,000. Aggregate Rockefeller donations, totaling $28,000 over the next five years, helped to organize several immigration bureaus or commissions, handle 5,100 immigrant-related complaints in New York City, establish Guide and Transfer services for those passing through Ellis Island, and draft laws regulating employment agencies in Pennsylvania. The New York Committee prepared a training course for groups providing social services to the foreign-born, and developed curriculum for immigrants in public and night schools. Publicity efforts, including newspaper editorials, special reports, briefs on legislation, and its own *Immigrants in America Review* enjoyed notable success.[36] Financial support from the Rockefellers showed their genuine concern for foreign-born workers and their families, but philanthropy comprised only part of the family's connection to working-class immigrants. In at least one instance, the industrialists' conduct as employers told a far different story.

What infamously became known as the Ludlow Massacre began in September 1913, with a strike against Colorado Fuel and Iron (CFI), of which the Rockefellers owned 40 percent. Among CFI's 3,500 workers, 506 were "white Americans," 248 were Black, and the rest were immigrants representing twenty-seven different groups. Over six hundred could not speak English. This ethnic diversity led critics to accuse the company of having imported workers to ensure a divided and therefore pliable labor force. Regardless of whether that had been the plan, strikers united to protest substandard company housing, failure to have a coworker oversee the weighing of each miners's daily production, and CFI's staunch opposition to collective bargaining. Contention intensified during the winter of 1913–1914. Several deadly skirmishes, involving strikers and CFI mercenaries, prompted the governor to call in the National Guard. At first welcomed by both sides, the Guard quickly demonstrated pro-management behavior, including the protection of strikebreakers, which further enraged the workers. On April 20, a major battle between Guardsmen and strikers occurred at the labor encampment near Ludlow. Tents caught fire, and the ensuing conflagration claimed numerous lives. Many of the dead were immigrants, including women and children, who either burned to death or suffocated while hiding in dugouts. Violence did not end with the Ludlow carnage. For the next ten days, angry miners prowled the region, destroying company property, killing 40 people, and generally wreaking havoc. Only the arrival of federal troops restored peace.[37]

Junior Rockefeller, who became the face of the family's culpability, struggled to understand the workers, especially their tragic fate. (Senior, well known for his opposition to unionism, largely avoided the Ludlow fallout.) In response to the massacre and a subsequent investigation by the Commission on Industrial Relations, Junior and his advisors created a plan for a company union, a middle ground between independent labor organizations and individual employment. Workers also received a pension plan. To try to connect with the workers, Junior personally visited Ludlow, where he danced with the immigrant women. The dance floor revealed a great divide. As shown by his previous philanthropic endeavors and now by his personal contact, Junior saw immigrant workers and their families as virtuous women and men, positive additions to their communities. Yet when it came to placing blame for the strike, notably its death and destruction, Junior followed the lead of CFI President C. F. Bowers. Rabble-rousers had exerted "a mighty influence" over the region's otherwise placid and content foreign-born laborers. Agitators had subverted the workers, and their ethnic identities had made them susceptible pawns. What Junior and those of his stripe apparently did not understand, parsing from the words of Industrial Relations Commissioner Florence J. "Daisy" Harriman, was that those who controlled capital were "in the last analysis responsible" for what happened in the industrial world. Instead, those same capitalists habitually found it easier to indict aliens—as either subversives or their targets—rather than themselves.[38] Others, however, stood ready to blame the barons.

The *Final Report of the Commission on Industrial Relations*, published in 1915, addressed the conflicts at Ludlow and elsewhere and recommended various strategies for their abatement. Primary attention centered on ascertaining the cause of recent turmoil and finding ways to alleviate it. The Commission was made up of nine generally progressive presidential appointees, of whom three had to be employers and three labor representatives. Members included AFL and Railway Conductors Brotherhood representatives, railroad executives, labor economist John R. Commons, socialite and social reformer Daisy Harriman, and pugnacious Missouri attorney Frank P. Walsh, who served as chair. Guidelines specifically called for investigation into the smuggling of "Asiatics" into the United States, but as the *Final Report* made clear, the commissioners had not limited their inquiry to this select group. They instead looked broadly at the overall effects of immigration on labor relations. Not surprisingly, given the polemic nature of their task, the commissioners could not agree on findings or recommendations, but the *Final Report*, both its primary text and various addendums, did provide insightful commentary on immigrant labor.[39]

The primary *report*—signed by Walsh and the three union representatives—began by heaping criticism on both employers and immigrants. Workers "emphatically" had not received their fair share of benefits and profits from American industrialization, and as a result, many now led impoverished lives. Cessation of immigration from northern and western Europe, because those men and women would not come to the United States given the situation that awaited them, offered proof of the "miserable condition of the mass of American workers." Labor now came only from "the backward and impoverished nations of southern and eastern Europe." Poor pay attracted these low-quality workers, and their willingness to accept pauper wages retarded any possible improvement. According to the *Report:* "The character and quality of the supply of labor have been affected by immigration and by the entrance into industry of women workers, both of which factors have caused an increase in the supply of cheap and unskilled labor." But, at least the immigrants had options, because they could return to their native countries during economic slowdowns. (Women apparently had contributed to the problem by leaving home to find work, but somehow they could not return to domestic life.) As a final indictment of foreign laborers, the *Report* connected reduced immigration resulting from the war in Europe with improving industrial conditions. The "salutary effects" would have been impossible had the influx remained high.[40]

Immigrants allegedly contributed to several serious maladies. For instance, "inequality of wealth and monopolization of land" contributed significantly to unemployment, but so, too, did immigration. The onrush of foreigners had been the "largest single factor" in impeding wage increases and had undermined American standards of living. Large numbers of non-English speakers, estimated at 50 percent of the industrial labor force, had "done much to prevent the development of better relations between employers and employees." Immigration had hampered the growth of unions, particularly "effective and responsible organizations," which clearly did not include the IWW. Although the *Report* did not mention specifically any of the recent strikes or labor conflicts in the sections dealing with immigrants, it generally connected recent strife to foreigners. Not only had the latter created "a number of our most difficult and serious industrial problems," they also bore responsibility "in a considerable measure for the existing state of industrial unrest." The *Report* did not elaborate on whether this was due to innate immigrant radicalism or their naïveté in following devious agitators. It did conclude that the involvement of immigrants in recent labor conflicts gave natives a convenient excuse for dismissing the underlying worker exploitation. Analysts could rationalize abuse by linking it to "ignorant foreigners."[41]

In suggesting corrective actions, however, the *Report* hedged, both endorsing more stringent restrictions and implying that employment opportunities would continue to attract some foreigners. Recommendations included endorsement of the literacy test (cited as having been advocated by the Dillingham Commission) as the best way to limit immigration to those most likely to become good citizens. By reducing the number of arrivals, the test also would bring immigration in line proportionally with industrial needs, and it would promote education in Europe. For those who continued to come to the United States, the *Report* emphasized the need for more aggressive Americanization. The US government should require all immigrants to declare their intent to become citizens—take out "first papers" in the parlance of the day—within six months of landing, and those who did not comply should have to register with authorities. If they did not declare in two years, or if they failed to complete the citizenship process, the government should deport them. Anyone so exiled would be barred from future reentry. State and local authorities, with possible federal assistance, also needed to develop programs to teach English to non-speakers, and employers must provide leisure time for its instruction.[42]

The *Report's* call for the federal government to do more to help workers and protect their rights also focused on the presence of foreigners. The Bureau of Immigration had taken initial steps to distribute incoming aliens, but more could be done to direct them to available jobs. Creation of a Division of Information had been an initial step in this direction, but more needed to be done. Current reduction in the number of annual arrivals, due to the war in Europe, made it possible to initiate and perfect other remedial programs on a smaller scale. In the case of securing the rights of labor, the

Report noted widespread worker distrust of government, due to perceptions of its collaboration with employers. This had special ramifications for immigrants, who routinely experienced employer exploitation. Suspicion of public officials left them with no one to whom they could turn for help, except perhaps radical agitators. Commissioners suggested changing the Bureau's name to Immigration and Employment—a clear indication of the extent to which they saw the two subjects as being interconnected—and appropriating additional funds for more extensive work. Commons and Harriman thought that a Federal Industrial Commission, independent of the official bureaucracy, should do the work. Regardless of the name, the expanded agency should have the power to protect the rights of all workers, specifically safeguard immigrants until they became citizens, and help laborers of any ethnicity find work.[43]

An interesting combination of the reformers Commons and Harriman plus the Commission's three business representatives filed a separate *report*, and it, too, indicted immigrants for causing social and economic problems. "Underlying the entire problem of self-government in this country, and placing a limit on the ability to remedy abuses either through politics or labor unions," they asserted, "is the great variety of races, nationalities, and languages." African Americans in the South showed the difficulties posed by ethnic diversity, problems compounded by the failure of Reconstruction. "Backward races or classes" coming from foreign countries now caused similar distress in other regions. From an employer's perspective, violent strikes and broken contracts could be traced to the hiring of immigrants. Multiple languages similarly stymied efforts by "Americanized" labor unions to organize and discipline industrial workers. The latter assertion conveniently ignored the AFL's frequent antipathy toward immigrant laborers, as shown by events at Patterson and Lawrence, and the commissioners summarily dismissed the presumably non-American IWW's successful organization of diverse ethnic groups as ineffective in allaying worker's "antagonism toward their employers." Problems such as violent strikes and broken contracts emanated from the unfortunate hiring of foreigners, and "paternal despotism of a corporation" was better than immigrant-led strikes. Statutes excluded one problematic group, the Chinese, and the time had come to stop admitting "others, less competent."[44]

Individual commissioners offered dissenting opinions. Frank Walsh voiced support for the primary *Report*, praising the whole of its recommendations "as wise and necessary for the welfare of the nation." Yet he opposed the literacy test, "as a matter of principle," as he did all restrictions on immigration. Walsh said nothing to counter the *Report's* overall negative assessment of foreign workers, but he did stress the need for new or improved government apparatuses to deal with immigrant and other labor problems. California businessman Harris Weinstock, part of the Commons cohort, similarly objected to calls for restriction, at least of those from Europe: "In normal times this country can profitably employ all the desirable and fit occidental immigrants that knock at our door, thereby adding greatly to the wealth and strength of the Nation." Although the United States already had enough laws—likely a reference to those barring "non-occidentals"—persistently lax officials had to enforce them properly. Kentucky grain-mill owner Samuel Thurston Ballard ignored existing statutes when he identified "encouraged, stimulated and probably assisted immigration" as the primary cause of labor unrest. War in Europe currently impeded the practice, but the situation would demand attention in the near future.[45]

Chinese immigration, which on the West Coast had become a scapegoat for labor troubles, drew especially strong condemnation. Multiple arguments likely influenced the commissioners who supported this assertion. The Commons *report* offered a veiled reference to events in 1905, when President Theodore Roosevelt and Secretary of Commerce and Labor Victor Metcalf took steps to reduce the harassment of Chinese, and Commissioner-General of Immigration Frank P. Sargent (a former union official) allegedly told his agents not to arrest or deport Chinese. As both Metcalf and Sargent supported Asian exclusion, the commissioners likely exaggerated application of their directives, but any policy or practice that showed leniency toward the Chinese fueled the rancor of their critics. So, too, did widely circulated stories of the continued admittance of high numbers of Asians. AFL leader Samuel Gompers purportedly had received evidence of the presence of illegal Chinese immigrants, whom he believed undermined the wages of other workers, from the National Civic Federation. Pacific Mail Steamship Company records for 1910–1915 did show thousands of Chinese passengers arriving at San Francisco. Most claimed to be "native," "son of native," "merchant," or "son of merchant," but a few did list "laborer" as their occupation. Authorities detained some, but most landed. Regardless of the legality of their entry, the Commissioners no doubt heard how their presence endangered the well-being of western workers.[46]

All of the Commission factions took for granted the propriety of Asian exclusion. Two staffers conducted a special inquiry, and a special subcommittee composed of Walsh, California businessman Harris Weinstock, and AFL representative James O'Connell then made extensive recommendations. Everyone concurred with their substance, but some disagreed with how best to administer laws and policies. Neither the main *Final Report* by

Walsh nor the Commons report included the inflammatory language used to describe Europeans. Instead, both stressed the need for better enforcement; in particular, smuggling had to be stopped. Immigration officers should be given the authority to detain suspected "contraband" (not inflammatory but certainly dehumanizing rhetoric), and to employ procedures streamlined to deport those who entered illegally more effectively. The primary *Report* also recommended enacting a constitutional amendment denying citizenship to native-born children of Chinese immigrants. Federal law prohibited the Asians from naturalization, but the Fourteenth Amendment defined anyone born in the United States as a citizen, theoretically with equal rights and privileges. The Commission now wanted to take away that legal status and protection, presumably from anyone of Asian ancestry. Yet concurrent with the Commission's inquiry, Delta Association of California president John P. Irish told the Pacific Northwest Immigration Convention that his state's economic development required more Asian labor, but from Japan.[47] Nothing was simple when it came to matters involving immigrants and employment.

A public weary of labor unrest and wary of potentially more violence no doubt wanted the Commission's recommendations to offer a definitive means of eliminating the disturbances, but the *Report's* conflicting conclusions precluded that result. This was particularly true in regard to immigrants. Even those who found problematic the number and types of immigrants arriving in the United States could not agree on the best corrective action. While the Commissioners demonstrated progressives' penchant for problem-solving, reaching a consensus on how to alleviate maladies arising from the convergence of ethnicity and labor eluded them. The same could be said for the nation as a whole. Soon the guns of war would complicate its quest.

IWW - linked to foreigness p.143
Ludlow Massacre report - p.155

CHAPTER 7

Effects of War

Immigrant Labor Dynamics during the Great War

"War has been declared against the Steel Trust and the independent mining companies of Minnesota by the Industrial Workers of the World," stated IWW leader William "Big Bill" Haywood, as he announced the return of labor turmoil to the Mesabi Iron Range during the summer of 1916. Reports circulated of strikers arming themselves for possible combat. Declared one unidentified IWW leader, after mine-owners had contracted for armed guards: "The strike is practically ended and war is started." Added Wobbly organizer Carlo Tresca, himself an unnaturalized Italian immigrant, after the guards had shot and killed a miner: "The strikers were previously warned to do nothing more violent than keep their hands in their pockets. Now we will arm for self defense." Beleaguered workers no doubt appreciated the passion conveyed by such rhetorical militancy, but even ardent supporters appreciated its potential consequences. "The Trust may send thousands of guns and millions of shells to the slaughter house of Europe—that is business. . . ," mused IWW stalwart Elizabeth Gurley Flynn. "But make a speech in free America and you are charged with murder. . . ." Her remarks came after the arrest of Tresca and other strike leaders for their purported involvement in a miner's death. Similar reaction to inflammatory rhetoric had characterized previous class conflicts, but new conditions involving a different war now intensified the backlash.[1]

The onset of World War I raised questions about if and how the United States should prepare itself for a military confrontation with a "foreign"

enemy, and gave added implications to any talk of armed class conflict, especially if it involved immigrant workers. Coincidental to the start of the 1916
Mesabi Range strike, the Duluth *News-Tribune* offered a telling observation.
Preparedness to defend the country against a potential invader (implied but
not stated to be Germany) logically had centered on the East Coast. In addition to abutting the Atlantic, which separated the United States from the
hostilities, the region was also America's commercial center and home to
its arms and munitions factories. The latter supplied the "blood and muscle
of national defense." But, the paper opined, the armaments industry relied
on iron ore from northern Minnesota, making it "fully as rich a prize." If
an enemy (in some far-fetched scenario) could invade through Canada or
the Great Lakes and occupy the Range, as Germany had done in parts of
France, it could strike at America's "chief resource for defense," thereby
crippling the nation. The warning implied the need to alleviate this threat,
and those to other similarly critical regions. Americans everywhere increasingly championed the need to provide adequate defense against a potential attack from abroad. But this bulwark alone would not suffice. Dangers
to national security also emanated from domestic sources, especially those
deemed foreign or un-American.[2] Millions of immigrants, already under
scrutiny for their involvement in labor unrest, became potentially dangerous internal enemies.

Preparedness for possible involvement in the European war, and its eventual actuality, would address this presumed domestic threat. How best to do
it would both consume and divide the nation, engendering questions that
went to the core of the country's collective essence. Devotees believed that
the nation needed to ready itself for a military engagement. This required
not just the enlargement of US armed forces and the training of potential
combatants; it also necessitated insuring the loyalty of all Americans and convincing them of the need to do whatever it would take to defeat the enemy.
The United States' declaration of war against Germany in April 1917 would
intensify these beliefs. "Teamwork," exhorted artist William Dodge Stevens
in his portrayal of American workers diligently completing a new merchant
ship, was the key to America's military success. Against such a backdrop,
labor unrest—already viewed dimly by many Americans—came to be seen
as inherently unpatriotic. Business leaders would use this heightened tension
to portray strikes, and the agitators who allegedly fostered them, as threats
to national security. Alleged perpetrators became saboteurs and traitors. In
pursuit of their eradication, what had been tacit connections between business interests and governmental agencies in the pursuit of labor tranquility
became more direct and the results more draconian. Tolerance, as President

Woodrow Wilson fearfully predicted, became an imperiled quality, and fears of disloyalty became especially keen when it came to aliens.[3]

Nationalistic Americans increasingly saw divided ethnic loyalty, colloquially called "hyphenism," as part of the threat to the United States. Any hint of affinity to an immigrant's country of origin attracted suspicion, and even innocuous use of foreign phrases drew condemnation. Anything in the nation's midst that was foreign now seemed menacing. Patriotic duty demanded the eradication of this insidious threat. Many believed that no more foreigners, or at least only the right kinds in reduced numbers, should be allowed to enter. From a "preparedness standpoint," declared principal Immigration Restriction League lobbyist James Patten, "no bill is more important" than those aimed at the proper control of immigration. Patten thought primarily in terms of exclusion, of getting Congress to pass a literacy test bill, but others placed more emphasis on cementing the fidelity of already-present immigrant laborers. As they responded to the realities of war, commercial leaders would join the latter effort, connecting it to their long-standing concerns about alien agitators and the proliferation of their dangerous creeds.[4]

American businessmen, while not necessarily promoting carnage for purposes of monetary gain, did recognize the Great War as an opportunity to make money. Most prognosticators, reported the *Literary Digest* in August 1914, expected the United States to benefit economically from the hostilities, or at least suffer less than other industrialized nations. A few spokesmen cautioned against being overly optimistic, but most anticipated positive results. "In more ways than one the folly of warfare which Europe has long been threatening to commit and at last seems determined to perpetuate must spell opportunity for the United States," concluded the New York *Sun*. The New York *Evening Mail* similarly foresaw the country increasing its exports of food stuffs, petroleum, munitions, iron and steel, and everything else the belligerent nations might consume. Perhaps looking back to past conflicts, rather than anticipating the machine-driven nature of modern warfare, this included cavalry horses. Trade also would increase with markets in Africa, Asia, and Latin America, and protracted hostilities would put the United States ahead of its European competitors in supplying products to those regions. "Such a war could hardly be otherwise than materially profitable," the *Sun* concluded. This proved to be the case, as the US economy initially declined but then recovered in the spring of 1915.[5] However, sustained profitability would require several key components.

When hostilities began, the *New York Mail* hinted at the importance of immigrant workers. Their labor would be essential for economic growth, and if they decided to return to their native lands, their exodus could create a labor shortage. By 1916, this had become a reality. Many alien residents had left the United States, some to serve in the military of their native country and others to take care of their families, and the war also impeded the travel of those who otherwise would have come to the United States. Even when the number of arrivals rose in April, they remained far below prewar levels. Other foreign residents, who wanted to visit family or ascertain the condition of property, were expected to leave the United States once cessation of hostilities allowed them to book safe passage. *Outlook* noted how the paucity of foreign-born residents had created a growing demand for unskilled workers: "Some railroad companies have been employing Southern Negroes and Mexicans in place of the Italian and Polish track hands who have left to fight for their native country or to secure higher wages." Similar shortages seemed likely to replicate these conditions in other industries. *Outlook* editors also wondered if postwar immigration would remain low, due to European nations wanting to keep their countrymen at home, where they could help to rebuild war-ravaged economies. This presumption proved to be faulty, as immigration in 1919 and 1920 would reach near-record highs, but that realization lay in the future.[6]

As Americans watched the Europeans rush headlong into war, they also focused attention on how to treat aliens who remained in the United States. The ensuing discussion centered on their loyalty. Especially the Germans, in spite of their long-standing presence in the United States, came under scrutiny. "The very term German-American is a contradiction," asserted a letter to the *Pawtucket Times* in early 1915, "for one cannot be politically both German and American, and the title describes the political status of its owner." A German could not, by this logic, be an American. Former President Theodore Roosevelt expanded this logic to include all men and women of foreign birth. Twenty years earlier, he called for the United States to remake its immigrants in its own image, saying "those of foreign origin who come here must become American; they must become like us, and not seek to make us like them." TR would show less negativity toward immigrants during his presidency, but in 1915, with the war bellows sounding in Europe, the old Rough Rider reiterated his impassioned calls for unmitigated assimilation. "The is no room in this country for hyphenated Americans," he remonstrated, for "a hyphenated American is not an American at all." The country's most visible nationalist may have tried to distinguish between his condemnation of aliens who remained foreign at heart and those who had assimilated by becoming naturalized citizens, but his message was clear. The United States could not tolerate even a hint of disloyalty among its immigrant residents. Interestingly, in the same speech to the Knights of Columbus, Roosevelt chastised employers who sought to profit from the war and urged them to pay their immigrant workers adequate wages.[7]

Conversely, those more appreciative of diversity argued that "love of his native land" was an essential component of an immigrant's Americanization. "A true citizen must be a true man, and a true man is ever true to his past," preached Unitarian pastor George R. Gebauer. Natives could not expect an immigrant—presumably of either sex—to become a thoroughly imbued patriot the moment she or he disembarked at Ellis Island, and to expect or demand such behavior would only make the foreigner a parasite, one who pledged shallow allegiance in order to maximize personal gain. Senator Robert La Follette (Wisconsin Republican) likewise sought to allay fears of divided loyalty: "The fact that the German, the Irishman, the Englishman, the Pole, the Hungarian, loves his home country, the country in whose bosom sleep his ancestors, does not weaken his allegiance to the government of his adoption." But, despite their passion, these pro-diversity voices soon became the exception. Criticism of hyphenated identity illustrated the growing sense of misgiving toward all things foreign, posing a special challenge for those who relied on immigrant labor.[8]

The National Security League (NSL) exemplified businessmen's wartime mentality. Although organized by corporate lawyer S. Stanwood Menken and heavily funded by such leading industrialists as Henry Frick and Cornelius Vanderbilt, the League abjured any intent to foster monetary gain by rejecting contributions from those who would accrue direct financial benefit from US preparedness. The NSL instead stressed "true patriotism" and the need for readiness of America's armed services. Originally this meant universal military training and compulsory service, but the League subsequently shifted its attention to promoting socioeconomic ideologies under the guise of "patriotic education." Americans, the League asserted, needed to protect their country from "dangerous proletarians," Bolsheviks, or adherents to any other doctrine or ideology that opposed capitalism. Too few of those who lived in the United States, native-born and immigrant alike, appreciated the fundamentally American "right of individual possession of property as guaranteed by the Constitution." Protection of this basic premise demanded assiduous and prompt remedial action. Coupled with an emphasis on naturalization and unity of language, the NSL's pro-capitalist education programs expectantly targeted immigrants.[9]

The League's wartime agenda focused on "the subject of Americanization, naturalization, and teaching the immigrants, bettering the ignorant." Through these endeavors, stated its president, Charles B. Leydecker, the NSL intended to be a force for "unifying the people in a nation of our American ideals, our principles of correct government, our respect for authority. . . ." The latter had long been a goal of business leaders, and the war had given it greater urgency by highlighting the dangers of disloyal proletarians. These were not, Lydecker explained, the "poorer" or working classes; instead, the term referred to "[a] member of society who is devoid of thrift, industry, or any accumulation by reason thereof." They composed only a small part of any "American constituency," "but our imported people are, unfortunately, some of them of that class." The unwanted elements emerged as "dangerous demagogues, or anti-American socialists or bolsheviki people. . . ." To combat their presence, at a time when the country stood on brink of war, the NSL sought to facilitate immigrant assimilation through the distribution of pro-naturalization literature and the teaching of patriotic lessons in schools.[10] Naturalization became the key element, and employers (both during the war and the subsequent Red Scare) would follow the NSL's pattern of its aggressive promotion.

During the months before the 1916 Mesabi Range miners' strike, the Oliver Company undertook concerted efforts to encourage the Americanization of its largely immigrant workforce. Oliver dominated mining on the Mesabi Range, owning more than half of the ore properties, employing upwards of 75 percent of the miners, and producing the largest share of the region's annual ore tonnage. Foreigners had made up the bulk of the Range's labor force since the onset of mining during the late 1800s, and during the 1907 strike, Oliver and other companies had added to their number by hiring "boatloads" of eastern Europeans to work as strikebreakers (see chapter 6). Managers no doubt appreciated the immigrants' availability and willingness to do the onerous work, but Oliver officials also recognized the prevalence of radical leanings among the aliens, as conveyed by the appellation "Socialist Finns." Comprising 15 percent of the regional labor force, the Finns were not the only miners whose presumed leftist leanings gave business operators a reason for forceful Americanization. At a time when war orders from European belligerents had raised the need for iron and steel, leading to an anticipated "big demand" at high prices during the coming year, Oliver and other mine operators had a special incentive to minimize labor problems.[11]

Company officials saw the pursuit of citizenship as a way to ensure worker fealty to both the United States and their employer, with the latter profiting from their laborers' loyalty. Foreigners who underwent naturalization would be less disruptive and more amenable to corporate policies, leading to a less contentious workplace and greater productivity. This would come at a time when war demands for steel, along with increased domestic consumption by the likes of Ford Motor Company, foretold growing profits, provided that there were no disruptions in ore extraction. To make this happen, Oliver managers encouraged the "naturalization of its employees, and the education of all, especially those who cannot speak English," and encouraged supervisors to get the message to the foreign-born workers. The company also rewarded those who became citizens: "I would also be in favor of making it clear to our men that when we make promotions, either from common labor to foremanship, or increases in the pay of foremen, that, other things being equal, that the man with full citizenship has a better chance for promotion and will be favored over the one without citizenship." Allegiance to the nation implied the assimilation of traits that apparently made the worker a more desirable employee. This meant one less likely to adhere to radical socioeconomic doctrines.[12]

Ironically, once a strike started in June 1916, immigrant laborers on the Mesabi showed the effects of other company-induced influences, although not those that management intended or endorsed. In the words of one sarcastic commentator, "these polyglot nationalities speaking thirty-six different tongues," many of whom had been brought to the Range as strikebreakers in 1907, "have become Americanized in the melting pot of the Mesaba mines." There, exploitation and the lack of union representation had created conditions ripe for "a struggle against industrial tyranny." Austrian and Italian miners, opined the *New Republic,* had been "helpless to make effective protest against actual abuses." "But in every large group of unorganized foreign-born workers," it continued, "are men who have espoused the doctrines and given their allegiance to the I.W.W." Efforts to homogenize the workers, regardless of the intent, gave the agitators a forum. Yet, in the mind of Committee on Industrial Relations agent George P. West, the aroused miners likely would teach elected officials "that public authority cannot be used brutally and recklessly on the side of the oppressors in a struggle against industrial tyranny."[13]

The pro-business Duluth *News-Tribune,* conversely, also found what it called an absence of patriotism among the immigrant workers. Cancellation of plans for the Range's "Americanization Day," which was to have included the distribution of thousands of copies of the pledge of allegiance, purportedly offered proof of the alien radicalism. "Little success has been made in efforts to secure delegations of foreign societies and other organizations to take part in the parade and flag raising ceremonies," proclaimed the paper's Independence Day edition. Interestingly, IWW leaders subsequently claimed that 65 percent of the strikers were citizens, and protesting strikers had insisted on having the American flag lead their processions. Despite these and other indications of American loyalty, many observers no doubt saw the miners' association with the radical Wobblies as a clear indication of failed or improper assimilation.[14] The 1916 strike would reinforce these perceptions.

Numerous contentions contributed to the work stoppage. During the decade since the region's last major labor confrontation, companies had reduced the length of the workday, but as a consequence, managers expected more productivity from fewer miners. Pay stagnated, leaving the largely immigrant workers struggling to provide for their families' subsistence. Companies also made payroll deductions for unspecified supplies and used a contract system based on production, in lieu of standard wages, for underground work. Foremen extorted bribes and other concessions from their crews. Adding insult to injury, corporate profits rose, but not workers' pay. Growing animus culminated on June 2 at a mine in Aurora, when disgruntled employees, reportedly led by Italian American Joe Greeni, initiated a walkout. It quickly spread throughout the Range. Given the AFL's persistent disinterest in organizing the region's largely unskilled workers, the strikers turned to the IWW for leadership and support. The killing of a striker by Oliver's hired guards—"pug uglies" in worker parlance—exacerbated an already tense situation. Local sheriffs took "possession of the laws to such an extent that they have disregarded the constitutional rights of the men and have not allowed them to meet in any hall." Although the miners mounted a spirited campaign, the arrest of striker leaders in connection with another killing, and the intransigence of corporate officials, eventually crushed the strike, but not before immigrant workers would play a prominent role.[15]

Typically, reaction to the unrest highlighted the presence of large numbers of alien laborers. Finns, Austrians, Slavs, and Italians comprised the majority of the strikers, and their ethnicity tended to attract more attention, almost all of it negative, than did their grievances. According to business leaders, the strike would not have happened except for the IWW's provocation of the foreign-born laborers. Ninety percent of those who had left their jobs were immigrants. "Italian strike leader" Carlo Tresca and other agitators conveyed their inflammatory messages not just in English, but also Finnish, Italian, and a host of "Slavonian languages." Notions of the strike's un-American character extended far beyond the Mesabi. At a hearing for IWW representatives in Michigan, who had been arrested while trying to elicit support for their Minnesota brethren, the presiding judge instructed the Wobblies as to "what constitutes American citizenship." As a first step toward their attainment of those qualities, the judge made each pledge "to wear the red, white and blue ribbon," and officials purportedly pinned an American flag on "each agitator" as he left the courtroom.[16] Apparently adherence to IWW ideology failed some sort of patriotic litmus test. If ever it had been "American" to promote issues of class conflict, it definitely was not so as the United States stood at the brink of war.

Wartime tensions likely prompted Mesabi operators to use another tactic, the threat of deportation, to try to intimidate striking immigrants. The Immigration Act of 1903 allowed for the exclusion of alien anarchists and for their expulsion within three years of their entry. Enforcement theretofore had been minimal. During the five years preceding the strike, the United States had sent home only a dozen anarchists and denied entrance to thirty-eight others, but these low numbers did not minimize the perceived threat. Oliver and other companies now intended to use it, and the remedial legislation, to their advantage. According to the Duluth *News-Tribune,* plans called for sending back to Europe four Mesabi strikers of each nationality, as a warning to other immigrant workers, and if disorder in their ranks persisted, "other aliens would be sent back to their homes until labor conditions become normal." In addition to other hardships, the returning deportees would face conscription into the warring armies. Realizing the adverse effects of wholesale removals and inadvisable loss of needed workers, business leaders hoped to use selective deportation of malcontents to frighten their compatriots and make them more amenable to managerial dictates.[17]

John Lind, former governor, US congressman, and current appointee to the pro-business Minnesota Commission of Public Safety (MCPS)—a wartime agency created "to maintain domestic law and order" and assure the state's contribution to national preparedness—articulated the strategy. Duluth newspapers arranged to have one of their Washington, DC, correspondents send "some rather lurid reports that the Government was planning to deport all unruly aliens who violated the law or caused disturbances." This provided the basis for the stories that appeared in the *News-Tribune.* Apocryphal, the reports intended to evoke fear among the immigrant workers, especially the Finns, whom authorities saw as the strike leaders. Dread of deportation, its advocates believed, would do more to quiet immigrant subversives than any other means, including the more difficult task of securing criminal convictions for their alleged transgressions. The latter necessitated adherence to due process, which the courts had concluded did not apply to alien removal. Those arrested on the Range, for such seemingly trivial offences as the distribution of handbills, made perfect deportation targets, for many "could not speak one word of English."[18] But, to make the possibility of being sent back to Europe seem real, at least one of the Range's foreign-born miners would have to serve as an example.

Authorities made good on their threat by arresting George Andreytchine, a strike leader and Bulgarian immigrant, and designating him for expulsion.

Andreytchine, an articulate speaker in several languages, had worked at Oliver before the strike, and when it started, he joined the IWW and served as a local organizer. At that point, he became a "dangerous alien." Grounds for Andreytchine's arrest centered on his ideology—he reportedly called himself a "Tolstoyan anarchist"—and his strike activities, which according to authorities "tended to incite violence." Moved to Ellis Island, his case attracted national attention and protest, leading Acting Secretary of Labor John Densmore to block his deportation. Densmore found Andreytchine to be "neither dangerous nor undesirable." A nationally circulated newspaper story hailed his release, calling it "the final defeat of the steel corporation," which had theretofore unleashed its "tyranny" "with the aid of gunmen and subservient officials." The miners could only wish for such results. In actuality, the mere prospect of deportation had its desired effect. "I soon discovered" Lind wrote to Attorney General Thomas W. Gregory, "that those aliens who were cussing American institutions and American conditions were very loath to leave them for their former plight. In fact, they would be rather good."[19] Managers and their supporters outside the Mesabi looked for similar ways to exploit workers' immigrant identities.

Operators' response to the September 1915 return of labor militancy at the Clifton-Morenci, Arizona, copper mines also tried to take advantage of their workers' national origins. Instead of embracing Americanization, particularly its expectations of ending ethnic distinctions among laborers, managers initially sought to exploit those differences. District mines relied on Mexicans, whom they paid lower wages than those earned by "white" workers elsewhere in the state. Beyond reducing labor costs, the practice had added value. According to union spokesmen: "The true facts are that these companies have tried there [at the Morenci area mines] employment of different races at different rates of wages for these races to prevent any cooperation among the men." Once the 1915 strike began, and workers showed solidarity, employers changed tactics and blamed the miners' participation on their ethnicity. "The federation [Western Federation of Miners] sent its agitators and organizers into the Clifton-Morenci district," asserted Phelps Dodge & Company managing director and antiunion zealot Walter Douglas, "knowing how easily the Mexican workmen are led and how easily they are intimidated." The subsequent unrest, contended another official, involved primarily "Mexicans and illiterate foreigners," usually one and the same. Public officials needed to impose prohibition, warned a third employer spokesman, in order to deter foreign-born strikers from committing "crazed deeds." Yet when the workers staged protest marches, they emulated comrades elsewhere by carrying American flags.[20]

Throughout the strike, press coverage associated the miners' ethnicity with allegations of unruly behavior. Accounts of violent Mexicans predominated. The Tucson *Daily Citizen,* a moderate-Republican and not pro-business paper, simultaneously reported "no sign of disorder" in the Morenci region and quoted statements from union leaders alleging the "increasing difficulty in controlling the Mexicans." Among a mob of twenty strikers, which behaved akin to a "pack of wolves," only three spoke English. Their bearing was not of the sort that one could expect from "intelligent white miners." According to the *Colorado Springs Gazette,* many of the latter had refused to join the union and left the region. Reports habitually identified ruffians who were accused of trying to intimidate those who did not belong to or support the union as Mexican. In an interesting footnote, not even the constabulary could escape ethnic scrutiny. Militiamen sent to police the region included a seventy-man Indian company, whose members were students at the government-run Phoenix Indian School. Praise for their involvement in the strike suggests that they comported themselves in ways appropriate for properly loyal nonwhites, even though they had been sent by pro-labor Governor George W. P. Hunt to preserve order rather than advance corporate interests.[21]

Mexicans who dug the copper at Clifton-Morenci, unlike the European immigrants who mined iron in Minnesota and Michigan, belonged to an ethnic group largely considered beyond the pale of Americanization. Both native-born Mexican Americans and those who migrated North experienced widespread discrimination and lived on the margins of "Anglo" society. An effectively open border between the United States and Mexico allowed workers to move back and forth frequently between the two nations. Likely on account of the journey's ease, coupled with the ill treatment that the immigrants encountered in the US, Mexicans had one of the lowest nationalization rates of any incoming group. Not surprisingly, mine operators' condemnation of the strikers did not stress the Mexicans' lack of loyalty to the United States, as they would have been presumed not to have had any, or even the capability to develop it. Only after the strike ended, and Pancho Villa had attacked an American town, did anxiety about Mexican Americans' lack of patriotism become an issue in Morenci and other US places where they lived in large numbers.[22]

With the help of federal mediators, the January 1916 strike settlement tried to mend ethnic and class divides. Mining companies pledged "the elimination so far as possible of all racial distinctions." Previously miners had backed a 1913–1914 initiative limiting a company's non-citizen employment—a provision clearly meant to affect Mexicans—to 20 percent of its workforce. Declared unconstitutional, the law had manifested working-class fears of what the *New Republic* called "an exploited body of aliens." Now, excepting those who had engaged in violence, "no individuals of any nationality will be banned from reemployment." Miners also received higher wages through a sliding scale based on the price of mined copper, and the companies agreed to the creation of a grievance committee. In exchange, workers terminated their association with the radical Western Federation of Miners and instead joined the AFL-affiliated Arizona State Federation of Labor.[23] All parties, including the denigrated Mexicans, seemed to have gained something from the settlement. This contrasted with the chain of events involving primarily white miners who labored across the state at Bisbee, during the summer of 1917.

After the United States had entered the war, and when combat in Europe was driving up copper prices, the IWW's Bisbee local demanded better pay and working conditions, leading to a walkout. European immigrants dominated the labor force. No Asians worked at area mines, and no Mexicans did underground mining. But "whiteness," in critics' minds, did not equate to loyalty. On July 12, local vigilantes belonging to the Bisbee Workingman's Loyal League and the Bisbee Citizens Protective League seized some 2,000 alleged radicals, 1,200 of whom were deported by rail to Columbus, New Mexico. Foreign-born miners predominated the ranks of deportees, but many of them had naturalized and registered for the draft. Ironically, few came from Germany and Austria, nations against which the United States was fighting. Press reports, when noting immigrant involvement, nonetheless emphasized their lack of patriotism and threat to national security. According to the *Colorado Springs Gazette*, "German propaganda" had engendered current labor strife in the Southwest, against which the federal government was prepared to take "drastic action." The local sheriff, according to the Portland *Daily Oregonian,* had called the deportees "a mob of aliens and enemies of my government," who promoted "bloodshed and anarchy." Such hardly was the case, as Governor Hunt and others proclaimed by citing the workers' compliance with draft laws and purchase of liberty bonds, and the President's Mediation Commission—created to improve labor conditions in the Southwest and on the Pacific Coast, found the deportations to be "wholly illegal and without authority in law, either state or federal." Unfortunately, more critical accounts had their inflammatory effect.[24]

Other papers harped on the same themes. Summarizing the news of the week for early August, one central states paper described the IWW's recent organizing efforts as a continuation of its "work of cooperating with the Germans," creating "various troubles for mine owners, lumber producers and themselves, in many western localities." The *Albuquerque Journal* incorrectly asserted that 65 to 85 percent of those removed from Bisbee were "aliens by birth and allegiance"; "they were not Americans and had no understanding of this form of government." After their arrival at an effective refugee camp in Columbus, the Tucson *Daily Citizen* published reports of "foreign elements" among the deportees attempting to organize an insurrection and seize weapons from a local Army depot. The leaders were said to be Austrians and Germans. Commenting on State Attorney General Wiley R. Jones's plans to investigate conditions in Bisbee, the *Daily Citizen* editorialized that he would find newly established policies designed to ensure that "only loyal American citizens" got employment at area firms. Ironically, the deportees and their supporters used almost the same phraseology, calling themselves "common American citizens" who were struggling to secure their rights.[25]

Progressive journalist Robert W. Bruere, an industrial relations expert, captured the essence of ethnic and labor relations in the Arizona copper country. In Fall 1917, the *New York Evening Post* sent him to investigate press reports of a widespread IWW conspiracy to thwart America's preparations "at the moment when our government was facing the most critical ordeal in its history. . . ." The German government purportedly provided funding for the IWW's subversive plot. Seeking to get a clear assessment of conditions in the Southwest, Burere visited the Clifton-Morenci mining communities, said to be "hotbeds of pro-German conspiracy." Such assertions, he found, could not have been further from the truth. The "terrible Mexicans" were in reality "the most docile people imaginable," who had struck only in hopes of securing an American standard of living. Yet a Phelps Dodge manager continued to intimate that they were subversives of the same stripe as the IWW. Bruere found similar conditions in Bisbee, leading him to conclude that managers used the mythical threat of a Wobbly-led insurrection to "camouflage" their failures to address the miners' legitimate grievances.[26] Such bargaining, however, would have undermined the operators' near-total authority, and they found it easier to paint the strikers as un-American subversives who were in treasonous collusion with a hostile foreign government.

US officials did see potential for the disruption of commercial preparedness. Secretary of Labor William B. Wilson feared Bill Haywood would succeed in getting Minnesota and Michigan miners to strike in support of the Bisbee deportees, demanding government intervention to secure their return. In Wilson's mind, the IWW agitation had nothing to do with improving the condition of workers but aimed "solely to coerce the United States government by interferring [*sic*] with preparations for defense." Even if true, the campaign emanated from a desire to help fellow workers, not from any overt objections to the war, but such logic escaped Secretary Wilson. He urged John Lind to use his influence with Mesabi mine operators "to so arrange wages and conditions of employment that there would no basis for agitation." This seemed unlikely, given that the Minnesota operators had just succeeded in quelling their own worker unrest without conceding to their demands. Noting the crackdowns during the recent strike, Lind dismissed Haywood's overtures to miners as "pure bluff." Relations between operators and workers were good, although one informant among the local Wobblies reported how "deprivation of beer" among local "Croats, Bosmans, and Montenegrins" might make them susceptible to subversive agitation. Lind disagreed, believing that it was "too hot" for subversives to have any sway on the Mesabi.[27]

Unsettled conditions in the state's agricultural regions, especially impediments to the recruitment of seasonal workers, presented "more menacing" problems. The Minnesota Nonpartisan League, seeking economic justice for northern Great Plains farmers and laborers, sowed seeds of discontent as it sought to rally the state's agrarian sector with its campaign against the "money trust" and other exploitative commercial interests. While it strived to show support for the war, the League's agitation—labeled Bolshevik and socialist by the conservative press—amplified concerns about the IWW's calls for better compensation of seasonal workers. Canadian agents also sought to poach their already low numbers. Lind, fearing that employers would not get enough hands for the fall-harvest, hoped for federal interdiction. "Many of the agitators infesting this state are aliens," he informed William Wilson, and their conduct justified deportation. Lind urged interdepartmental coordination to make alien expulsion "a most efficient instrumentality for combating the IWW menace." "Kindly instruct your representatives [in] Minneapolis and Duluth to cooperate with Department of Justice in instituting deportation proceedings promptly," he exhorted the Labor Secretary, while making similar overtures to Attorney General Thomas Gregory. Jail time posed no threat and thus proved to be an ineffective deterrent. Deportation of a few foreign-born reprobates, conversely, "would have a most wholesome effect on all aliens."[28]

Lind's consistent connection of aliens with radicalism showed the linkage's prevalence even among immigrant liberals. Born in Smaland, Sweden, Lind entered politics as a progressive Republican, becoming the first Swedish American elected to Congress in 1886. His partisan allegiance changed during the 1890s, when in 1898 he won the race for governor as a Silver Republican-Democrat-Populist fusion candidate. By 1900, he was an avowed Bryan Democrat and a pronounced enemy of the "trusts." Critics, he cynically noted, once called men like him anarchists. During World War I, Lind tried to give temperate support President Wilson's war aims, serving on the National War Labor Board and the Minnesota Commission of Public Safety. Yet he objected to the latter's extremism and eventually resigned. The *Minneapolis Journal* thereafter pronounced him to be of the same ilk as the "Bolsheviki, I.W.W., and uncatalogued flotsam and jetsam of the state."[29] Lind no doubt took issue with these unfounded characterizations, but however unfair he may have thought them, such ad hominem attacks did not deter him from attributing not just class conflict but also all other unpatriotic machinations to a foreign presence.

Radical labor leaders, for better or worse, contributed to this perception. Prior to his brutal lynching on August 1 at Butte, Montana, IWW spokesman Frank Little allegedly told the Arizona governor, Thomas E. Campbell: "I don't give a damn what your country is fighting; I am fighting for the solidarity of labor." Little made these remarks in support of the striking Arizona miners, and after coming to Butte, he continued his inflammatory rhetoric. His speeches there made reference to tearing up the US Constitution and the tyranny of President Woodrow Wilson. To make his point about the illegitimacy of US involvement in the Great War, Little called US troops "Uncle Sam's scabs in uniform." IWW loyalists, he asserted, would wage war against capitalism, but not Germany. In reality, most Wobblies—notably in the West where Little made his fiery speeches—had a more immediate interest in economics than geopolitics, and many foreign-born workers who objected to draft registration mistakenly thought it would lead to immediate conscription. Relatively few were actively opposed to the war.[30]

Some, but not all, socialists also objected to any American involvement in the hostilities. The war's sole purpose, opponents averred, was to reward capitalist interests and enhance corporate profits. Dismissing the Wilsonian idea of "making the world safe for democracy" and protecting the "humanity of civilization," one antiwar critic reportedly defined US participation as nothing more than a crass effort to safeguard "J. P. Morgan's money." The socialist *Call* refuted condemnations of antiwar agitators, instead declaring that the real traitors to the United States were "the mine-owners, the transportation-kings, and the food-speculators." While such rhetoric paled in comparison to Little's vitriol, few would have found it patriotic, especially at a time when foreign-born leaders dominated the Socialist Party and immigrant voters provided most of its electoral support. Numerous candidates based their message on opposition to the war, including the draft and the sale of war bonds. In 1917, the Bolshevik Revolution cemented, in the minds of many, a universal connection between immigrants, radicalism, and traitorous behavior. Combined, they produced a pervasive distrust that tainted even legitimate labor reform.[31]

A horrific mine fire had engendered a strike that brought Frank Little to Butte, and in its wake, the Metal Mine Workers' Union made a host of reasonable demands, reforms designed to improve safety, raise wages, and eliminate antiunion hiring practices. The latter centered on the use of "rustling cards," documents needed to look for work at the dominant Anaconda Copper Mining Company and many smaller operations. Predictably, labor advocates or others whom managers deemed to be undesirable could not obtain them. While these practices may have given workers proper cause to strike, the tenor and tone of Little's remarks provided ample fodder for critics who wished to focus attention on some alleged foreign conspiracy. "IWW Agitators in West Are Working in Cause of Germany" reported Butte *Daily Post,* and other press organs trumpeted similar allegations of treason. While not explicitly linking Little—himself of American Indian descent—to immigrants, the press made clear their belief that he was traitor, guilty of treasonous sedition.[32]

Vigilante murder of Frank Little turned vitriol to violence. During the early morning hours of August 1, six masked men—self-proclaimed "officers"—pulled Little from his Butte boardinghouse. After dragging the IWW leader behind their car, the assailants severely beat and then hanged him from a railroad bridge. A cryptic sign pinned to his underwear—all that he was wearing—seemed to threaten his compatriots with a similar fate. Most saw the lynching as an outrage, an exercise in mob violence. Three thousand miners marched in Little's funeral precession, and the banner draping his coffin proclaimed him "a martyr to solidarity." Others saw him as a "madman," "a cripple in mind and body," who appealed to the nation's "anarchist element." The Duluth *News-Tribune* made clear where national loyalty should fit into the sordid affair: "If the government is too busy to protect its loyal citizens from outspoken treason. . . [from] the oratory of traitors, their loyal, flag-loving citizens will do this for their country." Taking a more moderate stance, the Cheyenne *Wyoming State Tribune* lamented the government's failure to arrest Little and thereby silence his "revolting and odious" utterances. Authorities everywhere had an obligation to eliminate the menace of radicalism.[33]

Immigration figured prominently in considerations of what specific remedies to pursue, and discussion coalesced around the propriety of using illiteracy as a means of exclusion. The so-called literacy test had been a restrictionist favorite since the mid-1890s, but a combination of congressional setbacks and presidential vetoes had stymied its enactment. Now, proponents believed, its time had come. Some emphasized its purported progressive features—an exact test that would ensure entry of only the best quality foreigners. In this vein, University of Wisconsin professor Edward A. Ross considered the exclusion of illiterates to be an effective means of preserving and protecting America's civic foundations. Others connected the test to unabashed ethnic bigotry—its anticipated exclusion of large numbers of southern and eastern Europeans, believed to be largely illiterate. Seeking to dispel such narrow-mindedness, Yale sociologist Henry P. Fairchild argued that resolution of the nation's immigration problems transcended any ethnic interests, as well as those "of any individuals of any class."[34] Others disagreed.

Many pundits saw immigration primarily as a socioeconomic issue. Speaking for those with an anti-restriction bent, New York City Democratic Congressman W. Bourke Cochran bluntly extolled the commercial contributions made by foreign-born workers: "The immigrant performs that basic labor which is the fountain of all industry." He or she also provided employment opportunities for others. Skilled laborers, for example, in order to create their products, required raw materials drawn from the earth by unskilled hands. As the latter provided their essential services, they propelled the nation's economic growth and thereby lifted the wages and living standards of native workers. The foreigner, Cochran concluded, contributed significantly to his new nation, "to its material prosperity, to its wealth, and . . . its stability." Over a century of America's unparalleled commercial growth bore witness to immigration's myriad benefits, and if the country wanted to maintain its commercial edge, it needed an abundance of foreign-born laborers, those whose "calloused hand" revealed their commitment to hard work. They, and not their "loquacious" countrymen, should be welcomed by all Americans.[35]

Trade unionists, conversely, saw that the continued stream of aliens into the United States comprised a source of cheap labor that was "ruinous to the workers already here, whether native or foreign." Exclusion of illiterates, in the words of American Federation of Labor leader Samuel Gompers, would keep "greedy corporations" from importing low-cost workers, to the detriment of US laborers. The only opposition came "from steamship companies, steel corporations, coal-operators, and other employers whose financial interests were associated with the maintenance of large numbers of workers forced by their helplessness to work for low wages." Restriction's opponents, concurred AFL Secretary Frank Morrison, came mainly from the ranks of America's "great barons," who intended "to supply the United States Steel Company, the great manufacturing concerns, coal companies, packing houses, and railroads, with men willing to work at cheaper wages than those who are born here." America's industrial giants already had access to more workers than they could hire, and using the steady stream of immigrants to maintain high unemployment, employers could keep wages low and profits high. "With them it is always the dollar," Morrison lamented, "with never a thought for the success or comfort of our millions of wage workers or the hundreds of thousands who are continuously without sustaining employment." Workers had no option but to accept whatever compensation companies chose to offer.[36]

Antiradicalism also influenced the restriction debate. Reiterating several provisions of the Immigration Act of 1903, the literacy test bill passed by Congress in 1915 called for exclusion of anarchists or others who opposed organized governments, proponents of assassination for political purposes, and advocates of property destruction. It did not include the 1903 exemption for "persons convicted of an offence purely political, not involving moral turpitude." This omission drew sharp criticism. Socialist Charles E. Russell accepted the need for "some limitations and restrictions on immigration" but found fault with the bill's "abolition of the right of political asylum in the United States." Exclusion based on involvement in certain types of violent protest might rightfully apply to people coming from places where they enjoyed the rights of free speech, press, and assembly, but not where abusive governments oppressed those freedoms. Such conditions frequently pushed protesters to the extreme. "Who are we," Russell asked President Wilson, "in this country, that we should pass judgment upon the measures used by patriots in other countries to effect their liberties." The same could have been asked about the treatment of domestic dissenters, especially immigrants but also native-born. The Duluth *News- Tribune* may have exceeded the bounds of propriety by effectively endorsing the lynching of agitators the likes of Frank Little, but the newspaper's editorial sentiments captured the current state of American intolerance.[37]

Pointing to "the fullness of our national strength" and "the maturity of our great institutions," President Wilson disagreed. In vetoing the bill, he gave initial attention to the section designed to exclude radicals. "It seeks to all but close entirely the gates of asylum," he admonished to the act's supporters, "which have always been open to those who could find nowhere else the right and opportunity of constitutional agitation for what they conceived to be the natural and unalienable rights of men." Many an immigrant who previously had been "marked as an outlaw" in his or her native land had "become an ornament to our citizenship and to our public councils." To exclude them would be a mistake. Wilson acknowledged the propriety of excluding those who posed "a menace to our peace and order or to the wholesome and essential relationships of life." Acceptable legislation, then, needed to distinguish between the true subversive, to whom the nation should deny entry, and those who merely had struggled for basic rights, to whom the country should offer asylum.[38] This quest for balance between protection of legitimate dissent and promotion of internal security would challenge Wilson—and indeed the United States—throughout the war.

The president also objected to the literacy test. Its adoption, he concluded, would turn public policy "away from tests of character and of quality and impose . . . tests of opportunity." It would exclude those whose circumstances had prevented them from receiving a formal education, ironically the very condition that pushed many foreigners to come to the United States. While accepting America's long-standing practice of barring those with demonstrated incapacity for self-support, due to disease or other malady, and those with a record of inappropriate behavior, Wilson disapproved of any new law intending to change the focus and intent of US immigration policy from selection to exclusion. The president made no mention of economic considerations and likely did not consider them to be pertinent. Given his well-established views about the pernicious influences of big business, whose "material interests" had "threatened constitutional freedom in the United States," Wilson's veto should not be construed as a deliberate attempt to aid employers, by retaining their access to immigrant workers. Nor should it be viewed as anti-labor. Because present arrivals were far different than their unskilled predecessors who had displaced American laborers or lowered their wages, the president did not consider them to be a threat to workers' well-being.[39]

Wilson's veto may temporarily have ended congressional agitation, but not the national clamor. *Outlook* editors conveyed business leaders' worries about how the war's effective-reduction of immigration had engendered declining labor pools and rising wages (which to employers apparently was unabashedly bad). In the absence of Italian and eastern European immigrants, many railroads were turning to Mexicans and African Americans. Drawing on racial stereotypes, the editorial stressed the value of immigrant workers and the pressing need for their renewed influx. Immigration Restriction League leader Joseph Lee evaluated the same developments and came to the opposite conclusion. Reduced immigration benefitted American labor. Permanent reduction, the intended results of a literacy test, would improve living conditions among the working class. "People who do not want to restrict immigration," he asserted, "do not want wages to rise or to have the slightest possibility of rising." Lost in the rancor were voices such as immigrant advocate Kate Holladay Claghorn, who saw immigration's wartime decline as a good opportunity to explore new ideas for dealing with foreign-born residents, innovative ways that "would reduce to a minimum their troubles and ours." Instead, in the veto's after-math, lawmakers resumed their emotion-charged debate.[40]

Congress next sent a Wilson a literacy test bill in spring 1917, as the United States stood on the cusp of entering the Great War. The looming threat of belligerent involvement cast a pall over immigrant communities. If Germany's resumption of submarine warfare against merchant ships led the United States to enter the conflict, it would make many immigrants' home countries enemies of the United States. During the 1916 election, Wilson had expressed disapproval of disloyal aliens (even as he aggressively pursued ethnic voters), but when faced with endorsing aliens' exclusion for illiteracy, he again balked. Literacy, he reiterated in rejecting the new bill, was a matter of opportunity, and "our experience in the past has not been that the illiterate immigrant is as such an undesirable immigrant." This time, such sentiments did not carry the day. With heightened nation-alism influencing the results, Congress overrode Wilson's veto, establish-ing a precedent of general exclusion that would have significant economic repercussions. No longer could businesses rely on a virtually unlimited pool of foreign labor. Yet while this would not have pleased them, concur-rent measures offering protection from alien provocateurs no doubt drew their favor.[41]

Multiple wartime acts targeted radicalism. The 1917 Espionage Act pro-hibited any "willful obstruction" of America's mobilization and any attempt to induce such behavior in others. Enforcement included censorship of the mail, a practice aimed at left-wing and often pro-labor publications. Going further, the 1917 Trading with the Enemy Act required foreign-language newspapers to submit translations of war-related stories to the Postmaster General, who would determine their suitability for dissemination. Congress enhanced the Espionage Act with the Sedition Act of 1918, making criminal any "disloyal, profane, scurrilous, or abusive" remarks about the US govern-ment, military, and flag. President Wilson also invoked the last remaining vestige of the 1798 Alien and Sedition Acts, which during wartime gave him the authority to arrest and deport unnaturalized aliens who hailed from an enemy nation. To a limited extent, Wilson used this power to take action against German Americans. But the affected aliens had to have ties to an external enemy, one of the nations against which the US government was waging war.[42] It remained for Congress to link specifically the antiradical intent of the Espionage and Sedition Acts with xenophobia. The deportation provisions of the Literacy Test Act had done this, to some extent, and in 1918, at the height of American involvement in the Great War, a second immigra-tion act would enhance the government's ability to expel alien agitators.

Proponents of social control would have preferred a more extensive peacetime sedition act, one that would have targeted both native- and foreign-born radicals, but without it they turned to deportation as the best option for dealing with subversion. In the Northwest, growing uneasiness about IWW agitation led to mass arrests of alien members, with the intent to return them to their home countries. The business-backed plan called for the removal of between 3,000 and 5,000 alleged subversives. Secretary of Labor William B. Wilson and various judges thwarted the mass expulsions, specifying in April 1918 that the government would "not arrest, detain, or deport any alien simply for joining the IWW." Congress countered this directive in October with passage of the Immigration Act of 1918. It allowed alien deportation for no more than belonging to an organization, such as the Wobblies, which advocated or taught property destruction or the violent overthrow of the US government. It did not matter how long the individual had lived in the United States. Supporters included Commissioner of Immigration Anthony Caminetti, a staunch antiradical and also an Italian immigrant. Secretary Wilson, to the contrary, refused to brand the IWW a subversive group, and few deportations occurred during the war years. Still, the die had been cast.[43]

On November 11, 1918, an armistice brought the Great War to a close. But while the guns may have gone silent and the bullets stopped flying, domestic peace and harmony did not come to reign over the United States. Class tensions soon would erupt in the so-called Red Scare, with much of the dread directed at working-class aliens and the advocates who championed their cause. The recently passed immigration statutes would contribute to the responses. The literacy test had established in law the precept of general restriction, predicating it on the belief that the United States received too many immigrants and had to reduce their number. Future statutes would amplify this principle. Enhanced deportation would help to ameliorate the threat posed by subversive foreigners who were already in the United States. In combination, the new policies left business and commercial leaders concerned about finding enough immigrant workers and pleased to have new means of controlling those whom they did hire. Decades of contention would come to a head as employers sought to balance their competing needs.

CHAPTER 8

Addressing the Reds

Immigrants and the Postwar Great Scare of 1919–1921

"Radicalism, with its borrowed European ideas, is doing its best to destroy the American labor movement and American prosperity and peace," read an unidentified newspaper clipping preserved by Pennsylvania Railroad managers in memoranda dealing with labor unrest among its employees in the early 1920s. Its sentiments captured the essence of five decades of class conflict that frequently had verged into veritable warfare. The writer did not specifically mention immigrants but did make clear that such egregious behavior could not have been the work of "level headed Americans among the wage earners." Their elimination left only the foreign-born, and perhaps those of native birth who had fallen under their sinister influence, to bear responsibility for the era's widespread class antagonism. Yet all was not lost. "Every American," the unidentified writer opined, should fight against this insidious foreign malice, "until it is cleaned out, as it will be."[1] Drawing on a heightened sense of patriotism carried over from the Great War, Americans would respond enthusiastically to such metaphorical calls to arms.

Fear of radicalism—what Assistant Secretary of Labor Louis Post described as a "delirium derived . . . from reports of mysterious crimes attributed to aliens"—defined the post–Great War Red Scare.[2] Announcement on November 11, 1919, of an armistice ending the fighting in Europe had given Americans hope of a return to what future president Warren G. Harding would call normalcy, a renewed opportunity for the nation to enjoy its myriad benefits. Yet at least immediately this was not to be the case. Multiple manifestations of class-based dissent, in the form of strikes, protests, and horrific acts of violence, put the nation on edge. Much of the fervor focused on immigrants, as it had since the onset of industrialization, and Americans again turned their attention to the eradication of immigrant-engendered subversion. Ultimately, reaction to this Red Scare would set the stage for the implementation of new and more severe immigration policies.

Extensive labor unrest coupled with international developments fueled the 1919–1920 Scare. Thirty-six hundred strikes involving four million workers convinced many observers that the United States was on the verge of a Bolshevik revolution akin to that which recently had consumed Imperial Russia. Creation of the Third Communist International, pledged to spread the Revolution to the rest of the world, coincided with domestic violence perpetrated in the name of class warfare, fueling Americans' fears. Evidence abounded. During April 1919, for instance, thirty-six package bombs were sent to business leaders and government officials, including John D. Rockefeller and A. Mitchell Palmer, and suspicion centered on the followers of Italian immigrant-anarchist Luigi Galleani. Authorities suspected the same group of perpetrating the September 1920 wagon-bombing of Wall Street, which killed thirty-eight and injured hundreds. While decades of class conflict had suggested some sort of radical conspiracy intended to topple America's industrial capitalism, convergence of the Bolshevik Revolution and widespread domestic unrest seemed to prove its existence and thereby validate the need to repel its dire threat.[3]

Warnings of Bolshevism's looming danger pervaded the press. Its spread, warned social commentator Edward E. Purinton, an unabashed champion of business efficiency, "would mean the destruction of both the liberty of the nation and the prosperity of the individual." As the threat to the United States emanated from the ranks of its working class, its more enlightened members must fight its pernicious forces. Columbia University sociology and history professor Franklin H. Giddings, Purinton's fellow contributor to the *Independent,* compared Bolshevism's threat to that recently posed by Imperial Germany. A confidential informer, who had infiltrated an IWW meeting at Butte, Montana, held shortly after the Bolsheviks seized power in November 1917, offered a chilling account. One of the Wobbly leaders reportedly had asked if there was some way to establish "touch with the Russian Bolsheviki and secure some speakers who thoroughly understood the situation in Russia." Their public addresses would provide "the working man an opportunity of knowing how the Russians threw off the yoke of oppression." The proposer knew that such speeches would lead to arrests, or worse, but in his mind, class-conscious men could have no more righteous end than to die for the proletarian cause. However hyperbolic may have been the language of both the IWW spokesman and the informant-chronicler, his account conveyed what many Americans saw as a genuine theat.[4] Few gave thought to the possibility of pundits overstating their case.

Pronouncements by national and local public officials added to the din. Candidate Harding warned of the need to extinguish "the fires of Bolshevism" burning within the United States. Yet he did place at least partial blame for its appeal on business interests, when he called for more fair distribution of the profits of production. Cincinnati Mayor John Glavin invoked the dangers of Bolshevism when he condemned creation of the National Social Unit, a community betterment program focused on his city and headed by Secretary of the Interior Franklin K. Lane. Glavin deemed it a dangerous undertaking, one step removed from socialism. Its proponents, he contended, were working on the premise "that where Bolshevism does not exist it is necessary to manufacture it." He also condemned policemen's or firefighters' unions, calling them a "form of Bolshevism." The mayor and his peers gave similar appellation to numerous other organizations, ranging from boards of education to garment workers unions. Their bromides may have been little more than political pandering, but even so, they found a receptive audience. Readers and listeners took them much more seriously than those who tried to minimize the Bolshevik threat.[5]

The Seattle General Strike set the tenor and tone of postwar antiradicalism. During World War I, US government–funded orders for merchant vessels spurred the growth of Seattle's shipyards, where over a dozen companies eventually employed 35,000 workers. They added to the ranks of the city's highly unionized and generally aggressive labor force. In December 1918, as World War I came to a close, the Metal Trades Council, representing the shipyard workers, authorized a strike to secure higher wages, and when negotiations failed, union leaders set a walkout for January 21. To support their fellow tradesmen, Seattle's Central Labor Council approved a general strike, and sixty thousand workers then struck on February 6. Although the strike remained orderly and nonviolent, and lasted only until February 11, business leaders along with much of the general public considered the Council's actions to be part of a conspiracy to launch a Bolshevik revolution. Select IWW and other radical propaganda gave credence to these fears. Seeking to condemn the strike's origins and purpose, and to make clear that the perpetrators would not have their way, Seattle Mayor and spokesman for the law-and-order forces Ole Hanson proclaimed: "The anarchists in this city shall not rule its affairs."[6]

Effectively a voice for the city's commercial establishment and its supporters, Hanson would use his post-strike notoriety to assign more specific blame. A proclamation issued during the strike had instructed Seattle residents to show their "Americanism," and his later commentary, pointedly titled *Americanism Versus Bolshevism*, identified the salient source of contradictory behavior. "The irreconcilable agitating alien, bolshevik or anarchist," he pronounced, "should not be allowed to remain one hour longer than is necessary to go through the proper legal forms to send him back to the land from where he came." Under no circumstances should such recreants be allowed to stay in "*this land of the free.*" Hanson, himself the son of Norwegian immigrants, did try to differentiate between the good and bad aliens who sought to make the United States their home: "There are times when we need immigrants, and surely no American would want to close the door to those aspiring souls who want to escape from the thraldom and poverty of the Old World and become citizens and upbuilders of the New."[7] Protesters among his city's shipbuilders and their supporters would not qualify, even though their toils had helped to provide for America's defense. Instead they fell into the former lot, comprised of those whom the nation should purge. Hanson's beliefs extended far beyond Seattle and, in the eyes of many Americans, they applied to any alien who engaged in class conflict.

After a spring and summer of continued labor unrest, coupled with sensational acts of violence assumed to be the work of worker-revolutionaries, the Boston Police Strike perpetuated the notion of a far-flung radical conspiracy, which in this instance had an unusual immigrant connection. As with the era's other disgruntled workers, the city's angry officers took issue with inadequate pay, oppressively long shifts, and abysmal working conditions. The AFL's recent decision to charter police unions, with its promise of support for collective bargaining, offered a path to remediation. Boston's constabulary approved AFL affiliation on August 9, and one month later, on September 9, after the Police Commissioner suspended the union organizers, rank-and-file policemen voted to strike. Eleven hundred left their posts, leaving "bean-eaters without protection," in the words of Montana's *Anaconda Standard*. Two nights of larceny, vandalism, and general mayhem followed the walkout. Hoodlums smashed windows and looted stores. Attendant violence left eight dead and dozens wounded. "Boston," reported the *New York Times*, "a town nearly three hundred years old, has been thrown back into a state of primitive savagery by the strike of her policemen." Chaos and disorder ruled the day, making the city "an experiment station of the exotic revolutionary ideas that have been imported into the United States."[8]

"Imported" connoted a dubious alien source. Large numbers of Irish Americans did serve on the Boston police force, yet the days of their contentious presence lay largely in the past. Irish immigration had reached its height in the mid-1850s, and the generally impoverished unskilled workers had encountered significant prejudice. Animosity based on their socioeconomic status, religion, and presumed failure to assimilate peaked with the Know Nothing movement of the 1850s. Violent acts perpetrated during its ascendency included the 1834 burning of a convent in Charlestown. The Civil War, at least when it was viewed as a campaign to reunite the Union rather than one to free the slaves, had a unifying effect on the city's population that carried over to the postwar decades. To be sure, anti-Irish bigotry did not completely disappear, but the region's new generation of nativists, most notably US Senator Henry Cabot Lodge, directed their xenophobia at "newer" arrivals. However, this did not keep critics from focusing on the ethnicity of the striking police officers. It was time, declared one faultfinder, to appoint more "old-fashioned Yankees—full blooded Americans" to the police force. "There seems [sic] to be altogether too many Irishmen in these positions to impart the true Americanism which we so much need in these trying times."[9]

One questionable voice did connect the Irish American strikers to US communists. Benjamin Gitlow, who a week before the police strike had been instrumental in founding the Communist Party USA, would later claim that its adherents had played a leading role in the unrest. Writing thirty years later, he stated: "An outstanding figure in the policemen's union of Boston, a policeman of Irish extraction, was a close sympathizer of the Communist party and collaborated with the communists in the conduct of the strike." The radicals intended to "intensify the strike violence" and thereby move the city toward a general strike. Skeptics subsequently would question the veracity of Gitlow's claims, as well as other stories of imported subversive influences. But at the time of the strike, many did believe it to be part of a broader Bolshevik conspiracy. "Bolshevism in Boston" read the storyline for the *Charlotte Observer's* coverage of police walkout, and the *Kalamazoo Gazette* associated the strike with the "dangerous spirit," appropriately called either bolshevism or anarchism, which plagued the nation.[10]

Striking steelworkers brought postwar labor unrest to America's core industry, with its long-standing commitment to managerial prerogative, extensive use of immigrant labor, and the open shop. Dissatisfied workers wanted shorter workdays, wages commensurate with the cost of living, and—most importantly—union recognition. During the Great War, the National Labor Board had supported an eight-hour day and the right of employees to organize, fueling workers' hopes for collective bargaining. High demand for steel coupled with a shortage of labor did lead to higher pay, but not union recognition. Judge Elbert H. Gary, US Steel's paternalistic chief executive, spoke for the industry when he advocated fair treatment for its workers while assiduously rejecting collective bargaining. "We are not obligated to contract with unions if we do not choose to do so," Gary stressed to his industry colleagues in April 1919. The AFL brotherhoods, which represented many of the industry's workers, recognized the power behind Gary's pronouncement, as well as their own weaknesses when it came to confronting the "steel trust," but under the auspicious of its National Committee for Organizing Iron and Steel Workers, the Federation nonetheless felt obligated to support the angry laborers.[11]

On September 22, 1919, an estimated 250,000 steelworkers, or 50 percent of the industry labor force, initiated an ill-fated strike. Fears of Bolshevism bolstered the resolve of intransigent managers and disaffected even some workers, leading them to craft a universally anti-immigrant explication for the origin of the troubles. Ignorant misguided foreigners, not knowledgeable Americans, comprised the whole of the strikers and bore responsibility for the unrest. According to supervisors at the Homestead works, 99 percent of those on strike were unnaturalized immigrants who had been influenced by "the Bolshevik spirit," and at the National Tube Company in McKeesport, Pennsylvania, Americans and "the better grade of foreigners" reportedly had all come to work. Several laborers, most of whom held more highly skilled positions, also attested to the lack of "American" strikers. Their absence left only immigrants among the rebellious ranks. By one account, unions had distributed "inflammatory literature" among the immigrants, seeking to inculcate Soviet propaganda, and as a result, "some of these poor misguided foreigners" had concluded that worker committees could replace bosses in running the mills. A Youngstown, Ohio, machinist denounced the IWW for spreading Bolshevik and other "Un-American" doctrines among the foreign workers.[12]

Judge Gary offered a nuanced assessment of aliens, both their strike involvement and general character. Most immigrants were "good citizens, loyal to this country and loyal to their employers." Foreigners had worked in the industry for decades, and contrary to allegations made by AFL leader Samuel Gompers, steel companies had not recruited contract laborers in order to keep wages low. Rather, the immigrants came to the United States seeking higher pay than they could earn at home. Foreign-born workers had been especially valuable during the Great War, and the industry could not have maintained adequate wartime production without their labor. To facilitate their assimilation, US Steel had conducted extensive welfare work, including promotion of naturalization, and over time many of those who became "Americanized" moved into higher positions. But Judge Gary qualified his praise: "I ought to say there, though, if we had known there was a substantial number of the kind of foreigners who, I think, are now making the real trouble here, who are disturbing the peace, who are resorting to violence, and who I believe are under the leadership of outsiders, we would not have employed them." The strike, he averred, was the product of union leaders agitating this minority of foreign workers.[13]

Riots and unsanctioned demonstrations at Gary, Indiana, had engendered the deployment of state and federal troops, and officers at the scene also saw foreigners as the primary insurrectionists. Major General Leonard Wood, who commanded the federal forces, charged "reds" with fomenting the tumult. He imposed martial law in Gary, East Chicago, and Indiana Harbor, but this provided only a palliative, not a long-term solution. In his view, to preserve domestic order and stability the United States needed to do a better job of Americanizing immigrant workers, and must deport or otherwise prosecute any "alien or naturalized red." Wood had long-standing connections with various restrictionists with whom he shared concerns about the ability of America's proverbial melting pot to admix effectively the current foreign influx.[14] General Wood did not testify at the congressional hearings called to investigate the steel strike, but one of his subordinates who had been with the soldiers at Gary echoed his negativity toward the alien strikers.

Lieutenant Donald C. Van Buren reported on the tense situation that had greeted the arrival of the troops, where conditions confirmed reports of a radical conspiracy. One could "feel the tension in the air and see it in the street." Local officials had lists of "Red leaders, men who were agitating all sorts and forms of revolution." Subsequent inquiry by Van Buren and his associates verified their identities, and not surprisingly, not one leader or organizer of a subversive organization "was an American-born citizen." The same could be said of the radical strikers. Numerous of the offending aliens, "First Branch Russian Bolsheviki," belonged to the IWW, which Van Buren dubbed the "Russian Federation of Labor," and based on information he and other commanders had submitted to immigration authorities, several had been detained pending possible deportation. Searches of various meeting halls had uncovered "literally tons of Bolshevik literature," virtually all of it written in foreign languages. When, during the congressional hearing, Georgia Senator Hoke Smith tried to ask what would be the effect of shipping "all the alien agitators and organizers out of the country," the lieutenant interrupted him in mid-sentence, responding: "There would be no more trouble at all."[15]

Not everyone agreed with those nativistic assessments. *New Republic* editors blamed Judge Gary for the strike, calling him "an inciter of violence, a provoker of industrial war, an industrial barbarian," who sought to perpetuate "absolute power in his industry." While promoting himself as the unimpeachable source of order and tranquility, he unjustly vilified alien laborers, using any and all means "to have them regarded as dreadful aliens, dark, dirty people who have not been Americanized in those well-governed smiling spacious communities of the steel district." Yet despite Gary's exhortations, no actual striker connection to Bolshevism existed, and those on the picket line did not aim to start a revolution. US Steel's behavior, particularly its refusal to bargain collectively with its workers through their selected representatives, provided evidence of history's march away from the harmony that had characterized the preindustrial workplace. The editors hoped that the federal government would recognize the company's transgressions and take action to settle the strike.[16]

Claiming that all Americans could trace their lineage to immigration, AFL organizer John Fitzpatrick also exonerated the immigrant workers. US Steel had combined boatloads of iron ore from Minnesota and immigrants from southern Europe to maximize production and profits. This had led to exploitation of the foreigners. Corporate avarice, not worker radicalism, had precipitated the walkout. "The only Bolshevist I saw over there [at the various steel plants] are the mill town officials and the men who deliberately defy the Constitution of the United States," Fitzpatrick told congressional investigators, with the latter remark aimed at steel managers and their underlings. As for the immigrants, most had taken steps toward Americanization. Many prewar arrivals, for example, had continued to use only their native languages, but impediments to overseas travel during the Great War had strengthened the foreigners' connection to their new home. Most now spoke English. This and their other "American" attributes dispelled the prevalent accusations of their disloyalty.[17]

While the Federation generally supported restriction as a means of protecting labor, officials also spoke well of those confronting US Steel. William Z. Foster, representing the AFL's National Committee for Organizing Iron and Steel Workers, saw striking immigrants as management's bitter pill. For years, Steel Trust representatives "had scoured the countries of Eastern and Southern Europe, and packed its mills with poor, dispirited ignorant immigrants. . . ," whom they could treat little better than slaves. Their numbers came to dominate the industry's unskilled positions. But eventually the men had awakened to their condition, come to appreciate the union's efforts to ensure better benefits, and rushed to join the strike. Realizing the immigrants "in truth to be highly rebellious working men," Steel Trust leaders found themselves "making the welkin ring with inconsistent denunciation of the 'revolutionary foreigners' with whom just a short time ago it was so anxious to crowd its plants." Company priorities now became American interests, necessitating united resistance "against the foreigners who were about to overwhelm them." "Don't let the 'hunkies' rule the mills," employers warned their American hands. Foster, of course, disagreed, characterizing alien workers as conscientious unionists who sought unity with their native-born compatriots in the fight for fair and equitable treatment.[18]

Conversely, Foster spoke disparagingly of African American workers, whom he portrayed as adverse to union membership and amenable to strikebreaking. During the struggle, with few exceptions they had made a "wretched showing" and contributed significantly to the union's defeat. Management allegedly had recruited thirty to forty thousand Black scabs, largely from the South. And yet, partial fault for their behavior lay with the unions, which had established strict color lines and thereby effectively excluded nonwhites from many occupations. This hurt all workers, as employers could exploit blacks' resentment by enticing them to work as strikebreakers. The time had come, Foster believed, for unions to "open their ranks to negroes [sic], make an earnest effort to organize them, and then give them a square deal when they do join." Black leaders could contribute to labor solidarity by urging African Americans to abandon their prejudice and join unions.[19]

Religious leaders also supported or absolved immigrant strikers. In particular, an investigation conducted by the Interchurch World Movement—an evangelical and educational social welfare organization sponsored by several American protestant denominations—intended to provide a neutral and objective assessment of the steel industry's labor relations. To complete the study, the Movement's Department of Industrial Relations created a nine-member Commission of Inquiry composed of representatives from eight denominations. In November, strike leaders asked the Commission to attempt mediation between steel-industry workers and management. Commissioners met with Judge Gary, only to hear his standard denunciation of the strikers' interconnected demands for Bolshevism and the closed shop. His response effectively ended any hopes of mediation, but the investigation continued. Although industry and some religious leaders sought to stifle the report, no doubt fearing its divergence from standard accounts, the Commission published its findings in July 1920.[20]

Immigrant steelworkers, whom the Commission identified as those from southern and eastern Europe, did not deserve their disreputable characterization. Largely filling unskilled and semiskilled jobs, they worked long days and frequently did double shifts. These conditions attracted largely single men, who saw "what one day *can* bring in but not what the years *do* bring in, to him and his class." Yet even they recognized their exploitation by the mill operators, and many foreigners, especially those who were married, wanted to work "American hours." Slavic workers, the Commission determined, were "mad enough" to strike for better wages and benefits, but this did not put them in league with Bolshevik agitators, who found little sympathy for their cause among the strikers. Even those detained in Gary had not been arrested for radical agitation or actively waging any kind of revolution, but rather for membership in certain organizations. Regarding the claims that only foreigners went on strike, the immigrants had their own explanation. Domestic laborers who would not work the "Hunkie" twelve-hour days failed to appreciate the extent of the "un-American" worker abuse. Immigrants reportedly told the strike leaders: "When you 'Americanize' the Americans and the negroes [*sic*], we'll strike again."[21] Frustrated foreigners may have seen their native-born colleagues as the ones who were at fault and needed to change, but most observers perceived the aliens as the culprits behind any and all industrial unrest.

This put the business community in a predicament, and the views of the United States Chamber of Commerce (USCC) exemplified the dilemma. Inherently conservative, Chamber members overwhelmingly favored freedom of contract between worker and employer and the antiunion open shop. Virtually all of the USCC's precepts and proposals emphasized the propriety of managerial prerogative. Yet the Chamber also supported fair treatment and payment of adequate wages. Cooperation between management and labor would lead to appropriate remuneration and let the workers sustain "a proper standard of living." Shift scheduling should allow at least one rest day per week, to maintain employees' health and well-being, but any further reduction that would increase leisure time must acknowledge the "commensurate loss in the earning power of workers." Harkening back to an earlier era, the postwar Chamber promoted harmony, or a "community of interests," as the "true basis of sound industrial relations." Strikes, particularly against railroads and other "public utilities," conversely inflicted "great harm on the community." To deter their consequences, the Chamber supported the passage of laws that would prohibit workers or their representatives from interfering with the operation of essential businesses. Remedial measures, however, should not include immigrant exclusion. Instead, the Chamber advocated for more and better means of assimilation and distribution, which would serve the needs of US companies[22]

The pro-immigrant Inter-Racial Council (IRC), headed by business leaders including chemical maker T. Coleman du Pont and printing equipment

magnate Philip T. Dodge, with the support of four hundred industrial organizations, shared the Chamber's views regarding foreign workers. America's
major industries relied upon skilled and unskilled immigrants to meet their
labor needs. Given their essentiality, none should be judged on the basis of
"racial prejudice." "Character, thrift, industry," along with a sound mind
and body, should determine the measure of the man (and one can assume
that the same applied to women) and determine the fitness of anyone who
came to the United States in search of economic opportunity. Women and
men who came to this country also contributed their arts and cultures. The
Council's 1920 National Conference on Immigration attempted to publicize the totality of benefits provided by foreign-born labor, but this did not
alleviate misgivings about the problematic beliefs and behaviors of some
alien worker.[23]

Russian immigrants, from the home of the Bolshevik Revolution, were a
case in point. No doubt using its own exaggerated language, the Inter-Racial
Council sought to convey the extent of their radical inclinations and also
stress the need to see beyond this single characteristic: "The Russian extreme
Socialist or Bolshevik views largely dominate the thoughts of Russians in
America. Most of them are anti-clerical and pro-Bolshevik. . ." and "the only
leaders who are listened to in the Russian Communities in America today
are in full sympathy with the Bolsheviki." Socialist organizations flourished
within their ethnic enclaves, notably those in Boston, Massachusetts; Water-
bury, Connecticut; and Providence, Rhode Island. Yet people in the United
States who knew well the Russian immigrants realized that they were "no
more vicious or undesirable than the peasantry of other nations." Of simple
stock, they wanted no more than to share in the best of what Americans had
to offer. If recent events had showcased the "unfortunate features" of their
Old World home, Americans would do well "to re-member [sic] that no Russian can judge America by its lynchings." Fixation on either blight obscured
the true nature of the respective peoples.[24]

Egregious behavior by a few undesirables, emphasized business representatives, need not stigmatize all immigrants. "The activities of a handful
of aliens with destructive revolutionary tendencies," the IRC averred, "have
caused many of us to make the word 'alien' or 'foreign-born' synonymous
with bolshevism, I.W.W.'ism and other such discordant notes in our National
life." Recent anti-immigrant stereotypes had been formed "at a time when
there was considerable excitement throughout the country over so-called
red outrages, and when the people were unthinkingly condemning all immigrants, aliens and even foreign-born citizens of proved patriotism." Given
that there was "no danger to be feared from the immigrant who is honest and

works hard," such condemnation needed to stop. Xenophobic hysteria had "so unsettled the foreign-born population" that hundreds of employees at basic industries were preparing to leave the United States. Because this would hurt American commerce, the IRC championed education as the best means of countering the adverse effects of radical propaganda and maintaining a loyal immigrant workforce.[25]

Americans needed to do more to convince foreign-born residents to join "with us in good citizenship" and "to feel at home." Too often, unwarranted concerns about the immigrants' political inclinations biased those who could promote assimilation. Overzealous authorities habitually broke up meetings of Russian Americans and arrested their leaders, without so much as an explanation of the necessity for such actions. These behaviors sent entirely the wrong message. Instead, companies should seek to create a positive environment for alien workers, by providing books and other recreational materials, establishing information services at the plants, and taking steps to ensure that immigrant housing options were on a par with those "enjoyed by Americans." Employers also should help immigrants contact family members with whom they had lost touch during the Great War, and help those who wished to send for family members who remained in Europe. Even something as minor as making sure that the local post office could meet foreigner's needs might engender good will.[26]

Plant operators seeking to counteract Bolshevism also needed to make the importance of patriotism an appealing message. Heavy-handed or "coercive naturalization" too often failed to produce "true Americanization," as the desire to become an American "*must come from the alien himself.*" The "average immigrant" had little interest in "sermons on the Constitution and 'loyalty,'" but he or she would appreciate lessons that explained how the American economic system rewarded "thrift, ambition, and skill." If a company had to reduce its workforce during the current transition from military to civilian production, managers should clarify that the dismissals would be temporary. Layoffs then should be made "on the basis of identical treatment of native and foreign born. . . . The same policy should be extended to *all* races without discrimination." Managerial bigotry, stated Coleman du Pont, only motivated aliens to leave—not just leave particular employment but leave the United States—and when they left, they "would take back with them stories about America which will make this country less attractive to immigrants." Businesses should also do their part to protect the foreigners from "unscrupulous persons" who exploited the newcomers' "ignorance of American conditions." These positive steps could allay immigrants' fears and promote their fealty.[27]

All Americans, not just those seeking to hire workers, had to recognize immigrants' value. Similar to employers, the larger public too often allowed the actions of those few aliens who advocated violent revolution to taint perceptions of all immigrants. They, in turn, interpreted raids and deportations as part of "a campaign of repression against the foreign born in general." Seeking to move beyond antiradical hysteria, the Council stressed the need to promote more factual consideration of the nation's need for immigrant labor. The United States lacked four million workers, and with a million foreigners supposedly wanting to return home, making proper use of those who remained—or who might come in the future—an economic "imperative." If the United States was to transition successfully to a peacetime economy, it had to have more workers. Interestingly, in the early months of 1919, high unemployment, especially among returning veterans, had contributed to the national anxiety that had fueled the Red Scare, but as industrial production increased later that year, the IRC pressed its contention that the United States had "plenty of room" for compliant, hardworking aliens whose presence would engender multiple economic benefits.[28]

In addition to providing labor, a continued inflow of immigrants would contribute to efficiency. "We are suffering at the present time from a lack of disposition to work," the IRC contended, due to existent workers' realization that they could not easily be replaced, "and in some industries there is an apparent conspiracy of deliberate slacking." This mode of personal subversion, coupled with the "incompetency of the worker who is rated higher than he should be," resulted in markedly decreased productivity. Access to adequate numbers of immigrants offered the best solution. "A proper supply of labor," which to the IRC meant those from abroad, would "do more to eliminate the inefficient, to secure and increase production, than anything else." Calls for efficiency fit Frederick Winslow Taylor's popular belief in "scientific management." In theory, taking steps to get each employee to perform "the highest grade of work for which his natural abilities fit him. . ." would lead to "maximum prosperity" for both labor and management. Ironically, many applications involving immigrant laborers relied on strict adherence to managerial prerogative, behavior that fostered the labor radicalism abhorred by capitalists. Going full circle, workers' embrace of these leftist ideologies contributed to the public's negative impression of immigrants.[29]

The IRC found an enthusiastic supporter in Charles L. Huston, Vice President and Works Manager at Lukens Steel Company. Organized in 1810, Lukens manufactured boiler plate at its Coatsville, Pennsylvania, mill. The owners practiced paternalistic management, which they believed would secure loyalty and create harmony among the workers. This proved to be an effective approach, as the company did not have its first strike until 1886. Then, while officials at two other regional mills agreed to workers' demands, Lukens held firm. Managers shut down the plant, evicted workers from company housing, hired Pinkerton detectives, and eventually broke the strike. Even though Lukens's financial situation was such that it could have accepted the workers' demands without incurring serious fiscal burden, the senior managing partner made clear that they would not "be surrendering ourselves to the control of our workmen by yielding at present."[30]

Following the Great War, Lukens's officials retained their predecessors' aversion to worker agency. Too many contemporary voices, complained Charles Huston, "seem to take entirely the workers' side, without giving any fair consideration to the fundamental principles of capital, which is not an autocratic over-lord. . . ." Operators instead sought to use their legitimate authority to benefit all concerned parties. Agitation for the eight-hour day, perpetrated by "organized labor and a lot of short sighted sociologists," particularly perturbed him. Not only did it challenge the boss's authority, it also had a deleterious effect on workers themselves, causing them to earn less than a day's cost of living. Lukens had tried using eight-hour shifts in 1919, but finding it "absolutely unsatisfactory," had returned to its traditional twelve-hour workdays. In Huston's mind, even the employees preferred that schedule; certainly, they had no reason to complain. Working long hours "never seems to have resulted in premature aging of men. . . ," nor did the five-and-a-half-day week prevent the workers from pursuing "their normal social and religious life." While Huston no doubt believed in the propriety of his pronouncements regarding longer workdays, his swipe at reformers and labor advocates revealed the importance he placed on rebuffing even the most mild challenges to managerial prerogative.[31] Preoccupation with this focus also prevented him from seeing the substance of worker demands, such as standard pay for a shorter workday. This mentality defined Lukens's behavior toward its immigrant employees.

To meet its labor needs, in terms of both quantity and quality, Lukens relied on "industrious and dependable" foreigners. Here, had Huston contemplated his declarations regarding twelve-hour workdays, he could have seen a contradiction to his professed reason for hiring aliens. The "ordinary American born, white man, who has gone through our public schools and received the benefits of our educational system" would not do the requisite manual labor, which over the years had prompted the company to tap other sources. "A sturdy, carefully selected European immigrant," Huston averred, "has given satisfactory service, is industrious and frugal, saving up his money so that when depression comes on he does not become a burden

on the community even to the same extent that the average American workman does." An economic slowdown recently had slackened US business, but
the expected revival would require additional unskilled laborers, of the type
that immigration had consistently supplied.[32] Huston apparently gave no
credence to the possibility that exploitative work conditions deterred native-
born workers from seeking employment, or even that company practices
might arouse the ire of foreigners. In his mind, they somehow were inherently suited to doing oppressive unskilled labor.

This myopia, however, did not blind Huston to the possibility of radical
proclivities among immigrant workers, but he saw ways to minimize their
unruly behavior. Scores of long-serving "standard men," immigrants "of the
steady-going conservative type, many of them Christian," worked at Lukens
and posed no danger to harmonious labor relations. While Huston did not
clarify the importance of the aliens' religious affiliation, he saw theism as
a deterrent to the embrace of "godless" subversive doctrines. Corporate
benevolence could achieve the same ends. "Where the heart touch between
employer and employee is maintained," he paternalistically contended, "a
cordial relationship will exist and the details will not be hard to arrange, but
where strife exists nothing will satisfy, and if you take the heart out of a man
you will lose the man." The company strove to prevent the latter. Seeking to
promote good will among its immigrant employees and keep them on the job,
Huston welcomed the IRC's offer to make an analysis of "racial conditions" at
the Lukens plants. He also supported noncoercive Americanization.[33]

Anticipating the multiple benefits of assimilation, Lukens managers
endeavored to formulate and implement a corporate program. "There certainly ought to be everything possible done to have a right basis of relationship with our employees put into effect all over the plant," concluded
one company official, "to avoid dissatisfaction, and to make everyone feel
that he is given proper and consistent treatment." He and other leaders saw
little value in putting up posters, which the IRC offered to provide, and had
doubts about the efficacy of scheduling outside speakers. Immigrant workers likely would see both methods as unwanted intrusions. Instead, the company focused on training foremen to spread the proper message among the
immigrant workers. Immediate supervisors could promote the company's
message of patriotic benefits and duties without seeming to be engaged in
high-pressure indoctrination. Successful implementation would eliminate
unnecessary disruptions and increase efficiency. Growth of immigrants'
patriotism would lead to productivity, and presumably profitability.[34]

Pennsylvania Railroad managers also found favor with corporate-
sponsored Americanization. Detailed postwar records of employee ethnicity

indicated management's recognition of their significance. In 1922, its Central Region—stretching west from Altoona and Renovo, Pennsylvania, to Crestline and Columbus, Ohio—reported 12,163 foreign-born employees, or 23 percent of their workforce. They represented fifty-four nationalities, ranging from Albanians to Welsh, with Italians, Austrians, and Poles comprising the largest groups. Given the polyglot nature of the Austrian Empire, many of the designated Austrians likely considered themselves to be something different, further expanding the workforce's ethnic diversity. Almost all of the immigrants came from Europe, but the labor force also included 36 Mexicans, 2 Japanese, 1 Persian, and an Egyptian. The Northwest Region—stretching from central Ohio to Chicago—reported 4,363 immigrant workers, down from 5,197 in 1913, with Poles, Italians, Greeks, Czech-Slovaks, and other central and eastern Europeans predominating among thirty-seven groups.[35]

Particulars of their industry set the context for how Pennsylvania dealt with its workers. Following American entry into the Great War, President Woodrow Wilson had invoked the 1916 Federal Possession and Control Act to establish government operation of the nation's railroads. This arrangement lasted for three years, until the Esch-Cummins Transportation Act of 1920 restored private management effective March 1. The act also created the nine-member Railroad Labor Board (RLB), whose jurisdictional responsibilities included arbitration of workplace disputes. The Board, however, lacked explicit authority to compel either side's behavior, a limitation that in practice would prove to be decidedly pro-business. Concurrently, the Chamber of Commerce led a campaign to make the "open shop" the national norm. Workers thereby would not have to belong to a union in order to secure or continue to have employment. Calling it the "American Plan" and framing it as an alternative to the "foreign" idea of a "closed"—or fully unionized—shop allowed proponents to capitalize on the patriotic fervor stemming from World War I.[36] Yet despite the rhetoric's propaganda value, railroads encountered determined resistance when they tried to establish open shops.

On the Pennsylvania, an initial dispute over union representation, wages, and the closed shop commenced in early April 1920, shortly after the railroad's resumption of private operation. Shopmen struck on April 1, followed by switchmen a week later. Work stoppages created coincidental bad press, coming just as the company launched a multimillion-dollar bond sale. The concurrence could not have pleased corporate officials, but it did give them a chance to assert their authority. Potential disruption of service drew harsh rebukes and swift reprisal. "Public interest," averred one of the superintendents, "demands that the officers and management of the Company take immediate steps to provide the transportation needed to prevent further interference with the movement of food and other necessary commodities." Managers also made clear their intent to deal with their employees as they—and they alone—saw fit. Neither the RLB nor union negotiators would determine company practices. Accounts varied as to the amount of attendant violence or direct interference with railroad operations, but Pennsylvania supervisors acted quickly to make sure they had adequate labor to continue operations.[37]

Company officials contracted with the Pinkerton Detective Agency to procure replacement workers and deliver them safely, under guard if necessary, to their place of employment. The presence of Pinkerton agents paid dividends, at least from the operators' perspective. According to one labor recruiter, "the only reason we did not get beat up was because of the rough looking men we had with us." Detectives also undertook a clandestine operation to preclude possible interference in the hiring process. "If we have any machinist operative, or other suitable operative, who can associate with the men at the employment office, we are authorized [apparently by railroad officials] to use this man to determine any kind of agitation that is taking place so as to anticipate any trouble in shipments, etc." Interestingly, the Pennsylvania declined to give information about the strikers to the Bureau of Investigation without a grand jury subpoena. Attorney General A. Mitchell Palmer recently had used Bureau agents to target suspected radicals and now was searching for evidence of a "red" uprising scheduled for May 1. Pennsylvania officials did not elaborate on the reasons for this decision, but after three years of government control, coupled with the unwanted establishment of the RLB, the railroad's managers did make clear their aversion to federal interference, especially in labor matters.[38]

Both railroad personnel and the Pinkerton detectives justified their actions by drawing on notions of obligation that the Great War had popularized. Reporting for work became the unequivocally proper course of action. To do otherwise—in the words of one the track men—was dereliction of one's "call to duty." Management lauded the devotion of those who had stayed on the job, or otherwise provided meritorious service "in the most crucial time of trouble." Staying at one's post implied being faithful, not just to the company, but also to some higher national need for order and stability. A company official, in a speech to employees, sought to combine a sense of duty with workplace harmony: "It has been said that a man cannot serve more than one master. We serve three—first, the company; second the public, and third ourselves." Commitment to the first two entities would improve proportionately the interests of the last. Putting this into practice, the Pennsylvania gave bonuses to workers—often the "oldest and most reliable" employees—who stayed on the job and paid lesser amounts to the men who recruited strikebreakers and delivered them to understaffed locations. Officials also made clear that they would not reinstate strikers, except as new employees, and would not accept labor's demands for a closed shop.[39]

Pennsylvania managers did not specifically target immigrants during the 1920 unrest, but subsequent events soon provided another opportunity. In June 1922, four hundred thousand AFL-affiliated shopmen struck railroads throughout the eastern United States to protest wage reductions, work-rule changes, and outsourcing to nonunion contractors. Workers were determined to protect their wartime gains, and management was equally resolved to assert its prerogatives. The Pennsylvania challenged the authority of AFL locals to represent the railroad's employees, offering instead to create a company union, an approach to labor relations euphemistically called the American Plan. In response to the workers' grievances, the RLB issued a decidedly pro-business decision. The Board supported the shopmen on outsourcing, but otherwise the railroads triumphed. Board Chairman Benjamin W. Hooper deemed the strike to be illegal, backed the idea of company unions, and validated the railroads' authority to set work rules. Not even President Warren G. Harding's call for mediation could bring the railroads and workers to resolve their issues, in part due to management's intransigence on not restoring the strikers' seniority. Shopmen also thought that their skills would hamper the recruitment of strikebreakers, thereby increasing their chances of prevailing.[40]

Inflammatory rhetoric emanated from both sides. Pennsylvania managers emphasized a connection between the walkout, its potential for violence, and the role of foreign influences. Workers, asserted RLB Chairman Hooper, had rejected the Board's ruling on the several contractual issues and instead moved to strike, creating a climate replete "with all of its inevitable un-American subversion of law and order." These he described as "threats, intimidation, mobs, riots, bombs, touches [torches], murder, and all of the forces of violence incident to a strike." Unionists effectively validated his assessment with their public calls for the "'Shock Troops' of America's industrial Army" to establish "industrial justice" on the nation's railroads. Referencing the Bolshevik Revolution and recent US labor disputes, worker advocates issued a frightening portent: "Look long at Russia, do not underestimate the warning of Youngstown, Ohio, and Mingo County, West Virginia, the inborn tendencies of every man and women is for a better life. If it cannot be obtained by orderly procedure then it will be obtained by some other method."[41] To the railroad officials, not to mention the general public, rhetorical connections between the land of Bolshevism and places of recent US labor unrest could not have been more ominous.

Fearing the worst, Pennsylvania managers turned their attention to preserving order and protecting property. Shipments of weapons—repeating shotguns and Colt revolvers—went to Chicago and Fort Wayne, Indiana, and ensuring proper police presence became a major concern. The General Managers Association of Chicago warned that county sheriffs were likely to appoint strikers as deputies, "under the guise" of needing to police the radicals in their midst, but not give the same status to company guards. This potentially would allow the strikers to act with impunity. To maintain order and protect their property, railroads now planned to partner with the federal government to provide US Marshals, who in turn would deputize company guards. A US District Attorney promised to provide an ample number of federal officers to any railroad needing "immediate consideration and attention" to quell violence and vandalism. The Pennsylvania also got a temporary restraining order, which prohibited any interference with strikebreakers. These included immigrants, recruited through advertisements in several German-and Scandinavian-language papers.[42] The choice of organs indicated the railroad's desire to hire those nationalities, likely considering them to be congenial workers, as opposed to obstreperous eastern Europeans. Officials also would take steps to reform the latter.

Inauguration of an extensive assimilation campaign in the Northwestern Region, which included the volatile yards at Chicago and Fort Wayne, coincided with efforts to quell the shopmen's strike. Seeking to inculcate a socioeconomically conservative message, managers secured the help of Italian American Vincent Colelli to oversee the instruction of foreign-born workers. Colelli had authored *The American's Book*, a primer for would-be citizens. After opening with an epigraph from Daniel Webster, "'Thank God, I, too, am an American,'" he proceeded to make clear what message those words should convey to immigrant readers. Being an American meant more than casting an intelligent vote or defending the country in times of war, or if necessary even sacrificing one's life so that the nation might persevere; it also meant devotion to proper ideology. With the world tottering "under the numberless theories of 'isms' which aim at the destruction of our government" (to which railroad officials could well have added "our equally important industrial-capitalist system"), Colelli aimed to inspire every foreign-born American "to live up to those traditions" that had made the nation great. This necessitated rejection of any and all subversive creeds, coupled with strict adherence to "the spirit which has *safely guided* [italics added] this country at all times—the spirit of fair play, justice, and equality."[43] Application of these fundamental tenets, of course, depended on one's perspective.

Colelli used the words and deeds of America's forefathers to articulate a pro-business definition of patriotism and citizenship. The nation's history revealed how colonial inhabitants from various lands had established a tradition of individualism (as opposed to the collectivism of both trade unionists and socialists), specifically the "right to enjoy the reward of their own effort." Success stories among succeeding generations provided proof that pernicious isms had no place in the United States or among those who would call it home. "Theodore Roosevelt's Last Message to the American People Before He Died" made this clear. There could be no "sagging back" on Americanization, the twenty-sixth president stressed, now that the Great War had ended. The nation's enemies stood ready to promote foreign doctrines, which everyone should reject. Immigrants especially must be 100 percent American: "Any man who says he is an American but something else also, isn't an American at all." TR left little doubt as to the connotation of *something else*. "We have room for but one flag, the American flag," he insisted, "and this excludes the red flag, which symbolizes all wars against liberty, just as much as it excludes any foreign flag of a nation to which we are hostile." One could not be a good American if she or he embraced the ideas for which the red banner stood. Seeing this as the preeminent message that one could send to a foreign-born worker, Pennsylvania managers hoped to put a copy of Colelli's tome in the hands of every immigrant employee.[44]

Attaining citizenship, Pennsylvania officials believed, would also ingrain the correct beliefs. Some of the Railroad's regional-divisions previously had conducted successful "educational work," aimed at promoting naturalization among immigrant employees, and officials on the Northwestern Division now envisioned achieving similar benefits by "assisting foreign born to secure their papers or instructions in English etc." "This is a big question if developed fully," wrote vice president T. B. Hamilton of the proposed campaign, "but one I think we should get into." Becoming a citizen involved a two-step process, the immigrant's initial declaration of intent—taking out the so-called First Papers—and the application for naturalization filed after five years of residency. A canvas of the Northwest Division indicated that less than 50 percent of foreign-born employees had started the process, leading managers to conclude that the subject was not receiving the "active interest which we believe it merits." This lapse, in turn, retarded efforts at ideological indoctrination, the inculcation of conservative pro-business attitudes and precepts.[45]

To cultivate more enthusiasm for pursuing citizenship, managers implemented vertical teaming. Every supervisor would assist in interviewing employees and providing the foreign-born with information about how to file the requisite naturalization papers. The first step involved data collection, so as to determine the number of foreign-born employees, their citizenship status, their ability to read and write either English or their native language, their comprehension of English, and their enrollment in any educational programs. A "Naturalization and Education Record of Foreign Born Employees" card recorded this information for each individual, along with the worker's marital status and the location of the spouse and any children. It also indicated if the immigrant had served in the US military. Supervisors, after identifying those who had not yet begun the application process, were to stress the "advantages of becoming an American citizen" but also take care not to say or do anything "which can be construed as an attempt to coerce" a hesitant employee. Yet management did see naturalization as a key component in stilling worker unrest, and to maximize results, supervisors wanted to get a clear understanding of why some of the workers did not intend to become citizens.[46]

Completion of the naturalization process would lead to more indoctrination. Upon becoming a citizen, the Division Superintendent would present the worker with a congratulatory "felicitation" card. Wording continued the company's patriotic emphasis. Every card included William Tyler Page's "The American's Creed," a patriotic paean to the greatness of the United States. In 1916–1917, a contest sponsored by hereditary organizations and offering a one-thousand-dollar prize had solicited brief statements of the nation's political beliefs. Page, a descendant of President John Tyler and of one of the signers of Declaration of Independence, had submitted the winning entry. The Creed's first paragraph asserted the virtues of the United States, a democratic republic, "a sovereign nation comprised of several sovereign states, and a perfect union," established on the foundation of "freedom, equality, justice, and humanity for which American patriots sacrificed their lives and fortunes." The second paragraph was a single line that showed the spirit of the age: "I therefore believe it is my duty to my country to love it, to support its Constitution, to obey its laws, to respect its flag, and to defend it against all enemies." Certainly, its flag was not the "red" one, and supporters of that socialistic banner and its associated doctrines clearly were enemies of the United States.[47]

Naturalization award ceremonies served multiple purposes. Recipients received acclaim for their accomplishments, and being feted by supervisors encouraged other alien employees. Also, at a time when many Americans felt strongly about the need to assimilate immigrants, the award ceremonies garnered "valuable publicity for the Pennsylvania Railroad. . . ." K. D. Pulcipher, who edited the railroad's in-house *Pennsylvania News*, notified local media of upcoming presentations. When truckman Thomas B. Jones completed naturalization, the *Toledo Blade* publicized the festivities, calling them an Americanization party thrown by the railroad's "big bosses." Similar coverage by *Bloomfield's Labor Digest* attracted attention from officials at other railroads. The Santa Fe, which had been considering a similar program, but had not seen any indication "of the results accomplished in that direction," requested information about the Pennsylvania's procedures. Ironically, given the program's intent to create strong bonds between the immigrants and their new homeland, the only example of the felicitation card remaining among the Pennsylvania Railroad papers is for Julius C. Brant, an immigrant who took a furlough, returned to his European home, and never returned to the United States.[48]

Overall, however, positive results pleased corporate leaders. As of October 3, 1923, of 28,665 foreign-born employees, 20,949–73 percent—either had received citizenship or taken out first papers. Over five thousand had enrolled in English language or other courses, but unfortunately, there are no surviving texts that could reveal what, if any, was the ideological orientation of the language lessons. In the Northwestern Region, 513 foreign-born workers had applied for naturalization, and over one thousand had met with a supervisor to discuss the process. Some officials wondered if the results justified the financial costs, but their concerns were not enough to scuttle the project. "It does not seem to me from the information given in your letter" vice president E. T. Whiter replied to one skeptic, "that the actual savings by discontinuance of this work will justify its discontinuance." Senior management considered the outlays to be well worth the results, and as late as 1927, supervisors were compiling lists of recently nationalized employees who should receive a felicitation card.[49]

Pennsylvania officials also foresaw their assimilation practices as having gender benefits. General Manager Hamilton believed that Colelli's citizenship primer would address issues raised by the passage of the Nineteenth Amendment, which gave women the right to vote. Debate leading up to ratification had stressed the potential ramifications of adding foreign-born women to the electorate. Opponents had also linked women's suffrage with Bolshevism, condemning both as foreign and subversive. Other critics had contended that foreign-born women would lack the knowledge and insights necessary to cast informed votes. Now, with the Amendment's passage, Colelli's primer addressed how properly to accommodate the change. *The American's Book* would make proper conservative precepts clear to the Pennsylvania's largely male labor force, and their assimilation would extend to the immigrants' homes. Men would convey the correct tenets of citizenship and explain proper exercise of the franchise to their wives, daughters, and other female family members. Foreign-born women would learn the responsibilities that came with the new privilege and exercise it in an appropriately patriotic manner.[50]

Business leaders saw Americanization as a means of restoring workplace harmony. Through proper assimilation, the immigrant workers upon whom US companies had come to rely for their labor needs would develop loyalty to their employers. This would alleviate the contention that had dominated labor relations since the start of industrialization and reached its height during the postwar Red Scare. Yet even as officials at some of the country's largest businesses believed that they finally had found the key to curbing the presumptive immigrant radicalism, the nation was taking steps to eliminate the flow of virtually unlimited workers from Europe.

Bolshevism = Foreign

"Corporate Sponsored Americanism 195

CHAPTER 9

Restricting the Hordes

Implementation of Immigrant Quotas

"The big steamship lines, railroad companies, big employers of cheap labor and the larger owners of undeveloped land exercise such a powerful and deadening effect on legislation having for its purpose the restriction of immigration that nothing can be done by a few patriotic congressmen," asserted an angry correspondent to the *Morning Oregonian* in January 1920. Others shared his belief that the time had come to reduce significantly the numbers of immigrants annually entering the United States. Radical malcontents posed an obvious danger but so, too, did the hordes of ordinary foreigners who overcrowded American cities, leading to a host of economic problems and creating social decay. Under existing laws, the agitators could be expelled, but "why deport a few of the big fish and let in thousands of smaller ones?" The time had come to right this perceived wrong. If existing statutes did not provide sufficient means for reducing immigration, Congress and the president swiftly should enact new ones.[1] This would appease those who viewed current immigrants negatively, but what of those who welcomed the pool of unskilled labor?

During and after the Red Scare, 1919–1924, government officials took steps to address these issues, most notably with the enactment of new and more stringent restrictions. Their implementation would curtail employers' virtually unfettered access to immigrant labor, a benefit businesses had enjoyed since the onset of industrialization. Companies continued to want immigrant workers, but decades of associating foreigners with labor unrest had reached an apex. Fear of subversive aliens combined with nativism (the inherent dislike of foreigners) and progressivism (the amelioration of social problems allegedly caused by immigrant) to convince many Americans of the need for more extensive exclusion. Only through proactive diligence, contended the restrictionist ranks, could the immigrant danger be ameliorated. The pertinent question was not if the maleficence truly existed but rather how best to eliminate it. Dismissing employers' arguments to the contrary, lawmakers ultimately enacted sweeping new quota-based restrictions, significantly reducing European immigration. Their passage effectively ended an epic chapter of American business and labor history.

Government officials first looked to deportation as a solution to the postwar "immigration problem." Using the popular tempered-by-flame analogy, the *Literary Digest* captured removal's appeal. According to a 1919 editorial, most observers commended the "skimming of the great American melting-pot" as a means of making "America safe for Americans." A train from the West Coast carried fifty closely guarded aliens, "declared unfit to remain in the land of the free," to a date with expulsion. Deportation would eliminate these corrupting elements, while allowing others—the majority of the proverbial admixture—to make positive contributions to their new homeland. A few might see the offending provocateurs as laudatory agitators, in the same vein as George Washington and Patrick Henry, but theirs was a decidedly minority opinion. Yet, as the editors noted, other commentators did wonder if targeting allegedly dangerous aliens was an extreme reaction, one that threatened legitimate dissent or protest.[2]

Deportation reached it height under the direction of Attorney General A. Mitchell Palmer. In November 1919 and January 1920, he authorized the mass arrest of suspected alien radicals, intending their deportation under the 1917 and 1918 Immigration Acts (see chapter 7). In concert with the Department of Labor, Palmer first targeted the Union of Russian Workers, a national immigrant organization with some three thousand members. Its literature implored the working class "to abolish government" and "take possession by forcible social revolution of all the wealth of the world," but in reality, the Union was little more than a social club for Russian emigres. This did not deter Palmer and his subordinates, whose dragnets in New York City and elsewhere resulted in hundreds of arrests and the eventual deportation of 249 anarchists aboard the *Buford*, colloquially dubbed the "Red Ark." Raids conducted on January 2, centering on the Communist Party of America (CP) and the Communist Labor Party (CLP), led to the arrest and temporary detention of an additional three thousand immigrants. Characterizing the CLP as a "gang of cut-throat aliens," essentially of the same ilk as the "Bolsheviks" who comprised the CP, the FBI's J. Edgar Hoover left little doubt as to why the Justice Department had focused on these two groups.[3]

While commercial interests no doubt appreciated the efforts to remove dangerous aliens, several leading industrialists dismissed the effectiveness of the so-called Palmer Raids. Critics included Charles M. Schwab, president and principal owner of Bethlehem Steel, the nation's second largest steel company, known for its manufacture of armor and military ordnance. Given the dominance of Hungarian immigrants among the company's unskilled employees, Schwab appreciated the value of foreign-born workers and did not want to see them expelled from the labor pool. This came despite his personal experience with Hungarians' capacity for radicalism. Ten years earlier, during a bitter 1910 Bethlehem strike, recent arrivals had joined a walkout by skilled machinists. Violence first occurred on February 10, when striking Magyars reportedly resorted to physical force to keep foreign-born compatriots from going to work. Schwab heaped blame on outside agitators, who sought to advance a socialist agenda. Remaining obdurate, he refused to yield to the strikers' demands and eventually settled the dispute on his own unwavering terms.[4] Yet a decade later, he did not support the Attorney General's actions against the same type of alleged provocateurs.

Fearing negative repercussions, Schwab and other business leaders criticized the Palmer Raids and advocated for alternative approaches for dealing with immigrants. The steelmaker foresaw an end to the postwar recession, when "the great body of American business will emerge with a vigor and an energy the world has never known before." It would lead to full employment and higher wages, and also require the presence of immigrant labor. Arguing that "common sense of the people, capitalist and worker, will not permit anything that isn't good citizenship," Schwab dismissed the threat of Bolshevism as a bugbear. Lawmakers similarly needed to see beyond the hysteria. Fearing its influence on calls for new immigrant exclusions, he and fellow employers hoped to shift congressional focus toward the crafting of selective admission standards, emphasizing distribution and assimilation. Policies must welcome those whose presence would benefit economically both themselves and the United States, by giving them opportunities to pursue citizenship, employment, and education.[5]

Lukens Steel's Charles Huston championed Americanization as a beneficial alternative to new exclusions. He, too, dismissed the currently popular assertions of a connection between foreigners and radicalism (even though he previously had acknowledged the linkage as a danger; see chapter 8).

Proposals based on the purported threat were mere manifestations ". . . of our modern hysterical methods of leaping without much looking, and taking action that, with a little more foresight, would either not be taken or be considerably modified." Even a one-year moratorium, proposed as a compromise to either a two-year prohibition or quotas, would have serious consequences, thwarting commercial growth just as the recessed postwar economy was poised to recover. When Pennsylvania Representative Thomas S. Butler suggested that Huston himself would have voted for an admittedly imperfect restriction bill, Huston replied that Congress needed to replace the flawed bill with one that would serve the needs of business. He suggested creating a commission to examine all aspects of American immigration, including admission requirements and better distribution of those who were allowed to enter. Ironically, the Dillingham Commission (1907–1911) had recommended the increasingly popular quota system, after having conducted just such an investigation.[6] Regardless of its origins, it and other restrictionist schemes now drew the ire of Huston and other industrialists.

The National Association of Manufacturers (NAM) joined the opposition. Organized during the depression of 1895, originally to promote foreign trade, by 1920 the Association had become a prominent business-advocacy coalition. NAM advocated freedom of contract and opposed organized labor. Early leaders had disparaged certain ethnic groups, but NAM now stressed the assimilation of immigrant workers, "through teaching the American language and ideals." If necessary, Americanization could take place on "company time." Anticipating postwar demands for labor, NAM dismissed calls for more extensive immigrant exclusion as the product of "bigotry and selfishness." The latter likely referred to the AFL's long-standing support for limits on the entrance of foreign workers. "Not a moment should be lost," stated its 1920 Legislative Committee, "in launching the campaign in favor of restricting all immigration for at least two years." Thereafter, onset of high unemployment should trigger additional moratoriums, which would protect American workers from low-cost foreign competition.[7]

Conversely, NAM supported the formation of a "constructive policy of selective immigration," rather than an overall reduction in the number of foreigners coming to the United States. Disagreeing with Schwab, the Association saw radical aliens as a prevalent pestilence demanding immediate eradication. The United States needed to enact strict laws excluding anyone who opposed all forms of government or advocated violent revolution. Their interdiction would help to alleviate the "wide-spread social unrest which is destructive of individual happiness, unsettling to industry, and against the general welfare of all the people and which if continued threatens the very foundation of the nation itself. . . ." Yet, while in the Associate's opinion their danger could not be overlooked, these malcontents comprised a decided minority of the nation's immigrants, and the United States should continue to welcome the sturdy, hardworking majority.[8]

Immigration's critics saw even too many of these as a pernicious presence. Business leaders, editorialized the *Montgomery Advertiser,* had let avarice cloud their judgment: "The average American, however, who thinks mainly of good government and settled social conditions, sees the wisdom of cutting down the number of immigrants and improving the quality of those who are eligible to admission." A human tide of epic proportions, proclaimed "Ex Attache" writing for the *Baltimore American,* threatened to flood the United States unless lawmakers acted to keep it "under rigid control." At the very least, the nation needed to suspend immigration and use the respite to retool the enforcement of existing statutes. Rejecting the National Association of Manufacturers' differentiation between subversive and productive alien workers, restrictionists both emphasized the need to exclude alien radicals and called for an overall reduction of immigration. President-elect Warren G. Harding drew their praise for his previous support of more stringent exclusion and his efforts to override Woodrow Wilson's 1917 veto of the literacy test bill. Restrictionists now anticipated Harding's approval of any new legislation.[9]

Both sides looked to Congress to determine the scope of any additional statutes. During an April 1921 special session, Washington Representative Albert Johnson proposed limiting the number of immigrants from each country to 3 percent of their nationality as enumerated in the 1910 US Census. The temporary measure, to last for fourteen months, would cap immigration at 350,000 and allow the United States to exclude those "whom we can neither feed nor support nor assimilate." Unfettered immigration, Johnson insisted, contributed to the twin evils of radicalism and high unemployment. An ardent restrictionist since his election to Congress in 1912, he originally had wanted a total ban to stay in effect for two years, but he embraced the quota system introduced by Vermont Senator William P. Dillingham as a workable substitution, one he envisioned would garner broad-based support. Opposition to the bill, he insisted, came only from employers who wanted to have an unlimited supply of "the unintelligent" at their factory doors.[10]

Fellow representatives joined Johnson in vilifying selfish business interests. Ironically, critics equated the unmitigated thirst for labor with the importation of the very radicalism that employers decried. William N. Vaile of Colorado acknowledged the value of commercial productivity, but rhetorically questioned its cost when it came with a reliance on immigration:

"But, if increased production of goods could only be secured by reduction of Americanism, by lowering our standards of living . . . by changing the character of our race—then production is bought at too great a cost." High postwar unemployment contradicted employers' claims of a labor shortage. "On the contrary," Vaile contended, "there is a great and growing shortage of jobs." Lucian W. Parrish, from Texas, also stressed restriction's part in protecting the United States from "poisonous influences" emanating from Europe. To eliminate radical threats, the US government "must see to it that those who come here are loyal and true to our Nation, and impress upon them that it means something to have the privileges of American citizenship." South Carolinian William F. Stevenson, after incorrectly connecting native-born Eugene Debs to imported radicalism, praised the quota bill for its anticipated interdiction of foreign-born subversives. Others, such as Texan Thomas L Blanton, foresaw decreased immigration reducing unemployment and thereby alleviating labor's anger and frustration.[11]

Similar sentiments emanated from the Senate. There, too, the bill's supporters showed little sympathy for arguments pressing the need for immigrant labor. "I plead for the great army of wage earners of America," declared James T. Heflin of Alabama, "to protect and defend them against this horde of unfit foreigners who want to come here to take their places in our industrial establishments." Known for his animosity toward African Americans, Heflin now turned his vitriol toward foreigners, especially "red anarchists and bolsheviki. . . ." Congress needed to eradicate their ilk by promptly passing a proscriptive statute. Florida's Park Trammell, invoking images of idle US businesses that could not retain their present employees, wondered why the nation would want any more immigrants. "What service or what benefit will they be to America?" he asked rhetorically. Others questioned whether foreigners assimilated or retained their highest loyalty to another nation.[12]

Anti-restrictionists vainly tried to mount counter arguments. Meyer London, a Socialist Congressman representing New York City's immigrant-rich East Side, dismissed the bill's effectiveness in curbing domestic radicalism. Excluding foreigners was not the answer, as the origins of America's class conflicts emanated from within the nation. "Ideas can neither be shut in nor shut out," he contended, urging his colleagues to focus their attention on conditions closer to home. "There is only one way of contending with an idea, and that is the old and safe American rule of free and untrammeled discussion." This precept should apply to industrial disputes. Fellow New Yorker William B. Cockran focused on immigration's commercial benefits. Alien laborers were "essential to the production of commodities," and the United States needed their labor to engender a postwar economic recovery.

In the Senate, Missouri's James A. Reed, an ardent and particularly bigoted restrictionist when the exclusions would target Asians or Africans, now remonstrated against the proposed quotas. Immigrants, at least those from Europe, would help the United States increase its industrial output. While such orations reflected the views of powerful business interests, they failed to carry the day. Congress overwhelmingly passed the Emergency Quota Act, and on May 19, 1921, President Warren G. Harding signed it into law.[13]

Commercial spokesmen denounced the new restrictions. Dismissing currently high unemployment as a temporary ailment, business leaders cited the expected onset of postwar prosperity to make their case for immigration's value. "A certain class of worker," complained the New York *Journal of Commerce*, "is necessary to the progress of our industries, and the present immigration law has practically eliminated this class." Aliens, editorialized the *New York Herald*, did the work that underlay "the whole national structure of production and business." Aliens might swell the ranks of radical subversives, but this did not deter employers, including those on record as lambasting their disruptive presence, from wanting to hire foreigners. United States Steel Corporation, whose managers had blamed immigrants—as either seditious instigators or their easily seduced followers—for the company's recent labor problems, decried the paucity of common workers resulting from the recent restrictions. Representatives of the National Association of Manufacturers and the Chamber of Commerce joined the capitalist chorus calling for revision, if not repeal, of the 1921 Act.[14]

Largely deprived of new immigrant workers, companies searched for alternatives. The Chamber of Commerce queried businesses as to whether they were "finding difficulty in securing common labor?" Each company was asked to estimate its "probable shortage" for the coming year. The Chamber specifically inquired about the employment of southern and eastern Europeans, the groups most frequently targeted by restrictionists and affected by the quotas, and about the possibility of substituting workers from other ethnic groups, specifically African Americans and "Mexicans." The latter comprised both those who resided in the United States and those who lived south of the border. Because the Act of 1921 exempted western hemisphere immigrants from quotas and did not make them part of the outright exclusion imposed on most Asians, Mexicans were an available labor source. Their numbers had increased dramatically during the past decade, and in some industries, especially those in the Southwest, they already held key positions. African Americans, large numbers of whom had moved north as part of the Great Migration during the previous decade, also stood ready to fill any void caused by the absence of Europeans.[15]

African American newspapers optimistically envisioned the 1921 Quota Act leading to increased black employment. Assessing the anticipated effects, the Wichita *Negro Star* foresaw beneficial results: "The effect of this measure will be encouraging to the colored workers who hope to make permanent places in the industrial life of the nation." Blacks only recently had gained footholds in many occupations, concurred the *Topeka Plaindealer,* but increased exclusion of foreign laborers augured well for future improvements. Conversely, competition from immigration, "if permitted to continue as it has existed in past years, would tend to increase the influences which make the fight of Negro labor, for permanency of status, a difficult one." The *Plaindealer* advised African Americans to make the most of the conditions. Expected expansion of industrial employment for blacks led the editors of Chicago's *Broad Axe* to include immigration restriction on their list of prominent African American causes, along with such pressing matters as the passage of antilynching legislation.[16] Neither it nor economic gain would materialize quickly.

While black spokesmen may optimistically have anticipated increased hiring of African Americans, business leaders showed little enthusiasm for employing non-European workers. At Lukens Steel, for example, Charles Huston hesitated to hire nonwhites. Wartime collaboration with the Armstrong Association of Philadelphia, a social service organization dedicated to improving the lives of the city's African American residents, showed Huston's bias. In 1918, when hostilities limited immigration and defense needs increased demands for workers, the Association had urged Huston to hire blacks, many of whom had recently arrived from the South. Lukens had been considering "the necessity of employing a large number of negroes," and housing them in a segregated camp, "within our works enclosure, where our own police force can help keep order and where the men can be properly kept track of." The company did employ some African Americans, but to prevent problematic contact with white coworkers, it lodged them in company houses and required "police supervision there to keep them from being objectionable to their neighbors." Managers also accepted widely held cultural assumptions of African American brutality and licentiousness, dismissing as too "war-like" a plan for staging boxing matches and rejecting as too promiscuous the idea of holding dances. Yet the employees provided by Armstrong, along with a later contingent used as strikebreakers, reportedly did excellent work.[17]

Lukens continued to employ significant numbers of African Americans after the war, but the benefits implied by their prolonged presence did not change management's negative perceptions. Huston described recent African

American hires as being "absolutely unsatisfactory." Out of "their element in climatic conditions," "where social relations were strained," they had failed to take advantage of their employment opportunities. On payday, they purportedly would quit early, to spend their "fat" paychecks, and at other times "would leave their post of duty without warning"; on the night shift, they "could not be kept from lying down and going to sleep on the job." Following their dismissal, due to decreased need, foremen "were heartily glad to see them depart and never want to see them back again." Huston later qualified his statements, acknowledging that "a limited number of these colored men made good in their work, and proved to be dependable and satisfactory, but the great majority of them turn out as I described them, so that as a class the characterization I gave I feel is fully warranted by the facts." Still, in 1923 African Americans comprised 27 percent of the Lukens workforce, mainly in unskilled and semiskilled positions, possibly due to the absence of immigrant workers.[18]

Pennsylvania Railroad managers similarly dismissed African Americans as an alternative to European immigrants. In 1922, a year after implementation of the initial quotas, officials complained about having difficulty finding suitable common laborers, estimating a shortfall of 6,200 on the Northwest Division—stretching from Ohio to Chicago—during the coming year. Hiring problems occurred even in larger cities, such as Chicago and Toledo, Ohio. Much of the shortfall stemmed from the dearth of southern and eastern Europeans. In addition to being the ethnic groups most restricted by the quotas (excepting the completely excluded Asian laborers), they also were the company's most relied-upon source of workers. Seeking a remedy, some officials believed that they could use workers from different European groups, specifically northern and western Europeans, whom the Quota Act favored. But in reality, these groups no longer dominated the immigrant stream, and their numbers were not enough to meet the Railroad's needs, especially in manual or unskilled occupations. Some managers mentioned the possibility of using Mexicans or African Americans, but without much enthusiasm. Southern and eastern Europeans remained the preferred labor source.[19]

Some African Americans performed "common labor" in the Pennsylvania's Maintenance of Equipment [M. of E.] Department, in one case working with "some Syrians," but supervisors had doubts about expanding the range of jobs open to blacks. "We could not use negroes from the South, or from any other part of the Country for work in our M. of W. [Maintenance of Way] Department, or in freight warehouses," reported one official. Another agreed, saying, "This class of labor can be used [only in the] engine house; cinder pit and coal wharf." Given the menial nature of these jobs,

most managers apparently believed that other railroad jobs required apti-
tudes and skills beyond the African Americans' ken. Others simply rejected
the idea of their employment. Officials also doubted the efficacy of comin-
gling the so-called Negroes with white workers, fearing that it would lead to
racial strife. In many cases, some combination of these reasons likely influenced the reluctance of Pennsylvania managers to employ African American
labor. More certain was management's preference for hiring the now more-
restricted European immigrants to do manual and semiskilled work.[20]

The same held true in regard to Asians. Renewed animosity toward
their presence, especially on the West Coast, now centered on the Japanese.
Lothrop Stoddard, an advocate of white supremacy, proffered to speak for
agitated westerners: "Relatively insignificant in numbers, they see themselves
menaced by countless hordes of colored men threatening them with destruction of their living standards, with numerical submission, with social steril-
ization, and with ultimate racial extinction." White workers saw them as an
"evil" competition with which they could not contend. Californians objected
to their acquisition of large amounts of agricultural land. Although state
statute prohibited those ineligible for citizenship from owning real estate,
Japanese immigrants had found loopholes, sowing seeds of discontent. "The
Japanese," averred US Senator James D. Phelan, "by crowding out our population, produce disorder and Bolshevism among our own people, who properly
look to our Government to protect them against this destructive competition." New California legislation sought to eliminate the various landowning
schemes, and Phelan pressed the national government to do its part by adding
Japan to the Asian Zone from which immigrants were barred.[21]

Away from the emotionally charged West Coast, Lukens Steel's Huston
showed scant inclination to hire Japanese or other Asians, even as it became
harder to recruit European immigrants. His attitudes reveal a xenophobic
interrelationship between class and ethnicity, similar to his ideas about African Americans. "I do not believe that we want many Orientals, however," he
wrote to Pennsylvania Congressman Thomas S. Butler, "with their widely
different habits and their non-Christian religious practices and associations."
Huston's opposition to Asians could have been simply a ploy, or a means of
appeasement, showing support for one type of exclusion so as shift the focus
away from new exclusions targeting Europeans. Other sources, however,
show clearly his bigotry toward all but select Asian elites. In the early 1900s,
Huston had a close personal relationship with a counterpart at the Imperial Steel Works in Yawatamachi, Japan, with whom the American mogul
regularly exchanged gifts and family news. Huston lauded his friend's practice of Christianity, hoping that his son would grow to be "a good Christian

boy." Huston apparently found such westernized individuals to be acceptable associates but showed no such favor toward ordinary Japanese laborers. As the blanket prohibition against Japanese immigrants appeared to abrogate a gentlemen's agreement between the two nations, the US Chamber of Commerce opposed their exclusion. This could have given Huston an opportunity to support the use of Japanese workers, but he instead made clear his preference for white workers.[22]

Temporary quotas remained in place for three years until 1924, when Congress revised the formula and made them permanent. New provisions set national quotas at 2 percent of the number of a nationality residing in the United States as enumerated by the 1890 Census. After 1927, each group's quota would be proportional to the number of their "national origin" in the United States in 1920, as a percentage of the maximum of 150,000 immigrants from all nationalities combined. Restrictionists carefully crafted the law so as to give preference to "old immigrants," those from northern and western Europe, and continue the exclusion of Asians. The time had come, concluded bill supporter Fred N. Vinson, newly elected Congressman from Kentucky, to save America from certain doom, by barring the "untold millions from the orient and the undesirable from the eastern and southern portions of Europe." It exempted western hemisphere immigrants, opening the door to a potential increase in Mexican immigration, whose numbers did climb during the following decade.[23]

Business interests made a final effort to retain their access to traditional immigrant workers. Connecticut Congressman Patrick B. O'Sullivan presented a list of sixty groups opposing the bill. Signatories included the National Association of Manufacturers of the United States of America, the Railway Car Manufacturers' Association, the National Boot and Shoe Manufacturers of the United States, and numerous state organizations. Speaking on their behalf, O'Sullivan accepted the need for some restriction, the prudent exclusion of objectionable women and men, but decried the Johnson Bill's new quotas. He condemned proposed legislation, along with any measure that would either discriminate against some groups or deprive the United States of needed labor. Immigrants, he asserted, added to the nation's prosperity. As to the threats posed by domestic radicalism, virtually all of its "great leaders" came "from old time stock," while few were "the product of the newer immigration."[24]

Others presented more tailored opposition. Senator Walter E. Edge presented a petition from the New Jersey State Legislature objecting to the Johnson Bill's desultory effects on Italian immigration. Petitioners portrayed the Italians as industrious and thrifty people who had distinguished themselves as construction workers, notably on railroads and public projects. Without their contributions, "the greatness of this country would have been impossible." Georgia Senator William J. Harris presented a similar missive on behalf of the Albany, Georgia, Chamber of Commerce. Wanting to populate productive regions of the state, the Chamber requested "the admission of certain selected desirable agricultural immigrants without regard to the prescribed national quotas." With safeguards, the United States could absorb all of those who wanted to come from the Netherlands, Scandinavian, and other not named but presumably northern European countries. The Chamber did not seem to know the bill's particulars, as the nationalities it wanted to attract had quotas that exceeded the numbers of their current arrivals.[25]

Speaking for the other side, Congressman John C. Box from Texas presented a list of those for and against the enhanced quotas similar to that cited by Congressman O'Sullivan, but made contradictory assertions. Opposing signatories far outnumbered supporters, but the patriotic and labor organizations that comprised the latter offered more convincing arguments. Their judgments, not those of foreign-born groups, should hold sway. "The men of the American Legion turned the tide in one great life-and-death struggle," Box contended, alluding to the Great War. Members now correctly saw the same urgency in the fight for immigration restriction. "Let us now hope," he continued, combining patriotism with xenophobia to endorse the Legion's position, "that the Sons of Italy will not get the best of this momentous struggle." As to manufacturers' opposition to virtually any prohibition that might reduce their access to workers, their representatives had made clear their purpose: "the desire for labor in such abundance as to make it cheap is the main motive for their efforts."[26]

Other congressmen and petitioners concurred. Georgia's Harris, prior to presenting the Albany Chamber's resolution, also introduced an American Legion resolution supporting more exclusive restrictions, so as to eliminate subversives. Those who failed to appreciate American social standards, or maliciously intended "to undermine or destroy by propaganda or direct action our institutions and government," should be denied entrance. In Long Beach, California, the Brotherhood of Carpenters carried the antiradical motif further. "Soviet and other foreign propaganda of a radical nature," emanating from "foreign sources and here fostered by aliens," threatened the United States. More immigrants would only exacerbate the danger. Bill supporters also objected to the entry of Mexicans, on the grounds that they displaced American workers. As the Johnson-Reed Bill would not affect these laborers, it is not clear if the spokesmen were misinformed about its provisions or wanted to add western hemisphere quotas.[27]

On May 26, President Calvin Coolidge signed the Johnson-Reed Act into law. Although he objected strongly to the exclusion of Japanese, part of the larger ban on Asian laborers, he approved of the bill's overall intent. In signing it, Coolidge asserted "the imperative need of the country for legislation of this general character." The temporary quota act would expire on June 30, necessitating a replacement. "It is of great importance," he continued, "that a comprehensive measure should take its place. . . ." Massachusetts Senator Henry Cabot Lodge, a restrictionist leader since the 1890s, called the new act "a very great measure, one of the most important if not the most important, that Congress has ever passed. It reaches far into the future." Of that, there was no doubt. Passage of the Johnson-Reed Act effectively ended the great era of European immigration.[28]

Continuance of the Pennsylvania Railroad's Americanization ceremonies into the late 1920s offered a fitting epilogue. After decades of relying on overseas immigrants to meet their labor demands, US employers now faced the reality of their significantly reduced numbers. New ways and means— be they different sources of workers or less labor-intense production—now would have to suffice. Even as European immigration became a part of the historical past, managers and supervisors retained their aversion to radical and subversive ideologies, which they tied to immigrant workers. This predisposition ultimately had proved to be inimical to their larger interests. Determination to purge "un-American" proclivities in the form of radical immigrants contributed significantly to the passage of the legislation that effectively ended seventy years of large-scale European immigration.

Epilogue

Closing America's proverbial gates to the influx of European and Asian laborers ended the decades-long era when industrialization and immigration had combined to transform the United States. Big business had come to dominate the American economy, and millions of working-class foreigners had extensively increased its ethnic diversity. Their nexus created numerous benefits, yet it also engendered a host of socioeconomic maladies.

Industrial America's immigration mythology emphasized a positive welcome to a land of opportunity. In her poetic testament, Emma Lazarus identified the United States as a refuge for the world's oppressed, a sanctuary to its "huddled masses." The Statue of Liberty, to whose pedestal Lazarus's verse was affixed in 1903, symbolized the country's purported offer of a warm reception. With her lamp serving as a beacon to "the homeless, tempest-tossed," Liberty appeared to convey the prospect of a new beginning in a land synonymous with freedom, populated by men and women inexorably committed to the exercise of their unalienable rights.[1] Yet, during the decades between 1865 and 1924, immigrants' actual welcome frequently showed the antithesis of both Lazarus's famed sonnet and the statute's iconic mystique.

This divergence stemmed largely from the realities of industrial America. The gulf between the haves and the have-nots, identified by political economist Henry George in his best-selling social critique as the incongruence between "poverty and progress," gave meaning to the Gilded Age and set the stage for the reform mentality that characterized the Progressive Era. George was not alone in his observations and assessments. Author Matthew Hale Smith juxtaposed "sunshine and shadow" to portray late-1860s New York City, the hub of America's commercial ascension, as a place of coincident affluence and want. Emergence of the large and static working classes challenged the veracity of upward mobility, the idea that any American could rise from relative rages to riches. Many came to doubt that the axiom applied to industrial laborers, especially those employed by America's great corporations. Focusing on the residents of New York's tenements, author-photographer Jacob Riis spoke for myriad fellow observers when he portrayed the impoverished as recently arrived immigrants and designated them as the "other half."[2]

These "strangers in the land," whose labor built America's industrial colossus, certainly understood this socioeconomic dichotomy, and they also recognized the decided intolerance for those who would challenge the underlying capitalist system. "When, in the year 1872 I left Germany. . . ," Haymarket defendant George Engel told the court that would sentence him to die, "I concluded to fare with my family to the land of America, the land that had been praised to me by so many as the land of liberty." Upon arrival his heart had swelled with the thought that he would "live among free men, and in a free country." This had not proven to be the case. Engel chided the United States for purporting to offer political freedom to men who suffered from want and starvation: "I came to the opinion that as long as working-men are economically enslaved they cannot be politically free." Engels then voiced an even greater affront to liberty, intolerance of suspect ideals: "Nor do I deny, that I too, have spoken at meetings, saying that, if every working man had a bomb in his pocket, capitalistic rule would soon come to an end. That is my opinion, and my wish; it became my conviction, when I mentioned the wickedness of the capitalistic conditions of the day." Expression of these ideals, as much as any actual involvement in the bombing, would send him and most of his fellow defendants to the gallows.[3]

The tragedy of 1886, or 1892, or 1919–1920, was not necessarily the failure of socialism or anarchism to wage a successful revolution against American capitalism. Indeed, whether the doctrines advocated by working-class radicals would have made the United States a better nation invites speculation that exceeds the realm of historical analysis. Given the injustices of the time, socialism or anarchism may well have created a fair and equitable America, at least for its extensively immigrant working class. They frequently did live and labor under horrible conditions, while business elites lived in the proverbial lap of luxury. Conversely, radical isms may have been sirens' calls, sounding wonderful messages that held only false promise. Implementation may well have led only to rack and ruin. Moreover, industrial capitalism did provide the foundation for the material largesse of the later twentieth century, when the scions of earlier immigrant workers became a people of plenty, part of America's heralded middle class. Would adherence to socialism or another radical alternative of industrial capitalism have made their lives even better, or at least allowed earlier a more equal distribution of America's collective wealth? The repression of their advocates means that we never will know.

History can conclude how and why industrial-era Americans betrayed their most fundamental values. While they welcomed the arrival of immigrant workers who would transform the United States into a commercial giant and produce unparalleled economic gain, they stifled those who demanded radical alterations to the capitalist system in which they toiled, dismissing their alternative doctrines as un-American. Instead of allowing debate and considering the legitimacy of the workers' grievances, they branded their beliefs and behaviors as subversive, and identified their origins as inherently foreign, as having no place in and being inimical to the essence of the United States. The land of liberty did not hesitate to place limits on working-class dissent, by effectively making it foreign. Here, may the lessons of history show, was true un-Americanism.

NOTES

Introduction: Capitalists and Immigrants in Historical Perspective, 1865–1924

1. Alfred D. Chandler, *The Visible Hand* (Cambridge: Harvard University Press, 1977), 1; Richard F. Bensel, *The Political Economy of American Industrialization, 1877–1900* (New York: Cambridge University Press, 2000), 207–16; Nell Irvin Painter, *Standing at Armageddon: The United States, 1877–1919* (New York: W. W. Norton, 1978); Gabriel Kolko, *The Triumph of Conservatism: A Reinterpretation of American History, 1900–1916* (New York: Free Press, 1963); John A. Garraty, *The New Commonwealth, 1877–1900* (New York: Harper & Row, 1968).

2. Painter, *Standing;* John A. Fitch, *The Causes of Industrial Unrest* (New York: Harper and Brothers, 1924); Louis Adamic, *Dynamite: The Story of Class Violence in America* (New York: Viking Press, 1931); Gwendolyn Mink, *Old Labor and New Immigrants in American Political Development* (Ithaca: Cornell University Press, 1986).

3. Adamic, *Dynamite,* 4; John Higham, *Strangers in the Land: Patterns of American Nativism, 1860–1925* (New York: Atheneum, 1978), 4. Higham's nativist interpretation has dominated the historical field. He does acknowledge the extent to which Americans denoted class conflict as "an un-American product of foreign agitators" (30), but his thesis stresses nativism. Works that build on his primarily sociocultural or "racial" explication include: David R. Roediger, *Working toward Whiteness: How America's Immigrants Became White* (New York: Basic Books, 2005); Andrew Gyory, *Closing the Gates: Race, Politics, and the Chinese Exclusion Act* (Chapel Hill: University of North Carolina Press, 1998); Matthew Frye Jacobson, *Whiteness of a Different Color: European Immigrants and the Alchemy of Race* (Cambridge: Harvard University Press, 1998); Jeanne E. Petit, *The Men and Women We Want: Gender, Race, and the Progressive Era Literacy Test Debate* (Rochester: University of Rochester Press, 2010).

4. Chandler, *Visible Hand,* 1; Matthew Josephson, *The Robber Barons: The Great American Capitalists, 1861–1901* (New York: Harcourt, Brace, 1934), vii–viii; Leon Fink, *The Long Gilded Age: American Capitalism and the Lessons of a New World Order* (Philadelphia: University of Pennsylvania Press, 2015), passim; Edward Morris, *Wall Streeters: The Creators and Corrupters of American Finance* (New York: Columbia Business School Publishing, 2015), 1–62; Morton Keller, *Affairs of State: Public Life in Late Nineteenth Century America* (Cambridge: Harvard University Press, 1977), 405–7.

5. Milton Derber, "The Idea of Industrial Democracy," *Labor History* 7 (September 1966): 259–86; New Jersey *Trenton Evening Times,* August 22, 1916; [Editors], "Industrial and Commercial Barons Determined to Flood United States With Chinese Laborers," *Brotherhood of Locomotive Firemen and Engineers Magazine* 64 (March 1918): 5–6; Gregorio and Eastman, both quoted in Steve Golin, "Defeat Becomes Disaster:

The Paterson Strike of 1913 and the Decline of the IWW," *Labor History* 24 (Spring 1983): 232 and 242; Louis Galambos, "AFL's Concept of Big Business: A Quantitative Study of Attitudes toward Large Corporations, 1894–1931," *Journal of American History* 57 (March 1971): 847–63. Fink makes a case for the so-called barons' complexity, but fails to undermine the basic premise of their persistent and unapologetic wielding of socioeconomic power; see *Long Gilded Age*, 38–62.

6. Kenneth Warren, *Triumphant Capitalism: Henry Clay Frick and the Industrialization of America* (Pittsburgh: University of Pittsburgh Press, 1996), 5–7; Naomi R. Lamoreaux, *The Great Merger Movement in American Business, 1895–1904* (Cambridge, UK: Cambridge University Press, 1985), 1–46; Elizabeth Esch and David Roediger, "One Symptom of Originality: Race and Management of Labor in the United States," *Historical Materialism* 17 (2009): 1–41; Thomas C. Cochran, "The Business Revolution," *American Historical Review* 79 (December 1974): 1449–66; Richard White, *Railroaded: The Transcontinentals and the Making of Modern America* (New York: W. W. Norton, 2011), xxv; Robert Wiebe, *Businessmen and Reform: A Study of the Progressive Movement* (Cambridge: Harvard University Press, 1962), 10–15; Painter, *Standing*, 75. For an interpretation that dismisses the idea of robber baron as "simplistic" and misleading, and thus gets "in the way of understanding what was going on," see Maury Klein, *The Life and Legend of Jay Gould* (Baltimore: Johns Hopkins University Press, 1986), 495–97 and passim.

7. United States Strike Commission, *Report of the Chicago Strike of June–July 1894, by the United States Strike Commission*, 53rd Cong., 3rd sess., Ex. Doc. 7 (Washington: Government Printing Office, 1895), George M. Pullman Testimony, p. 556; Parry quoted in Albion G. Taylor, *Labor Policies of the National Association of Manufacturers* (Urbana: University of Illinois Press, 1927; reprint, New York: Arno Press, 1973), 37–38; Pope quoted in Wiebe, *Businessmen*, 190; Walter Licht, *Working for the Railroad: The Organization of Work in the Nineteenth Century* (Princeton: Princeton University Press, 1983), 79–124.

8. [Marcus Hanna], *Mark Hanna, His Book* (Boston: Chapple Publishing Company, 1904), 40; "Mr. Pullman's Statement" to the New York *Tribune*, July 14, 1894, in [George M. Pullman], *The Strike at Pullman* [privately printed, ca. 1894], 36–37; Andrew Carnegie, *Problems of Today* (reprint, Garden City: Doubleday, Doran, 1933), 43.

9. Kirby quoted in Taylor, *National Association*, 126–27; Andrew Carnegie, *Triumphant Democracy; or Fifty Years' March of the Republic* (New York: Charles Scribner's Sons, 1886; reprint, New York: Johnson Reprint Corp., 1971), 348. My language regarding immigrant "militancy" draws on Donna R. Gabaccia, *Militants and Migrants: Rural Sicilians Become American Workers* (New Brunswick, NJ: Rutgers University Press, 1988).

10. John R. Commons, *Races and Immigrants in America* (New York: Macmillan, 1907), 61–64, quoted 63; Henry P. Fairchild, *Immigration: A World Movement and Its American Significance* (New York: Macmillan, 1913), 123–24 and 144–62; Richmond Mayo-Smith, *Emigration and Immigration: A Study in Social Science* (New York: Charles Scriber's Sons, 1890), 95; Thomas G. Andrews, *Killing for Coal: America's Deadliest Labor War* (Cambridge: Harvard University Press, 2008), 117–20.

11. [Editor], "Immigration," *Locomotive Firemen's Magazine* 22 (April 1897): 221–22; W. R. Jones to E. V. McCandless, February 25, 1875, in James H. Bridge, *The Inside History of Carnegie Steel Company: A Romance of Millions* (New York: Aldine Book,

1903), 81; Commons, *Races*, 107–8, 112–13, and 156; Esch and Roediger, "Race and Management"; Foster Rhea Dullas, *Labor in America: A History* (New York: Thomas Y. Crowell, 1949), 78–79, 88, and 97–99; David Roediger and Philip Foner, *Our Own Time: A History of Labor and the Working Day* (New York: Greenwood Press, 1989), 124–25; Garraty, *New Commonwealth*, 148–49; Victoria Hattam, *Labor Visions and State Power: Origins of Business Unionism in the United States* (Princeton: Princeton University Press, 1993), 22–23.

12. *Reports of the Immigration Commission*, vol. 1, *Abstracts of Reports of the Immigration Commission, with Conclusions and Recommendations and Views of the Minority* (Washington, DC: Government Printing Office, 1911), 25; [Nelson A. Miles], "The Lessons of the Recent Strikes," *North American Review* 159 (August 1894): 184; Henry P. Fairchild, "Immigration and Crisis," *American Economic Review* 1 (December 1911): 753; Commons, *Races*, 63; Renqiu Yu, *To Save China, to Save Ourselves: The Chinese Hand Laundry Alliance of New York* (Philadelphia: Temple University Press, 1992), 19.

13. For general background on the immigrant experience, this study relies heavily on Leonard Dinnerstein, Roger Nichols, and David Reimers, *Natives and Strangers: A History of Ethnic Americans*, 5th ed. (New York: Oxford University Press, 2010); Roger Daniels, *Coming to America: A History of Immigration and Ethnicity in American Life* (New York: HarperCollins, 1990); and Alan M. Kraut, *The Huddled Masses: The Immigrant in American Society, 1880–1921* (Arlington Heights, IL: Harlan-Davidson, 1982). *Reports of the Immigration Commission*, vol. 5, *Dictionary of Races and Peoples* (Washington, DC: Government Printing Office, 1911), passim, provides an example of how contemporaries used *race* to designate immigrant groups.

14. Melvyn Dubofsky, *Industrialism and the American Worker, 1865–1920* (Arlington Heights, IL: Harlan Davidson, Inc., 1985), 1–5; Garraty, *New Commonwealth*, 128–78; Terence Powderly, "The Army of the Discontented," *North American Review* 140 (April 1885): 369–77; *The Nation* 4 (June 27, 1867): 519. John Higham, for example, emphasized common attitudes between organized labor and capital regarding immigrants by 1900, but organized workers comprised less then 10 percent of the labor force; see Higham, *Strangers*, 69, and Joseph B. Bishop, "President Roosevelt's First Year," *International Quarterly* 6 (December 1902): 450–62.

15. Gompers quoted in Roediger and Foner, *Own Time*, 180; Melvyn Dubofsky, "The 'New' Labor History: Achievements and Failures," *Reviews in American History* 5 (June 1977): 249–54; H. M. Gidelman, "Perspectives on American Industrial Violence," *Business History Review* 47 (Spring 1973): 1–23; James Livingston, "The Social Analysis of Economic History and Theory," *American Historical Review* 92 (February 1987): 69–96; Tom Goyens, *Beer and Revolution: The German Anarchist Movement in New York City, 1880–1914* (Urbana: University of Illinois Press, 2007).

16. Tyler Stovall, "White Freedom and the Lady of Liberty," *American Historical Review* 123 (February 2018): 20–21; Hasia Diner, "The Encounter between Jews and America in the Gilded Age and Progressive Era," *Journal of the Gilded Era and Progressive Era* 11 (January 2012): 2–25; John Higham, *Send These to Me: Immigrants in Urban America* (Baltimore: Johns Hopkins University Press, revised ed., 1984), 71–80. Diner notes that upward mobility, into the ranks of business owners, was not uncommon among Jewish immigrants, but even of these, most began as low-wage workers; see 17–18.

17. J. W. C. Pennington, "The Position and Duties of the Colored People," in Donald Yacovone, ed., *Freedom's Journey: African American Voices of the Civil War*

(Chicago: Lawrence Hill Books, 2004), 76–89, quoted 81; [Editors], "The Crime of Competition," *Railroad Trainmen's Journal* 15 (November 1898): 917–22, quoted 917; Eric Arnesen, " 'Like Banquo's Ghost, It Will Not Down': The Race Question and the American Railroad Brotherhoods," *American Historical Review* 99 (December 1994): 1601–34; Thomas C. Holt, *Children of Fire: A History of African Americans* (New York: Hill and Wang, 2010), 185–202; Eric Foner, *Reconstruction: America's Unfinished Revolution, 1863–1877* (New York: Harper & Row, 1988), 479–90; Licht, *Working*, 67–69, 221–25, and 297–305.

18. Diane C. Vecchio, *Merchants, Midwives, and Laboring Women: Italian Migrants in Urban America* (Urbana: University of Illinois Press, 2006), passim; Susan Levine, *Labor's True Woman: Carpet Weavers, Industrialization, and Labor Reform in the Gilded Age* (Philadelphia: Temple University Press, 1984), passim; William H. Carwardine, *The Pullman Strike*, 4th ed. (Chicago: Charles H. Kerr, 1894), 86; Helen C. Camp, *Iron in Her Soul: Elizabeth Gurley Flynn and the American Left* (Pullman: Washington State University Press, 1995), passim; Frankel Oz, "Whatever Happened to 'Red Emma'? Emma Goldman, From Alien Radical to American Icon," *Journal of American History* 83 (December 1996): 903–5; Stovall, "Lady," 7.

19. Bensel, *Political Economy*, passim.

20. General Plan of Safety & Welfare Work at Bethlehem Steel Company, October 26, 1913, Bethlehem Steel Corporation Papers, Hagley Library, Wilmington, Delaware. Other parts of the collection deal almost exclusively with corporate organization and financial matters.

21. Joseph Wall discusses this issue regarding the study of Andrew Carnegie, in *Andrew Carnegie* (New York: Oxford University Press, 1970), 379.

22. For a discussion of newspaper subjectivity, see White, *Railroaded*, 98.

23. My conceptual framework borrows from that developed by William Cronon; see *Nature's Metropolis: Chicago and the Great West* (New York: W. W. Norton, 1991), 223.

1. Harmonic Dissidence: Immigrants and the Onset of Industrial Strife

1. Wendell Phillips, "The Outlook," *North American Review* 127 (July–August 1878): 110–11; James B. Stewart, *Wendell Phillips: Liberty's Hero* (Baton Rogue: Louisiana State University Press, 1986), 210–11, 291–92, and 297; quoted 292. It is notable that Phillips used other *Review* columns to praise violent European radicals; see Stewart, 322.

2. Charlotte Erickson, *American Industry and the European Immigrant, 1860–1885* (New York: Russell & Russell, 1957), passim; Daniels, *Coming to America*, 121–84; Marcus L. Hansen, *The Atlantic Migration* (Cambridge: Harvard University Press, 1940. reprint ed. New York: Harper & Row, 1961), 280–88; Eric Foner, *Reconstruction*, 419–20; Walter D. Kamphoefner, "Immigrant Epistolary and Epistemology: On the Motivators and Mentality of Nineteenth-Century German Immigrants," *Journal of American Ethnic History* 28 (Spring 2009): 34–54; David Montgomery, *Beyond Equality: Labor and the Radical Republicans, 1862–1872* (New York: Alfred A. Knopf, 1967), 35.

3. Washington, DC *The National Era*, September 21, 1854; *Boston Recorder*, December 28, 1854; *New York Mirror* reprinted in the *Boston Evening Transcript*, January 11, 1854; R. B. Hayes to S. Birchard, October 13, 1854, in Charles Richard Williams, ed.,

The Diary and Letters of Rutherford B. Hayes (Columbus: Ohio State Archeological and Historical Society, 1922; digital ed., http://apps.ohiohistory.org/hayes/), 470; Ray Allen Billington, *The Protestant Crusade, 1800–1860* (New York: Macmillan, 1938), passim; Tyler Anbinder, *Nativism and Slavery: The Northern Know Nothings and the Politics of the 1850s* (New York: Oxford University Press, 1990), passim; Sean Wilentz, *The Rise of American Democracy: Jefferson to Lincoln* (New York: W. W. Norton, 2005), 679–96; Michael F. Holt, *The Rise and Fall of the American Whig Party: Jacksonian Politics and the Onset of the Civil War* (New York: Oxford University Press, 1999), 845–57, 912–19, and 949–60. Holt and Anbinder disagree on class support for the Know Nothing movement, but it clearly was pre-industrial; see Holt, *Rise and Fall*, 1147–48n14. Anbinder notes that in New York City, a center to Irish immigration, working-class violence did not fit well into either class or ethnic-based explications, but is better described as working-class men ever ready to resort to fisticuffs; see Anbinder, *Five Points: The 19th-Century New York City Neighborhood that Invented Tap Dance, Stole Elections, and Became the World's Most Notorious Slum* (New York: Free Press, 2001), 180–81, 290–91, and passim.

4. Holt, *Rise and Fall*, 83, 188, 190–91, and 203–6; Eric Foner, *Free Soil, Free Labor, Free Men: The Ideology of the Republican Party before the Civil War* (New York: Oxford University Press, 1970), 33–34 and 227–37; Alexander Saxton, *The Rise and Fall of the White Republic: Class, Politics, and Mass Culture in Nineteenth Century America* (London: Verso, 1990), 71–72; Kerby A. Miller, *Emigrants and Exiles: Ireland and the Irish Exodus to North America* (New York: Oxford University Press, 1985), 264–70, 316–20, and 323.

5. Edmund Frye to Zebina Eastman, March 14, 1852, Zebina Eastman Papers, Chicago Historical Museum, Chicago, Illinois; B. F. Johnson to W. H. Osborn, July 21, 1855, Illinois Central Railroad Collection, The Newberry Library, Chicago, Illinois; Pennsylvania Railroad Company Memorandum, February 20, 1855, Pennsylvania Railroad Company Archives, Hagley Library, Wilmington, Delaware; Paul W. Gates, *The Illinois Central Railroad and Its Colonization Work* (Cambridge: Harvard University Press, 1934), 94–98 and 149–238; Theodore Belgen, "The Competition of the Northwestern States for Immigrants," *Wisconsin Magazine of History* 3 (September 1919): 1–11; Albert Fishlow, *American Railroads and the Transformation of the Antebellum Economy* (Cambridge: Harvard University Press, 1965), 200–4.

6. Henry C. Carey, *Principles of Political Economy* (Philadelphia: Carey, Lea & Blanchard, 1837; reprint ed., New York: Augustus M. Kelley, 1965), 1:8–10; *Principles of Social Science* (Philadelphia: J. B. Lippincott, 3 vols., 1856–1858), 3: 247; *The Harmony of Interests: Agricultural, Manufacturing & Commercial* (Philadelphia: J. S. Skinner, 1851; reprint ed., New York: Augustus M. Kelly, 1967), 19–20, 28, 121, and 130.

7. Carey to Schuyler Colfax, January 2, 1865, and January 16, 1865, in [Henry C. Carey], *Miscellaneous Works of Henry C. Carey* (Philadelphia: Henry Carey Baird, 1868), 2:7 and 39; Eric Foner, *Reconstruction, 1863–1877* (New York: Harper and Row, 1988), 299–300; Willard H. Smith, *Schuyler Colfax: The Changing Fortunes of a Political Idol* (Indianapolis: Indiana Historical Bureau, 1952), 204, 240–42, and 307.

8. Henry Ward Beecher to Thomas H. Dudley, February 13, 1865, Henry Bates to Dudley, June 20, 1864, and John Williams to Dudley, February 18, 1865, Dudley Collection, Huntington Library, Pasadena, California; Clifford E. Clark Jr., *Henry Ward Beecher: Spokesman for a Middle-Class America* (Urbana: University of Illinois Press, 1978), passim; John R. Commons et al., eds., *A Documentary History of American*

Industrial Society (Cleveland: Arthur H. Clark Company, 1910), 9:74–80; Philip M. Katz, "'Lessons From Paris': The American Clergy Responds to the Paris Commune," *Church History* 68 (September 1994): 393–406.

9. John Williams to Thomas Haines Dudley, September 24, 1864, March 25, 1865, and September 29, 1864, Dudley Collection; Commons, *Documentary History*, 74–80; Erickson, *American Industry*, 7–31.

10. John Williams to Thomas Haines Dudley, September 24, 1864, and March 25, 1865, Henry C. Carey to Dudley, September 22, 1864, C. H. Marshall to [Dudley], August 30, 1864, and Henry Bates to Dudley, June 20, 1864, Dudley Collection; Montgomery, *Beyond*, 21–25.

11. "Letter IV" in Francis Lieber, *The Stranger in America* (Philadelphia: Carey, Lea, and Blanchard, 1835), 59–90; Peter W. Becker, "Prologue: Lieber's Place in History," in Charles R. Mack and Henry H. Lesesne, ed., *Francis Lieber and the Culture of the Mind* (Columbia: University of South Carolina Press, 2005), 1–7; Paul Finkelman, "Lieber, Slavery, and Free Thought in Antebellum South Carolina," ibid., 11–22; Bradley C. S. Watson, "Who Was Francis Lieber?" *Modern Age* 42 (2001): 304–10; John R. Vile, "Francis Lieber and the Process of Constitutional Amendment," *Review of Politics* 60 (1998): 525–43.

12. Francis Lieber, "Proposal of a Constitution for an Association to Promote German Immigration," Francis Lieber Collection, Huntington Library, Pasadena, California. Lieber's references to Germans obviously refers to Germanic-speaking peoples, as a untied Germany did not yet exist.

13. Lieber, "Proposal"; William B. West, Vice Consul in Dublin, to Dudley, August 11, 1863, and Thomas Mathison to Dudley, May 30, 1864, Dudley Collection; Lecture by J. W. C. Pennington, August 24, 1863, in Yacovone, *Freedmen's Journey*, 79; James McPherson, *Battle Cry of Freedom, The Civil War Era* (New York: Oxford University Press, 1988), 600–1; Iver Bernstein, *The New York City Draft Riots: Their Significance for American Society and Politics in the Age of the Civil War* (New York: Oxford University Press, 1990), 186–87 and passim.

14. *New York Times*, August 19, 1865; Hamilton Fish to Francis Lieber, April 5, 1869, Lieber Collection; Fish quoted in Marlene J. Mayo, "A Catechism of Western Diplomacy: The Japanese and Hamilton Fish, 1872," *Journal of Asian Studies* 26 (May 1967): 396; National Immigration Convention to the Pennsylvania Railroad Company, April 18, 1871, Board Meeting Minutes, May 24, 1871, and Henry W. Gwinner to the National Immigration Convention, April 28, 1871, Pennsylvania Railroad Archives; Wisconsin *Milwaukee Sentinel*, December 16, 1870; South Dakota *Yankton Press*, January 11, 1871; Montgomery, *Beyond*, 73–74.

15. Gilead A. Smith to Eastman, February 22, 1869, Eastman Papers; Blegen, "Competition," 11–29; Christina A. Ziegler-McPherson, *Selling America: Immigrant Promotion and the Settlement of the American Continent, 1607–1914* (Santa Barbara: Praeger, 2017): 73–132. Unfortunately, existing manuscripts do not reveal the extent of the Eastman-Burritt endeavors. It is not known if they every got beyond the discussion stage.

16. *The Nation* 4 (June 27, 1867): 518; Board of Immigration of Virginia to the People of Scotland, England, and Wales, April 20, 1866, Board of Immigration Collection, Albert and Shirley Small Special Collections Library, University of Virginia, Charlottesville, Virginia; Richmond, Virginia, *Whig*, April 5, 1867; James Loewenberg, "Efforts of the South to Encourage Immigration, 1865–1900," *South Atlantic Quarterly* 33 (October 1934), 363–84; Foner, *Reconstruction*, 213–14.

17. Macon, Georgia, *Georgia Weekly Telegram*, January 10, 1868; New Orleans *The Daily Picayune* 3 October 1869; Loewenberg, "Efforts"; J. Vincent Lowery, "'Another Species of Race Discord': Race, Desirability, and the North Carolina Immigration Movement of the Early Twentieth Century," *Journal of American Ethnic History* 35 (Winter 2016): 32–59; Matthew Furrow, "Samuel Gridley Howe, the Black Population of Canada West, and the Racial Ideology of the 'Blueprint for Radical Reconstruction,'" *Journal of American History* 97 (September 2010): 344–70; Moon-Ho Jung, *Coolies and Cane: Race, Labor, and Sugar in the Age of Emancipation* (Baltimore: Johns Hopkins University Press, 2006), 74–106. Tye Kim Ore quoted in Jung, 98.

18. Immigration Society of Newberry, South Carolina, Broadside, September 6, 1869, South Caroliniana Library, University of South Carolina, Columbia, South Carolina; *Financial Index* quoted in Loewenberg, 382; Foner, *Reconstruction*, 419–20 and 424.

19. Hamilton Fish to Francis Lieber, April 5, 1869, Lieber to Fish, April 15, 1869, and Fish to Lieber, August 7, 1869; Lieber Collection; Dudley to Fish, June 19, 1869, Dudley Collection; [Lieber] to Fish, April 3, 1870, in Thomas S. Perry, ed., *The Life and Letters of Francis Lieber* (Boston: James R. Osgood and Company, 1882), 396–97; Hansen, *Migration*, 288–92. For background on Fish, see: Allan Nevins, *Hamilton Fish: The Inner History of the Grant Administration* (New York: F. Ungar Publishing, reprint ed., 1957), passim; Saxton, *Rise and Fall*, 228.

20. Lieber to Fish, April 15, 1869, Lieber Collection; [Lieber] to Bluntschli, August 21, 1868, in *Life and Letters*, 389, and [Lieber] to Fish, April 3, 1870, Perry, ed., *Letters*, 396–97.

21. Roland J. Jensen, "The Politics of Discrimination: America, Russia, and the Jewish Question," *American Jewish History* 75 (March 1986): 280–95, quoted 290; Mayo, "Catechism," 389–410.

22. John Williams to Dudley, September 24, 1864, and Thomas Dudley to Hamilton Fish, January 6, 1870, and January 19, 1870, Dudley Collection.

23. Hamilton Fish to Francis Lieber, April 5, 1869, Lieber to Fish, April 15, 1869, and Fish to Lieber, August 7, 1869, Lieber Collection; Dudley to Fish, June 19, 1869, Dudley Collection; [Lieber] to Franz von Holtzendorff, August 11, 1872, in *Life and Letters*; Fish quoted in Mayo, "Catechism."

24. Carey, *Political Economy*, 1:339; Lincoln is quoted in Eric Foner, *The Fiery Trial: Abraham Lincoln and American Slavery* (New York: W. W. Norton, 2010), 114; D. O. Kellogg, "Thoughts on the Labor Question" (Philadelphia: Philadelphia Social Science Association, 1879; reprinted in Leon Stein and Philip Taft, eds., *Labor Politics: Collected Pamphlets*, New York: Arno & and the New York Times, 1971), 1–14, quoted 8; Foner, *Free Soil*, 11–39. Kellogg is discussed in Rosanne Currarino, "The Politics of 'More': The Labor Question and the Idea of Economic Liberty in Industrial America," *Journal of American History* 93 (June 2006), 31–32.

25. Westmoreland Coal Company, Notice of Incorporation, June 27, 1854, Westmoreland Coal Company Papers, Hagley Library, Wilmington, Delaware; Christopher T. Baer, "A Guide to the Historical Records of the Penn Virginia Corporation and the Westmoreland Coal Company," Unpublished Finding Aid, Hagley Museum and Library, 1984; New York *Commerical Advertiser*, March 4, 1869; Montgomery, *Beyond Equality*, 8–11. Similar background information on Westmoreland may be found at the Company's website, www.westmoreland.com/history.

26. Notes from the Directors' Meetings, May 20, 1857, December 16, 1857, January 6, 1858, December 15, 1858, January 5, 1859, and September 21, 1859, Westmoreland Papers.

27. Notes from the Directors' Meetings, September 14, 1862, November 19, 1862, December 17, 1862, May 20, 1863, and June 17, 1863, Westmoreland Papers. On the Westmoreland-Pennsylvania Railroad connection, see Albert J. Churella, *The Pennsylvania Railroad Volume 1: Building An Empire, 1846–1917* (Philadelphia: University of Pennsylvania Press, 2013), 632–38.

28. Notes from the Directors' Meetings, January 7, 1863, and March 18, 1863, Westmoreland Papers.

29. Notes from the Directors' Meetings, January 6, 1864, February 14, 1864, and March 16, 1864, Westmoreland Papers.

30. Notes from Directors' Meetings, May 15, 1867, February 19, 1873, and September 19, 1877, Westmoreland Papers.

31. Notes from Directors' Meetings, September 21, 1864, November 15, 1865, March 21, 1866, February 20, 1867, March 20, 1867, April 17, 1867, January 15, 1868, November 18, 1868, January 20, 1869, October 20, 1869, November 17, 1869, May 14, 1871, September 18, 1872, September 17, 1873, March 17, 1875, June 16, 1875, and March 15, 1876, Westmoreland Papers.

32. Henry Collins and Chimen Abramsky, *Karl Max and the British Labour Movement: Years of the First International* (London: Macmillan, 1965), v–vii and 44–51, Marx quoted 50; Mark A. Lause, "The American Radicals & Organized Marxism: The Initial Experience," *Labor History* 33 (Winter 1992): 55–80.

33. New York *Herald*, July 3, 11, and 17, 1871; passim; Edward S. Mason, *The Paris Commune: An Episode in the History of the Socialist Movement* (New York: Howard Fertig, 1967), Philip M. Katz, *From Appomattox to Montmartre: Americans and the Paris Commune* (Cambridge: Harvard University Press, 1988), 69–70, 80–81, 123–31, and passim.

34. Josephson, *Robber Barons*, 165–73; Foner, *Reconstruction*, 512–16; Samuel Rezneck, "Distress, Relief, and Discontent in the United States during the Depression of 1873–78," *Journal of Political Economy* 58 (December 1950): 498–500.

35. Katz, *Appomattox*, 168; Herbert Gutman, "The Tomkins Square Riot in New York City" *Labor History* 6 (1965): 44–70, Commissioner Gardner quoted 48.

36. Kevin Kelly, *Making Sense of the Molly Maguires* (New York: Oxford University Press, 1998), passim; Edward G. Quinn, "Of Myth and Men: An Analysis of Molly Maguireism in Nineteenth Century Pennsylvania," *Eire-Ireland* 23 (Winter 1988): 52–61.

37. Marvin W. Schlegel, *Ruler of the Reading: The Life of Franklin B. Gowen, 1836–1889* (Harrisburg: Archives Publishing Company of Pennsylvania, 1947), 62–76 and 84–152, quoted 84; Wayne G. Broehl Jr., *The Molly Maguires* (Cambridge: Harvard University Press, 1965), 289–306.

38. J. A. Dacus, *Annals of the Great Strikes in the United States* (Chicago: L. T. Palmer & Co., 1877), 125; Robert V. Bruce, *1877: Year of Violence* (Chicago: Ivan R. Dee, Inc., reprint ed., 1989), passim; Philip S. Foner, *The Great Labor Uprising of 1877* (New York: Monad Press, 1977), passim; Churella, *Pennsylvania*, 476–92; Katz, *Appomattox*, 172–74; John F. Stover, *History of the Baltimore and Ohio Railroad* (West Lafayette, IN: Purdue University Press, 1987), 135–40; George H. Burgess and Miles C. Kennedy, *Centennial History of the Pennsylvania Railroad Company, 1846–1946* (Philadelphia: Pennsylvania Railroad Company, 1949), 365–73.

39. Edgar T. Wells to Thomas A. Scott, August 24, 1877, Pennsylvania Railroad Archives, file 1807, roll 78, BF46.

40. Edward W. Martin [James D. McCabe], *The History of the Great Riots* (Philadelphia: National Publishing, 1877), passim, quoted 4, 281, and 371; Goyens, *Beer*, 43–45; John J. Clancy Jr., "A Mugwump on Minorities," *Journal of Negro History* 51 (July 1966): 189.

41. Dacus, *Annals*, 23–25, 57, 76–87, and 307–42; quoted 308.

42. Frank Thompson to Thomas A. Scott, October 30, 1877, Pennsylvania Railroad Archives; Thomas A. Scott, "The Recent Strikes," *North American Review* 125 (September 1877): 351–62; James A. Ward, "Power and Accountability on the Pennsylvania Railroad, 1846–1878," *Business History Review* 49 (Spring 1975): 37–59.

43. Pennsylvania General Assembly, *Report of the Committee Appointed to Investigate the Railroad Riot in July 1977* (Harrisburg, PA: Lane S. Hart, State Printer, 1878), 30, 36, 245, 266, 270, 323–24, 381, 492, 730, and 800.

44. *Chicago Inter-Ocean*, August 31, 1877; *Boston Daily Advertiser*, July 28, 1877; Boston, *The Congregationalist*, August 22, 1877; Washington, DC, *National Republican*, quoted in Bruce, 225.

45. Kenton J. Clymer, *John Hay: The Gentleman as Diplomat* (Ann Arbor: University of Michigan Press, 1975), 1–3 and 34–48.

46. John Hay, *The Bread-winners: A Social Study* (New York: Harper and Brothers, 1883; reprint ed., Ridgewood, NJ: Gregg Press, 1967), 78, 81, 89–90, 192, 225, 244, and 247; Hay to J. W. Foster, June 23, 1900, in William R. Thayer, *The Life and Letters of John Hay* (Boston: Houghton Mifflin, 1929), 2:235; Clymer, 71–81 and 102–12.

47. Allan Pinkerton, *Strikers, Communists, Tramps and Detectives* (New York: G. W. Carleton, Publishers, 1878), ix–xii, 20–23, 46–47, 67–79, 87, 95–96, 132–34, and 277.

48. Ibid., 161, 229–31, 354, 370–72, 387–90, 397–98, and 404.

49. Ibid., 380–83; Foner, *Reconstruction*, 421–22.

50. *Chicago Inter-Ocean*, July 27, 1877; Foner, *Uprising*, 154–55.

51. Westmoreland Annual Report for 1877, submitted March 20, 1878, Westmoreland Papers.

52. Westmoreland Board Meeting, June 19, 1878, October 19, 1878, and September 18, 1878; Westmoreland Annual Report for 1881, submitted March 15, 1882, Westmoreland Papers; [Francis A. Walker, comp.], *Statistics of the Population of the United States [1870]* (Washington, DC: Government Printing Office, 1872), 370. None of the primary histories of the Molly Maguires or their sensational trials note their extension beyond the anthracite region. Conceivably, there could have been similar organizations in western Pennsylvania's bituminous regions, but if so, they have not received attention from historians; see notes 36 and 37.

53. Notes from Directors' Meeting, June 19, 1878, Westmoreland Papers; Jeremiah P. Shalloo, *Private Police, with Special Reference to Pennsylvania* (Philadelphia: American Academy of Political and Social Sciences, 1933), 58–61 and 82–85; Kenny, *Making Sense*, 107–8.

54. Notes from Directors' Meeting, September 18, 1878, and October 19, 1881, Westmoreland Papers; Select Committee to Investigate Armed Bodies of Men for Private Purposes [Untitled Report], 52nd Cong., 2nd sess., 1893, S. Rept. 1280, Testimony of Andrew C. Robertson, p. 225.

2. No Danger among Them: Asian Immigrants as Industrial Workers

1. Crocker to Coles, April 12, 1865, quoted in Catherine C. Phillips, *Cornelius Cole: California Pioneer and United States Senator* (San Francisco: John Henry Nash, 1929), 138; Ping Chiu, *Chinese Labor in California, 1850–1880* (Madison: State Historical Society of Wisconsin, 1967), 40–48.

2. Stuart Creighton Miller, *The Unwelcome Immigrant: The American Image of the Chinese, 1785–1882* (Berkeley: University of California Press, 1969), passim; Lucy E. Salyer, *Laws Harsh as Tigers: Chinese Immigrants and the Shaping of Modern Immigration Law* (Chapel Hill: North Carolina University Press, 1995), passim; Charles Nordhoff, *California for Health, Pleasure, and Residence. A Book for Travelers and Settlers* (New York: Harper & Brothers Publishers, 1875), 91; Mary Roberts Coolidge, *Chinese Immigration* (New York: Henry Holt, 1909), passim.

3. Nordhoff, *California*, 84–92.

4. Charles T. Blake to Mother and Father, February 3, 1850, Charles T. Blake Papers, California Historical Society, San Francisco, California; Malcolm J. Rohrbough, *Days of Gold: The California Gold Rush and the American Nation* (Berkeley: University of California Press, 1977), 1–16. Sucheng Chan argues that the Chinese "cannot be called an industrial proletariat." He defines them instead as "an emergent Chinese working class," but I think that it is best to combine the two phraseologies and identify them as part of an "emergent proletariat." In the eyes of industrialist employers, Chinese by the 1860s were as much part of the region's growing working class as were any other immigrants; see Sucheng Chan, *This Bittersweet Soil: The Chinese in California Agriculture, 1860–1910* (Berkeley: University of California Press, 1986), 64.

5. Caspar T. Hopkins, *Common Sense Applied to the Immigration Question: Showing Why the "California Immigrant Union" was Founded and What It Expects To Do* (San Francisco: Turnbull & Smith, 1869), 12–16; Albert L. Hurtado, "California Indians and the Workaday West: Labor, Assimilation, and Survival," *California History* 69 (Spring 1990): 2–11; Mae M. Ngai, "Chinese Gold Miners and the 'Chinese Question' in Nineteenth-Century California and Victoria," *Journal of American History* 101 (March 2015): 1082–105.

6. Rossiter W. Raymond, *Mines and Mining in the States and Territories West of the Rocky Mountains* (Washington, DC: Government Printing Office, 1877), 70 and 185; [Editors], "Monthly Record of Current Events," *Hutchings' Illustrated California Magazine* 41 (November 1859): 238; Ngia, "Chinese Gold Miners," 1093–94, 1099–100, and 1102.

7. Charles Blake to Mother, April 15, 1861, Blake Papers; Robert J. Chandler, "Integrity Amid Tumult, Wells Fargo & Co's Gold Rush Banking," *California History* 70 (Fall 1991): 271–73; Chiu, *Chinese Labor*, 10–25; David Lavender, *California: Land of New Beginnings* (New York: Harper and Row, 1972), 257.

8. G. G. Vliet to Leland Stanford, April 10, 1889, Stanford Papers, Green Library, Stanford University, Palo Alto, California; Chan, *Bittersweet*, 26; Coolidge, *Chinese Immigration*, 41–54; Chui, *Chinese Labor*, 35–37 and 89–93; Matthew Guterl and Christine Skwiot, "Atlantic and Pacific Crossings: Race, Empire, and 'the Labor Problem' in the Late Nineteenth Century," *Radical History Review* 91 (Winter 2005): 40–61; Jean Pfaelzer, *Driven Out: The Forgotten War Against Chinese Americans* (New York: Random House, 2007), 8–16, 29–38, and passim; Sue Fawn Chung, *In Pursuit of Gold: Asian Miners and Merchants in the American West* (Urbana: University of Illinois Press, 2011), 1–45.

9. Wendell Phillips, "The Chinese," *National Standard*, July 30, 1870.

10. "Inaugural Address of Leland Stanford, Governor of the State of California, January 10, 1862" (Sacramento: Benj. P. Avery, State Printer, 1862), p. 4, copy in Stanford Papers; Noah Pickus, *True Faith and Alliance: Immigration and American Civic Nationalism* (Princeton: Princeton University Press, 2005), 22–33.

11. "Annual Address of Leland Stanford, Governor of the State of California, at the Fourteenth Session of the Legislature [January 1863]" (Sacramento: Benj. P. Avery, State Printer, 1863), copy in Leland Stanford Papers; Pickus, *True Faith,* 52–63. On the issue of immigrant whiteness, see: Jacobson, *Whiteness,* 1–12 and passim; Roediger, *Working toward Whiteness,* 3–132. During Reconstruction, when the Fourteenth Amendment gave citizenship and its attendant rights to African Americans, Congress retained this vestige of legal bigotry, when it refused to extend the same privilege to Asian immigrants.

12. Stanford, "Annual Address," January 1863.

13. Leland Stanford to [Josiah Stanford], May 21, 1841, Stanford to Mother and Father, May 4, 1860, Stanford to W. H. Rogers, August 8, 1862, Stanford Papers; Norman T. Tutorow, *Leland Stanford: Man of Many Careers* (Menlo Park, CA: Pacific Coast Publishers, 1971), 24–35 and 42–50. Tutorow comes to different conclusions, such as that the school's racially diverse student body was a deterrent to Stanford's attending, but the document does not support this.

14. Tutorow, *Leland Stanford,* 177, 192–93, and 207.

15. Leland Stanford to My Dear Mother, December 24, 1865, Stanford to Mark Hopkins, May 18, 1867, quoted, and June 9, 1868, and Stanford to E. B. Crocker, December 18, 1868, Stanford Papers; Chiu, *Chinese Labor,* 40–51; David H. Bain, *Empire Express: The Building of the Transcontinental Railroad* (New York: Viking, 1999), 205–9; John H. Williams, *A Great and Shining Road: The Epic Story of the Transcontinental Railroad* (New York: Times Books, 1988), 30–40, 90–100, and 117; Richard J. Orsi, *Sunset Limited: The Southern Pacific Railroad and the Development of the American West, 1850–1930* (Berkeley: University of California Press, 2005), 1–17.

16. "Second Annual Message of Leland Stanford, Governor of the State of California, at the Fifteenth Session of the Legislature" (Sacramento: O. M. Clayes, State Printer, 1863), copy in Stanford Papers.

17. Stanford to E. B. Crocker, December 18, 1868, and January 3, 1869, and Stanford to Mark Hopkins, November 9, 1868, Stanford Papers; Stanford quoted in [J. J. Warner or A. W. Bishop?], "The Pacific Railroad: 1836–1869," manuscript copy, HM 4257–4266, Huntington Library, pp. 2–3.

18. J. B. Harris to Mark Hopkins, October 21, 1876, Mark Hopkins Papers, Stanford University, Palo Alto, California; Chiu, *Chinese Labor,* 40–48; Williams, *Shining Road,* 90–94 and 117. Stanford is quoted in Williams, 117.

19. San Francisco *Evening Bulletin,* January 4, 1867, February 15 and 21, 1867, and March 11, 1867; San Francisco *Mercantile Gazette and Prices Current,* February 16, 1867; San Francisco *California Farmer and Journal of Useful Sciences,* March 7 and 14, 1867; Sacramento *Weekly Rescue,* March 2, 1867.

20. [Casper T. Hopkins], "California Reflections of Casper T. Hopkins [Originally composed in 1888]," *California Historical Society Quarterly* 25 (June 1946): 97–120 and 27 (June 1948): 168–71; Charles A. Baker, "Henry George and the California Background of *Poverty and Progress,*" *California Historical Society Quarterly* 24 (June 1945): 108–12; C. T. Hopkins, *Common Sense,* 23–64.

21. *Common Sense*, 16–18. For background on Asian naturalization, see Pickus, *True Faith*, 52–66.

22. *Common Sense*, 18–23.

23. [Hopkins], "California Reflections," 27:170.

24. *Common Sense*, 20; San Francisco *Daily Evening Bulletin*, April 5, 1869, April 6, 1869, and April 8, 1869.

25. California State Senate, Special Committee on Chinese Immigration, *Chinese Immigration: Its Social, Moral, and Political Effect* (Sacramento: State Printing Office, 1878), 14–5 and 25–9; Coolidge, *Chinese Immigration*, 83–95.

26. Special Committee Report, 46–47. Mary Robert Coolidge also notes: "No representative of the large employers of Chinese labor . . . appear[s] on the list"; see *Chinese Immigration*, 85.

27. Special Committee Report, 30, 52, 114–17, and 219–21.

28. Stanford to H. H. Ellis [1877], Stanford Papers; Bruce, *Violence*, 267–70.

29. Constitution of the State of California, 1879. On the invalidation of the anti-Chinese provisions, see Hiroshi Motomura, *Americans in Waiting* (New York: Oxford University Press, 2006), 63–64.

30. *An Act to Execute Certain Treaty Stipulations Relating to Chinese*, Forty-Seventh Cong., 1st Sess., Chapter 126, May 6, 1882, https://catalog.archives.gov/id/5752153. For background, see Gyory, *Closing*, 1–2, 212–41, and 254–59.

31. Stanford to Collis Huntington, May 1, 1875, Stanford Papers; Orsi, *Sunset Limited*, 1–27 and 32; and White, *Railroaded*, 118–30.

32. Crocker to Huntington, April 5, 1883, and May 12, 1882, Crocker-Huntington Correspondence, Huntington Library, Pasadena, California.

33. Charles Crocker to Collis Huntington, August 27, 1881, September 13, 1881, Crocker-Huntington Correspondence; Josephson, *Barons*, 221–30.

34. Crocker to Huntington, January 4, 1882, January 10, 1882, and January 21, 1882, Crocker-Huntington Correspondence.

35. Crocker to Huntington, January 21, 1882, January 24, 1882, and January 27, 1882, Crocker-Huntington Correspondence.

36. Crocker to Huntington, September 13, 1881, and January 4, 1882, Crocker-Huntington Correspondence. For the connection between Chinese exclusion and demands for the exclusion of contract laborers, see Gyory, *Closing*, 20–27. On the CP's recruitment of Chinese laborers, see Williams, *Shining Road*, 97 and 162, and Chiu, *Chinese Labor*, 44–47.

37. Crocker to Huntington, January 5, 1882, January 10, 1882, January 24, 1882, and January 5, 1882, Crocker-Huntington Correspondence.

38. Crocker to Huntington, February 17, 1882, March 29, 1883, and June 8 and 22, 1883, Crocker-Huntington Correspondence.

39. Crocker to Huntington, July 10, 1883, Huntington Papers; San Francisco *Evening Daily Bulletin*, July 5, 11, and 17, 1883.

40. N. Hoag to T. H. Goodman, September 20, 1883, and October 3, 9, and 18, 1883, Hoag to H. G. Baker, October 4, 1883, Hoag to C. P. Huntington, October 14, 1883, Hoag to S. M. Gillman, October 16, 1883, and Hoag to Geo. C. Perkins, November 19, 1883, California Immigration Commission of the Central Pacific Railroad Papers, Huntington Library, Pasadena, California; Cerinda W. Evans, *Collis Potter Huntington* (Newport News, Virginia: The Mariners' Museum, 1954), 1:154–56.

41. Denis Kearney to Stanford, May 7, 1884, Stanford Papers.

3. Alien Anarchism: Immigrants and Industrial Unrest in the 1880s

1. Charles Heath Diary, May 4 and 5, 1886, Charles Andrew Heath Papers, Newberry Library, Chicago, Illinois.

2. "The Red Flag," editorial, *Frank Leslie's Illustrated Newspaper*, May 15, 1886.

3. Carroll D. Wright, "The Factory System as an Element in Civilization," *Journal of Social Science* 16 (December 1882): 101–26, quoted 108; Charles C. Coffin, "Labor and the Natural Forces," *Atlantic Monthly* 43 (May 1879): 553–66; Rev. James O'Connor, "Capital and Labor," *American Catholic Quarterly Review* 8 (October 1883): 477–95.

4. United States House of Representatives, *Statistical Abstract of the United States. 1883*, 48th Cong., 1st sess., H. Exec. Doc. 32 (Washington: Government Printing Office, 1884), 123–28; Philip S. Foner, *History of the Labor Movement in the United States*, vol. 2, *From the Founding of the American Federation of Labor to the Emergence of American Imperialism* (New York: International Publishers, 1955), 2:11–16; Garraty, *New Commonwealth*, 78–88.

5. Coffin, "Labor," 558; William E. Griffis, *Charles Carleton Coffin: War Correspondent, Traveller, Author, and Statesman* (Boston: Estes and Lauriat, 1898), passim; Nathan Allen, "Changes in New England Population," *Popular Science Monthly* 22 (August 1883): 433–44; [Editors], "Fact and Rumor," *Christian Union* 21 (January 21, 1880): 71; *Statistical Abstract, 1883*, 131–32.

6. [Richard E. Thompson], "Political Economy of Immigration," *American* 4 (April 1882): 262–63; D. McGregor Means, "Chinese Immigration and Political Economy," *The New England and Yale Review* 36 (January 1877): 1–10; Albion Tourgee, "Aaron's Rod in Politics," *North American Review* 132 (February 1881): 139–62.

7. George M. Fredrickson, "Introduction," in Albion W. Tourgee, *A Fool's Errand* (Cambridge: Harvard University Press, 1961; New York: Harper & Row, 1966), vii–xxv; Tourgee, *Errand*, 24, 132–33, and 136.

8. Lucy Larcom, "American Factory Life," *Journal of Social Science* 16 (December 1882): 141–46; Shirley Marchalonis, "Lucy Larcom," *Legacy* 5 (Spring 1988): 45–52.

9. Chicago *Daily Inter Ocean*, June 21, 1882; *Boston Daily Advertiser*, June 23 and 30, 1882; Milwaukee *Daily Republican Sentinel*, June 23, 1882; *St Louis Globe-Democrat*, July 20, 1882; *Frank Leslie's Illustrated Newspaper*, July 8, 1882; San Francisco *Daily Evening Bulletin*, July 8, 1882.

10. *Frank Leslie's Illustrated Newspaper*, July 8, 1882, and August 5, 1882; Foner, *Labor Movement*, 1:497–524 and 2:16–19, Freighthandlers Union quoted 2:17.

11. Samuel Reznick, "Patterns of Thought and Action in an American Depression, 1882–1886," *American Historical Review* 61 (February 1956): 303–5; Gyory, *Closing*, 19–27, 247–48, and 279; Foner, *Labor Movement*, 1:497–524, Federation quoted 521. Gyory clearly shows that workers, except on the West Coast, wanted exclusion of contracted immigrants, not merely the Chinese.

12. Powderly, "Army," 369–78, quoted 371; *New York Times*, April 15, 1885; Samuel Reznick, "Patterns," 284–307; Delber L. McKee, "'The Chinese Must Go!' Commissioner General Powderly and Chinese Immigration, 1897–1902," *Pennsylvania History* 44 (Winter 1977): 37–51.

13. *Raleigh News and Observer*, December 16, 1883; *Boston Daily Advertiser*, April 3, 1882; *St. Louis Globe-Democrat*, April 4, 1882; Philip T. Sylvia, "The Position of Workers

in a Textile Community: Fall River in the Early 1880s," *Labor History* 16 (Spring 1975): 230–48; Eric Foner, "Class, Ethnicity, and Radicalism in the Gilded Age: The Land League and Irish America," in *Politics and Ideology in the Civil War* (New York: Oxford University Press, 1980), 175–76.

14. *Boston Daily Advertiser*, January 28, 1884, February 1, 1884, February 4, 1884, February 7, 1884, and April 25, 1884; *St. Louis Globe-Democrat*, January 28, 1884, and February 16, 1884; *Milwaukee Sentinel*, March 19, 1884; *New York Times*, April 28, 1884; Boston, *The Congregationalist*, May 15, 1884; *Milwaukee Daily Journal*, October 16, 1884.

15. *New York Times*, January 21, 1884, April 29, 1884, and July 7, 1884; *Chicago Daily Tribune*, January 26, 1884, and July 7, 1884; *Milwaukee Sentinel*, July 15, 1884; Edward W. Bemis, "Mine Labor in the Hocking Valley," *Publications of the American Economic Association* 3 (July 1888): 27–42, quoted 27; George B. Cotkin, "Strikebreakers, Evictions, and Violence: Industrial Conflict in the Hocking Valley," *Ohio History* 87 (April 1978): 140–50; Andrew Birtle, "Governor George Hoadly's Use of the Ohio National Guard in the Hocking Valley Coal Strike of 1884," *Ohio History* 91 (August 1982): 37–57. Bemis emphasized the onset of harmony in the strike's aftermath, a conclusion with which others disagreed.

16. *Michigan Farmer* 15 (July 22, 1884): 4; *Milwaukee Sentinel*, July 17, 1884; Lucy Parsons, *Famous Speeches of the Eight Chicago Anarchists* (New York: Socialistic Publishing Society; New York: Arno Press, 1969), 13; Paul Avrich, *The Haymarket Tragedy* (Princeton: Princeton University Press, 1984), 96, 111, and 286; Foner, *Labor Movement*, 2:16–19.

17. Henry B. Leonard, "Ethnic Cleavage and Industrial Conflict in Late 19th Century America: The Cleveland Rolling Mill Company Strikes of 1882 and 1885," *Labor History* 20 (Fall 1979): 524–48.

18. Ibid., quoted 538; Eric Rauchway, *Murdering McKinley: The Making of Theodore Roosevelt's America* (New York: Hill and Wang, 2003), 166.

19. Philip Foner, *History of the Labor Movement in the United States*, vol. 1, *From Colonial Times to the Founding of the American Federation of Labor* (New York: International Publishers, 1947), 1:497–524; Eric Foner, "Class," 165 and 177–79; Matthew Frye Jacobson, *Barbarian Virtues: The United States Encounters Foreign Peoples at Home and Abroad, 1876–1917* (New York: Hill and Wang, 2000), 73–97; Fairchild, *Immigration*, 106 and 123; Wheeling, West Virginia *Sunday Register*, March 21, 1886; *New York Herald*, April 13, 1886.

20. Terence V. Powderly, "The Organization of Labor," *North American Review* 135 (July 1882): 118–26; [Editors], "The Eight Hour Day," *Science* 7 (January 1886): 59; Carlotta R. Anderson, *All-American Anarchist: Joseph A. Labadie and the Labor Movement* (Detroit: Wayne State University Press, 1998), 37–38 and 119–24. For general coverage of the eight-hour-day movement, see Roediger and Foner, *Our Own Time*, passim.

21. Klein, *Life and Legend*, 151–52; Jessica Smith Rolston, *Mining Coal and Undermining Gender: Rhythms of Work and Family in the American West* (New Brunswick, NJ: Rutgers University Press, 2014), 39.

22. Frank W. Taussig, "The South-Western Strike of 1886," *Quarterly Journal of Economics* 1 (January 1887): 184–222; Theresa A. Case, *The Great Southwest Railroad Strike and Free Labor* (College Station: Texas A&M University Press, 2010), 97–220; Theresa A. Case, "Blaming Martin Irons: Leadership and Popular Protest in the 1886

Southwest Strike," *Journal of the Gilded Age and Progressive Era* 8 (January 2009): 52–81; Klein, *Life and Legend*, 357–63. The Knights statement of grievances, from the St. Louis *Republican*, March 11, 1886, is quoted in Taussig, 197.

23. Taussig, "South-Western Strike," quoted 192 and 217; Case, "Blaming," 68, 77–79. Case states that Iron's longtime residence and his ethnicity explain the lack of focus on his immigrant past (79).

24. Bureau of Labor Statistics and Investigation, comp., *The Official History of the Great Strike of 1886 on the Southwestern Railway System* (Jefferson City: Tribune Printing Company, 1886), 11; Case, *Southwest*, 88–93; Edward J. M. Rhodes, "The Chinese in Texas," *The Southwest Historical Quarterly* 81 (July 1977): 1–36.

25. Heath diary, April 17, 1886; *Chicago Daily Tribune*, April 18, 1886, April 20, 1886, and April 22, 1886; Dallas *Morning News*, April 21, 1886; Harrisburg, Pennsylvania *Patriot*, April 22, 1886; New York *Herald*, April 24, 1886; Donald L. McMurray, "Labor Policies of the General Managers Association of Chicago, 1886–1994," *Journal of Economic History* 13 (Spring 1953): 160–79; Thomas C. Cochran, *Railroad Leaders, 1845–1890: The Business Mind in Action* (Cambridge: Harvard University Press, 1953), 26–28.

26. James McCosh to Mrs. McCormick, May 7, 1886 and Cyrus H. McCormick Jr. to McCosh, May 25, 1886, McCormick Papers, Series 2X, State Historical Society of Wisconsin, Madison, Wisconsin; Avrich, *Haymarket*, xi–xii, 181–214; James Green, *Death in the Haymarket* (New York: Pantheon Books, 2006), 104–17; Robert Ozanne, *A Century of Labor Management: Relations at McCormick and International Harvester* (Madison: University of Wisconsin Press, 1967), 9–25; Cronon, *Nature's Metropolis*, 313–18.

27. James McCosh to Mrs. McCormick, May 7, 1886 and Thomas Fray to Mr. McCormick, February 17, 1886, McCormick Papers; *Chicago Daily Tribune*, May 5, 1886; *Los Angeles Times*, May 5, 1886; *New York Times*, May 5, 1886; Ozanne, *Century*, 7.

28. Heath Diary, November 11, 1887; *Boston Daily Advertiser*, November 12, 1887; Avrich, *Tragedy*, xi–xii, 181–214.

29. Arvich, *Tragedy;* Timothy Messer-Kruse, *The Trial of the Haymarket Anarchists: Terrorism and Justice in the Gilded Age* (New York: Palgrave Macmillan, 2011). Messer-Kruse uses extensive research in trial records to explicate the particulars of the case but does not make a convincing argument for the defendants' guilt.

30. Avrich, *Tragedy*, 3–8, 107–8, 120–23, 128–29, 150–54.

31. Ibid., 157–58 and 231–32; Parsons, *Speeches*, 42; H. C. Adams, "Shall We Muzzle Anarchists?" *The Forum* 1 (July 1886): 449.

32. [August Spies], "Revenge Circular" [n.p.: Chicago, 1886], Haymarket Collection, Chicago Historical Society; "Attention Workingmen," Broadside [n.p.: Chicago, 1886], Rudy Lamont Ruggles Collection, Newberry Library; Avrich, *Haymarket*, 189–93.

33. Avrich, 268; Walker and Grinnell quoted in Messer-Kruse, *Trial*, 118–19; Joseph E. Gary, "The Chicago Anarchists of 1886: The Crime, the Trial, and the Punishment," *The Century Magazine* 45 (April 1893): 803–37, quoted 812.

34. *Spectator* 59 (May 8, 1886): 605–6; Troy, New York, *Weekly Times*, May 5, 1886; Dallas *Morning News*, May 9, 1886; *Galveston Daily News*, May 21, 1886; *Cherokee Advocate*, May 12, 1886. For background on Chicago's large immigrant population, see Bessie L. Pierce, *A History of Chicago*, vol. 2: *From Town to City* (New York: Alfred A. Knopf, 1940), 13–26.

35. *Leslie's Illustrated*, May 15, 1886.

36. H. C. Adams, "Anarchists," 445–54, quoted 446 and 449; S. Lawrence Bigelow, I. Leo Sharfman, and R. M. Wenley, "Henry Carter Adams," *Journal of Political Economy* 30 (April 1922): 201–11.

37. William M. Salter, "A Cure for Anarchy: A Lecture Delivered before the Society of Ethical Culture," Chicago: Press of H. M. Shabad & Co., 1887, and "What Shall Be Done with the Anarchists?: A Lecture," Chicago: Open Court Publishing, 1887, Anarchist Pamphlets Collection, Newberry Library, Chicago Illinois; Amy Kittelstrom, "Dedicated Spirits: Religious Mediators and Romantic Ideas in the Late Nineteenth Century," *The European Legacy* 9 (February 2004): 31–42; Avrich, 304.

38. Parsons, *Famous Speeches*, 4–5, 26–27, and 43–44. Parsons uses "Michel" as the spelling of Schwab's first name.

39. Jerry M. Cooper, "The Wisconsin National Guard in the Milwaukee Riots of 1886," *Wisconsin Magazine of History* 55 (Autumn 1971): 31–48. Cooper spells the Guards *Kosciusko*, but other sources spell their namesake *Kosciuszko*.

40. *Milwaukee Daily Journal*, May 15, 1886.

41. *Dunn County News*, May 8 and 15, 1886.

42. *The Nation*, November 17, 1887, p. 383, December 8 and 22, 1887; *Public Opinion*, May 14, 1887, pp. 97–99; A. Cleveland Coxe, "Government by Aliens," *The Forum* 7 (August 1889): 597–608; W. M. F. Pound, "Immigration and Crime," *The Forum* 8 (December 1889): 428–40; Terence V. Powderly, "A Menacing Irruption," *North American Review* 147 (August 1888): 165–74; Rabbi Solomon Schindler, "Immigration," *Arena* 16 (March 1891): 416–20; Arthur Mann, "Solomon Schindler: Boston Radical, *The New England Quarterly* 23 (December 1950): 453–76.

43. Theodore Roosevelt, "The Immigration Problem," *The Harvard Monthly* 7 (December 1888): 85–90, quoted 85 and 88. For background on Most and Rossa, see Messer-Kruse, *Trial*, 65 and 69, and Foner, "Class," 163–64.

44. Hjalmar Boyesen, "Dangers of Unrestricted Immigration," *Forum* 3 (July 1887): 532–42; Clarence A. Glasrud, "Boyesen and Norwegian Immigration," *Norwegian-American Studies & Records* 19 (1956): 15–46.

45. John P. Altgeld, "The Immigrant's Answer," *Forum* 8 (February 1890): 684–96, quoted 690.

46. Edward W. Bemis, "Restriction of Immigration," *Andover Review* 9 (March 1888): 252–64, quoted 251 and 263. For background on the literacy test, see Robert Zeidel, *Immigrants, Progressives, and Exclusion Politics: The Dillingham Commission, 1900–1927* (DeKalb: Northern Illinois University Press, 2004), 7–20 and 116–30.

47. Bemis, "Restriction," 262. Bemis's appeal for the literacy test appeared in print at the same time as his assessment of the Hocking Valley strike, yet therein, he made no mention of immigrant involvement; see "Mine Labor."

48. Gunther Peck, *Reinventing Free Labor: Padrones and Immigrant Workers in the North American West, 1880–1930* (Cambridge, UK: Cambridge University Press, 2000), 84–89; Higham, *Strangers*, 48–50 and 99–100; Gyory, *Closing*, 254–59.

4. Confronting the Barons: Immigrant Workers and Individual Moguls

1. Toledo, Ohio, *Commercial*, reprinted in Chicago *Daily Inter Ocean*, July 9, 1892 and Worcester, Massachusetts, *Daily Spy*, July 8, 1892.

2. Chauncey F. Black, "The Lessons of Homestead: A Remedy for Labor Troubles," *The Forum* 16 (September 1892): 14–25; Thomas K. McGraw, *Prophets of Regulation: Charles Francis Adams, Louis D. Brandeis, James M. Landis, Alfred E. Kahn* (Cambridge: Harvard University Press, 1984), 65–74; Garraty, *New Commonwealth*, 117–27; Kolko, *Triumph*, 11–25; Glenn Porter, *The Rise of Big Business* (Wheeling, IL: Harlan Davidson, Inc., 1973), 23–25.

3. Herold C. Livesay, *Andrew Carnegie and the Rise of Big Business* (New York: Longman, 2nd ed., 2000), 1–119; Bridge, *Carnegie Steel*, passim.

4. Andrew Carnegie, "The Gospel of Wealth," in *The Gospel of Wealth and Other Timely Essays* (New York: Doubleday, Doran, 1933), 1–39, quoted 1 and 11, originally published in *North American Review*, June and December 1889.

5. Andrew Carnegie, "An Employer's View of the Labor Question," "The Results of the Labor Struggles," and "How I Served My Apprenticeship," in *The Gospel of Wealth and other Timely Essays*, 97–111, 113–33, and vii–xix; "Results" quoted 128. "Employer's View" originally published in *Forum*, April 1886; "Result," *Forum*, August 1886, and "Apprenticeship," *Youth's Companion*, April 1886.

6. Andrew Carnegie, "The Scottish American: Speech to the Annual Dinner of the St. Andrews Society," November 30, 1891, in Ashley H. Thorndike, ed., *Modern Eloquence* (New York: Lincoln Scholarship Fund, 1928): 1:216–23.

7. Select Committee to Investigate the Armed Bodies of Men for Private Purposes [Untitled Report], 52nd Cong., 2nd sess., S. Rept. 1280, Testimony of Henry C. Frick, p. 158; Carnegie and Frick quoted in Warren, *Triumphant Capitalism*, 64–65 and 398n18, 69, and 86.

8. Warren, *Triumphant Capitalism*, 43–49. By putting pressure on his partner, Carnegie purportedly strained their relationship, and this may have contributed to Frick's subsequent hard line against the Homestead workers.

9. *Chicago Inter Ocean*, January 17, 1886, January 19, 1886, and May 5, 1887; *Frank Leslie's Illustrated Newspaper*, February 6, 1886; *Milwaukee Daily Journal*, January 21, 1886, December 1, 1886, and June 11, 1887; Milwaukee *Sentinel*, January 22, 1886, February 2, 1886, and February 21, 1886; Philadelphia *North American*, January 20, 1886, January 28, 1886, and February 3, 1886; St. Louis *Globe-Democrat*, January 17, 1886, and January 21, 1886.

10. St. Louis *Globe-Democrat*, June 28, 1886.

11. *Milwaukee Daily Journal*, January 21, 1886; *Milwaukee Sentinel*, February 2, 1886; Philadelphia *North American*, January 20, 1886; *St. Louis Globe-Democrat*, January 21, 1886.

12. *Milwaukee Sentinel*, February 7, 1886; Philadelphia *North American*, January 28, 1886, and February 10, 1886, quoted; *St. Louis Globe-Democrat*, January 22, 1886,

13. *Chicago-Inter Ocean*, February 15, 1888, February 28, 1888, April 25, 1888, May 18, 1889, May 26, 1889, July 11 and 14, 1889; St. Paul *Daily News*, June 29, 1889; Atchison, Kansas *Daily Globe*, July 12, 1889.

14. Paul Krause, *The Battle for Homestead, 1880–1892: Politics, Culture, and Steel* (Pittsburgh: University of Pittsburgh Press, 1992), 12–43, 246–49, 315–28, 369–72, 390, and 413n14; Edward Slavishak, "Working-Class Muscle: Homestead and Bodily Disorder in the Gilded Age," *Journal of the Gilded Age and Progressive Era* 3 (October 2004): 339–68. Carnegie later indicated that he disagreed with Frick's handling of Homestead,

resulting in a permanent fissure between the two men. But this should not erase what he did at the time; see Warren, *Triumphant Capitalism*, 85–86 and 207–21.

15. Krause, *Battle*, 354–55, Frick quoted 355; Paul Avrich and Karen Avrich, *Sasha and Emma: The Anarchist Odyssey of Alexander Berkman and Emma Goldman* (Cambridge: Harvard University Press, 2012), 61–79; Warren, *Triumphant Capitalism*, 88–89; Richard Drinnon, "The *Blast:* An Introduction and Appraisal," *Labor History* 11 (Winter 1970): 82–88.

16. *New York Times*, July 24 and 25, 1892; Portland *Oregonian*, July 24, 1892, *New York Herald*, July 24, 1892, *Chicago Daily Inter-Ocean*, July 24, 1892.

17. Gompers quoted in *Irish World and American Industrial Liberator*, July 23, 1892; *New York Herald*, July 4 and 5, 1892; Boston *Daily Journal*, July 7, 1892.

18. Authur G. Burgoyne, *The Homestead Strike of 1892* (Pittsburgh: Rawsthorne Engraving and Printing, 1893; Pittsburgh: University of Pittsburgh Press, 1992), v, quoted 85, quoted 94, and 146, 184; Myron R. Stowell, *"Fort Frick" Or the Siege of Homestead* (Pittsburgh: Pittsburgh Printing Co., 1893), quoted 38 and 71.

19. Edward W, Bemis, "The Homestead Strike," *Journal of Political Economy* 2 (June 1894): 369–96.

20. Edward W. Bemis, "Restriction of Emigration," *Bibliotheca Sacra* 53 (July 1896): 560–73, quoted 563.

21. Reverend W. F. Crafts, "Questions to Specialists: Why Did the Working Men in the Homestead Labor Riots Injure Their Cause by Lawlessness," *Our Day* 9 (October 1892): 760–63. Stowell, in *"Fort Frick,"* indicates the immigrants' religious convictions in his descriptions of funerals; see 86 and 96.

22. Hamlin Garland, "Homestead and Its Perilous Trades: Impressions of a Visit," *McClures Magazine* 3 (June 1894): 3–20, and L. W. "Homestead as Seen by One of Its Workers," *McClures Magazine* 3 (July 1894): 163–69. For background on Hamlin's progressive orientation, see Donald Pizer, *Hamlin Garland's Early Work and Career* (Berkeley: University of California Press, 1960), 1–3 and 49–54.

23. House Committee on the Judiciary, "Investigation of the Employment of Pinkerton Detectives in Connection with the Labor Troubles at Homestead, PA," 52nd Cong., 2nd sess., H. Rept. 2247 (Washington, DC: Government Printing Office, 1892), ix, 96, and 141; Senate Select Committee, [Investigation of Labor Troubles], 52nd Cong., 2nd sess., S. Rept. 1280, February 10, 1893, 31, 43–44, 111–12, 133, and 209.

24. "Pinkerton Detectives," Testimony of Hugh O'Donnell, 90, 93, and 96.

25. [Investigation of Labor], Testimony of Henry Frick, 158–59.

26. [Investigation of Labor], Testimony of William Weihe, 197–98 and 215–16. Weihe did not specifically mention *padrones*, or laborer contractors, but they did effectively continue to hire immigrant workers for companies who wanted them; see Peck, *Reinventing*, passim.

27. "Pinkerton Detectives," 210–11 and 214; [Investigation of Labor], 30; Chauncey F. Black, "The Lessons of Homestead: A Remedy For Labor Troubles," *The Forum* 14 (September 1892): 14–25.

28. Paul Krause, "East-Europeans in Homestead," in David P. Demarest Jr., ed., *"The River Ran Red," Homestead 1892* (Pittsburgh: University of Pittsburgh Press, 1992), 62–65; Krause, *Battle*, 390.

29. House Committee on Immigration, "Immigration Investigation," 52nd Cong., 1st sess., H. Rept. 2090, Testimony of Henry Cabot Lodge, 733–38 and 740–42;

Senate Committee on Immigration, "Investigation by the Committee of Immigration of the United States Senate, on the Proposition of the Suspension of Immigration for One Year," 52nd Cong., 2nd sess., S. Rept. 1333, Testimony of Henry Cabot Lodge, 143–48, Testimony of William A. Peffer, 148–52, and Testimony of William C. Oates, 742–48; William C. Oates, "The Homestead Strike, I. A Congressional View," *North American Review* 155 (September 1892): 355–64; Fairchild, *Immigration*, 110–13.

30. W. G. Yeager to Stuyvesant Fish, November 13, 1893, and December 2, 1893, Fish to Yeager, November 16, 1893, and undated response to December 2nd letter, IC Land Commissioner [to Fish], March 14, 1894, Aiello & Co. to Fish, March 29, 1894, President's Office Files—Letters of Stuyvesant Fish, Illinois Central Collection.

31. J. F. Duncombe to James Fentress, July 11, 1894, and Fish to Yeager, November 16, and undated response, Illinois Central Collection; Arnesen, "Like Banquo's Ghost," 1601–34.

32. Booker T. Washington, "Manuscript Version of the Atlantic Exposition Address" and "Standard Version of the Atlanta Exposition Remarks," September 18, 1895, in Louis R. Harlan, ed., *The Booker T. Washington Papers* (Urbana: University of Illinois Press, 1974), 3:578–87; Frederick Douglass quoted in the *Cleveland Gazette*, June 2, 1894. For background on Mississippi race relations during the late nineteenth century, see Foner, *Reconstruction*, 558–63, and Holt, *Children*, 223–24.

33. Harry C. Ager, "Causes of the Present Business Depression," *The American Journal of Politics* 4 (March 1894): 233–44; Frederic C. Howe, "Commercial Depression and Business Crisis," *The American Journal of Politics* 5 (November 1894): 449–60; Samuel W. Dike, "The Wage-Earners Loss During the Depression," *The Forum* 18 (November 1894): 369–78, McKinley quoted 369; Higham, *Strangers*, 68–77, Steel Association representative quoted 70.

34. *New York Herald*, January 28, 1894; Carlos Schwantes, *Coxey's Army: An American Odyssey* (Lincoln: University of Nebraska Press, 1985), passim; quote from the *Kansas City Star*, 273.

35. Schwantes, *Army*, 188 and 299–300n5; Henry Frank, "The Crusade of the Unemployed," *The Arena* 10 (June 1894): 239–44; William N. Black, "The Coxey Crusade and Its Meaning," *Engineering Magazine* 7 (June 1884): 307–13; T. B. Veblen, "Army of the Commonweal," *Journal of Political Economy* 2 (1893–94): 456–61, quoted 460.

36. George M. Pullman to Mrs. George Pullman, February 25, 1894, and August 7, 1894, Benjamin Harrison to Pullman, February 7, 1896, and Wayne MacVeagh to Pullman, January 10, 1894, Pullman Miller Collection, Chicago Historical Society, Chicago, Illinois; United States Strike Commission, *Report of the Chicago Strike of June–July 1894, by the United States Strike Commission*, 54th Cong., 3rd sess., Ex. Doc. 7 (Washington: Government Printing Office, 1895, testimony of George Pullman, 555–56.

37. Almont Lindsey, *The Pullman Strike: The Story of a Unique Experiment and of the Great Labor Upheaval* (Chicago: University of Chicago Press, 1942), 1–106; *Report of the Chicago Strike*, passim; Richard T. Ely, "Pullman: A Social Study," *Harper's New Monthly Magazine* 70 (February 1885), 452–66; [Untitled Senate Pinkerton Report], 28–29.

38. Lindsey, *Pullman*, 50; *Chicago Strike Report*, Testimony of Rev. Morris L. Wickman, 462 and Testimony of Rev. Henry O. Lindeblad, 638–41; Carwardine, *Pullman*, 44–46, 48, 53–54, and 101.

39. Carwardine, *Pullman*, 32; *New York Times*, June 27, 1894, quoted Lindsey, *Pullman*, 136.

40. J. H. Harakan to Stuyvesant Fish, March 11, 1893, and August 2, 1894, and Fish to IC Railroad Solicitor James Fentress, June 30, 1894, Illinois Central Collection; Grover Cleveland, "The Government in the Chicago Strike of 1894," in Leon Stein, ed., *The Pullman Strike* (New York: Arno & The New York Times, 1969), 1–49, quoted 6 and 23; McMurray, "Labor Politics," 160–79; Lindsey, *Pullman*, 107–273, Olney quoted 245.

41. [Multiple Authors], "The Lessons of the Recent Strikes," *North American Review* 159 (August 1894): 180–206, quoted 188, 189, and 190.

42. Pullman to Mrs. Pullman, August 7, 1894, Pullman Miller Collection; Lindsey, *Pullman*, 339–41. The Pullman Company Archives at the Newberry Library have only minimal records pertaining to the 1894 Strike, and they reveal little about the company's attitude or behavior.

43. A. N. Towne to Pullman, June 6, 1894, William A. Talcott to Pullman, July 13, 1894, and Wm. Franklin to Pullman, August 22, 1894, Pullman Miller Collection.

44. J. McGregor Adams to Pullman, May 15, 1894, Almer Hegler to Pullman, July 13, 1894, F. E. Kittredge to Pullman, July 13, 1894, Geoge S. Bang to Pullman, August 29, 1894, and Mrs. John A. Logan to Pullman, July 2, 1894, Pullman Miller Collection; Goyens, *Beer*, 59–60, Johann Most quoted 60.

45. Frank B. Abbott to Pullman, July 19, 1894, M. C. Britain to Pullman, July 28, 1894, "Old Rebel" to Pullman, July 22, 1894, and George H. Stone to Pullman, July 8, 1894, Pullman Miller Collection.

46. *Chicago Strike Report*, Testimony of Malcomb McDowell, 360, Testimony of Herald Cleveland, 371–74, Testimony of Victor M. Harding, 376 and 380, Testimony of N. D. Hutton, 400–1, and Testimony of Jennie Curtis, 434.

47. *Chicago Strike Report*, Testimony of Eugene Debs, 169–71; Nick Salvatore, *Eugene V. Debs: Citizen and Socialist* (Urbana: University of Illinois Press, 1982), 104–8. Ironically, involvement in the Pullman Strike did convert Debs to Socialism.

48. *Chicago Strike Report*, 45–46 and 53–55, and Testimony of Edward Bemis, 650; Shelton Stromquist, *A Generation of Boomers* (Urbana: University of Illinois Press, 1987), 131 and 189.

49. Henry Cabot Lodge to H. L. Gray, January 18, 1896, and Lodge to Charles Gralton, March 13, 1896, Henry Cabot Lodge Papers, Massachusetts Historical Society, Boston, Massachusetts; *Cong. Rec.*, 54th Cong., 1st session, 28: 26 and 33, and 54th Cong., 2nd sess., 29: 1677 and 1967; Petit, *Men and Women*, 14–30.

50. *"Immigration Laws." Message from the President of the United States, Returning to the House of Representatives Without His Approval, House Bill Numbered 7864, Entitled "An Act to Amend the Laws of the United States,"* 54th Cong., 2nd sess., S. Doc 185 (Serial 3471).

51. Andrew Carnegie, "Wealth's Duty," *Charities Review* 5 (November 1895): 33–35.

52. *New York Herald*, July 11, 1892.

5. Into the New Century: Economic Expansion and Continued Discord

1. Rauchway, *Murdering*, 1–28, quoted 16 and 53.

2. Montana *Anaconda Standard*, September 7, 1901; Charlotte *Daily Observer*, September 7, 1901; Dallas *Morning News*, September 7, 1901; Duluth *News-Tribune*, September 7, 1901; Rauchway, *Murdering*, 60–61, 100–11, and 114–15.

3. Philadelphia *Inquirer*, September 11 and 12, 1901; Jackson, Michigan, *Daily Citizen*, September 11, 1901.

4. Emporia *Gazette*, September 7, 1901; Rauchway, *Murdering*, 120.

5. Theodore Roosevelt to Henry Cabot Lodge, September 9, 1901, in Henry Cabot Lodge, ed., *Selections from the Correspondence of Theodore Roosevelt and Henry Cabot Lodge, 1884–1918* (New York: Henry Scribner's Sons, 1924), 1:499–502.

6. Portland *Morning Oregonian*, January 26, 1901; St. Louis *Globe-Democrat* editorial, reprinted in the *Colorado Springs Gazette*, April 18, 1901, Cleveland *Plain Dealer*, November 21, 1901.

7. Lodge to T. A. Carroll, December 5, 1901, Lodge Papers; Theodore Roosevelt to Henry Cabot Lodge, September 9, 1901, and Lodge to Roosevelt, September 19, 1901, in Lodge, *Correspondence*, 1:499–506; *Annual Message of the President, Transmitted to Congress, December 3, 1901*, 54th Cong., 1st Sess., H. Doc. 1.

8. [William McKinley], *Speeches and Addresses of William McKinley* (New York: Double Day and McClure, 1900), 10; "Immigration Restriction Defeated," *The Outlook* 60 (December 24, 1898): 990; Fairchild, *Immigration*, 113; William Preston Jr., *Aliens and Dissenters: Federal Suppression of Radicals, 1902–1933* (Cambridge: Harvard University Press, 1963; New York: Harper & Row, 1966), 29–34 and 66–67.

9. J. M. Dickinson, General Council, Illinois Central Railroad Company, to Stuyvesant Fish, October 23, 1902, with copy of Dickinson to Senator McLaurin, October 23, 1902, James A. Wright to Fish, November 5, 1902, and Fish to Dickinson, October 21, 1902, Illinois Central Collection; Henry Cabot Lodge to Prescott Hall, March 3, 1903, Lodge Papers; William B. Shattuc to Prescott Hall, March 3, 1903, Immigration Restriction League Papers, Harvard Houghton Library, Cambridge, Massachusetts.

10. Dickinson to Fish, October 23, 1902, Dickinson to McLaurin, November 8, 1902, W. W. Finley to Dickinson, October 27, 1902, Fish to Dickinson, October 21, 1902, and Fish to Charles Scott, January 5, 1903, Illinois Central Collection; Montgomery, Alabama, *Advertiser*, September 1, 1901.

11. Philadelphia *Inquirer*, July 5, 1901; Jean Strouse, *Morgan: American Financier* (New York: Random House, 1999), 396–409 and 427–29; Lewis Corey, *The House of Morgan: A Social Biography of the Masters of Money* (New York: G. Howard Watt, 1930), 245–89. For background on the new economic order, see Foner, *Labor Movement*, vol. 3, *The Policies and Practices of the American Federation of Labor* (New York: International Publishers, 1964), 3:11–26; James Weinstein, *The Corporate Ideal in the Liberal State* (Boston: Beacon Press, 1968), 26–27; Wiebe, *Businessmen*, 18–20 and passim.

12. Philadelphia *Inquirer*, July 5, 1901, and August 14, 1901; *Pawtucket Times*, July 15, 1901; Tucson *Daily Citizen*, August 5, 1901; Harrisburg, Pennsylvania, *Patriot*, August 7, 1901; St. Albans, Vermont, *Daily Messenger*, August 22, 1901; Duluth, Minnesota *News Tribune*, September 11, 1901; Carroll D. Wright, "The Homestead Strike of 1892 and the National Amalgamated Association of Iron, Steel, and Tin Workers, 1892–1901," *Quarterly Journal of Economics* 16 (November 1901): 37–68; Ernest L. Bogart, "The Steel Strike," *Bibliotheca Sacra* 59 (January 1902): 108–28; Foner, *Labor Movement*, 3:78–86.

13. Eliot Jones, *The Anthracite Coal Combination in the United States, With Some Account of the Early Development of the Anthracite Industry* (Cambridge: Harvard University Press, 1914), 151–58.

14. *New York Times*, September 11, 1902; Joseph B. Bishop, "The Coal Strike," *International Quarterly* 6 (December 1902): 456; John Cummings, "The Passing of the Coal Strike," *Journal of Political Economy* 11 (December 1902): 56; John Birkinbine, "Anthracite Coal Mining in Pennsylvania," *Cassier's Magazine* 22 (August 1902): 507–20; R. M. Benjamin, "Legislation to Control the Anthracite Coal Corporations," *Albany Law Review* 64 (1902): 418; Edwin Maxey, "Private Property and Public Rights," *Arena* 28 (December 1902): 561–62; Arthur T. Hadley, *Railroad Transportation: Its History and Its Laws* (New York: G. P. Putnam's Sons, 1885), 68; Robert Wiebe, "The Anthracite Coal Strike of 1902: A Record of Confusion," *Mississippi Valley Historical Review* 48 (September 1961): 229–51.

15. Peter Roberts, "The Anthracite Coal Situation," *Yale Review* 11 (May 1902): 29–37; "Pennsylvania Laws, 1889," and "Pennsylvania Legislative Record, 1897," quoted in Alexander Trachtenberg, *The History of Legislation for the Protection of Coal Miners in Pennsylvania, 1824–1915* (New York: International Publishers, 1942), 134 and 137; Victor R. Greene, "A Study of Slavs, Strikes, and Unions: The Anthracite Strike of 1897," *Pennsylvania History* 31 (April 1964): 199–215.

16. Frank Norris, "A Study in Strike-Time of the Conditions of Living in Representative Mining Towns," *Everybody's Magazine* 7 (July–December 1902): 241–48, quoted 248; Richard Cartwright, "An Economic Study of the Miner as He Is," *Catholic World* 75 (September 1902): 715–26; *The Irish World and Industrial Liberator*, September 6, 1902; Green, "Study."

17. John Mitchell, *Organized Labor: Its Problems, Purposes, and Ideals and the Present and Future of American Wage Earners* (Philadelphia: American Book and Bible House, 1903), 177–85, quoted 179.

18. Mitchell, *Labor*, quoted 177 and 180; John Mitchell, "The Coal Strike," *McClures Magazine* 20 (December 1902): 219–24; Mitchell quoted on "drove" in Wiebe, "Anthracite," 235.

19. *Bovey Iron News* quoted in Duluth, Minnesota *News Tribune*, December 31, 1912; Strouse, *Morgan*, 74–75, 160, 218, 537–38, and passim.

20. Corey, *House*, 76–78; Strouse, *Morgan*, 218–22, 292–93, and 296–99.

21. Philadelphia *Inquirer*, July 5, 1901; [Editorial], "J. P. Morgan's Greatest Failure—The Steamship Trust," *Current Literature* 53 (August 1912): 172–74; Thomas R. Navin and Marian V. Sears, "A Study in Merger: Formation of the International Mercantile Marine Company," *Business History Review* 28 (December 1954): 291–328; Corey, *House*, 304–7, and photograph insert, 314–15; Strouse, *Morgan*, 457–81.

22. Immigration Department, National Civic Federation, *Facts About Immigration* (privately published, 1907), 92–93 and passim; Barbara Miller Solomon, *Ancestors and Immigrants: A Changing New England Tradition* (Cambridge: Harvard University Press, 1956; reprint ed., Boston: Northeastern University Press, 1989), 123; Franklin J. Warne, *The Immigrant Invasion* (New York: Dodd, Mead, 1913), passim.

23. Marcus A. Hanna, "Industrial Conditions and Arbitration," *Annals of the American Academy of Political and Social Science* 20 (July–December 1902): 21–26, quoted 24; James Weinstein, "Big Business and the Origins of Workmen's Compensation," *Labor History* 8 (Spring 1967): 156–75.

24. Hanna, "Industrial," quoted 25 and 26.

25. *Colorado Springs Gazette*, August 2, 1902; Frederick Luebke, "Introduction," in *European Immigrants in the American West* (Albuquerque: University of New Mexico

Press, 1998), vii–xix; Melvin Dubofsky, *We Shall Be All: A History of the Industrial Workers of the World* (Chicago: Quadrangle Books, 1969): 19–37 and 62–63. Dubofsky concludes that "unlike other American industrial centers of that era, all of the major mining districts of Colorado, Idaho, and Montana were dominated by native-born majorities" (24). But newspaper accounts of strikes occurring after 1900 make frequent reference to immigrant workers from multiple ethnic groups.

26. Tucson *Daily Citizen*, July 10, 1903; New York City *Worker*, March 8, 1903; Joseph F. Park, "The 1903 'Mexican Affair' at Clifton," *Journal of Arizona History* 19 (Summer 1977): 119–48.

27. Olympia, Washington, *Daily Recorder*, June 4, 1903, quoted; Tucson *Daily Citizen*, June 9 and 10, 1903, quoted; *Colorado Springs Gazette*, June 10 and 12, 1903; *Salt Lake Telegram*, June 10 and 12, 1903; Acting Governor Stoddard to President Roosevelt, quoted in Springfield, Massachusetts *Republican*, June 11, 1903.

28. New York City *Daily People*, June 13, 1903; Boise *Idaho Daily Statesman*, June 13, 1903; Donald T. Garate, "Wenceslao (Three-Fingered Jack) Loustaunau: Blacksmith with a Cause," *Journal of Arizona History* 48 (Summer 2007): 111–42, Haywood quoted 124.

29. *Colorado Springs Gazette*, September 11, 1903, October 26, 1903, October 30, 1903, November 16, 1903, and November 21, 1903; Mother Jones, "We Must Stand Together," Speech at Louisville, Colorado, November 21, 1903, in Philip S. Foner, ed., *Mother Jones Speaks: Collected Writings and Speeches* (New York: Monad Press, 1983), 106–7; Andrews, *Killing*, Palmer quoted p. 48, see also 240–44.

30. Stephen Brier and Ferdinando Fasce, "Italian Migrants and the Language of Solidarity in the Early-Twentieth-Century Western Coal Fields," *Labor: Studies in Working Class History of the Americas* 20 (Summer 2011): 89–121.

31. Brier and Fasce, "Italian Migrants."

32. Brier and Fasce, "Italian Migrants"; *Colorado Springs Gazette*, December 14, 1903.

33. *Colorado Springs Gazette*, October 20, 1903, November 8 and 20, 1903, December 8, 1903, March 25, 1904, and September 9, 1904.

34. Cartright, "Economic Study"; Brier and Fasce, "Italian Migrants"; *Colorado Springs Gazette*, August 2, 1903.

35. [Editors], "The Situation in Colorado," *The Independent* 56 (June 16, 1904): 1396–97; Foner, *Labor Movement*, 3:395–400; Dubofsky, *Be All*, 49–55; New York *Daily People*, October 5, 1903.

36. New York *Daily People*, October 17, 1903; *Boston Journal*, October 12, 1903; *Salt Lake Telegram*, December 2, 1903; *Colorado Springs Gazette*, January 28, 1904, July 12, 1904, and September 27, 1904.

37. Dubofsky, *Be All*, 24, 57–87, and 128; Anna H. Tripp, *The I.W.W. and the Paterson Silk Strike of 1913* (Urbana: University of Illinois Press, 1987), 3–16; New York City *The Worker*, January 18, 1903; Duluth *News-Tribune*, November 27, 1907. I have used Mesabi, the preferred spelling; however, contemporary sources used several variations, which I have not corrected in quotations.

38. Philip Foner, *History of the Labor Movement in the United States*, vol. 4: *The Industrial Workers of the World, 1905–1917* (New York: International Publishers, 1965), 486–87; Theodore C. Blegen, *Minnesota: A History of the State* (Minneapolis: University of Minnesota Press, 1964; 2nd ed., 1975), 359–72.

39. [United States Immigration Commission], *Reports of the Immigration Commission*, vol. 16, *Immigrants in Industries* (Washington, DC: Government Printing Office, 1911), 291–327, quoted 291 and 304–5; Charles B. Cheney, "A Labor Crisis and A Governor," *Outlook* (May 2, 1908): 24–30, quoted 25.

40. Reminiscence of Loren D. Lammon, sent to Rudolph Elstad, December 27, 1954, L. D. Lammon Papers, Minnesota Historical Society, St. Paul, Minnesota; Cheney, "Labor Crisis," quoted 24 and 26; Timo Riippa, "The Finns and Swede-Finns," in June D. Holmquist, *They Chose Minnesota: A Survey of the State's Ethnic Groups* (St. Paul: Minnesota Historical Society, 1981), 308–9. For a discussion of the controversy surrounding whiteness, see Roediger, *Working toward Whiteness*, 1–54.

41. Neil Betten, "Strike on the Mesabi—1907," *Minnesota History* 40 (Fall 1967): 340–47; Commission, *Reports*, 16: 329–37.

42. William W. Bates to Gov. Johnson, August 8 and 12, 1907, Julius Moersch to W. H. Williams, August 12, 1907, Williams to Johnson, September 10, 1907, and Thomas D. O'Brien et al., to Johnson, August 2, 1907, Labor and Industries Department—Labor Problems on the Iron Range, 1907 [Hereafter cited as Johnson Papers], Minnesota State Archives, Minnesota Historical Society, St. Paul, Minnesota; Duluth *News-Tribune*, July 14, 1907.

43. Lafayette Bliss to Governor Johnson, January 14, 1907, and O'Brien et al., to Johnson, August 2, 1907, Johnson Papers; Betten, "Strike"; Commission, *Reports*, 16:336–37; Charles B. Cheney, "Johnson of Minnesota," *Outlook* 40 (January 25, 1908): 167–73; Cheney, "Labor Crisis"; Lammon, "Reminiscences." Lammon, who published the *Itasca Iron News*, in Coleraine, Minnesota, remembered after fifty years that many of the Finns were so angry that they would not go back to work at Oliver Mining.

44. Commission, *Reports*, quoted 16:337; Duluth *News-Tribune*, July 5, 1907, July 14, 1907, July 23 and 25, 1907; Cleveland *Plain Dealer*, July 21, 1907; Aberdeen, South Dakota, *Daily American*, July 24, 1907; *Colorado Springs Gazette*, July 27, 1907.

45. Commission *Reports*, 16:322 and 373–83, quoted 374; Duluth *News-Tribune*, June 30, 1907.

46. Commission *Reports*, 16:340–41.

47. Ibid.

48. Louis Levine [Louis Lorwin], *The Women's Garment Workers: A History of the International Ladies' Garment Workers' Union* (New York: B. W. Huebsch, Inc., 1924; reprint, New York: Arno & The New York Times, 1969), 1–143; Woods Hutchinson, "The Hygienic Aspects of the Shirt-Waist Strike," *The Survey* 23 (January 22, 1910): 541–50.

49. Levine, *Garment Workers*, 144–67, quoted 147; [Editorial], "A Women's Strike," *The Outlook* 93 (December 11, 1909): 799–801.

50. Constance D. Leupp, "The Shirtwaist Makers' Strike," *The Survey* 23 (November 18, 1909): 383–86, quoted p. 384; Hutchinson, "Hygienic," 550; William Mailly, "The Working Girls' Strike," *The Independent* 67 (December 23, 1909): 1416–20; [Editors], "Strike of the Lady Shirtwaist Makers," *The Survey* 23 (November 23, 1909): 228; [Editors], "Girl Strikers Protest Against Magistrates," *The Survey* 23 (January 8, 1909): 489–90.

51. Levin, *Garment Workers*, 168–95, 577n26, and 591; [The Cloak, Suit and Skirt Manufacturers' Protective Association, ed.], *The Cloak Makers' Strike* [New York:

Manufacturers' Association, 1910], p. 78; John H. M. Laslett, *Labor and the Left: A Study of Socialist and Radical Influences in the American Labor Movement* (New York: Basic Books, 1970), 101–10.

52. Zeidel, *Immigrants*, quoted p. 1 and passim.

53. Commission, *Reports: Immigrants in Industries, Part 23, Summary Reports of Immigrants in Manufacturing and Mining*, 19:17–34.

54. Commission, *Reports: Immigrants in Industries, Part 21, Diversified Industries; Part 22, The Floating Labor Supply*, 18:331–469, quoted 331, 453, and 458–59.

55. Commission, *Reports: Statements and Recommendations Submitted by Societies and Organizations Interested in the Subject of Immigration*, 41:15–20, 103–38, and 369–71, quoted 18, 106, and 271.

56. *Reports*, 41:7, 33–36, 81–87, 97–99, 140–57, quoted 7, 34, 81, 87, 154, and 156.

6. Turmoil Amid Reform: Immigrant Worker Protest and Progressivism

1. News Report to the Friendly Sons of St. Patrick of Montclair, New Jersey [March 18, 1912], and News Report [May 17, 1912], in Arthur Link, ed., *The Papers of Woodrow Wilson* (Princeton: Princeton University Press, 1977), 24:252 and 405; Woodrow Wilson, *A History of the American People* (New York: Harper and Brothers, 1901), 212–13.

2. Colonel George Pope, " 'Business' and the Manufacturers," *American Industries* 14 (September 1913): 15; Wiebe, *Businessmen*, passim; McGraw, *Profits*, 1–142; Zeidel, *Immigrants*, 1–20.

3. Immigration Restriction League to Charles D. Hilles, March 15, 1912, Joseph Lee Papers, Massachusetts Historical Society, Boston Massachusetts; Charles Nagel to William Howard Taft, Immigration and Naturalization Service Records, Record Group 85, 53139/10, National Archives, Washington, DC; Zeidel, *Immigration*, 118–26.

4. [Editors], "Heavy Increase in Immigration," *Literary Digest* 47 (October 23, 1913): 787–88; Fairchild, "Immigration and Crisis," 753–65, quoted 761–62. See also Fairchild, *Immigration*.

5. Isaac Hourwich, *Immigration and Labor: The Economic Aspects of European Immigration to the United States* (New York: G. P. Putnam's Sons, 1912), 11–35, quoted 11, 12, and 25; Yael Schacher, "A Contrarian Expertise: Isaac Hourwich's *Immigration and Labor*," unpublished paper in the hands of the author. For a criticism of Hourwich's methods, but not necessarily his overall conclusions, see Robert F. Forester, "Hourwich's Immigration and Labor," *Quarterly Journal of Economics* 27 (August 1913): 656–71.

6. Hourwich, *Immigration*.

7. Olympia, Washington, *Morning Olympian*, February 4 and 17, 1912; Portland, Oregon, *Morning Oregonian*, February 23, 1912, and June 16, 1916; Boise, Idaho, *Statesman*, July 8, 1913; [Editors], "Immigrants and the Northwest," *The Survey* 27 (March 23, 1912): 1951–52; [Editors], "To Send Immigrants South," *Literary Digest* 47 (October 11, 1913): 617–18.

8. Franklin MacVeagh to Henry L. Higginson, January 27, 1913, and February 24, 1913, Franklin MacVeagh Papers, Library of Congress, Washington, DC; Lucius Beers to Elihu Root, April 17, 1912, Italian-American Businessmen's Association to Root, May 9, 1912, Root to Lawrence S. Conkling, February 26, 1914, Root to Prescott Hall, May 10, 1912, Elihu Root Papers, Library of Congress, Washington, DC.

9. Herbert Shapiro, "The McNamara Case: A Window on Class Antagonism in the Progressive Era," *Southern California Quarterly* 70 (March 1988): 64–95; Graham Adams Jr., *The Age of Violence, 1910–15: The Activities and Findings of the United States Commission on Industrial Relations* (New York: Columbia University Press, 1966), 1–24; Avrich and Avrich, *Sasha and Emma*, 240–51.

10. [Editors], "Special Focus: The Federal Commission on Industrial Relations," *The Survey* 27 (February 3, 1912): 1659–60; [Editors], "Notes To the President of the United States," *The Chautauquan* 66 (March 1912): 22–26; [Editors], "For a Peace Commission, *The Outlook* 100 (January 13, 1912): 67–68; [From the President's Message, February 2, 1912], "The Need for a Federal Commission," *The Survey* 27 (February 17, 1912): 1775–76; [Editors], "Hughes-Borah Bill," *The Survey* 27 (March 9, 1912): 1898–99; Allen T. Burns, "For a Just Industrial Peace," *The Survey* 27 (March 16, 1912): 1925–27; John B. Clark, "Commission on Industrial Relations," *The Survey* 28 (July 6, 1912): 493–95; Adams, *Age*, 25–74.

11. Philip S. Foner, *History of the Labor Movement in the United States*, vol. 5, *The Industrial Workers of the World* (New York: International Publishers, 1965), 306–50, quoted 314 and 332; Tripp, *Paterson*, 17–35; [Editors], "Developments at Lawrence," *The Survey* 27 (February 10, 1912): 1725–26; [Editors], "The Lawrence Settlement," *The Survey* 27 (March 23, 1912): 1949–50.

12. W. Jett Lauck, "The Lesson From Lawrence," *North American Review* 195 (May 1912): 665–72, quoted 668 and 671; [Editors], "The Lawrence Strike: A Review," *The Outlook* 100 (March 9, 1912): 531–36, quoted 536; [Editors], "Social Forces: After the Battle," *The Survey* 28 (April 6, 1912): 1–2; Walter E. Weyl, "The Strikers at Lawrence: Special Correspondence to *The Outlook*," *The Outlook* 100 (February 10, 1912): 309–12.

13. [Editors], "Salem Trial of the Lawrence Case," *The Outlook* 102 (December 1912): 739–40; W. J. Lauck, "The Significance of the Situation at Lawrence: The Condition of the New England Woolen Mill Operator," *The Survey* 27 (February 17, 1912): 1772–74; Walter E. Weyl, "It Is Time to Know," *The Survey* 28 (April 6, 1912): 65–67; Weyl, "The Strikers," quoted 309; [Editors], "Two Hours, Reduced Wages, and a Strike," *The Survey* 27 (January 27, 1912): 1633–34; Lewis E. Palmer, "A Strike For Four Loaves of Bread," *The Survey* 27 (February 3, 1912): 1690–97, quoted 1691; Robert A. Woods, "The Clod Strike," *The Survey* 27 (March 16, 1912): 1929–32; [Editors], "Settlement," 1949–50.

14. Lauck, "Significance," quoted 1774; Weyl, "Time to Know," quoted 66; [Editors], "Two Hours," quoted 1633; [Editors], "Lawrence and the Industrial Workers of the World," *The Survey* 28 (April 6, 1912): 79–80.

15. Lorin F. Deland, "The Lawrence Strike: A Study," *Atlantic Monthly* 109 (May 1912): 694–704, quoted 797 and 798; [Letter to the *Outlook* Editors], referenced in "Strike: A Review," 533; Diana Reep, "Margaret Deland (1857–1945)," *Legacy* 14 (April 30, 1997): 44.

16. *Colorado Springs Gazette*, February 25, 1912; [Editors], "Children of a Strike," *The Survey* 27 (February 24, 1912): 1791; [Editors], "Foster Homes Investigated," *The Survey* 27 (February 24, 1912): 1791–92; Foner, *Industrial Workers*, 325–28.

17. [Editors], "Ettor in Jail: Strike Goes On," *The Survey* 27 (February 10, 1912): 1726–27; Owen R. Lovejoy, "The Right of Free Speech," *The Survey* 17 (March 9, 1912): 904–5; Foner, *Industrial Workers*, 335–38 and 343–46. Several spellings appear for LoPezzo and I have used that found in Foner.

18. [Editors], "Salem," *Outlook*, quoted 739; [Editors], "Aftermath of a Strike," *The Outlook* 101 (June 1, 1919): 237–38; James P. Heaton, "The Legal Aftermath of the Lawrence Strike," *The Survey* 28 (July 6, 1912): 503–10; James P. Heaton, "The Salem Trial," *The Survey* 29 (December 7, 1912): 301–4, quoted 302.

19. Constance D. Leupp, "The Lawrence Strike," *The Survey* 27 (March 23, 1912): 1953–54; [Editors], "Social Forces: After the Battle," *The Survey* 28 (April 6, 1912); John D. Adams, "Clod or Brother?: To The Editor," *The Survey* 27 (March 30, 1912): 2014–15; Weyl, "The Strikers," 312; [Editors], "Salem," 739.

20. Lauck, "Lesson," quoted 672, and "Significance," 1772 and 1774; Deland, "Lawrence," quoted 698 and 705.

21. Lauck, "Significance," and "Lesson," quoted 668 and 672.

22. [A Manufacturer], "The Situation as Seen by a Manufacturer," *The Survey* 28 (April 6, 1912): 75; "A Mill Owner's View," *The Survey* 28 (April 6, 1912): 75–76; Woods, "Clod Strke," quoted 1929.

23. [Editors], "Lawrence and the Industrial Workers of the World," *The Survey* 28 (April 6, 1912): 79–80; [Editors], "The Lawrence Strike: A Review," *The Outlook* 100 (March 9, 1912): 531–36, quoted 533; Robert A. Woods, "The Clod Stirs," *The Survey* 27 (March 16, 1912): 1929–32; [Editors], "A Needless Labor War," *The Outlook* 100 (January 27, 1912): 151–52; [Editors], "The Real Question," *The Outlook* 100 (February 24, 1912): 385–86; Edwin T. Brewster, "Free Speech In Lawrence: To the Editors," *The Survey* 27 (March 30, 1912): 2015–16.

24. [Editors], "Social Forces," 1; [Editors], "Strike Review," quoted 533; Woods, "Clod Stirs," 1930; Weyl, "Strikers," 309; [Editors], "A Needless Labor War," *The Outlook* 100 (January 27, 1912): 151–52; [Editors], "The Real Question," *The Outlook* 100 (February 24, 1912): 385–86.

25. Mary K. O'Sullivan, "The Lessons of War at Lawrence," *The Survey* 28 (April 6, 1912): 72–74; Vida D. Scudder, "For Justice Sake," *The Survey* 28 (April 6, 1912): 77–79; Portland, Oregon, *The Morning Oregonian*, May 25, 1912.

26. Haywood quoted in the *New York Times*, May 25, 1913; [Editors], "The Strike of the Jersey Silk Workers," *The Survey* 30 (April 19, 1913): 81–82; [Editors], "The Strike of the Jersey Silk Workers," *The Survey* 30 (May 31, 1913): 300; Steven Golin, *The Fragile Bridge: Paterson Silk Strike, 1913* (Philadelphia: Temple University Press, 1988), 18 and passim; Foner, *Industrial Workers*, 351–72, quoted 362; Tripp, *Paterson*, 71, 78, 216 and passim.

27. [Editors], "Work of the I.W.W. in Paterson," *Literacy Digest* 46 (May 10, 1913): 1043–44; Mason, "Industrial," quoted 284; [Editors], "Pageant of the Paterson Strike," *The Survey* 30 (June 28, 1913): 428; Foner, *Industrial*, 362.

28. Mason, "Industrial War," 287; Boise *Idaho Daily Statesman*, December 30, 1912; John N. Ingham, "A Strike in the Progressive Era: McKees Rocks, 1909," *Pennsylvania Magazine of History and Biography* 90 (July 1966): 353–77.

29. Judith Sealander, *Public Wealth & Private Life: Foundation Philanthropy and the Reshaping of American Social Policy From the Progressive Era to the New Deal* (Baltimore: Johns Hopkins University Press, 1997), 1–34; Weibe, *Businessmen*, 7, 17, and 186.

30. Star Murphy to Junior, December 29 and 30, 1905, and Murphy to Nathaniel Meyer, January 8, 1906, Family Papers III-2-P, folder 30–324, Rockefeller Family Papers, Rockefeller Archive Center, Tarrytown, New York. More full coverage of this and other aspects of Rockefeller philanthropy was published previously as "Pursuit

of 'Human Brotherhood': Rockefeller Philanthropy and American Immigration, 1900–1933," *New York History* 90 (Winter/Spring 2009): 85–106.

31. Jane E. Robbins to Mr. Rockefeller, February 8, 1909, Lawrence F. Abbott to Starr Murphy, March 8, 1909, and William B. Howland to Murphy, March 11, 1909, Murphy to Robbins, March 3 and 18, 1909, Robbins to Rockefeller, May 4, 1910, Murphy to Junior, May 27, 1910, Murphy to Robbins, June 2, 1910, Allessandro Fabbri to Rockefeller, March 17, 1911 and [undated] March 1914, Murphy to Junior, April 1, 1911, Murphy to Junior, March 5, 1912, Murphy to Umberto Coletti, March 7, 1912, Richardson to Murphy, March 6, 1913, and Murphy to Howland, March 11, 1913, Family Papers, III-2-P, folder 30–314.

32. Murphy to Junior, March 16, 1909, Umberto M. Coletti, Executive Secretary, Italian Immigrant Society, to J. D. Rockefeller, February 1, 1912, Richardson to Murphy, March 17, 1915, Richardson to Murphy, May 17, 1917, [JDR-Secretary] to Richardson, May 21, 1917, Richardson to Fabbri, May 25, 1917, Fabbri to JDR, May 4, 1918, Richardson to Murphy, with Murphy's handwritten comments, May 4, 1918, and Richardson to Murphy, May 18, 1918, Family Papers, III-2-P, folder 30–314.

33. Frances A. Kellor, "Who Is Responsible for the Immigrant?" *The Outlook* 106 (April 25, 1914): 912–17.

34. Kellor, "Responsible," quoted 914 and 917.

35. Starr J. Murphy to John D. Rockefeller Jr., November 10, 1910, Family Papers, III-2-P, folder 30–313; Higham, *Strangers*, 239–42; Robert A. Carlson, "Americanization as an Early Twentieth-Century Adult Education Movement," *History of Education Quarterly* 10 (Winter 1970): 440–64.

36. Starr J. Murphy to John D. Rockefeller Jr., November 10, 1910, Frederick Gates Memorandum, November 11, 1910, Murphy to Frances A. Kellor, November 11, 1910, Murphy to Grace E. J. Parker, Financial Secretary, Civic League [various dates between January 24, 1911, and July 2, 1915], indicating Rockefeller contributions, W. S. Richardson to Kellor, August 3, 1915, Murphy to Junior, with handwritten comments from Junior, August 6, 1915, and Murphy to Kellor, August 7, 1915, Memorandum from W. S. Richardson to Starr Murphy, November 11, 1915, Family Papers, III-2-P, folder 30–313.

37. [Editors], "The Colorado Coal Strike Report," *Journal of Political Economy* 23 (April 1913): 394–96; Zeidel, "Pursuit," 96; Howard M. Gitelman, *The Legacy of the Ludlow Massacre: A Chapter in American Industrial Relations* (Philadelphia: University of Pennsylvania Press, 1988), 133–35 and passim; Andrews, *Killing*, 2, 268–82, and 365–66n77.

38. Ibid.; *New York Times*, December 28, 1914; George S. McGovern and Leonard F. Guttridge, *The Great Coalfield War* (Boston: Houghton Mifflin, 1972), 195 and 332; Zeese Papanikolas, *Buried Unsung: Louis Tikas and the Ludlow Massacre* (Salt Lake City: University of Utah Press, 1982), 243–45. As Papanikolas notes, history likely never will be able to explicate exactly how Junior felt about what happened at Ludlow, but existing sources support the contradictory beliefs here conveyed.

39. [US Senate], *Final Report of the Commission on Industrial Relations* (Washington, DC: Government Printing Office, 1915): vi, 283, and 303; Adams, *Age*, 25–74; Derber, "Industrial Democracy," 262–65.

40. *Report on Relations*, 8–11, 36, 163, and 236.

41. *Report on Relations*, 235–36.

42. *Report on Relations*, 236–37.

43. *Report on Relations*, 59–61, 133–34, and 178–81.

44. *Report on Relations*, 396–97.

45. *Report on Relations*, 302, 404, and 443.

46. Pacific Mail Steamship Company Records, vol. 428, Record of Immigrant Passengers, 1910–1913, and vol. 429, 1913–1915, Huntington Library, Pasadena, California; *Report and Relations*, 397–98; Erika Lee, *At America's Gate: Chinese Immigration During the Exclusion Era, 1882–1943* (Chapel Hill: University of North Carolina Press, 2003), 67–68 and 125–26.

47. *Report on Relations*, 243–51 and 397–98; Olympia, Washington *Morning Oregonian*, February 23, 1912.

7. Effects of War: Immigrant Labor Dynamics during the Great War

1. Haywood quoted in *Literary Digest* 53 (September 23, 1916): 732; Duluth *News-Tribune*, June 23, 1916; Flynn quoted in Dorothy Gallagher, *All the Right Enemies—The Life and Times of Carlo Tresca* (New Burnswick, NJ: Rutgers University Press, 1988), 61; on the Mesabi strike, see Philip S. Foner, *History of the Labor Movement in the United States*, vol. 4, *The Industrial Workers of the World, 1905–1917* (New York: International Publishers, 1965), 486–517.

2. Duluth *News-Tribune*, June 6, 1916; David M. Kennedy, *Over Here: The First World War and American Society* (New York: Oxford University Press, 1980), 30–36.

3. William Dodge Stevens, "Teamwork Builds Ships," in David H. Mihaly, "Riveting Imagery," *Huntington Frontiers* (Spring/Summer 2014): 14–15; John M. Cooper Jr., *The Warrior and the Priest: Woodrow Wilson and Theodore Roosevelt* (Cambridge: Harvard University Press, 1983), 320; Painter, *Standing*, 292–342; Kennedy, *Over Here*, 30–44.

4. James Patten to Prescott Hall, March 31, 1916, Joseph Lee Papers, Massachusetts Historical Society, Boston, Massachusetts; Higham, *Strangers*, 197–201.

5. [Editors], "Europe's Call to Arms," *Literary Digest* 49 (August 8, 1914): 215–16; "How the War Affects America," *Literary Digest* 49 (August 15, 1914): 256–57; C. Whit Pfeiffer, "From 'Bohunks' to Finns: The Scale of Life among the Ore Strippers of the Northwoods," *The Survey* (April 1, 1916): 8–14.

6. [Editors], "War Affects America," 256–57; [Editors], "More Immigration Coming in Spite of the War" *Literary Digest* 53 (July 1, 1916): 46; [Editors], "The Immigration of the Year," *The Outlook* 113 (August 30, 1916): 1023–24.

7. "Real Americanism," Pawtucket, Rhode Island, *Pawtucket Times*, February 10, 1915; Theodore Roosevelt, Remarks at the Appomattox Day Banquet of the Hamilton Club of Chicago, January 20, 1893, Theodore Roosevelt Collection, Harvard Widener Library, Cambridge, Massachusetts; *New York Times*, October 13, 1915; Higham, *Strangers*, 199–200. On war-induced hostility toward foreigners, see Frederick C. Luebke, *Bonds of Loyalty: German Americans and World War I* (DeKalb: Northern Illinois University Press, 1974), passim.

8. Robert M. LaFollette, "Speech in Oconomowoc, Wisconsin," December 30, 1915, in La Follette Family Papers—Robert M. La Follette, Senior, Series B, Library of Congress, Washington, DC; Duluth *News-Tribune*, July 5, 1915.

9. [Editors], "The Security League Conference," *The Outlook* 111 (December 8, 1915): 853–54; [Editors], "The National Security League," *The Outlook* 112

(February 16, 1916): 35; [Editors], "Constructive Patriotism," *The Outlook* 114 (December 13, 1916): 784–85; Robert D. Ward, "The Origins and Activities of the National Security League," *Mississippi Valley Historical Review* 47 (June 1960): 51–65, quoted 59 and 60.

10. [United States Congress], *National Security League—Hearings Before A Special Committee of the House of Representatives*, 65th Cong., 3rd sess., December 19, 1918, pp. 17, 174–75, 194, 197, 203, and 220–21.

11. Louis W. Hill to J. J. Mitchell, December 17, 1915, Louis Hill Papers, Minnesota Historical Society, St. Paul, Minnesota; Marion B. Cotbern, "When Strike Breakers Strike: The Demands of the Miners on the Misaba Range," *The Survey* 36 (August 26, 1916): 535–36; [Editors], "The Mesaba Strike," *The New Republic* 8 (September 2, 1916): 108–9; Mary Heaton Vorse, "The Mining Strike in Minnesota—From the Miners' Point of View," *The Outlook* 113 (August 30, 1916): 1036 and 1045–46; Tyler Dennett, "The Other Side," *The Outlook* 113 (August 30, 1916): 1046–48; Foner, *Industrial Workers*, 486–93.

12. [LRS] to H. F. Downing et al., February 19, 1916, and LRS to George W. Morgan, May 22, 1916, Oliver Mining Company Papers, Minnesota Historical Society, St. Paul, Minnesota; Louis Hill to J. J. Mitchell, December 17, 1915, Hill to E. C. Rice, June 30, 1916, Rice to Hill, July 8, 1916, and August 1, 1916, Louis Hill Papers.

13. LRS to Morgan, May 22, 1916, Oliver Papers; George P. West, "The Mesaba Range Strike," *The New Republic* 8 (2 September 1916):108–9.

14. Duluth *News-Tribune*, June 18, 1916, June 23, 1916, July 4 and 13, 1916. The IWW had lost some of its prowess in the aftermath of the Paterson Strike, but it still retained its reputation as a diabolical radical organization; see Golin, "Defeat," 223–48.

15. House of Representatives, State of Minnesota, "Hearing Before Committee on Labor and Labor Legislation: Labor Troubles in Northern Minnesota," January 30, 1917, passim, Testimony of Sigmund A. Slonin, quoted 75; Foner, *Industrial Workers*, 486–517; Gallagher, *Right Enemies*, 55–62.

16. Duluth *News-Tribune*, June 18, 1916, June 27, 1916, July 1, 1916, July 7, 1916, and August 27, 1916; Michigan, *Jackson Citizen Press*, August 21, 1916.

17. Duluth *News-Tribune*, July 1, 1916, and August 26, 1916; Preston, *Aliens*, 31–33, 99–100, and 290n72.

18. John Lind to Thomas W. Gregory, July 26, 1917, John Lind Papers, Minnesota Historical Society, St. Paul, Minnesota; "Labor Troubles" Hearing, Sigmund A. Slonin Testimony, p. 83; Carl H. Chrislock, *Watchdog of Loyalty: The Minnesota Commission on Public Safety During World War I* (St. Paul: Minnesota Historical Society Press, 1991), ix.

19. Ibid., Duluth *News-Tribune*, August 26, 1916; Belleville, Illinois, *New Democrat*, August 14, 1916; Aberdeen, South Dakota, *Daily News*, August 23, 1916; Columbus, Georgia, *Daily Express*, August 28, 1916; Mary Heaton Vorse, *A Footnote to Folly: Reminiscence of Mary Heaton Vorse* (New York: Farrar and Rinehart, 1935), 135.

20. Tucson, Arizona, *Daily Citizen*, September 14, 17, and 29, 1915, and October 5, 1915; Portland, Oregon, *Daily Oregonian*, September 19, 1915; *Colorado Springs Gazette*, October 24, 1915; Dallas, Texas, *Morning News*, October 5, 1915; [Editor], "A Strike Without Disorder," *The New Republic* 6 (January 22, 1916): 304–6; John A. Fitch, "Arizona's Embargo on Strike-Breakers," *The Survey* 36 (May 6, 1916): 143–46.

21. Tucson *Daily Citizen*, October 7 and 11, 1915; *Colorado Springs Gazette*, October 7, 1915; Billingham, Washington, *Herald*, October 7, 1915; Boise, Idaho, *Daily Stateman*, December 2, 1915.

22. Columbia, South Carolina, *The State*, March 27, 1916; Elliott R. Barkan, *From All Points: America's Immigrant West, 1870s–1952* (Bloomington: Indiana University Press, 2007), 194–202.

23. *Salt Lake Telegram*, January 11, 1916; Tucson *Daily Citizen*, January 16, 1916; Fitch, "Arizona's Embargo," 145; James W. Byrkit, *Forging the Copper Collar: Arizona's Labor-Management War of 1901–1921* (Tucson: University of Arizona Press, 1982), 52–62; *New Republic*, November 6, 1915, quoted in Byrkit, 54. Byrkit suggests that the Clifton-Morenci strike prepared the copper operators to take a more aggressive stand during subsequent strikes, but their rhetoric indicates that they were willing to use any strategy to undermine the Morenci strikers. That they did not use patriotism therefore much be seen as by design.

24. Max Lowenthal to Guy E. Logan, with Commission's "Report of the Bisbee Deportations," November 10, 1917, Herbert Metcalf Papers, Iowa Historical Society, Des Moines, Iowa; Portland *Daily Oregonian*, August 1 and 19, 1917; Byrkit, *Forging*, 1–3, 157–215, 221–22, and 230.

25. *Colorado Springs Gazette*, August 3, 1917 and September 13, 1917; Tucson *Daily Citizen*, August 7 and 16, 1917; Albuquerque, New Mexico, *Journal*, August 8, 1917; Perry, Oklahoma *Republican*, August 9, 1917.

26. Robert W. Bruere, "The Three-Cornered Fight," in the *Dallas Morning News*, November 14, 1917.

27. W. B. Wilson to John Lind, telegram, July 31, 1917, Lind to Wilson, telegram, July 31, 1917, and Anthony Pleva to Lind, July 30, 1917, Lind Papers.

28. Lind to Wilson, July 31, 1917, Lind to Thomas G. Gregory, July 26, 1917, and H. W. Libby to Lind, February 21, 1918, Lind Papers; Robert L. Morlan, *Political Prairie Fire: The Nonpartisan League, 1915–1922* (St. Paul: Minnesota Historical Society Press, 1955; revised ed., 1985), 188–201; Carl H. Chrislock, *The Progressive Era in Minnesota, 1899–1918* (St. Paul: Minnesota Historical Society Press, 1971), 130–81.

29. George M. Stephenson, *John Lind of Minnesota* (Port Washington, NY: Kennikat Press, 1935; reprint edition, 1971), 154–55, 178–86, and 332–38; *Minneapolis Journal*, November 4, 1918, quoted in Stephenson, *Lind*, 341.

30. Tucson *Daily Citizen*, August 1, 1917; Philadelphia *Daily Inquirer*, August 2, 1917; Arnon Gutfeld, "The Murder of Frank Little: Radical Labor Agitation in Butte, Montana, 1917," *Labor History* 10 (Spring 1969): 177–92; Benjamin G. Rader, "The Montana Lumber Strike of 1917," *Pacific Historical Review* 36 (May 1967): 189–207.

31. [Editors], *Literary Digest* 55 (September 1, 1917): 9–11; Luebke, *Bonds*, 293–94.

32. *Butte Daily Post* quoted in Gutfeld, "Murder," 182; Paul F. Brissenden, "The Butte Miners and the Rusting Card," *American Economic Review* 10 (December 1920): 755–75.

33. Gutfeld, "Murder"; Montana *Anaconda Standard*, August 2, 1917; Washington *Olympia Daily News*, August 2, 1917; Duluth *News-Tribune*, August 2, 1917; Cheyenne *Wyoming Tribune*, August 3, 1917.

34. [Editors], "The Reading Test for Immigrants," *Literary Digest* 52 (April 22, 1916): 1133–34, and "Japanese Immigration-Grievance," 1138; Fairchild and Ross testimony in Transcript of a Hearing Before the President of the United States on the

Immigration Bill (H. R. 6060), January 22, 1915, Papers of Woodrow Wilson, Library of Congress, Washington, DC. For background on the literacy test, see Zeidel, *Immigrants*, 116–32, and Preston, *Aliens*, 63–80.

35. Cochran and Frank Morrison Testimony, "Hearings," Wilson Papers.

36. *Literary Digest*, "Reading Test," and Morrison Testimony, "Hearing," Wilson Papers.

37. Charles E. Russell Testimony, "Hearings," Wilson Papers; Duluth *News-Tribune*, August 2, 1917. For background on the 1915 Immigration Bill, see Link, *Papers*, 32:144n1.

38. Woodrow Wilson, "To the House of Representatives," January 28, 1915, *Papers*, 32:143. For background on the debate over Wilson's position on the protection of civil liberties, see Jerold S. Auerbach, "Woodrow Wilson's 'Predictions' to Frank Cobb: Words Historians Should Doubt Ever Got Spoken," *Journal of American History* 54 (December 1967): 608–17, and Arthur Link, "That Cobb Interview," *Journal of American History* 72 (June 1985): 7–17.

39. Wilson, "To the House," 143–44; "A News Report of Three Addresses in Milwaukee," March 24, 1912, in *Papers*, 24:259–61.

40. [Editors], "The Immigration of the Year," *The Outlook* 113 (August 30, 1916): 1023–24; Joseph Lee, "Immigration," *The Survey* 37 (December 30, 1916): 368; Kate Holladay Claghorn, "Immigration's Ebbing Tide," *The Survey* 35 (January 29, 1916): 524–25; [Editors], "The Illiteracy Test Again Before Congress," *The Survey* 35 (March 4, 1916): 651.

41. Woodrow Wilson, "To the House of Representatives," January 29, 1917, in *Papers*, 47:52–53; Cong. Rec., 64th Cong., 2nd sess., February 5, 1917, 2629; John Milton Cooper Jr., *The Vanity of Power: American Isolation and the First World War* (Westport, CT: Greenwood Publishing, 1969), 122–23.

42. Donald Johnson, "Wilson, Burleson and Censorship in the First World War," *Journal of Southern History* 28 (February 1962): 46–58; Painter, *Armageddon*, 334–35; Higham, *Strangers*, 210 and 219–20.

43. Kate Holladay Claghorn, *The Immigrant's Day in Court* (New York: Harper and Brothers, 1923; reprint ed., New York: Arno Press, 1969), 315–16 and 339–57; Preston, *Aliens*, 163–207, Labor Department Memorandum quoted 169; Higham, *Strangers*, 221 and 228–29.

8. Addressing the Reds: Immigrants and the Postwar Great Scare of 1919–1921

1. "Outlaw Strike" [unidentified and undated newspaper clipping], Pennsylvania Railroad Papers, collection 1810, box 1047, folder 013.01(2), Hagley Library, Wilmington, Delaware. An accompanying Memorandum from A. F. Whitney, VP Brotherhood of Railroad Trainmen, to All Members, April 4, 1920, suggests that the clipping may have come from a labor paper, or it could have been found by Whitney and sent with his antistrike message urging them not to join the "illegal strike."

2. Louis F. Post, *The Deportations Delirium of Nineteen-Twenty: A Personal Narrative of and Historic Official Experience* (New York: Charles H. Kerr, 1923; reprint ed., New York: Da Capo Press, 1970), quoted 305 and passim.

3. *Literary Digest*, March 1, 1919, p. 16; *Survey*, 41 (February 22, 1919): 722–24; Robert K. Murray, *Red Scare: A Study in National Hysteria, 1919–1920* (Minneapolis:

University of Minnesota Press, 1955), passim; Stanley Coben, *A. Mitchell Palmer: Politician* (New York: Columbia University Press, 1963), 196–245; Post, *Deportations*, 1–147.

4. Edward Earle Purinton, "The Workers Foes Within—Another Article on 'Wake Up Americans," *The Independent* 97 (January 21, 1919): 443–44 and 452–58; Franklin H. Giddings, "What Is Fair," *The Independent* 97 (January 21, 1919): 437; "Report of an I.W.W. Meeting Held at Butte, Montana, December 30th, 1917, sent by John F. McGee to John Lind, Lind Papers.

5. Harding quoted in *Cleveland Plain Dealer*, January 22, 1919; Duluth *News-Tribune*, January 22, 1919; [Editors], "Who Makes Bolshevism in Cincinnati?" *The New Republic* 18 (April 19, 1919): 65–67; C. M., "All in the Day's Work," *The New Republic* 18 (April 1919): 372–73.

6. *New York Times*, February 8, 1919; Robert L. Friedheim, *The Seattle General Strike* (Seattle: University of Washington Press, 1964), passim; Terje I. Leiren, "Ole and the Reds: The 'Americanism' of Seattle Mayor Ole Hanson," *Norwegian American Studies* 30 (1985): 75–95.

7. Ole Hanson, *Americanism Versus Bolshevism* (Garden City: Doubleday, Page, 1920), 244 and 247.

8. *Anaconda Standard*, September 10, 1919; "Disorder in Boston," *New York Times*, September 11, 1919, quoted; Joseph Slater, "Public Workers: Labor and the Boston Police Strike of 1919," *Labor History* 38 (Winter 1996/1997): 7–27; Francis Russell, *A City in Terror—1919—The Boston Police Strike* (New York: Viking Press, 1975), passim. Russell provides the most complete account of the strike, but while it is clearly researched, neither its prose, analysis, nor documentation meet academic standards.

9. Russel, *City in Terror*, 195; Oscar Handlin, *Boston's Immigrants: A Study in Acculturation*, revised ed. (Cambridge: Harvard University Press, 1959), 184–229.

10. Benjamin Gitlow, *The Whole of Their Lives: Communism in America—A Personal History and Intimate Portrayal of its Leaders* (New York: Charles Scribner's Sons, 1984), 55–57; *Charlotte Observer*, September 11, 1919; *Kalamazoo Gazette*, September 11, 1919. For a critique of the assertions of communist involvement, see Melvin Dubofsky, "Review of *City In Terror*," *Labor History* 17 (Summer 1976): 436–40. Dubofsky calls such stories "outrageous, undocumented, and unsubstantiated."

11. David Brody, *Labor in Crisis: The Steel Strike of 1919* (Urbana: University of Illinois Press, revised ed., 1987), passim; Gary quoted 95.

12. Testimony of W. M. Mink, October 10, 1919, US Senate, 66th Cong., 1st sess., *Investigation of Strike in Steel Industries: Hearings Before the Committee on Education and Labor* (Washington, DC: Government Printing Office, 1919), 491; Testimony of J. S. Oursler, October 10, 1919, 478; Testimony of William A. Cornelius, October 10, 1919, 528; Testimony of William Rumberger, October 1, 1919, 286 and 290; Testimony of John J. Martin, October 1, 1919, 310 and 313; Testimony of T. J. Davis, October 4, 1919, 440 and 449; and Testimony of Joseph Smith, October 4, 1919, 454.

13. Testimony of Elbert Gary, October 1, 1919, 152–248, and Testimony of Samuel Gompers, September 26, 1919, 88–89, *Steel Hearings*.

14. *Colorado Springs Gazette*, October 8, 1919; Testimony of Lieut. Donald C. Van Buren, October 24, 1919, 910, *Steel Hearings*; Robert DeC. Ward, "Some Thoughts on Immigration," *The Scientific Monthly* 15 (October 1922): 313–19, Wood quoted 316; Brody, *Steel Strike*, 134–36, Wood quoted 134.

15. Testimony of Lieut. Van Buren, October 24, 1919, 906–52, quoted 909, 911, 929, 940–41, and 942, *Steel Hearings*.

16. [Editors], "The Steel Strike," *The New Republic* 20 (October 1, 1919): 245–46, and "The Depth of Garyism," 20 (October 8, 1919): 279–82.

17. Testimony of John Fitzpatrick, September 25, 1919, 28–29 and 66–67, *Steel Strike*.

18. William Z. Foster, *The Great Steel Strike and Its Lessons* (New York: B. W. Huebsch, 1920), 10, 166, and 201–2; Foster Testimony, October 3, 1919, 425, *Steel Strike*.

19. Foster, *Great Steel*, 205–12, quoted 210.

20. William Hard, "After the Strike," *The New Republic* 21 (January 28, 1920): 559–62; Philip C. Ensley, "The Interchurch World Movement and the Steel Strike of 1919," *Labor History* 13 (Spring 1972): 217–31.

21. Commission of Inquiry, The Interchurch World Movement, *Report on the Steel Strike of 1919* (New York: Harcourt, Brace and Howe, 1920), 8, 38–39, 76–79, 99–100, 132–33, 151–54, and 179.

22. [Editors], "Referendum of the United States Chamber of Commerce on Employee Relations," *Monthly Labor Review* 11 (September 1920): 424–26; Higham, *Strangers*, 203 and 244–45.

23. Coleman du Pont and William H. Barr, Inter-Racial Council to A. F. Huston, March 12, 1920, and George K. Irvin to C. L. Huston, Report on the National Conference on Immigration, April 10, 1920, Lukens Steel Company Papers, Hagley Library, Wilmington, Delaware; Albuquerque, New Mexico, *Journal*, January 11, 1920.

24. Inter-Racial Council, "Conditions among Russians in the United States," Bulletin, August 9, 1919, Lukens Papers.

25. Du Pont and Barr to Huston, March 12, 1920, Joseph Mayper to Charles L. Huston, March 10, 1920, and Inter-Racial Council Memorandum, March 2, 1920, Inter-Racial Council Memorandum, March 5, 1920, Inter-Racial Council, Weekly Letter No. 4, March 19, 1920, box 1993, Lukens Papers; Albuquerque *Journal*, January 18, 1920; Norman Hapgood, ed., *Professional Patriots* (New York: Albert & Charles Boni, 1925), 16, 44, 132–35; Murray, *Red Scare*, 84–86.

26. Ibid., and IRC Memorandum, June 16, 1919, Lukens Papers.

27. Du Pont to Huston, March 12, 1920, and IRC Memorandum, June 16 and 23, 1919, Lukens Papers; Du Pont quoted in Twin Falls, Idaho, *Daily News*, January 13, 1920.

28. Du Pont to Huston, March 12, 1920, Lukens Papers; Macon, Georgia, *Daily Telegraph*, January 18, 1929; Murray, *Red Scare*, 6–8.

29. IRC Memorandum, March 19, 1920, Lukens Papers; Frederick Winslow Taylor, *Principles of Scientific Management* (New York: Harper & Brothers, 1919), 9.

30. Julian C. Skaggs and Richard L. Ehrlich, "Profits, Paternalism, and Rebellion: A Case Study in Industrial Strife," *Business History Review* 54 (Summer 1980): 155–74, quoted 174.

31. Charles L. Huston to Albert Shiels, April 2, 1920, Huston to John R. Dunlap and John H. Van Deventes, eds., *Industrial Management*, October 11, 1921, Huston to George Smart, August 20, 1924, Lukens Papers.

32. Charles Huston to George K. Irvin, June 2, 1920, Charles Huston to T. S. Butler, December 11, 1920, Huston to Boise Penrose, January 13, 1921, and February 25, 1921, Lukens Papers.

33. Charles Huston to Clarence E. Howard, Commonwealth Steel Company, July 11, 1922, Huston to George Smart, August 13, 1924, Huston to George K. Irvin, June 2, 1920, and W. H. Barr to Huston, June 5, 1920, Lukens Papers.

34. Charles Huston to George K. Irvin, March 4, 1920, March 31, 1920, and June 2, 1920; Huston to W. T. Barr, June 14, 1920; Huston to Joseph Mayper, March 20, 1920; W. H. Barr to Huston, June 5, 1920; W. H. Hamilton to Huston, June 10, 1920 (2 letters); George Irwin to Huston, April 15, 1920, quoted, Lukens Papers.

35. Chart sent by J. A. McCrea to Vice-Presidents, March 2, 1923, Pennsylvania Railroad Papers; Burgess and Kennedy, *Centennial History*, 567–68.

36. Kennedy, *Over Here*, 257–58; John F. Stover, *The Life and Decline of the American Railroad* (New York: Oxford University Press, 1970), 175–78; Murray, *Red Scare*, 267–69.

37. J. W. Roberts to T. B. Hamilton, April 6, 1920; Pennsylvania Railroad Papers, file 1819, boxes 1046–47; Michigan, *Grand Rapids Press*, April 1, 1920; Lexington, Kentucky, *Herald*, April 9, 1920; Portland, Oregon, *Oregonian*, April 10, 1920; Colin J. Davis, *Power At Odds: The 1922 Shopmen's Strike* (Urbana: University of Illinois Press, 1997), 51–56.

38. W. H. Scriven to Whom It May Concern, April 21, 1920, B. H. Hudson to W. B. Wood, telegram, April 1, 1920, Loesch, Scofield, Loesch & Richards, to W. W. Burrell, April 3, 1920, W. E. Webster, Pinkerton Agency, to T. B. Hamilton, April 3, 1920, C. R. Duff to W. W. Burrell, November 13, 1920, and W. E. Blanchley to R. C. Caldwell, July 27, 1920, Pennsylvania Railroad Papers; Davis, *Power*, 54; Coben, *Palmer*, 234–45. Louis Post, *Deportations*, asserts the use of "labor spies," "private detectives" in creating the Red Scare, 56, 82, and 102.

39. Webster to Hamilton, April 6, 1920, W. W. Burrell to R. E. McGarty, May 21, 1920, R. E. McGarty to T. B. Hamilton, August 10, 1920, with undated statement by employee A. J. Bruechner, W. B. Wood to T. B. Hamilton, September 22, 1920, J. G. Rogers, Notice, April 27, 1920 and Rogers to T. B. Hamilton, May 3, 1920, W. H. Scriven to W. B. Wood, July 27, 1920, and August 9, 1920, Memorandum of W. C. Pitman, July 25, 1920, Union-Management Meeting Minutes, September 11, 1920, and Memorandum, Fort Wayne Office, April 8, 1920, Pennsylvania Railroad Papers; Harrisburg, Pennsylvania, *Patriot*, April 9, 1920.

40. Collin J. Davis, "Bitter Conflict: The 1922 Railroad Shopmen's Strike," *Labor History* 33 (Fall 1992): 433–55; Selig Perlman and Philip Taft, *History of Labor in the United States, 1896–1932*, Vol. 4, *Labor Movements* (New York: Macmillan, 1935), 515–24; John F. Stover, *American Railroads* (Chicago: University of Chicago Press, 1961), 195–97.

41. Memorandum Calling for Strike Vote, June 12, 1922, T. G. Rogers to G. L. Peck, Telegram, July 1, 1922, Statement of Railroad Labor Board Chairman Ben W. Hooper, July 8, 1922, Railway Employees' Department of the AFL, Strike Bulletins No. 7 and No. 10, August 1922, Pennsylvania Railroad Papers.

42. J. W. Higgins, General Managers Association–Chicago, to All Members, July 3, 1922, W. J. Betts, Chief of Police, to W. H. Scriven, July 8, 1922 and to W. W. Burrell, July 10, 1922, T. R. Colfer to Burrell, July 9, 1922, J. G. Rogers to G. L. Peck, July 7 and 19, 1922, Pennsylvania Railroad Company Memorandum, Temporary Restraining Order, July 15, 1922, L. Stein to General Managers, July 12, 1922, and E. N. Lewis to W. W. Burrell, July 24, 1922, Pennsylvania Railroad Papers.

43. Vincent Colelli, *The American's Book* (Philadelphia: The Pennsylvania Railroad, 1923), ii.

44. Ibid., 1–3 and 77–78.

45. J. A. McCrea to J. G. Rogers, March 7, 1922, J. G. Rogers to T. B. Hamilton, with Hamilton's handwritten comments, December 28, 1922, J. A. McCrea to G. L. Peck, January 27, 1923, W. W. Burrell to J. B. Hutchinson, February 15, 1923, and W. B. Wood to J. B. Hutchinson et al., July 6, 1923, Pennsylvania Railroad Papers. Several letters refer to American efforts in other regions, but there are no related papers among the Hagley Pennsylvania Collection; see J. G. Rogers to T. B. Hamilton, January 31, 1923, and T. B. Hamilton to C. S. Krick, January 9, 1923, Pennsylvania Railroad Papers. A published report indicates that the Americanization began in the Eastern Region in 1913; see *Industrial Relations: Bloomfield's Labor Digest* 17 (October 13, 1923): 1699.

46. Charles S. Krick to T. B. Hamilton, January 17, 1923, with "Naturalization and Education of Foreign Born Employees" form, W. B. Wood to E. T. Whiter, February 26, 1923, Wood to J. B. Hutchinson et al., April 10, 1923, and September 5, 1923, Americanization Campaign Memorandum, April 21, 1923, Pennsylvania Railroad Papers.

47. Felicitation Card, Pennsylvania Railroad Papers. Colelli's *American's Book* also included the Creed, along with an explanation of its origins (80).

48. T. B. Hamilton to W. B. Wood, September 5, 1923, H. B. Hudson to W. B. Wood, October 3, 1923, Wood to Hamilton, October 6, 1923, R. H. Pinkham to Wood, October 12, 1923, W. H. Scriven to H. H. Garrigues, January 9, 1924, Woods to Garrigues, December 27, 1923, with copy to K. D. Pulcipher, Pulchiper to Hamilton, January 3, 1924, *Toledo Blade*, February 19, 1924, with commentary by Pulchiper on clipping, T. A. Gregg to W. W. Burrell, October 13, 1923, and Felicitation Card for Robert Syers, Pennsylvania Railroad Papers; *Bloomfield's*, October 6, 1923.

49. Memorandum "For Public Information," Pennsylvania Railroad System, October 3, 1923, R. H. Pinkham to H. E. Newcoment, November 30, 1927, Pennsylvania Railroad Papers.

50. Ellen Carol Dubois, "Working Women, Class Relations, and Suffrage Militance: Harriot Stanton Blatch and the New York Suffrage Movement, 1894–1909," *Journal of American History* 74 (June 1987): 34–58; Anna Peterson, "Making Women's Suffrage Support an Ethnic Duty: Norwegian American Identity Construction and the Women's Suffrage Movement, 1880–1925," *Journal of American Ethnic History* 30 (Summer 2011): 5–23; Julia L. Mickenberg, "Suffragettes and Soviets: American Feminism and the Specter of Revolutionary Russia," *Journal of American History* 100 (March 2014): 1021–51.

9. Restricting the Hordes: Implementation of Immigrant Quotas

1. *Morning Oregonian*, January 20, 1920.

2. [Editors], "Skimming the Melting Pot," *Literary Digest* 60 (March 1919): 16–17.

3. Coben, *Palmer*, 208–34, Hoover quoted 208; Post, *Deportations*, 1–147, quoted 23.

4. Philadelphia *Inquirer*, February 9 and 10, 1910; Robert Hansen, "The Bethlehem Steel Strike of 1910," *Labor History* 15 (Winter 1974): 3–18.

5. Du Pont to Huston, March 12, 1920, IRC Memorandum, March 5, 1920, IRC Memorandum, March 24, 1920, and IRC Memorandum, June 16, 1920, Lukens

Steel Papers; *Jackson (Michigan) Citizen Patriot*, December 12, 1920; *New York Times*, February 1, 1920; Post, *Deportations*, 236–37; Coben, *Palmer*, 239. Schwab also may have had personal animus toward Palmer. During the 1910 Bethlehem strike, then-congressman Palmer had been supportive of the strikers; see Hansen, "Steel Strike," 12–14.

6. Charles L. Huston to T. S. Butler, January 13, 1921, January 18, 1921, and March 31, 1921; Butler to Huston, December 13, 1920, January 14, 1921, and January 20, 1921; Huston to Boise Penrose, January 13, 1921, February 25, 1921, and March 31, 1921; Penrose to Huston, March 15, 1921, Lukens Papers. On the Dillingham Commission, see Zeidel, *Immigrants,* 131–44.

7. Taylor, *Labor Policies*, 56–58, 65, 71, and 126–27; *New York Times*, November 28, 1920.

8. Taylor, *Labor Policies*, 126–27.

9. *Montgomery Advertiser*, June 1, 1920; *Idaho Daily Statesman*, August 30, 1920; *Grand Rapids Press*, November 20, 1920; *Baltimore American*, December 5, 1920.

10. Congressional Record, 67th Cong., 1st Sess., April 21, 1921, 61: 417 and 495–501; Kristofer Allerfeldt, "'And We Got Here First': Albert Johnson, National Origins and Self-Interest in the Immigration Debate of the 1920s," *Journal of Contemporary History* 45 (January 2010): 7–26.

11. Congressional Record, 67th Cong., 1st Sess., April 21, 1921, 61: 501–2 and 508–9.

12. Ibid., May 2, 1921, 915–17, 922, and 928–29.

13. Ibid., April 21, 1921, 512 and 516–17, and May 3, 1921, 953;

14. [Editors], "The Cry for More Immigration," *Literary Digest* 75 (November 18, 1922): 18–19; *New York Times*, June 30, 1921; Higham, *Strangers*, 300–30.

15. G. L. Peck to John Ihlder, Secretary, Immigration Committee, US. Chamber of Commerce, December 28, 1922, Pennsylvania Railroad Papers; *Industrial Relations: Bloomfield's Labor Digest* 17 (October 6, 1923): 1690–92; Topeka, Kansas *Plaindealer*, November 21, 1924. Ihlder had requested the information in a letter, not in the collection, dated October 9, 1922.

16. Wichita, Kansas *Negro Star*, January 11, 1924; Topeka, Kansas *Plaindealer*, February 22, 1924, and April 18, 1924; Chicago *Broad Axe*, March 22, 1924.

17. John T. Emlen to Abram F. Huston, March 5, 1918, Charles Huston to Emlen, March 21, 1918, November 23, 1918, February 6, 1919, February 27, 1919, March 2, 1919, and Huston to Armstrong Association, August 9, 1923, Lukens Papers.

18. Huston to Butler, December 11, 1920, and January 1, 1921, Lukens Papers. There is no evidence that explains the contradiction between Huston's negative characterization of black workers and his company's relative willingness to hire them, but the dates of the latter suggest that it may have been due to a lack of immigrants.

19. T. B. Hamilton to G. L. Peck, December 1, 1922, G. L. Peck to John Ihlder, December 28, 1922, Pennsylvania Railroad Papers.

20. Hamilton to Peck, December 1, 1922, Chicago and Fort Wayne Reports, October 24, 1922 [damaged and partial], Hutchinson to Burrell, November 15, 1922, and Thomas A. Roberts to Burrell, November 24, 1922, Pennsylvania Railroad Papers.

21. "Amendment, California Alien Land Law, Adopted November 2, 1920," *Annals of the American Academy of Political and Social Sciences* 93 (January 1921): 13–16; Paul Scharrenberg, "The Attitudes of Organized Labor towards the Japanese,"

ibid., 34–38; James D. Phelan, "Why California Objects to the Japanese Invasion," ibid., 16–17; Lothrop Stoddard, "The Japanese Question in California," ibid., 42–46, quoted 42.

22. Charles Huston to T. S. Butler, December 11, 1920, Huston to Boise Penrose, February 25, 1921, Huston to T. Aramaki, November 7, 1905, September 27, 1906, April 19, 1907, Aramaki to Huston, February 23, 1909, and April 16, 1924, Lukens Papers; *New York Times*, May 8, 1924.

23. "An Act To limit the immigration of aliens into the United States," 68th Cong., Sess. 1., Chap. 190, *The Statutes At Large of the United States of America from December, 1923 to March, 1925* (Washington, DC: Government Printing Office, 1925), 153–69; Cong. Rec., 68th Cong., 1st sess., April 11, 1924, 65: 6117–21; Allerfeldt, "Albert Johnson," 11–16.

24. Cong. Rec., 68th Cong., 1st sess., April 8, 1924, 5998–6001.

25. Ibid., March 6, 1924, 3668–69; ibid., April 18, 1924, 6600 and 6627–28.

26. Ibid., March 15, 1924, 4265–74, quoted 4268 and 4269.

27. Ibid., January 7, 1924, 580; ibid., February 1, 1924, 1774–75; ibid., February 18, 1924, 2324.

28. *New York Times*, May 27, 1924.

Epilogue

1. Heinrich Edward Jacob, *The World of Emma Lazarus* (New York: Schocken Books, 1949), 178. How and when Lady Liberty came to symbolize America's immigrant identity can be debated; see Stovall, "White Freedom," 1–27.

2. Henry George, *Poverty and Progress: An Inquiry into the Cause of Industrial Depressions and the Increase of Want with Increase of Wealth* (New York: Modern Library, 50th anniversary ed., 1929; originally published 1879); Matthew Hale Smith, *Sunshine and Shadow in New York* (Hartford, CT: J. B. Burr and Company, 1969), quoted 708; Jacob Riis, *How the Other Half Lives: Studies among the Tenements of New York* (New York: Charles Scribner's Sons, 1890).

3. Parsons, Speeches, 32–3.

BIBLIOGRAPHY

Archives and Manuscripts

Anarchist Pamphlets Collection, Newberry Library, Chicago, Illinois

Bethlehem Steel Corporation Papers, Hagley Library, Wilmington, Delaware

Board of Immigration Collection, Albert and Shirley Small Special Collections
   Library, University of Virginia, Charlottesville, Virginia

Charles Andrew Heath Papers, Newberry Library, Chicago, Illinois

Charles T. Blake Papers, California Historical Society, San Francisco, California

Crocker-Huntington Correspondence, Huntington Library, Pasadena, California

Dudley Collection, Huntington Library, Pasadena, California

Elihu Root Papers, Library of Congress, Washington, DC

Francis Lieber Collection, Huntington Library, Pasadena, California

Franklin MacVeagh Papers, Library of Congress, Washington, DC

Haymarket Collection, Chicago Historical Society, Chicago, Illinois

Henry Cabot Lodge Papers, Massachusetts Historical Society, Boston, Massachusetts

Herbert Metcalf Papers, Iowa Historical Society, Des Moines, Iowa

Illinois Central Railroad Collection, The Newberry Library, Chicago, Illinois

Immigration Restriction League Papers, Harvard Houghton Library, Cambridge,
   Massachusetts

John Lind Papers, Minnesota Historical Society, St. Paul, Minnesota

Joseph Lee Papers, Massachusetts Historical Society, Boston Massachusetts

L. D. Lammon Papers, Minnesota Historical Society, St. Paul, Minnesota

Labor and Industries Department—Labor Problems on the Iron Range, 1907, Minnesota State Archives, Minnesota Historical Society, St. Paul, Minnesota

La Follette Family Papers—Robert M. La Follette, Senior, Series B, Library of Congress, Washington, DC

Louis Hill Papers, Minnesota Historical Society, St. Paul, Minnesota

Lukens Steel Company Papers, Hagley Library, Wilmington, Delaware

Mark Hopkins Papers, Stanford University, Palo Alto, California

McCormick Papers, State Historical Society of Wisconsin, Madison, Wisconsin

Newberry, South Carolina, Immigration Society, Caroliniana Library, University of
   South Carolina, Columbia, South Carolina

Oliver Mining Company Papers, Minnesota Historical Society, St. Paul, Minnesota

Pacific Mail Steamship Company Records, Record of Immigrant Passengers, 1910–
   1915, Huntington Library, Pasadena, California

"Pacific Railroad: 1836–1869," Manuscript copy, Huntington Library, Pasadena,
   California

Pennsylvania Railroad Company Archives, Hagley Library, Wilmington, Delaware

Pullman Company Archives, Newberry Library, Chicago, Illinois

Pullman Miller Collection, Chicago Historical Society, Chicago, Illinois
Rockefeller Family Papers, Rockefeller Archive Center, Tarrytown, New York
Rudy Lamont Ruggles Collection, Newberry Library
Stanford Papers, Green Library, Stanford University, Palo Alto, California
Theodore Roosevelt Collection, Harvard Widener Library, Cambridge, Massachusetts
Westmoreland Coal Company Papers, Hagley Library, Wilmington, Delaware
Woodrow Wilson Papers, Library of Congress, Washington, DC
Zebina Eastman Papers, Chicago Historical Museum, Chicago, Illinois

Books

Adams, Graham, Jr. *The Age of Violence, 1910–15: The Activities and Findings of the United States Commission on Industrial Relations*. New York: Columbia University Press, 1966.
Adamic, Louis. *Dynamite: The Story of Class Violence in America*. New York: Viking Press, 1931.
Anderson, Carlotta R. *All-American Anarchist: Joseph A. Labadie and the Labor Movement*. Detroit: Wayne State University Press, 1998.
Anbinder, Tyler. *Five Points: The 19th-Century New York City Neighborhood that Invented Tap Dance, Stole Elections, and Became the World's Most Notorious Slum*. New York: Free Press, 2001.
——. *Nativism and Slavery: The Northern Know Nothings and the Politics of the 1850s*. New York: Oxford University Press, 1990.
Andrews, Thomas G. *Killing for Coal: America's Deadliest Labor War*. Cambridge: Harvard University Press, 2008.
Avrich, Paul. *The Haymarket Tragedy*. Princeton: Princeton University Press, 1984.
Avrich Paul, and Karen Avrich. *Sasha and Emma: The Anarchist Odyssey of Alexander Berkman and Emma Goldman*. Cambridge: Harvard University Press, 2012.
Bain, David H. *Empire Express: The Building of the Transcontinental Railroad*. New York: Viking, 1999.
Barkan, Elliott R. *From All Points: America's Immigrant West, 1870s–1952*. Bloomington: Indiana University Press, 2007.
Bensel, Richard F. *The Political Economy of American Industrialization, 1877–1900*. New York: Cambridge University Press, 2000.
Bernstein, Iver. *The New York City Draft Riots: Their Significance for American Society and Politics in the Age of the Civil War*. New York: Oxford University Press, 1990.
Billington, Ray Allen. *The Protestant Crusade, 1800–1860*. New York: Macmillan, 1938.
Bridge, James H. *The Inside History of Carnegie Steel Company: A Romance of Millions*. New York: Aldine Book, 1903.
Blegen, Theodore C. *Minnesota: A History of the State*. Minneapolis: University of Minnesota Press, 1964; 2nd ed., 1975.
Brody, David. *Labor in Crisis: The Steel Strike of 1919*. Urbana: University of Illinois Press, revised ed., 1987.
Broehl, Wayne G., Jr. *The Molly Maguires*. Cambridge: Harvard University Press, 1965.
Bruce, Robert V. *1877: Year of Violence*. Chicago: Ivan R. Dee, Inc., reprint ed., 1989.

Burgess, George H. and Miles C. Kennedy, *Centennial History of the Pennsylvania Railroad Company, 1846–1946*. Philadelphia: Pennsylvania Railroad Company, 1949.

Burgoyne, Authur G. *The Homestead Strike of 1892*. Pittsburgh: Rawsthorne Engraving and Printing, 1893; Pittsburgh: University of Pittsburgh Press, 1992.

Camp, Helen C. *Iron in Her Soul: Elizabeth Gurley Flynn and the American Left*. Pullman: Washington State University Press, 1995.

Carey, Henry C. *The Harmony of Interests: Agricultural, Manufacturing & Commercial*. Philadelphia: J. S. Skinner, 1851; reprint ed., New York: Augustus M. Kelly, 1967.

——. *Miscellaneous Works of Henry C. Carey*. Philadelphia: Henry Carey Baird, 1868.

——. *Principles of Political Economy*. Philadelphia: Carey, Lea & Blanchard, 1837; reprint ed., New York: Augustus M. Kelley, 1965.

——. *Principles of Social Science*. Philadelphia: J. B. Lippincott, 3 vols., 1856–1858.

Carnegie, Andrew. *The Gospel of Wealth and Other Timely Essays*. New York: Doubleday, Doran, 1933.

——. *Problems of Today*. Reprint, Garden City: Doubleday, Doran, 1933.

——. *Triumphant Democracy; or Fifty Years' March of the Republic*. New York: Charles Scribner's Sons, 1886; reprint, New York: Johnson Reprint Corp., 1971.

Carwardine, William H. *The Pullman Strike*. 4th ed. Chicago: Charles H. Kerr, 1894.

Case, Theresa A. *The Great Southwest Railroad Strike and Free Labor* (College Station: Texas A&M University Press, 2010.

Chandler, Alfred D. *The Visible Hand*. Cambridge: Harvard University Press, 1977.

Chan, Sucheng. *This Bittersweet Soil: The Chinese in California Agriculture, 1860–1910*. Berkeley: University of California Press, 1986.

Chiu, Ping. *Chinese Labor in California, 1850–1880*. Madison: State Historical Society of Wisconsin, 1967.

Chrislock, Carl H. *The Progressive Era in Minnesota, 1899–1918* (St. Paul: Minnesota Historical Society Press, 1971), 130–81.

——. *Watchdog of Loyalty: The Minnesota Commission on Public Safety During World War I*. St. Paul: Minnesota Historical Society Press, 1991.

Chung, Sue Fawn. *In Pursuit of Gold: Asian Miners and Merchants in the American West*. Urbana: University of Illinois Press, 2011.

Churella, Albert J. *The Pennsylvania Railroad Volume 1: Building An Empire, 1846–1917*. Philadelphia: University of Pennsylvania Press, 2013.

Claghorn, Kate Holladay. *The Immigrant's Day in Court*. New York: Harper and Brothers, 1923; reprint ed., New York: Arno Press, 1969.

Clark, Clifford E., Jr. *Henry Ward Beecher: Spokesman for a Middle-Class America*. Urbana: University of Illinois Press, 1978.

[The Cloak, Suit and Skirt Manufacturers' Protective Association, ed.]. *The Cloak Makers' Strike*. New York: Manufacturers' Association, 1910.

Clymer, Kenton J. *John Hay: The Gentleman as Diplomat*. Ann Arbor: University of Michigan Press, 1975.

Coben, Stanley. *A. Mitchell Palmer: Politician*. New York: Columbia University Press, 1963.

Cochran, Thomas C. *Railroad Leaders, 1845–1890: The Business Mind in Action*. Cambridge: Harvard University Press, 1953.

Colelli, Vincent. *The American's Book*. Philadelphia: The Pennsylvania Railroad, 1923.

Collins, Henry and Chimen Abramsky. *Karl Max and the British Labour Movement: Years of the First International*. London: Macmillan, 1965.

Commons, John R. *Races and Immigrants in America*. New York: Macmillan, 1907.

Commons, John R., et al., eds. *A Documentary History of American Industrial Society*. Cleveland: Arthur H. Clark Company, 1910.

Coolidge, Mary Roberts. *Chinese Immigration*. New York: Henry Holt, 1909.

Cooper, John M., Jr. *The Vanity of Power: American Isolation and the First World War*. Westport, CT: Greenwood Publishing, 1969.

——. *The Warrior and the Priest: Woodrow Wilson and Theodore Roosevelt*. Cambridge: Harvard University Press, 1983.

Corey, Lewis. *The House of Morgan: A Social Biography of the Masters of Money*. New York: G. Howard Watt, 1930.

Cronon, William. *Nature's Metropolis: Chicago and the Great West*. New York: W. W. Norton, 1991.

Dacus, J. A. *Annals of the Great Strikes in the United States*. Chicago: L. T. Palmer & Co., 1877.

Daniels, Roger. *Coming to America: A History of Immigration and Ethnicity in American Life*. New York: HarperCollins, 1990.

Davis, Colin J. *Power At Odds: The 1922 Shopmen's Strike*. Urbana: University of Illinois Press, 1997.

Demarest, David P. Jr., ed. *"The River Ran Red," Homestead 1892*. Pittsburgh: University of Pittsburgh Press, 1992. See esp. sidebar, Paul Krause, "East-Europeans in Homestead."

Dinnerstein, Leonard, Roger Nichols, and David Reimers. *Natives and Strangers: A History of Ethnic Americans*. 5th ed. New York: Oxford University Press, 2010.

Dubofsky, Melvyn. *Industrialism and the American Worker, 1865–1920*. Arlington Heights, IL: Harlan Davidson, Inc., 1985.

——. *We Shall Be All: A History of the Industrial Workers of the World*. Chicago: Quadrangle Books, 1969.

Dullas, Foster Rhea. *Labor in America: A History*. New York: Thomas Y. Crowell, 1949.

Erickson, Charlotte. *American Industry and the European Immigrant, 1860–1885*. New York: Russell & Russell, 1957.

Evans, Cerinda W. *Collis Potter Huntington*. Newport News, Virginia: The Mariners' Museum, 1954.

Fairchild, Henry P. *Immigration: A World Movement and Its American Significance*. New York: Macmillan, 1913.

Fink, Leon. *The Long Gilded Age: American Capitalism and the Lessons of a New World Order*. Philadelphia: University of Pennsylvania Press, 2015.

Fitch, John A. *The Causes of Industrial Unrest*. New York: Harper and Brothers, 1924.

Foner, Eric. *The Fiery Trial: Abraham Lincoln and American Slavery*. New York: W. W. Norton, 2010.

——. *Free Soil, Free Labor, Free Men: The Ideology of the Republican Party before the Civil War*. New York: Oxford University Press, 1970.

——. *Politics and Ideology in the Civil War*. New York: Oxford University Press, 1980.

——. *Reconstruction: America's Unfinished Revolution, 1863–1877*. New York: Harper & Row, 1988. See esp. chap. 8, "Class, Ethnicity, and Radicalism in the Gilded Age: The Land League and Irish America."

Foner, Philip S. *The Great Labor Uprising of 1877*. New York: Monad Press, 1977.

——. *History of the Labor Movement in the United States*. 10 vols. New York: International Publishers, 1947–1994.

——, ed. *Mother Jones Speaks: Collected Writings and Speeches*. New York: Monad Press, 1983.

Foster, William Z. *The Great Steel Strike and Its Lessons*. New York: B. W. Huebsch, 1920.

Friedheim, Robert L. *The Seattle General Strike*. Seattle: University of Washington Press, 1964.

Gabaccia, Donna R. *Militants and Migrants: Rural Sicilians Become American Workers*. New Brunswick, NJ: Rutgers University Press, 1988.

Gallagher, Dorothy. *All the Right Enemies—The Life and Times of Carlo Tresca*. New Burnswick, NJ: Rutgers University Press, 1988.

Garraty, John A. *The New Commonwealth, 1877–1900* (New York: Harper & Row, 1968.

Gates, Paul W. *The Illinois Central Railroad and Its Colonization Work*. Cambridge: Harvard University Press, 1934.

George, Henry. *Poverty and Progress: An Inquiry into the Cause of Industrial Depressions and the Increase of Want with Increase of Wealth*. New York: Modern Library, 50th anniversary ed., 1929; originally published 1879.

Gitelman, Howard M. *The Legacy of the Ludlow Massacre: A Chapter in American Industrial Relations*. Philadelphia: University of Pennsylvania Press, 1988.

Gitlow, Benjamin. *The Whole of Their Lives: Communism in America—A Personal History and Intimate Portrayal of its Leaders*. New York: Charles Scribner's Sons, 1984.

Golin, Steven. *The Fragile Bridge: Paterson Silk Strike, 1913*. Philadelphia: Temple University Press, 1988.

Goyens, Tom. *Beer and Revolution: The German Anarchist Movement in New York City, 1880–1914*. Urbana: University of Illinois Press, 2007.

Green, James. *Death in the Haymarket*. New York: Pantheon Books, 2006.

Griffis, William E. *Charles Carleton Coffin: War Correspondent, Traveller, Author, and Statesman*. Boston: Estes and Lauriat, 1898.

Gyory, Andrew. *Closing the Gates: Race, Politics, and the Chinese Exclusion Act*. Chapel Hill: University of North Carolina Press, 1998.

Hadley, Arthur T. *Railroad Transportation: Its History and Its Laws*. New York: G. P. Putnam's Sons, 1885.

Handlin, Oscar. *Boston's Immigrants: A Study in Acculturation*. Revised ed. Cambridge: Harvard University Press, 1959.

[Hanna, Marcus]. *Mark Hanna, His Book*. Boston: Chapple Publishing Company, 1904.

Hansen, Marcus L. *The Atlantic Migration*. Cambridge: Harvard University Press, 1940; reprint ed. New York: Harper & Row, 1961.

Hanson, Ole. *Americanism Versus Bolshevism*. Garden City: Doubleday, Page, 1920.

Hapgood, Norman, ed., *Professional Patriots*. New York: Albert & Charles Boni, 1925.

Harlan, Louis R., ed. *The Booker T. Washington Papers*. 14 volumes. Urbana: University of Illinois Press, 1972–74.

Hattam, Victoria. *Labor Visions and State Power: Origins of Business Unionism in the United States*. Princeton: Princeton University Press, 1993.

Hay, John. *The Bread-winners: A Social Study*. New York: Harper and Brothers, 1883; reprint ed., Ridgewood, NJ: Gregg Press, 1967.

Higham, John. *Send These to Me: Immigrants in Urban America*. Baltimore: Johns Hopkins University Press, revised ed., 1984.

———. *Strangers in the Land: Patterns of American Nativism, 1860–1925*. New York: Atheneum, 1978.

Holmquist, June D., ed. *They Chose Minnesota: A Survey of the State's Ethnic Groups*. St. Paul: Minnesota Historical Society, 1981.

Holt, Michael F. *The Rise and Fall of the American Whig Party: Jacksonian Politics and the Onset of the Civil War*. New York: Oxford University Press, 1999.

Holt, Thomas C. *Children of Fire: A History of African Americans*. New York: Hill and Wang, 2010.

Hopkins, Caspar T. *Common Sense Applied to the Immigration Question: Showing Why the "California Immigrant Union" was Founded and What It Expects To Do*. San Francisco: Turnbull & Smith, 1869.

Hourwich, Isaac. *Immigration and Labor: The Economic Aspects of European Immigration to the United States*. New York: G. P. Putnam's Sons, 1912.

Immigration Department. National Civic Federation. *Facts About Immigration*. Privately published, 1907.

Interchurch World Movement. *Report on the Steel Strike of 1919*. New York: Harcourt, Brace and Howe, 1920.

Jacob, Heinrich Edward. *The World of Emma Lazarus*. New York: Schocken Books, 1949.

Jacobson, Matthew Frye. *Barbarian Virtues: The United States Encounters Foreign Peoples at Home and Abroad, 1876–1917* (New York: Hill and Wang, 2000.

———. *Whiteness of a Different Color: European Immigrants and the Alchemy of Race*. Cambridge: Harvard University Press, 1998.

Jones, Eliot. *The Anthracite Coal Combination in the United States, With Some Account of the Early Development of the Anthracite Industry*. Cambridge: Harvard University Press, 1914.

Josephson, Matthew. *The Robber Barons: The Great American Capitalists, 1861–1901*. New York: Harcourt, Brace, 1934.

Jung, Moon-Ho. *Coolies and Cane: Race, Labor, and Sugar in the Age of Emancipation*. Baltimore: Johns Hopkins University Press, 2006.

Katz, Philip M. *From Appomattox to Montmartre: Americans and the Paris Commune*. Cambridge: Harvard University Press, 1988.

Keller, Morton. *Affairs of State: Public Life in Late Nineteenth Century America*. Cambridge: Harvard University Press, 1977.

Kelly, Kevin. *Making Sense of the Molly Maguires*. New York: Oxford University Press, 1998.

Kennedy, David M. *Over Here: The First World War and American Society*. New York: Oxford University Press, 1980.

Klein, Maury. *The Life and Legend of Jay Gould*. Baltimore: Johns Hopkins University Press, 1986.

Kolko, Gabriel. *The Triumph of Conservatism: A Reinterpretation of American History, 1900–1916*. New York: Free Press, 1963.

Krause, Paul. *The Battle for Homestead, 1880–1892: Politics, Culture, and Steel*. Pittsburgh: University of Pittsburgh Press, 1992.

Kraut, Alan M. *The Huddled Masses: The Immigrant in American Society, 1880–1921*. Arlington Heights, IL: Harlan Davidson, 1982.

Lamoreaux, Naomi R. *The Great Merger Movement in American Business, 1895–1904*. Cambridge, UK: Cambridge University Press, 1985.

Lavender, David. *California: Land of New Beginnings*. New York: Harper and Row, 1972.

Laslett, John H. M. *Labor and the Left: A Study of Socialist and Radical Influences in the American Labor Movement*. New York: Basic Books, 1970.

Lee, Erika. *At America's Gate: Chinese Immigration During the Exclusion Era, 1882–1943*. Chapel Hill: University of North Carolina Press, 2003.

Levine, Louis [Louis Lorwin]. *The Women's Garment Workers: A History of the International Ladies' Garment Workers' Union*. New York: B. W. Huebsch, Inc., 1924; reprint, New York: Arno & The New York Times, 1969.

Levine, Susan. *Labor's True Woman: Carpet Weavers, Industrialization, and Labor Reform in the Gilded Age*. Philadelphia: Temple University Press, 1984.

Licht, Walter. *Working for the Railroad: The Organization of Work in the Nineteenth Century*. Princeton: Princeton University Press, 1983.

Lieber, Francis. *The Stranger in America*. Philadelphia: Carey, Lea, and Blanchard, 1835.

Lindsey, Almont. *The Pullman Strike: The Story of a Unique Experiment and of the Great Labor Upheaval*. Chicago: University of Chicago Press, 1942.

Link, Arthur, ed. *The Papers of Woodrow Wilson*. Princeton: Princeton University Press, 1966–1994.

Livesay, Herold C. *Andrew Carnegie and the Rise of Big Business*. New York: Longman, 2nd ed., 2000.

Lodge, Henry Cabot, ed. *Selections from the Correspondence of Theodore Roosevelt and Henry Cabot Lodge, 1884–1918*. New York: Henry Scribner's Sons, 2 volumes, 1924.

Luebke, Frederick. *Bonds of Loyalty: German Americans and World War I*. DeKalb: Northern Illinois University Press, 1974.

———. *European Immigrants in the American West*. Albuquerque: University of New Mexico Press, 1998.

Mack, Charles R. and Henry H. Lesesne, eds. *Francis Lieber and the Culture of the Mind*. Columbia: University of South Carolina Press, 2005. See esp. Peter W. Becker, "Prologue: Lieber's Place in History" and Paul Finkelman, "Lieber, Slavery, and Free Thought in Antebellum South Carolina."

Martin, Edward W. [James D. McCabe]. *The History of the Great Riots*. Philadelphia: National Publishing, 1877.

Mason, Edward S. *The Paris Commune: An Episode in the History of the Socialist Movement*. New York: Howard Fertig, 1967.

Mayo-Smith, Richmond. *Emigration and Immigration: A Study in Social Science*. New York: Charles Scriber's Sons, 1890.

McGovern, George S., and Leonard F. Guttridge. *The Great Coalfield War*. Boston: Houghton Mifflin, 1972.

McGraw, Thomas K. *Prophets of Regulation: Charles Francis Adams, Louis D. Brandeis, James M. Landis, Alfred E. Kahn*. Cambridge: Harvard University Press, 1984.

[McKinley, William]. *Speeches and Addresses of William McKinley*. New York: Double Day and McClure, 1900.

McPherson, James. *Battle Cry of Freedom, The Civil War Era*. New York: Oxford University Press, 1988.

Messer-Kruse, Timothy. *The Trial of the Haymarket Anarchists: Terrorism and Justice in the Gilded Age*. New York: Palgrave Macmillan, 2011.

Miller, Kerby A. *Emigrants and Exiles: Ireland and the Irish Exodus to North America*. New York: Oxford University Press, 1985.

Miller, Stuart Creighton. *The Unwelcome Immigrant: The American Image of the Chinese, 1785–1882*. Berkeley: University of California Press, 1969.

Mink, Gwendolyn. *Old Labor and New Immigrants in American Political Development*. Ithaca: Cornell University Press, 1986.

Mitchell, John. *Organized Labor: Its Problems, Purposes, and Ideals and the Present and Future of American Wage Earners*. Philadelphia: American Book and Bible House, 1903.

Montgomery, David. *Beyond Equality: Labor and the Radical Republicans, 1862–1872*. New York: Alfred A. Knopf, 1967.

Morlan, Robert L. *Political Prairie Fire: The Nonpartisan League, 1915–1922*. St. Paul: Minnesota Historical Society Press, 1955; revised ed., 1985.

Morris, Edward. *Wall Streeters: The Creators and Corrupters of American Finance*. New York: Columbia Business School Publishing, 2015.

Motomura, Hiroshi. *Americans in Waiting*. New York: Oxford University Press, 2006.

Murray, Robert K. *Red Scare: A Study in National Hysteria, 1919–1920*. Minneapolis: University of Minnesota Press, 1955.

Nevins, Allan. *Hamilton Fish: The Inner History of the Grant Administration*. New York: F. Ungar Publishing, reprint ed., 1957.

Nordhoff, Charles. *California for Health, Pleasure, and Residence. A Book for Travelers and Settlers*. New York: Harper & Brothers Publishers, 1875.

Orsi, Richard J. *Sunset Limited: The Southern Pacific Railroad and the Development of the American West, 1850–1930*. Berkeley: University of California Press, 2005.

Ozanne, Robert. *A Century of Labor Management: Relations at McCormick and International Harvester*. Madison: University of Wisconsin Press, 1967.

Papanikolas, Zeese. *Buried Unsung: Louis Tikas and the Ludlow Massacre*. Salt Lake City: University of Utah Press, 1982.

Parsons, Lucy. *Famous Speeches of the Eight Chicago Anarchists*. New York: Socialistic Publishing Society; New York: Arno Press, 1969.

Peck, Gunther. *Reinventing Free Labor: Padrones and Immigrant Workers in the North American West, 1880–1930*. Cambridge, UK: Cambridge University Press, 2000.

Perlman Selig, and Philip Taft, *History of Labor in the United States, 1896–1932*, Vol. 4, *Labor Movements* (New York: Macmillan, 1935

Perry, Thomas S. ed. *The Life and Letters of Francis Lieber*. Boston: James R. Osgood and Company, 1882.

Petit, Jeanne E. *The Men and Women We Want: Gender, Race, and the Progressive Era Literacy Test Debate*. Rochester: University of Rochester Press, 2010.

Pfaelzer, Jean. *Driven Out: The Forgotten War Against Chinese Americans*. New York: Random House, 2007.

Phillips, Catherine C. *Cornelius Cole: California Pioneer and United States Senator*. San Francisco: John Henry Nash, 1929.

Pickus, Noah. *True Faith and Alliance: Immigration and American Civic Nationalism*. Princeton: Princeton University Press, 2005.

Pierce, Bessie L. *A History of Chicago*. Vol. 2: *From Town to City*. New York: Alfred A. Knopf, 1940.

Pinkerton, Allan. *Strikers, Communists, Tramps and Detectives*. New York: G. W. Carleton, Publishers, 1878.

Pizer, Donald. *Hamlin Garland's Early Work and Career*. Berkeley: University of California Press, 1960.

Porter, Glenn. *The Rise of Big Business*. Wheeling, IL: Harlan Davidson, Inc., 1973.

Post, Louis F. *The Deportations Delirium of Nineteen-Twenty: A Personal Narrative of and Historic Official Experience*. New York: Charles H. Kerr, 1923; reprint ed., New York: Da Capo Press, 1970.

Preston, William Jr. *Aliens and Dissenters: Federal Suppression of Radicals, 1902–1933*. Cambridge: Harvard University Press, 1963; New York: Harper & Row, 1966.

[Pullman, George M.]. *The Strike at Pullman*. Privately printed, ca. 1894.

Rauchway, Eric. *Murdering McKinley: The Making of Theodore Roosevelt's America*. New York: Hill and Wang, 2003.

Riis, Jacob. *How the Other Half Lives: Studies among the Tenements of New York*. New York: Charles Scribner's Sons, 1890.

Roediger, David R. *Working towards Whiteness: How America's Immigrants Became White*. New York: Basic Books, 2005.

Roediger, David R., and Philip Foner. *Our Own Time: A History of Labor and the Working Day*. New York: Greenwood Press, 1989.

Rohrbough, Malcolm J. *Days of Gold: The California Gold Rush and the American Nation*. Berkeley: University of California Press, 1977.

Rolston, Jessica Smith. *Mining Coal and Undermining Gender: Rhythms of Work and Family in the American West*. New Brunswick, NJ: Rutgers University Press, 2014.

Russell, Francis. *A City in Terror—1919—The Boston Police Strike*. New York: Viking Press, 1975.

Salvatore, Nick. *Eugene V. Debs: Citizen and Socialist*. Urbana: University of Illinois Press, 1982.

Salyer, Lucy E. *Laws Harsh as Tigers: Chinese Immigrants and the Shaping of Modern Immigration Law*. Chapel Hill: North Carolina University Press, 1995.

Saxton, Alexander. *The Rise and Fall of the White Republic: Class, Politics, and Mass Culture in Nineteenth Century America*. London: Verso, 1990.

Schlegel, Marvin W. *Ruler of the Reading: The Life of Franklin B. Gowen, 1836–1889*. Harrisburg: Archives Publishing Company of Pennsylvania, 1947.

Schwantes, Carlos. *Coxey's Army: An American Odyssey*. Lincoln: University of Nebraska Press, 1985.

Sealander, Judith. *Public Wealth & Private Life: Foundation Philanthropy and the Reshaping of American Social Policy from the Progressive Era to the New Deal*. Baltimore: Johns Hopkins University Press, 1997.

Shalloo, Jeremiah P. *Private Police, with Special Reference to Pennsylvania*. Philadelphia: American Academy of Political and Social Sciences, 1933.

Smith, Matthew Hale. *Sunshine and Shadow in New York*. Hartford, CT: J. B. Burr and Company, 1969.

Smith, Willard H. *Schuyler Colfax: The Changing Fortunes of a Political Idol*. Indianapolis: Indiana Historical Bureau, 1952.

Solomon, Barbara Miller. *Ancestors and Immigrants: A Changing New England Tradition*. Cambridge: Harvard University Press, 1956; reprint ed., Boston: Northeastern University Press, 1989.

Stein, Leon, ed. *The Pullman Strike*. New York: Arno & The New York Times, 1969. See esp. Grover Cleveland, "The Government in the Chicago Strike of 1894."

Stein, Leon and Philip Taft, eds. *Labor Politics: Collected Pamphlets*. New York: Arno & and the New York Times, 1971. See esp. Kellogg, D. O. "Thoughts on the Labor Question-."

Stephenson, George M. *John Lind of Minnesota*. Port Washington, NY: Kennikat Press, 1935; reprint edition, 1971.

Stewart, James B. *Wendell Phillips: Liberty's Hero*. Baton Rouge: Louisiana State University Press, 1986.

Stover, John F. *American Railroads*. Chicago: University of Chicago Press, 1961.

——. *History of the Baltimore and Ohio Railroad*. West Lafayette, IN: Purdue University Press, 1987.

——. *The Life and Decline of the American Railroad*. New York: Oxford University Press, 1970.

Stowell, Myron R. *"Fort Frick" Or the Siege of Homestead*. Pittsburgh: Pittsburgh Printing Co., 1893.

Stromquist, Shelton. *A Generation of Boomers*. Urbana: University of Illinois Press, 1987.

Strouse, Jean. *Morgan: American Financier*. New York: Random House, 1999.

Taylor, Albion G. *Labor Policies of the National Association of Manufacturers*. Urbana: University of Illinois Press, 1927; reprint, New York: Arno Press, 1973.

Taylor, Frederick Winslow. *Principles of Scientific Management*. New York: Harper & Brothers, 1919.

Thayer, William R. *The Life and Letters of John Hay*. Boston: Houghton Mifflin, 1929.

Thorndike, Ashley H., ed., *Modern Eloquence*. New York: Lincoln Scholarship Fund, 1928. See esp. Andrew Carnegie, "The Scottish American: Speech to the Annual Dinner of the St. Andrews Society," November 30, 1891.

Tourgée, Albion W. *A Fool's Errand*. Cambridge: Harvard University Press, 1961; New York: Harper & Row, 1966.

Trachtenberg, Alexander. *The History of Legislation for the Protection of Coal Miners in Pennsylvania, 1824–1915*. New York: International Publishers, 1942.

Tripp, Anna H. *The I.W.W. and the Paterson Silk Strike of 1913*. Urbana: University of Illinois Press, 1987.

Tutorow, Norman T. *Leland Stanford: Man of Many Careers*. Menlo Park, CA: Pacific Coast Publishers, 1971.

Vecchio, Diane C. *Merchants, Midwives, and Laboring Women: Italian Migrants in Urban America*. Urbana: University of Illinois Press, 2006.

Vorse, Mary Heaton. *A Footnote to Folly: Reminiscence of Mary Heaton Vorse*. New York: Farrar and Rinehart, 1935.

Wall, Joseph. *Andrew Carnegie*. New York: Oxford University Press, 1970.

Warne, Franklin J. *The Immigrant Invasion.* New York: Dodd, Mead, 1913.

Warren, Kenneth. *Triumphant Capitalism: Henry Clay Frick and the Industrialization of America.* Pittsburgh: University of Pittsburgh Press, 1996.

Weinstein, James. *The Corporate Ideal in the Liberal State.* Boston: Beacon Press, 1968.

White, Richard. *Railroaded: The Transcontinentals and the Making of Modern America.* New York: W. W. Norton, 2011.

Wiebe, Robert. *Businessmen and Reform: A Study of the Progressive Movement.* Cambridge: Harvard University Press, 1962.

Wilentz, Sean. *The Rise of American Democracy: Jefferson to Lincoln.* New York: W. W. Norton, 2005.

Williams, Charles Richard, ed. *The Diary and Letters of Rutherford B. Hayes.* Columbus: Ohio State Archeological and Historical Society, 1922.

Williams, John H. *A Great and Shining Road: The Epic Story of the Transcontinental Railroad.* New York: Times Books, 1988.

Wilson, Woodrow. *A History of the American People.* New York: Harper and Brothers, 1901.

Yacovone, Donald, ed. *Freedom's Journey: African American Voices of the Civil War.* Chicago: Lawrence Hill Books, 2004.

Yu, Renqiu. *To Save China, to Save Ourselves: The Chinese Hand Laundry Alliance of New York.* Philadelphia: Temple University Press, 1992.

Zeidel, Robert. *Immigrants, Progressives, and Exclusion Politics: The Dillingham Commission, 1900–1927.* DeKalb: Northern Illinois University Press, 2004.

Ziegler-McPherson, Christina A. *Selling America: Immigrant Promotion and the Settlement of the American Continent, 1607–1914.* Santa Barbara: Praeger, 2017.

Government Documents

Bureau of Labor Statistics and Investigation, comp. *The Official History of the Great Strike of 1886 on the Southwestern Railway System.* Jefferson City: Tribune Printing Company, 1886.

California State Senate, Special Committee on Chinese Immigration. *Chinese Immigration: Its Social, Moral, and Political Effect.* Sacramento: State Printing Office, 1878.

Constitution of the State of California, 1879.

Congressional Records

[Grover Cleveland.] *"Immigration Laws." Message from the President of the United States, Returning to the House of Representatives Without His Approval, House Bill Numbered 7864, Entitled "An Act to Amend the Laws of the United States."* 54th Cong., 2nd sess., S. Doc 185 (Serial 3471).

Immigration and Naturalization Service Records. Record Group 85, 53139/10. National Archives, Washington, DC.

Pennsylvania General Assembly. *Report of the Committee Appointed to Investigate the Railroad Riot in July 1977.* Harrisburg, PA: Lane S. Hart, State Printer, 1878.

Raymond, Rossiter W. *Mines and Mining in the States and Territories West of the Rocky Mountains.* Washington, DC: Government Printing Office, 1877.

[Roosevelt, Theodore.] *Annual Message of the President, Transmitted to Congress, December 3, 1901.* 54th Cong., 1st Sess., H. Doc. 1.

[Stanford, Leland]. "Annual Address of Leland Stanford, Governor of the State of California, at the Fourteenth Session of the Legislature [January 1863]." Sacramento: Benj. P. Avery, State Printer, 1863.

——. "Inaugural Address of Leland Stanford, Governor of the State of California, January 10, 1862." Sacramento: Benj. P. Avery, State Printer, 1862.

——. "Second Annual Message of Leland Stanford, Governor of the State of California, at the Fifteenth Session of the Legislature." Sacramento: O. M. Clayes, State Printer.

State of Minnesota. House of Representatives. "Hearing Before Committee on Labor and Labor Legislation: Labor Troubles in Northern Minnesota," January 30, 1917

[United States Congress.] *An Act to Execute Certain Treaty Stipulations Relating to Chinese.* Forty-Seventh Cong., 1st Sess., Chapter 126, May 6, 1882. National Archives, https://catalog.archives.gov/id/5752153.

[United States Congress]. An Act To limit the immigration of aliens into the United States, 67th Cong., 1st sess.

——. "An Act To limit the immigration of aliens into the United States," 68th Cong., Sess. 1.

——. *National Security League—Hearings Before A Special Committee of the House of Representatives.* 65th Cong., 3rd sess., December 19, 1918.

United States House of Representatives. House Committee on Immigration. "Immigration Investigation," 52nd Cong., 1st sess., H. Rept. 2090.

——. House Committee on the Judiciary. "Investigation of the Employment of Pinkerton Detectives in Connection with the Labor Troubles at Homestead, PA." 52nd Cong., 2nd sess., H. Rept. 2247. Washington, DC: Government Printing Office, 1892.

——. *Statistical Abstract of the United States. 1883.* 48th Cong., 1st sess., H. Exec. Doc. 32. Washington: Government Printing Office, 1884.

United States Immigration Commission. *Reports of the Immigration Commission.* 41 volumes. Washington, DC: Government Printing Office, 1911.

United States Senate. *Final Report of the Commission on Industrial Relations.* Washington, DC: Government Printing Office, 1915.

——. *Investigation of Strike in Steel Industries: Hearings Before the Committee on Education and Labor.* Washington, DC: Government Printing Office, 1919.

——. Select Committee to Investigate the Armed Bodies of Men for Private Purposes [Untitled Report], 52nd Cong., 2nd sess., S. Rept. 1280.

——. Senate Committee on Immigration. "Investigation by the Committee of Immigration of the United States Senate, on the Proposition of the Suspension of Immigration for One Year," 52nd Cong., 2nd sess., S. Rept. 1333,

——. Senate Select Committee. [Investigation of Labor Troubles]. 52nd Cong., 2nd sess., S. Rept. 1280, February 10, 1893.

United States Strike Commission. "Report on the Chicago Strike of June–July 1894, by the United States Strike Commission." Washington, DC: Government Printing Office, 1895.

[Walker, Francis A., comp.] *Statistics of the Population of the United States [1870].* Washington, DC: Government Printing Office, 1872.

Journal Articles

Allerfeldt, Kristofer. "'And We Got Here First': Albert Johnson, National Origins and Self-Interest in the Immigration Debate of the 1920s." *Journal of Contemporary History* 45 (January 2010): 7–26.

Arnesen, Eric. "'Like Banquo's Ghost, It Will Not Down': The Race Question and the American Railroad Brotherhoods," *American Historical Review* 99 (December 1994): 1601–34.

Auerbach, Jerold S. "Woodrow Wilson's 'Predictions' to Frank Cobb: Words Historians Should Doubt Ever Got Spoken." *Journal of American History* 54 (December 1967): 608–17.

Baker, Charles A. "Henry George and the California Background of *Poverty and Progress*." *California Historical Society Quarterly* 24 (June 1945): 97–115.

Belgen, Theodore. "The Competition of the Northwestern States for Immigrants." *Wisconsin Magazine of History* 3 (September 1919): 1–11.

Betten, Neil. "Strike on the Mesabi—1907." *Minnesota History* 40 (Fall 1967): 340–47.

Birtle, Andrew. "Governor George Hoadly's Use of the Ohio National Guard in the Hocking Valley Coal Strike of 1884." *Ohio History* 91 (August 1982): 37–57.

Brier, Stephen and Ferdinando Fasce. "Italian Migrants and the Language of Solidarity in the Early-Twentieth-Century Western Coal Fields." *Labor: Studies in Working Class History of the Americas* 20 (Summer 2011): 89–121.

Carlson, Robert A. "Americanization as an Early Twentieth-Century Adult Education Movement." *History of Education Quarterly* 10 (Winter 1970): 440–64.

Case, Theresa A. "Blaming Martin Irons: Leadership and Popular Protest in the 1886 Southwest Strike." *Journal of the Gilded Age and Progressive Era* 8 (January 2009): 52–81.

Chandler, Robert J. "Integrity Amid Tumult, Wells Fargo & Co's Gold Rush Banking." *California History* 70 (Fall 1991): 271–73.

Clancy, John J., Jr. "A Mugwump on Minorities." *Journal of Negro History* 51 (July 1966): 174–92.

Cochran, Thomas C. "The Business Revolution." *American Historical Review* 79 (December 1974): 1449–66.

Cooper, Jerry M. "The Wisconsin National Guard in the Milwaukee Riots of 1886." *Wisconsin Magazine of History* 55 (Autumn 1971): 31–48.

Cotkin, George B. "Strikebreakers, Evictions, and Violence: Industrial Conflict in the Hocking Valley." *Ohio History* 87 (April 1978): 140–50.

Currarino, Rosanne. "'The Politics of 'More': The Labor Question and the Idea of Economic Liberty in Industrial America." *Journal of American History* 93 (June 2006), 17–36.

Davis, Collin J. "Bitter Conflict: The 1922 Railroad Shopmen's Strike." *Labor History* 33 (Fall 1992): 433–55.

Derber, Milton. "The Idea of Industrial Democracy." *Labor History* 7 (September 1966): 259–86.

Diner, Hasia. "The Encounter between Jews and America in the Gilded Age and Progressive Era." *Journal of the Gilded Era and Progressive Era* 11 (January 2012): 2–25.

Drinnon, Richard. "The *Blast:* An Introduction and Appraisal." *Labor History* 11 (Winter 1970): 82–88.

Dubofsky, Melvyn. "The 'New' Labor History: Achievements and Failures." *Reviews in American History* 5 (June 1977): 249–54.

———. "Review of *City in Terror.*" *Labor History* 17 (Summer 1976): 436–40.

Dubois, Ellen Carol "Working Women, Class Relations, and Suffrage Militance: Harriot Stanton Blatch and the New York Suffrage Movement, 1894–1909." *Journal of American History* 74 (June 1987): 34–58.

Ensley, Philip C. "The Interchurch World Movement and the Steel Strike of 1919." *Labor History* 13 (Spring 1972): 217–31.

Esch, Elizabeth and David Roediger. "One Symptom of Originality: Race and Management of Labor in the United States." *Historical Materialism* 17 (2009): 1–41.

Fishlow, Albert. *American Railroads and the Transformation of the Antebellum Economy.* Cambridge: Harvard University Press, 1965.

Furrow, Matthew. "Samuel Gridley Howe, the Black Population of Canada West, and the Racial Ideology of the 'Blueprint for Radical Reconstruction.'" *Journal of American History* 97 (September 2010): 344–70.

Galambos, Louis. "AFL's Concept of Big Business: A Quantitative Study of Attitudes toward Large Corporations, 1894–1931." *Journal of American History* 57 (March 1971): 847–63.

Garate, Donald T. "Wenceslao (Three-Fingered Jack) Loustaunau: Blacksmith with a Cause." *Journal of Arizona History* 48 (Summer 2007): 111–42.

Gidelman, H. M. "Perspectives on American Industrial Violence." *Business History Review* 47 (Spring 1973): 1–23.

Glasrud, Clarence A. "Boyesen and Norwegian Immigration." *Norwegian-American Studies & Records* 19 (1956): 15–46.

Golin, Steve. "Defeat Becomes Disaster: The Paterson Strike of 1913 and the Decline of the IWW." *Labor History* 24 (Spring 1983): 223–48.

Greene, Victor R. "A Study of Slavs, Strikes, and Unions: The Anthracite Strike of 1897." *Pennsylvania History* 31 (April 1964): 199–215.

Guterl, Matthew and Christine Skwiot. "Atlantic and Pacific Crossings: Race, Empire, and 'the Labor Problem' in the Late Nineteenth Century." *Radical History Review* 91 (Winter 2005): 40–61.

Gutfeld, Arnon. "The Murder of Frank Little: Radical Labor Agitation in Butte, Montana, 1917." *Labor History* 10 (Spring 1969): 177–92.

Gutman, Herbert. "The Tomkins Square Riot in New York City." *Labor History* 6 (1965): 44–70.

Hansen, Robert. "The Bethlehem Steel Strike of 1910," *Labor History* 15 (Winter 1974): 3–18.

[Hopkins, Casper T.]. "California Reflections of Casper T. Hopkins [Originally composed in 1888]." *California Historical Society Quarterly* 25 (June 1946): 97–120 and 27 (June 1948): 165–74.

Hurtado, Albert L. "California Indians and the Workaday West: Labor, Assimilation, and Survival." *California History* 69 (Spring 1990): 2–11.

Ingham, John N. "A Strike in the Progressive Era: McKees Rocks, 1909." *Pennsylvania Magazine of History and Biography* 90 (July 1966): 353–77.

Jensen, Roland J. "The Politics of Discrimination: America, Russia, and the Jewish Question." *American Jewish History* 75 (March 1986): 280–95.

Johnson, Donald. "Wilson, Burleson and Censorship in the First World War." *Journal of Southern History* 28 (February 1962): 46–58.

Kamphoefner, Walter D. "Immigrant Epistolary and Epistemology: On the Motivators and Mentality of Nineteenth-Century German Immigrants." *Journal of American Ethnic History* 28 (Spring 2009): 34–54.

Katz, Philip M. "'Lessons From Paris': The American Clergy Responds to the Paris Commune." *Church History* 68 (September 1994): 393–406.

Kittelstrom, Amy. "Dedicated Spirits: Religious Mediators and Romantic Ideas in the Late Nineteenth Century." *The European Legacy* 9 (February 2004): 31–42.

Lause, Mark A. "The American Radicals & Organized Marxism: The Initial Experience." *Labor History* 33 (Winter 1992): 55–80.

Leiren, Terje I. "Ole and the Reds: The 'Americanism' of Seattle Mayor Ole Hanson." *Norwegian American Studies* 30 (1985): 75–95.

Leonard, Henry B. "Ethnic Cleavage and Industrial Conflict in Late 19th Century America: The Cleveland Rolling Mill Company Strikes of 1882 and 1885." *Labor History* 20 (Fall 1979): 524–48.

Link, Arthur. "That Cobb Interview." *Journal of American History* 72 (June 1985): 7–17.

Livingston, James. The Social Analysis of Economic History and Theory." *American Historical Review* 92 (February 1987): 69–96.

Loewenberg, James. "Efforts of the South to Encourage Immigration, 1865–1900." *South Atlantic Quarterly* 33 (October 1934), 363–84.

Lowery, J. Vincent. "'Another Species of Race Discord': Race, Desirability, and the North Carolina Immigration Movement of the Early Twentieth Century." *Journal of American Ethnic History* 35 (Winter 2016): 32–59.

Mayo, Marlene J. "A Catechism of Western Diplomacy: The Japanese and Hamilton Fish, 1872." *Journal of Asian Studies* 26 (May 1967): 389–410.

Marchalonis, Shirley. "Lucy Larcom." *Legacy* 5 (Spring 1988): 45–52.

McKee, Delber L. "'The Chinese Must Go!' Commissioner General Powderly and Chinese Immigration, 1897–1902." *Pennsylvania History* 44 (Winter 1977): 37–51.

McMurray, Donald L. "Labor Policies of the General Managers Association of Chicago, 1886–1994." *Journal of Economic History* 13 (Spring 1953): 160–79.

Mickenberg, Julia L. "Suffragettes and Soviets: American Feminism and the Specter of Revolutionary Russia." *Journal of American History* 100 (March 2014): 1021–51.

Mihaly, David H. "Riveting Imagery." *Huntington Frontiers* (Spring/Summer 2014): 14–15.

Navin Thomas R. and Marian V. Sears. "A Study in Merger: Formation of the International Mercantile Marine Company." *Business History Review* 28 (December 1954): 291–328.

Ngai, Mae M. "Chinese Gold Miners and the 'Chinese Question' in Nineteenth-Century California and Victoria." *Journal of American History* 101 (March 2015): 1082–1105.

Oz, Frankel. "Whatever Happened to 'Red Emma'? Emma Goldman, From Alien Radical to American Icon." *Journal of American History* 83 (December 1996): 903–42.

Park, Joseph F. "The 1903 'Mexican Affair' at Clinton." *Journal of Arizona History* 19 (Summer 1977): 119–48.

Peterson, Anna. "Making Women's Suffrage Support an Ethnic Duty: Norwegian American Identity Construction and the Women's Suffrage Movement, 1880–1925." *Journal of American Ethnic History* 30 (Summer 2011): 5–23.

Quinn, Edward G. "Of Myth and Men: An Analysis of Molly Maguireism in Nineteenth Century Pennsylvania." *Eire-Ireland* 23 (Winter 1988): 52–61.

Rader, Benjamin G. "The Montana Lumber Strike of 1917." *Pacific Historical Review* 36 (May 1967): 189–207.

Reep, Diana. "Margaret Deland (1857–1945)." *Legacy* 14 (April 30, 1997): 43–50.

Rezneck, Samuel. "Distress, Relief, and Discontent in the United States during the Depression of 1873–78." *Journal of Political Economy* 58 (December 1950): 498–500.

——. "Patterns of Thought and Action in an American Depression, 1882–1886." *American Historical Review* 61 (February 1956): 284–307.

Rhodes, Edward J. M. "The Chinese in Texas." *The Southwest Historical Quarterly* 81 (July 1977): 1–36.

Shapiro, Herbert. "The McNamara Case: A Window on Class Antagonism in the Progressive Era." *Southern California Quarterly* 70 (March 1988): 64–95.

Skaggs, Julian C. and Richard L. Ehrlich. "Profits, Paternalism, and Rebellion: A Case Study in Industrial Strife." *Business History Review* 54 (Summer 1980): 155–74.

Slater, Joseph "Public Workers: Labor and the Boston Police Strike of 1919." *Labor History* 38 (Winter 1996/1997): 7–27.

Slavishak, Edward. "Working-Class Muscle: Homestead and Bodily Disorder in the Gilded Age." *Journal of the Gilded Age and Progressive Era* 3 (October 2004): 339–68.

Stovall, Tyler. "White Freedom and the Lady of Liberty." *American Historical Review* 123 (February 2018): 1–27.

Sylvia, Philip T. "The Position of Workers in a Textile Community: Fall River in the Early 1880s." *Labor History* 16 (Spring 1975): 230–48.

Vile, John R. "Francis Lieber and the Process of Constitutional Amendment." *Review of Politics* 60 (1998): 525–43.

Ward, James A. "Power and Accountability on the Pennsylvania Railroad, 1846–1878." *Business History Review* 49 (Spring 1975): 37–59.

Ward, Robert D. "The Origins and Activities of the National Security League." *Mississippi Valley Historical Review* 47 (June 1960): 51–65.

Watson, Bradley C. S. "Who Was Francis Lieber?" *Modern Age* 42 (2001): 304–10.

Weinstein, James. "Big Business and the Origins of Workmen's Compensation." *Labor History* 8 (Spring 1967): 156–75.

Wiebe, Robert. "The Anthracite Coal Strike of 1902: A Record of Confusion." *Mississippi Valley Historical Review* 48 (September 1961): 229–51.

Zeidel, Robert. "Pursuit of 'Human Brotherhood': Rockefeller Philanthropy and American Immigration, 1900–1933," *New York History* 90 (Winter/Spring 2009): 85–106.

Periodicals

Adams, H. C. "Shall We Muzzle Anarchists?" *The Forum* 1 (July 1886): 449.

Adams, John D. "Clod or Brother?: To The Editor." *The Survey* 27 (March 30, 1912): 2014–15.

"Aftermath of a Strike." *The Outlook* 101 (June 1, 1919): 237–38.

Ager, Harry C. "Causes of the Present Business Depression." *The American Journal of Politics* 4 (March 1894): 233–44.

Allen, Nathan. "Changes in New England Population." *Popular Science Monthly* 22 (August 1883): 433–44.

Altgeld, John P. "The Immigrant's Answer." *Forum* 8 (February 1890): 684–96.

"Amendment, California Alien Land Law, Adopted November 2, 1920." *Annals of the American Academy of Political and Social Sciences* 93 (January 1921): 13–16.

Bemis, Edward W. "The Homestead Strike." *Journal of Political Economy* 2 (June 1894): 369–96.

——. "Mine Labor in the Hocking Valley." *Publications of the American Economic Association* 3 (July 1888): 27–42.

——. "Restriction of Immigration." *Andover Review* 9 (March 1888): 252–64.

——. "Restriction of Emigration," *Bibliotheca Sacra* 53 (July 1896): 560–73.

Benjamin, R. M. "Legislation to Control the Anthracite Coal Corporations." *Albany Law Review* 64 (1902): 418.

Bigelow, S. Lawrence, I. Leo Sharfman, and R. M. Wenley. "Henry Carter Adams." *Journal of Political Economy* 30 (April 1922): 201–11.

Birkinbine, John. "Anthracite Coal Mining in Pennsylvania." *Cassier's Magazine* 22 (August 1902): 507–20.

Bishop, Joseph B. "The Coal Strike." *International Quarterly* 6 (December 1902): 456.

——. "President Roosevelt's First Year." *International Quarterly* 6 (December 1902): 450–62.

Black, Chauncey F. "The Lessons of Homestead: A Remedy for Labor Troubles." *The Forum* 16 (September 1892): 14–25.

Black, William N. "The Coxey Crusade and Its Meaning." *Engineering Magazine* 7 (June 1884): 307–13.

[Bloomfield & Bloomfield]. *Industrial Relations: Bloomfield's Labor Digest* 17 (October 13, 1923): 1699.

Boyesen, Hjalmar. "Dangers of Unrestricted Immigration." *Forum* 3 (July 1887): 532–42.

Bogart, Ernest L. "The Steel Strike." *Bibliotheca Sacra* 59 (January 1902): 108–28.

Brewster, Edwin T. "Free Speech In Lawrence: To the Editors." *The Survey* 27 (March 30, 1912): 2015–16.

Brissenden, Paul F. "The Butte Miners and the Rusting Card." *American Economic Review* 10 (December 1920): 755–75.

Burns, Allen T. "For a Just Industrial Peace." *The Survey* 27 (March 16, 1912): 1925–27.

C. M. "All in the Day's Work." *The New Republic* 18 (April 1919): 372–73.

Cartwright, Richard. "An Economic Study of the Miner as He Is." *Catholic World* 75 (September 1902): 715–26.

Carnegie, Andrew. "Wealth's Duty." *Charities Review* 5 (November 1895): 33–35.

Cheney, Charles B. "A Labor Crisis and A Governor." *Outlook* (May 2, 1908): 24–30.

"Children of a Strike." *The Survey* 27 (February 24, 1912): 1791.

Claghorn, Kate Holladay. "Immigration's Ebbing Tide." *The Survey* 35 (January 29, 1916): 524–25.

Clark, John B. "Commission on Industrial Relations." *The Survey* 28 (July 6, 1912): 493–95.

Coffin, Charles C. Johnson of Minnesota." *Outlook* 40 (January 25, 1908): 167–73.

——. "Labor and the Natural Forces." *Atlantic Monthly* 43 (May 1879): 553–66.

"Colorado Coal Strike Report." *Journal of Political Economy* 23 (April 1913): 394–96.

"Constructive Patriotism." *The Outlook* 114 (December 13, 1916): 784–85.

Cotbern, Marion B. "When Strike Breakers Strike: The Demands of the Miners on the Misaba Range," *The Survey* 36 (August 26, 1916): 535–36.

Coxe, A. Cleveland. "Government by Aliens." *The Forum* 7 (August 1889): 597–608.

"Crime of Competition," *Railroad Trainmen's Journal* 15 (November 1898): 917–22.

"Cry for More Immigration." *Literary Digest* 75 (November 18, 1922): 18–19.

Cummings, John. "The Passing of the Coal Strike." *Journal of Political Economy* 11 (December 1902): 56.

Deland, Lorin F. "The Lawrence Strike: A Study." *Atlantic Monthly* 109 (May 1912): 694–704.

Dennett, Tyler. "The Other Side." *The Outlook* 113 (August 30, 1916): 1046–48.

"The Depth of Garyism." *The New Republic* 20 (October 8, 1919): 279–82.

"Developments at Lawrence." *The Survey* 27 (February 10, 1912): 1725–26.

Dike, Samuel W. "The Wage-Earners Loss During the Depression." *The Forum* 18 (November 1894): 369–78.

"Double Labor War." *The Outlook* 104 (May 3, 1913): 11.

"The Eight Hour Day." *Science* 7 (January 1886): 59.

Ely, Richard T. "Pullman: A Social Study." *Harper's New Monthly Magazine* 70 (February 1885), 452–66.

"Ettor in Jail: Strike Goes On." *The Survey* 27 (February 10, 1912): 1726–27.

"Europe's Call to Arms." *Literary Digest* 49 (August 8, 1914): 215–16.

"Fact and Rumor." *Christian Union* 21 (January 21, 1880): 71.

Fairchild, Henry P. "Immigration and Crisis." *American Economic Review* 1 (December 1911): 753.

Fitch, John A. "Arizona's Embargo on Strike-Breakers." *The Survey* 36 (May 6, 1916): 143–46.

"For a Peace Commission. *The Outlook* 100 (January 13, 1912): 67–68.

Forester, Robert F. "Hourwich's Immigration and Labor." *Quarterly Journal of Economics* 27 (August 1913): 656–71.

"Foster Homes Investigated." *The Survey* 27 (February 24, 1912): 1791–92.

Frank, Henry. "The Crusade of the Unemployed." *The Arena* 10 (June 1894): 239–44.

Garland, Hamlin. "Homestead and Its Perilous Trades: Impressions of a Visit," *McClures Magazine* 3 (June 1894): 3–20.

Gary, Joseph E. The Chicago Anarchists of 1886: The Crime, the Trial, and the Punishment." *The Century Magazine* 45 (April 1893): 803–37.

Giddings, Franklin H. "What Is Fair." *The Independent* 97 (January 21, 1919): 437.

"Girl Strikers Protest Against Magistrates." *The Survey* 23 (January 8, 1909): 489–90.

Hanna, Marcus A. "Industrial Conditions and Arbitration." *Annals of the American Academy of Political and Social Science* 20 (July–December 1902): 21–26.

Hard, William. "After the Strike." *The New Republic* 21 (January 28, 1920): 559–62.

"Haywood's Battle in Paterson." *Literary Digest* 46 (May 10, 1913): 1043–44.

Heaton, James P. "The Legal Aftermath of the Lawrence Strike." *The Survey* 28 (July 6, 1912): 503–10.

——. "The Salem Trial." *The Survey* 29 (December 7, 1912): 301–4.

"Heavy Increase in Immigration." *Literary Digest* 47 (October 23, 1913): 787–88.

"How the War Affects America." *Literary Digest* 49 (August 15, 1914): 256–57.

Howe, Frederic C. "Commercial Depression and Business Crisis." *The American Journal of Politics* 5 (November 1894): 449–60.

"Hughes-Borah Bill." *The Survey* 27 (March 9, 1912): 1898–99.

Hutchinson, Woods. "The Hygienic Aspects of the Shirt-Waist Strike." *The Survey* 23 (January 22, 1910): 541–50.

"Illiteracy Test Again Before Congress." *The Survey* 35 (March 4, 1916): 651.

"Immigrants and the Northwest." *The Survey* 27 (March 23, 1912): 1951–52.

"Immigration." Locomotive Firemen's Magazine 22 (April 1897): 221–22.

"Immigration of the Year." *The Outlook* 113 (August 30, 1916): 1023–24.

"Immigration Restriction Defeated." *The Outlook* 60 (December 24, 1898): 990.

"Industrial and Commercial Barons Determined to Flood United States With Chinese Laborers." *Brotherhood of Locomotive Firemen and Engineers Magazine* 64 (March 1918): 5–6.

"J. P. Morgan's Greatest Failure—The Steamship Trust." *Current Literature* 53 (August 1912): 172–74.

"Japanese Immigration-Grievance." *Literary Digest* 52 (April 22, 1916): 1138.

Kellor, Frances A. "Who Is Responsible for the Immigrant?" *The Outlook* 106 (April 25, 1914): 912–17.

Kinkead, W. L. "The Paterson Strike: To the Editor." *The Survey* 30 (May 31, 1913): 315–16.

L. W. "Homestead as Seen by One of Its Workers." *McClures Magazine* 3 (July 1894): 163–69.

Larcom, Lucy. "American Factory Life." *Journal of Social Science* 16 (December 1882): 141–46.

Lauck, W. Jett. "The Lesson From Lawrence." *North American Review* 195 (May 1912): 665–72.

——. "The Significance of the Situation at Lawrence: The Condition of the New England Woolen Mill Operator." *The Survey* 27 (February 17, 1912): 1772–74.

"Lawrence and the Industrial Workers of the World." *The Survey* 28 (April 6, 1912): 79–80.

"Lawrence Settlement." *The Survey* 27 (March 23, 1912): 1949–50.

"Lawrence Strike: A Review." *The Outlook* 100 (March 9, 1912): 531–36.

Lee, Joseph. "Immigration." *The Survey* 37 (December 30, 1916): 368.

"Lessons of the Recent Strikes." *North American Review* 159 (August 1894): 180–206.

Leupp, Constance D. "The Lawrence Strike." *The Survey* 27 (March 23, 1912): 1953–54.

——. "The Shirtwaist Makers' Strike." *The Survey* 23 (November 18, 1909): 383–86.

Lovejoy, Owen R. "The Right of Free Speech." *The Survey* 17 (March 9, 1912): 904–5.

Mailly, William. "The Working Girls' Strike." *The Independent* 67 (December 23, 1909): 1416–20.

[Manufacturer]. "The Situation as Seen by a Manufacturer." *The Survey* 28 (April 6, 1912): 75.

Mason, Gregory. "Industrial War in Paterson." *The Outlook* 104 (June 7, 1913): 283–87.

Maxey, Edwin. "Private Property and Public Rights." *Arena* 28 (December 1902): 561–62.

Means, D. McGregor. "Chinese Immigration and Political Economy." *The New England and Yale Review* 36 (January 1877): 1–10.

"Mesaba Strike." *The New Republic* 8 (September 2, 1916): 108–9.

[Miles, Nelson A.], "The Lessons of the Recent Strikes," *North American Review* 159 (August 1894): 184.

"Mill Owner's View." *The Survey* 28 (April 6, 1912): 75–76.

Mitchell, John. "The Coal Strike." *McClures Magazine* 20 (December 1902): 219–24.

"Monthly Record of Current Events." *Hutchings' Illustrated California Magazine* 41 (November 1859): 238.

"More Immigration Coming in Spite of the War." *Literary Digest* 53 (July 1, 1916): 46.

"National Security League." *The Outlook* 112 (February 16, 1916): 35.

"Need for a Federal Commission." *The Survey* 27 (February 17, 1912): 1775–76.

"A Needless Labor War." *The Outlook* 100 (January 27, 1912): 151–52.

Norris, Frank. "A Study in Strike-Time of the Conditions of Living in Representative Mining Towns," *Everybody's Magazine* 7 (July–December 1902): 241–48.

"Notes To the President of the United States." *The Chautauquan* 66 (March 1912): 22–26.

Oates, William C. "The Homestead Strike, I. A Congressional View." *North American Review* 155 (September 1892): 355–64.

O'Connor, Rev. James. "Capital and Labor." *American Catholic Quarterly Review* 8 (October 1883): 477–95.

O'Sullivan, Mary K. "The Lessons of War at Lawrence." *The Survey* 28 (April 6, 1912): 72–74.

"Pageant of the Paterson Strike." *The Survey* 30 (June 28, 1913): 428.

Palmer, Lewis E. "A Strike for Four Loaves of Bread." *The Survey* 27 (February 3, 1912): 1690–97.

Pfeiffer, C. Whit. "From 'Bohunks' to Finns: The Scale of Life among the Ore Strippers of the Northwoods." *The Survey* (April 1, 1916): 8–14.

Phelan, James D. "Why California Objects to the Japanese Invasion." *Annals of the American Academy of Political and Social Sciences* 93 (January 1921): 16–17.

Phillips, Wendell. "The Chinese." *National Standard*, July 30, 1870.

——. "The Outlook." *North American Review* 127 (July–August 1878): 110–11.

Pope, Colonel George. "'Business' and the Manufacturers." *American Industries* 14 (September 1913): 15.

"Possible Paterson." *The Outlook* 104 (June 14, 1913): 318–21.

Pound, W. M. F. "Immigration and Crime." *The Forum* 8 (December 1889): 428–40.

Powderly, Terence. "The Army of the Discontented." *North American Review* 140 (April 1885): 369–77.

——. "A Menacing Irruption." *North American Review* 147 (August 1888): 165–74.

——. "The Organization of Labor." *North American Review* 135 (July 1882): 118–26.

Purinton, Edward Earle. "The Workers Foes Within—Another Article on 'Wake Up Americans." *The Independent* 97 (January 21, 1919): 443–44 and 452–58.

"Reading Test for Immigrants." *Literary Digest* 52 (April 22, 1916): 1133–34.

"Real Question." *The Outlook* 100 (February 24, 1912): 385–86.

"Referendum of the United States Chamber of Commerce on Employee Relations." *Monthly Labor Review* 11 (September 1920): 424–26.

Roberts, Peter. "The Anthracite Coal Situation." *Yale Review* 11 (May 1902): 29–37.

Roosevelt, Theodore. "The Immigration Problem." *The Harvard Monthly* 7 (December 1888): 85–90.

"Salem Trial of the Lawrence Case." *The Outlook* 102 (December 1912): 739–40.

Scharrenberg, Paul. "The Attitudes of Organized Labor towards the Japanese." *Annals of the American Academy of Political and Social Sciences* 93 (January 1921): 34–38.

Schindler, Rabbi Solomon. "Immigration." *Arena* 16 (March 1891): 416–20.

Scott, Thomas A. "The Recent Strikes." *North American Review* 125 (September 1877): 351–62.

Scudder, Vida D. "For Justice Sake." *The Survey* 28 (April 6, 1912): 77–79.

"Security League Conference." *The Outlook* 111 (December 8, 1915): 853–54.

"Send Immigrants South." *Literary Digest* 47 (October 11, 1913): 617–18.

"Situation in Colorado." *The Independent* 56 (June 16, 1904): 1396–97.

"Skimming the Melting Pot." *Literary Digest* 60 (March 1919): 16–17.

"Social Forces: After the Battle." *The Survey* 28 (April 6, 1912): 1–2.

"Special Focus: The Federal Commission on Industrial Relations." *The Survey* 27 (February 3, 1912): 1659–60.

"Steel Strike," *The New Republic* 20 (October 1, 1919): 245–46.

"Strike of the Jersey Silk Workers." *The Survey* 30 (April 19, 1913): 81–82 and (May 31, 1913): 300.

"Strike of the Lady Shirtwaist Makers." *The Survey* 23 (November 23, 1909): 228.

"Strike Without Disorder." *The New Republic* 6 (January 22, 1916): 304–6.

Stoddard, Lothrop. "The Japanese Question in California." *Annals of the American Academy of Political and Social Sciences* 93 (January 1921): 42–46.

Taussig, Frank W. The South-Western Strike of 1886." *Quarterly Journal of Economics* 1 (January 1887): 184–222.

[Thompson, Richard E.]. "Political Economy of Immigration." *American* 4 (April 1882): 262–63.

Tourgee, Albion. "Aaron's Rod in Politics." *North American Review* 132 (February 1881): 139–62.

"Two Hours, Reduced Wages, and a Strike." *The Survey* 27 (January 27, 1912): 1633–34.

Veblen, T. B. "Army of the Commonweal." *Journal of Political Economy* 2 (1893–1894): 456–61.

Vorse, Mary Heaton. "The Mining Strike in Minnesota—From the Miners' Point of View." *The Outlook* 113 (August 30, 1916): 1036 and 1045–46.

Ward, Robert DeC. "Some Thoughts on Immigration." *The Scientific Monthly* 15 (October 1922): 313–19.

Weyl, Walter E. "It Is Time to Know." *The Survey* 28 (April 6, 1912): 65–67.

——. "The Strikers at Lawrence: Special Correspondence to *The Outlook*," *The Outlook* 100 (February 10, 1912): 309–12.

"What is Hostility to Government?" *The Outlook* 104 (June 21, 1913): 351.

"Who Makes Bolshevism in Cincinnati?" *The New Republic* 18 (April 19, 1919): 65–67.

"Women's Strike." *The Outlook* 93 (December 11, 1909): 799–801.

Woods, Robert A. "The Clod Stirs." *The Survey* 27 (March 16, 1912): 1929–32.

——. "The Clod Strike." *The Survey* 27 (March 16, 1912): 1929–32.

"Work of the I.W.W. in Paterson." *Literacy Digest* 46 (May 10, 1913): 1043–44.

Wright, Carroll D. "The Factory System as an Element in Civilization." *Journal of Social Science* 16 (December 1882): 101–26.

——. "The Homestead Strike of 1892 and the National Amalgamated Association of Iron, Steel, and Tin Workers, 1892–1901." *Quarterly Journal of Economics* 16 (November 1901): 37–68.

Unpublished Papers

Schacher, Yael. "A Contrarian Expertise: Isaac Hourwich's *Immigration and Labor*."

Newspapers

Advertiser (Montgomery, Alabama)
Anaconda Standard (Montana)
Baltimore American
Boston Daily Advertiser
Boston Evening Transcript
Boston Journal
Boston Recorder
Broad Axe (Chicago)
California Farmer and Journal of Useful Sciences [San Francisco]
Charlotte Observer (North Carolina)
Cherokee Advocate
Chicago Daily Tribune
Chicago Inter-Ocean
Cleveland Gazette
Cleveland Plain Dealer
Colorado Springs Gazette
Commercial Advisor
The Congregationalist (Boston)
Daily American (Aberdeen, South Dakota)
Daily Citizen (Jackson, Michigan)
Daily Citizen (Tucson)
Daily Evening Bulletin (San Francisco)
Daily Express (Columbus, Georgia)
Daily Globe (Atchison, Kansas)
Daily Inquirer (Philadelphia)
Daily Journal (Boston)
Daily Messenger (St. Albans, Vermont)
Daily News (Aberdeen, South Dakota)
Daily News (Twin Falls, Idaho)
Daily News (St. Paul)
Daily Observer (Charlotte, North Carolina)
Daily People (New York)
The Daily Picayune

Daily Recorder (Olympia, Washington)
Daily Republican Sentinel (Milwaukee)
Daily Spy (Worcester, Massachusetts)
Daily Stateman (Boise, Idaho)
Daily Telegraph (Macon, Georgia)
Dunn County News (Wisconsin)
Evening Bulletin (San Francisco)
Frank Leslie's Illustrated Newspaper
Galveston Daily News
Gazette (Colorado Springs)
Gazette (Emporia, Kansas)
Georgia Weekly Telegram
Grand Rapids Press (Michigan)
Herald (Bellingham, Washington)
Herald (Lexington, Kentucky)
Idaho Daily Statesman (Boise)
Inquirer (Philadelphia)
Irish World and American Industrial Liberator (New York)
Jackson Citizen Press (Michigan)
Journal (Albuquerque, New Mexico)
Kalamazoo Gazette
Los Angeles Times
Mercantile Gazette and Prices Current (San Francisco)
Michigan Farmer
Milwaukee Daily Journal
Milwaukee Sentinel
Montgomery Advertiser (Alabama)
Morning News (Dallas, Texas)
Morning Olympian (Olympia, Washington)
Morning Oregonian (Portland)
The Nation
The National Era
Negro Star (Wichita, Kansas)
New Democrat (Belleville, Illinois)
New York Herald
New York Times
News-Tribune (Duluth, Minnesota)
North American (Philadelphia)
Olympia Daily News (Washington)
Oregonian (Portland)
Patriot (Harrisburg, Pennsylvania)
Pawtucket Times
Plain Dealer (Cleveland)
Plaindealer (Topeka, Kansas)
Public Opinion
Raleigh News and Observer
Republican (Perry, Oklahoma)

Republican (Springfield, Massachusetts)
St Louis Globe-Democrat
Salt Lake Telegram
Spectator (Great Britain)
The State (Columbia, South Carolina)
Statesman (Idaho, Boise)
Sunday Register (Wheeling, West Virginia)
Trenton Evening Times
Yankton Press
Whig (Richmond, Virginia)
Worker (New York)

INDEX

Foreign?
Socialism
German Propaganda

Re-tells pivotal moments
in labor history +
examine the discourse
around them w/ a focus on
w

WTUL ?   p. 131

when does this intersect w/
other progressive currents
Eugenics ?
Settlement houses ?
Race Riots ?

More about how business leaders
shifted to anti-im
was it political ? But my
believe it was for the
best ?

Interesting omission — Henry
Ford
Ford Motor Co. — barely a mention